Coming of Age in the Holocaust

The Last Survivors Remember

Mary J. Gallant

University Press of America,® Inc.
Lanham · New York · Oxford

Copyright © 2002 by
University Press of America,® Inc.
4720 Boston Way
Lanham, Maryland 20706
UPA Acquisitions Department (301) 459-3366

PO Box 317
Oxford
OX2 9RU, UK

All rights reserved
Printed in the United States of America
British Library Cataloging in Publication Information Available

Library of Congress Cataloging-in-Publication Data

Gallant, Mary J.
Coming of age in the Holocaust : the last survivors remember /
Mary J. Gallant.
p. cm
Includes bibliographical references and index.
1. Holocaust, Jewish (1939-1945)—Personal narratives.
2. Holocaust, Jewish (1939-1945)—Psychological aspects.
3. Holocaust survivors—Psychology. 4. Holocaust survivors—
Interviews. 5. Stress management. 6. Adjustment (Psychology)
I. Title.

D804.3 .G353 2002
940.53'18'0922—dc21   2002073206 CIP

ISBN 0-7618-2403-0 (paperback : alk. ppr.)

∞™ The paper used in this publication meets the minimum
requirements of American National Standard for Information
Sciences—Permanence of Paper for Printed Library Materials,
ANSI Z39.48—1984

*For my students
and all who with hearts full and true
seek after wisdom*

CONTENTS

1.	Introduction	1
2.	In the Shadow of the *Endlosung*	5
3.	The Children	27
4.	The Adolescents	97
5.	Young Women	163
6.	Young Men	225
7.	Reflections; The Challenged Identity Model	275
	Appendices	301

Methodological Appendix I
Methodological Appendix II

Bibliography	309
Index	319

PREFACE

We learn most things in life from others--how to conduct ourselves wisely, how to express emotions appropriate to each context and, in consonance with the expected rises and falls appropriate to flows in the structure of interaction, how to be ourselves *authentically*. We learn to love, to show gratitude, to have anger or loathing, to cherish. We learn ways in which to live well, ways to die, ways to show pain or dread, ways to show exhileration and gladness. But, once the ordered patterning of life changes as it did during the Holocaust for those remembered in these pages, a destructive vortex ensues in which the self loses its supportive scaffolding. At that point, what social processes, if any, are part of survival? is there any standard way of proceeding that would afford the survivor more of an edge? In situations that seem to be beyond hope, what role has wisdom ?

What Holocaust survivors tell us in their return from the abyss is that, when all we take for granted in life is stripped away, it is in fact essential to hold fast to the principles which shaped life in that other, more accommodating reality. And when nothing else makes any kind of sense, take comfort in caring for each other. Holocaust survivor narratives stand out in witnessing not just the past--the frailty of social institutions, but in underscoring the importance of cherishing *the other* as well as ourselves, and by this simple means, at least, begin to transcend the errors of history.

ACKNOWLEDGEMENTS

I wish to recognize the following organizations who provided funding or other assistance for this work: Social Sciences and Humanities Council of Canada-Ottawa, the Holocaust Memorial Society of Vancouver, Temple Emmanuel of Victoria, the YIVO Institute for Jewish Research--New York, National Archives and Records Administration, District of Columbia, the Holocaust Memorial Resource and Education Center of Central Florida at Maitland, the University of West Florida and Rowan University. Special thanks are due to Rabbi Victor Reinstein, Robert Krell, Barry Dunner, Lewis and Kay Killian, Ruth and Paul Tasch and my research assistant, Jay Cross for their help and encouragement during the early stage of the research. As the work progressed it prospered because of the kind insights and support of members of the Goldner Symposium-Wroxton, Seth Lichter-Northwestern University, my colleagues at Rowan University--Dean Pearl Bartelt, Cindy Carson, Harriet Hartman, Cindy Vitto, and members of the Sociology Department.

There are those whose influence was felt in a different and more perduring sense than those whom I already mentioned. In this regard I want to acknowledge my teachers, Harold Finestone, Robert Habenstein, J. Clyde Mitchell, Don Martindale, Roberta Simmons, Gregory P. Stone; my parents, brother and sister; and the Holocaust survivors who are part of this work--Bertha, Elsie, Klara, David, Chaim, Robbie, Rene, Mariette, Harry, Leon, Peter, Louise, Michel, Polla, Ruth, Leo, Serge, and Vera.

INTRODUCTION

The children were crying, their mommies were begging and shouting, and the uncles were shooting. My mommy picked me up and ran over to one such angry uncle dressed in a green suit. He had a gun. She took his arm and pulled it, and pointed to me and then my mommy fell on her knees and she wept... She wept quite a lot. And then there was a loud noise and she fell down and her face was on the ground. I don't remember what happened then... When I woke up, my mommy was no longer there...

> Report of a slaughter of Jews in Latvia given by a child in Camp Kaiserwald. From the memoirs of Galina Raicin-Klebanow in *The Unfinished Road: Jewish Survivors of Latvia Look Back* edited by Gertrude Schneider. 1991:138-149.

Coming of Age in the Holocaust is a narrative analysis of surviving persecution and terror as part of growing up. The work takes a sociological approach to in-depth interviews with eighteen Holocaust survivors. The depth and quality of memories that these survivors held untapped for so many years is considerable. They provide a vivid witness to history using ordinary words portraying the various contexts and situations of persecution for Jews in Europe, 1933-45. Each survivor's narrative is the portrait of a life put together in the shadow of the Holocaust. They tell of fears, worries and plans, their fight against hopelessness; they witness the small miracles and gentle mercies that somehow were also part of that time.

In the 1933-45 period when the Holocaust took place, these survivors were either children, adolescents or young women or men. What they had faced was extraordinary in many respects. Nothing of that magnitude or degree of coordination had ever before this been directed against a people in so many geographical locations at the same time. Each of them in their specific national contexts experienced society against the self, fully and cruelly (see also Eckhardt 1988:432-442) in a way that went beyond merely bringing death to an aggregate of people sharing a social designation. In the Holocaust, as Abba Kovner put it (Eckhardt and Eckhardt 1982), Jews were a people defiled to the depths of their soul. Innocent of the intentions of their tormentors and the nature of the insidious abuse that awaited them, they had to deal with lies, betrayal and corruption. Contradiction, degradation and confusion coupled with the pain of physical torment eventually made the individual long for death rather than merely fall prey to it by accident or the course of events. How did they endure this? Did what they practiced during their ordeal have any effect on their lives afterward, on who they became?

My sense overall is that transcendence processes in which the survivors engaged during their ordeal were an intrinsic part of their ability to successfully construct new lives afterward. What are these transcendence processes exactly? And, how may we trust that there was any kind of articulation of reality across the barrier between normal life and this bleak time of great horror? Survivors discussed by Hass (1995) and Helmreich (1992) clearly highlight the significance of transcendence as an important component of the complex of meanings survivors experienced during ordeal as well as life afterward. Levinas (1969), a Holocaust survivor himself, formally develops a conceptualization of transcendence in his work titled *Totality and Infinity*. From his philosophical position, transcendence cannot be separated from wider historical processes, human nature and the question of goodness. It may be familiarly construed as as belief in goodness, with individual and collective representation.

> Transcendence or goodness is produced as pluralism. The pluralism of being is not produced as a multiplicity or a constellation spread out before a possible gaze, for thus it would be already totalized, joined into an entity. Pluralism is accomplished in goodness proceeding from me to the other...(Levinas 1969:305-306)

Transcendence is a concept which I use to refer to an implicit, discursive, meaning-based uptake of self and other. With it the interpretation of reality at crisis points where gaps in the structure of meaning leave us imperilled can be constructively addressed, allowing us to more effectively conduct ourselves as to be creditable players in interpersonal interaction, to take up the challenge cast upon us by fate and turn it to advantage. In a trauma setting, however, the shock, debasement, the constant unbalancing by what horrifies, allows the interpersonal regenerative processes appropriate to everyday life only a mild salience. In fact, certain scholars (Erickson 1976; Herman 1996), see this relational dimension as key to understanding traumatic response to severe threat and abuse. Such considerations add to the conviction that it is the reganing of at least discursive agency during ordeal which affords the creative, sociative self the ability to mobilize an inner defense against the ineffable so as to confront it in terms of challenge rather than capitulation. Survivor narratives suggest that the will to survive extreme ordeal may be associated with interpretive processes that mobilize meanings from the past so that they are oriented toward action and agency both alone and with others using already internalized maps with cultural and communal referents.

Given these considerations, I determined to focus my analysis on self-other processes as part of surviving extremity and to construct a model that pulled together many of the ideas suggested by what was said by the eighteen survivors represented in this work. My analysis is formally presented in Chapter 7 where the Challenged Identity Model is developed. In no way did I want this analytical pursuit to overshadow the primary goal of these survivors which was to provide witness to the Holocaust in a period of revisionism. Their narratives therefore constitute the main body of this work and are presented in Chapters 2 through 6.

Were the particular survivors who participated in my work any different from those who gave earlier accounts? Most of them were among the youngest of the European Jews to have made it through the 1939-45 period alive. They all revealed stress patterns from achieving survival. My assessment of their background characteristics (see Appendices I and II) shows them to represent the full range of variation in Jewish community life and the contexts of persecution in the times. They all went on to various expressions of successful recovery as professionals, artisans and entrepreneurs while also being actively involved to some extent in community. Most married and had families. But it was fifty years later that the study was done, and each of them had lived a full life since the time of terror. Would this have amplified their focus on the social rather than the physiological dimensions of their early struggles? Whatever the answers to these questions may be, the reader will, I believe, be assured by the clarity of the survivors' thoughts and the vividness of their memories.

CHAPTER 2

IN THE SHADOW OF *ENDLOSUNG*

> If injustice is bad..., it is not because it contradicts an eternal idea of justice, but because it... kills the small part of existence that can be realized on this earth through mutual understanding...
> Albert Camus, *The Rebel*, 1956:283.

INTRODUCTION

The twentieth century has been described by some as an age of genocides. The Holocaust[1] (1933-45) provides us with an archetype of genocide. The fact that this the largest and most systematized of genocides had been perpetrated by a western nation once known for its great humanism leaves us with doubt about ourselves and casts shadow upon our times that cannot reasonably be shrugged off. The Nazis had used the term *die endlosung*[2] to refer to the final solution of centuries of abuse of the European Jews (Eckhardt and Eckhardt 1988). The term refers to the ultimate degradation and dehumanization of Jews through a torture process that transfigured death into a form of mercy.

Survivors of the Holocaust experienced both society against the self during their ordeal, and society in denial of the wounded self[3] afterwards. Within formal centers of knowledge in the postwar era survival of persecution and abuse was not widely seen as a problematic worthy of extensive study. Like all of previous history, in the immediate postwar decades, we had with some degree of adequacy recorded atrocity and massacre, then, as a community, turned our attention to other things (Abzug 1992), expecting those still bearing deep wounds from the past to gladly comply. Given this, the silence of the survivors was hardly remarkable. In recent years, however, we have turned to survivors for remembrance and wisdom.[4]

By the 1990s, the overriding cultural tendency was toward compassionate discourse on human endurance.[5] Given the enormity of the crime against life which the shoah represents, however, this cultivated sensitivity may have been more superficial and passive than profound and active. Above all, it was late. Survivors had not been given voice by a community of liberation which at first could not begin to fathom the enormity of what had happened or how to deal with its effects (see also Segev 1993). Most survivors had to find their own means of dealing with what at the time was a fairly uncharted region in the annals of science.

Memory of traumatic events is compelling and painful, unlike any other in terms of its effect on self rocesses. One possessing such memories is in a sense possessed by them. Traumatic memories cannot be snuffed out; they have an extraordinary, even horrific substance which will not blend in with what is routine, normal or harmonious. They will not fall into oblivion despite survivors wanting this.[6] In short, they *happen* to survivors rather than being chosen by them, much like the generating circumstances. Survivors were abandoned to their haunting memories and subjected to a skepticism from others that springs out of the absence of social structures to accommodate belief. Since memory of a vicious past is the basic focus of narrative analysis in this book, it is worth examining the various conceptual frameworks which were used to interpret survivors' attempts to share what they had passed through in the Nazi *sonderbehandlung* of the Jews.

Models of surviving that prepondered in the immediate postwar period and subsequent decades up to the present time are discussed in the next section. As I see it, these models form an apparent continuum. Although the categories I have chosen are intuitive and sensitizing rather than exhaustive, I see a general trajectory from the early postwar period to the present as moving from a distanced, object-oriented position to a compassionate and embracing treatment of survivors and surviving.

MODELS OF SURVIVING:
Early Versions

The survivor as *antiman* was an early postwar view of what was involved in persecution, imprisonment and prolonged suffering. It was a view encouraged by "experts" who had some form of firsthand knowledge about the KZ system[7] and unfortunately cultivated a suspicion of survivors. It was not clear just how unblemished and resilient someone could be who had confronted the worst side of the human condition and not succumbed (see also Segev 1993:113-122). Krystal's (1968) or Bettelheim's (1980) works, for instance, suggest a portrait of survivors as clinging to life, rising on the bodies of others, as being more aggressive and instrumental than the dead. The subtextual message is that it was the best and noblest who perished.

Some instances of this kind of approach were more sensitive and appealing than others. Jean Amery (1984; 1980), for instance, wrote that once one had encountered the Other as torturer there was no turning back; life was tainted forevermore by the vision of antiman. For the survivor-victim, there would never again be a full sense of trust in the Other; society, the ground for all defining, had betrayed its commitment to goodness and no longer could be seen as unequivocally safe or just. Holocaust survivors who had encountered the ineffable were permanently altered by it.

The term "survivor guilt" entered the vernacular at about the same time as the antiman model, and complemented it. Initially it was coined to denote anxiety related to severe loss during violence and betrayal. But the term in use took on a more sinister aspect, implicitly binding together the fate of the survivor with that of the perpetrator. By contrast, in the lived experience of survivors the "guilt" was passive, having to do with being alive when family, friends, and the network of those representing community and life itself had perished. The connotation of guilt contributed to the image of survivor as "monster" or at least as having done something for which "guilt" was the price. The survivor was not accorded the same status as the martyred, though they may both have faced equal torments. It was a most unfortunate if unintended burden to put upon the innocent whom history had already so cruelly molested. The medical literature of the time gave little respite from this retreat of reason and compassion.

This early skepticism concerning Holocaust survivors never really disappeared over the nearly sixty years since 1945, and keeps recurring in the reviews and commentaries of critics. In the literature on the Holocaust, the ***critic's model*** of surviving is an implicit one, emerging from the subtle nuances, turn of phrase and suggestion, in which critics take on approaches to the victims. It does so with impunity having been given the cultural license to judge. With objectivity assumed, the critic[8] is the guardian of truth, the protector of conventional scions of good taste, appropriateness, and fit. Ideally, sound criticism plays evenhandedly to both the tragic and the comedic, the banal and the sublime. But, with regard to traumatic experience, such objectivity may handicap insight, leaving a flat kind of cynicism to portray survival less in terms of human uniqueness than in factual inconsistencies. With regard to the Holocaust, the most knowledgeable critics have a widened sense of various works that represent the contrasting contexts in which the persecution occurred, but even they often afford little more than a scathing sarcasm, depicting it in terms of the antiheroic.

Istvan Deak (1992a; 1992b) is a critic who in his review of Tec's *In the Lion's Den: the Life of Ostvald Rufelsen* (1992) represents the survivor as one who is willing to make a Faustian bargain. Deak's dim view of Rufelsen carries against the author's who has in other works (see also Tec 1986) portrayed survivors as both victims and rescuers, as humans pressed to the limits of their endurance, as neither saints nor idiots. Actions of anyone being hunted and persecuted when taken out of the urgency and confusion of the generating contexts may be deprived of what afforded them any measure of cogency. In any case, the critic's soothsaying role would hardly be crippled by insight from a sympathetic understanding of the survivor. It is indeed ironic that where rare or unique realities are being considered, a cynicism devoid of any such gentling is made to appear central to balanced judgement. So it has come to pass that the dialogue between critic and accused[9] leaves even the most innocent among the victims of extremity twice abused: first by the generating conditions of persecution and torture and then by withering frameworks of interpretation in which their victimage is trussed up for viewing.

The early *medical model* of survivors grew out of science and the professions during the immediate postwar period. Survivors were known in the socio-medical literature in terms of "syndrome" (see also Dimsdale 1974; Eitinger 1964; Krystal 1968; Szalet 1945) and could then be declared "cured," "chronic" or "incurable" by specific segments of the knowledge community.[10] Being overshadowed by the powerful and prestigious aura of the medical establishment, counterpositions were slow to arise and so this model extended itself through institutional channels associated with medical practice well into the present time. It left the dignity of the survivor as a person somewhat unexplored while making a clear, clinical picture of the kind of damage that can occur under prolonged privation. In short, it pathologized the survivor. As Segev (1993:113-122) points out, even those wanting to save the remnant of Judaism in Europe were daunted by the degree of injury in those surviving the concentration camps. The researchers pulled back in alarm from what could not be fully comprehended and into what their methodologies and field of practice could legitimate.

Much of the initial research contributing to the medical model grew out of research with children or young adults in displaced person camps after 1945. It was here that Friedman (1949) identified survivor syndrome (see also Bluhm 1948; Dreifuss 1980:40; Rosenfeld 1986), describing it as dysfunctional orientations appearing after the removal of life threatening circumstance. Survivors continued to show effects associated with hurt and damage long after the primary traumata had been contained. Contrary to our naive expectations of how survivors *should* act after release from their agonies, Friedman maintained that, in fact, their ability to buoy and return to emotional wholeness was severely depleted. The process was influenced by loss and damage to valuable elements of past selves and identifications during their struggle to survive.

Survivors were observed to have developed depressive disorders and were aggressive or psychosomatic as they never had been before. Symptomatology included profound fatigue and emotional shallowness. Survivors could recount horrifying events with a lack of expression and a marked detachment, part of a numbing associated with longstanding repression of severe fear and anxiety. Some of the survivors examined by Friedman (1949:602-604) also exhibited narcolepsy, were incapable of crying, or felt guilt for being alive while so many among them had died. They showed a general withdrawal of libido and, with this, other conditions such as amenorrhoea for women and sexual impotence for men.[11] Overall it could be said that the greater the fear and helplessness survivors felt during prolonged trauma, the more profound their symptoms afterward. There was no medical precedent in place to "cure" the wide variety of socio-emotional effects survivors were manifesting, and so it became a labelled form of deviance suspended somewhere at the margins of the normal life they were supposed to have rejoined after liberation.

The *theological model* concerning the Holocaust and survivors was associated with radical humanistic theology (see also Bonhoeffer 1971; Fackenheim 1970; 1978; 1982; Littell 1986; Niemoller 1947; Roth 1979; Rubenstein 1966; Rubenstein and Roth 1987). In the immediate postwar period, it struck a needed balance against the negativity and uncertainty shown survivors. It provided a view of survivors and surviving that, despite the weightiness of the larger issues being discussed, portrayed humanity with wisdom and decency. In the theological approach,[12] survivors are seen as victims of some vicious force, and it is this force, not the victims, that falls under scrutiny. Reasoning in this approach focuses a critique on civilization and the human inability at the time of the conflagration to stop the persecution. Collective orientations in the movement of civilization, larger streams of historical life in which humanity is caught up, and continuing structures of prejudice and hate, are all seen in the theological model as having played a role in generating the Holocaust.

So far from taking a diminishing view of the survivor, the theological model celebrates the ideal of martyr. Literature in this genre is resplendent with the imagery and conviction that each human who either perished or survived was sanctified by the injustice she or he faced. Theology on the Holocaust calls for positive change through critical analysis of social and religious structures that contributed to the conflagration--the apathy that condoned it, the technology that affected it, and the siege mentality which made it work; Nazism was seen by it as merely the sociohistorical device which acted as catalyst. From this point of view, it is an easy jump to contend that we in Western civilization are condemned as moral actors by our own hand. We have donned a righteous objectivity that masks a factual complicity.

A final kind of postwar approach to survival is what may be referred to as *survivors' own model* of surviving. In the memoirs, diaries, first hand accounts and testimonials of various kinds which survivors wrote, the image presented of those caught up in the circumstance was generally more compelling and credible than other attempts at describing what they had endured.[13] These survivor-authors knew firsthand what it took to survive. Many had made it through just by sheer will and a determination to become witnesses to the most unthinkable moment in history. Most had been prisoners or had in other ways endured specific abuse and could never forget any of it. They had known constant fear, horror, and privation beyond what they could have imagined possible in an earlier time. Theirs is the testament that shook Western awareness and with a persistent, unabating sound cried out "never forget." Their view of surviving is full of sadness and pain; it contains a fierce moral sensibility and a perduring optimism.

The "Anus Mundi" Kielar described gripped our memories and would not let go. He and the others who wrote (e.g., Frankl 1965; Levi 1965; Muller 1979) works of this kind speak of martyrs, heroes, thieves and cowards. The oppressor is seen through a commission of violence. Examples of works fitting this model even in their titles show the pressing nature of the truth they contain. The authors want, as Primo Levi (1982) suggested, to turn fear and shame into justice and virtue. Titles of this kind include Gill's *The Journey Back from Hell*, Wieslaw Kielar's *Anus Mundi* (1971), Victor Frankl's *The Doctor and the Soul* (1965), and Primo Levi's *The Reawakening* (1965). It details a world of crushing misery, yet there is an existential awareness that is beyond the fright and terror, a belief that evil will consume itself and perversity fall of its own contradictions.

NEW MODELS
General Approaches

In light of the inadequacies of earlier models to sensitively deal with the complex issues involved in surviving prolonged terror and abuse, some authors working in the last quarter of the twentieth century have provided a reconceptualization. Information available at that time had provoked sensibilities that led to new questions being asked. The response in the literature represented an attempt to compassionately assess rather than criticize survivors of either man-made or natural disasters. They began to interpret survival in terms of lived experience, relations, emotions and the socially constructed self, that is, to examine the dynamics of survival as a social process (see also Herman 1992).

Some of the new work offered a reprise of material already received. Others explored in a more personalized way the lives of remaining survivors.[14] I refer to this body of work as the *second generation's model*. It uniquely places a richly sympathetic light on survivors (see also Greenspan 2000) and the effect of their wounds on both their own lives and the next generation's. Aaron Hass' *The Aftermath* (1995) offers a fine example of this approach. The strength of this kind of work is in its examination of the socio-emotional dimensionality of surviving extremity (see also Herman 1992; Terr 1990). Hass acknowledges the difficulties associated with applying the medical model to survivors and then goes on to develop his own polished, original synthesis of what had been rehashed for decades but never quite with his insight.

Hass explores the normalizing strategies survivors engaged as they dealt with memories too heavy for the human heart. His metaphors emerge out of his acquaintance with survivors who want to be understood as whole and strong in the present--"normal"--yet freighted with a past that consumes the light of their being. His analysis of survival "guilt" focuses on mourning. Hass sees the "guilt" in terms of survivors' denial frames, as displacement strategies for holding on to the past and the loved ones remembered in it. Failing to mourn meant postponing feared loss. At the same time, it delayed the possibility of making a healing closure. Survivors continued to hold on to their loved ones in suspended time and so could not, in Hass' terms, "excrete" the pain (Hass 1995:41-42) of losing them to death so as to enter the world renewed. The logic of their choice may involve other considerations as well. Western socialization trains us to mourn the loss of individual life. But, when all of a large extended family or even entire communities are removed by violence as though with one stroke, extant rituals consecrating the dead and honoring the injured lose efficacy. Nor can these rituals effectively take place within a coercion setting. In both instances, emotional gaps are left in the self structure of survivors, fostering disorientation followed by an emotional paralysis. This interpretation of what survivors face leaves us with a way of understanding their wounds, going beyond a merely intellectual labelling of agony incorporated within the self as sickness or flaw.

The *feminist model* flowered in the 1970s and continued to grow within many fields of interest as a critical approach to taken for granted institutional structures within postmodern life, particularly those associated with gender disparity. In the area of Holocaust studies, this model expands the relational and humanistic aspects of surviving violence, terror and abuse. Specifically, it looks at women's ways of getting through violence and privation. Works in this genre examine how women, following gender cultural patterns, remained with the victims even at the height of their ordeal, and through passive and spiritual resistance denied full victory to the enemy. The images women survivors painted of the ghettos and concentration camps were heavily peopled. They spoke of families, friends, neighbors and strangers as they depicted the tragedy. Those who write in this genre are at pains to portray the inner space of individuals in the crowd scenes of genocide (see also Holliday 1995; Leitner 1978; Nomberg-Pryztyck 1985; Perl 1948). They show survivors as people experiencing the unbelievable. The survivors and victims in the pages of their works are human, active, aware.

Examples of this approach are contained in Rittner and Roth's *Different Voices* (1993), which puts together a series of excerpts from larger works written by women either during or following the Holocaust. The words of these women authors convey urgency and a commitment to salvage life where death was the norm. Etty Hillesum, for instance, writes of serving the needs of other women prisoners and their children at Ravensbruck. Gisella Perl resolved by whatever means possible to save pregnant women from being thrown alive into the body burning pits of Auschwitz. The focus is on helping the helpless. They tell us of victims facing a behemoth while having only the flimsiest of means to stay the force against their spirit and of the small gestures of caring which in some cases may have kept many from death. Through talk and the ideals underscored in it, staying alive became a quest, a duty fostered onto the living[15] by their peers. This view of survival goes well beyond seeing it as the gift of luck or "instinct." But more importantly, it treats survival as engaging spheres of meaning and socio-emotional continuities.

Feminist scholars noted that work on the Holocaust in the postwar period tended to overlook the experience of women survivors while ironically, by its very logic, genocide specifically targets women and children, with women facing a kind of double jeopardy (Ringelblum 1993). This in no way is intended to deny the suffering of men. They, too, from this approach, live and die within the meaning frameworks of gender, not just as bodies, but as providers, brothers and public leaders, sharing in the Holocaust the same hell as women but different horrors (Goldenberg 1994; 1991). This approach to the Holocaust, above all, hallows humanity, embracing survivors as the honorably wounded, as comrades, beloved strangers, friends, and neighbors. Women as well as men are acknowledged not just as victims but as rescuers, resisters and culture bearers. The message in the feminist interpretation of surviving goes beyond picturing humanity under extremity; it implores the reasoning mind to move toward a heightened compassion and a more inclusive embrace.

The Symbolic Interactionist Approach to Surviving

Sociology's contribution to the study of the Holocaust has been scattered[16] and may be for the most part characterized by random bursts of good intention rather than by offering a consistent focus on it in theory and research.[17] It was not until the 190's and the effective conceptualization of the social nature of emotion that the politics of the field (see also Fine 1993) allowed the study of survivors and surviving to be addressed more seriously.[18] The socially constructed nature of emotion was by that time being convincingly handled by researchers like Hochschild (1983)[19] and others (Denzin 1984) who were concerned with the sociology of lived experience (Denzin 1985; Ellis 1990). There was a growing awareness in the discipline of the potential in narrative analysis and multimethod research designs for expanding the boundaries of insight, especially with regard to rare or sporadically recurring events that were best accessed by firsthand accounts, narrative analysis or documentary data from single sources.

Interactionism, with its theoretical emphasis on understanding and emancipation from constricting frameworks of meaning (Becker 1967; Blumer 1969), had the unique methodological strengths to lead sociological research into the study of the embattled or tortured self. In the interactionist approach to surviving, assumptions about the social nature of the self are central[20] and guide the study of surviving[21] extremity, taking it as a social process. From the interactionist perspective, the self is conceptualized as socially constructed; the integral and consistent self is seen as problematic. Interaction within specific contexts is seen as generating ameliorative strategies for positive change and personal healing. Survival of extremity in this approach involves effectively manipulating symbols representing the connection between society and the self. From this point of view, during genocide, the join between self and society is brutally compromised. Normal lifecourse processes are disrupted, relational networks obliterated, parents are separated from children and family units destroyed. The child, like the adult, in such conflict and loss, experiences a profound tendency to disidentify (see also Rosenblatt 1983), with little in place structurally to effect a palliative.

This approach leads us to expect that the survivor as discursive self would use interaction during extremity to weave something confirming into experience so as to recast identity and mend the self fractured by terror and abuse[22], thus enabling survival within the trauma context. Under reduced conditions, threatened by imprisonment, torture or death, self processes must be turned toward reengagment of life sustaining actions. There is a discursive framing of events using reference groups from the past and close ties in the present to transcend complete obliteration, terror and pain (see also Hutter 1966). Such an approach legitimates the exploration of the social dimensions of survival. The model of survival which developed out of the interpretation of the narratives of the eighteen Holocaust survivors is part of this symbolic interactionist tradition. It is briefly acknowledged in the next section and more fully elaborated in Chapter 7.

The Challenged Identity Model

The human ability to innovate, to transcend frightful limitations by constructing new meaning structures, is humanity's most distinctive hallmark. Hannah Arendt (1963) in *The Human Condition* noted that what makes humanity unique is its peculiar ability to transform as much as conform, to act more than behave, and to generate, through interpersonal interaction, a new and emergent reality even under extremity. Within a trauma setting, however, the individual capacity for sociation or role-taking is either handicapped, or for whole periods of time, shut down. The trust necessary to identify with and personify others is compromised. In order to slow an unfettered deterioration of self under extreme oppression, victims must replace shock and retreat with a willingness to endure. They must assess the forbidding landscape, dividing it into smaller negotiable bits (Gallant 1994), taking on identities and meanings that foster the will to keep on going (see also Des Pres 1976). This involves socio-emotional as well as relational factors.[23] The self must recover *in* the coercion setting the means to symbolically reassert a bridge to others, generating a new set of effective meanings (see also Frankl 1965). Through interaction among those sharing a similar ship of fate, survivors must rename the world so as to reweave threads of past values and normative understandings into a meshwork that saves the self from collapse. Social structures promoting persecution, torture and death resist the kind of naming (see also Hochschild 1983) that fosters victims' revitalization of being. There must be a process that reengages the self disenfranchised by oppression[24] so as to offset irreversible damage.

Drawing on elements in both feminist and interactionist scholarship, my own interpretation of the in-depth interviews I conducted with survivors led to the construction of a model of surviving terror and oppression that I have called ***The Challenged Identity Model***. It highlights three conceptual mainstays of the self under attack: 1) the discursive, negotiative stance in which **challenged identity** begins to shape up as a way of keeping the self whole during prolonged extremity, 2) the transactional flow in which **interactional emergents** cue the formation of meanings and strategies related to surviving threat, and 3) the emergence of a collective consciousness or **survival communality**, one that highlights beliefs, practices and values associated with hope and renewal during oppression.

Discussion

There appears to be a trend in Holocaust studies over the past fifty or so years since 1945, one that recognizes an increased humanism and a heightened understanding of what surviving involves. There have been inconsistencies and contradictions along the way. Scholarship on surviving extremity has been tied very strongly in the social sciences to medical research, partially because for quite a while it was the only legitimized model around for dealing with pain and personal dysfunction. The term *survivor syndrome*, which has proven to be a label of mixed usefulness, is associated with this approach. Across the various treatments of surviving identified in this chapter, Holocaust survivors have gone from being pathologized and denied to being blamed for their silence.

In the last twenty years models have focused on relational elements in the survival process. They form the basis for a new literature that guides our comprehension of traumatic memory. Work connected with this approach suggests that a critical part of the survival process had to do with managing socio-emotional resources. But the lens through which they give this impression remains unfocused. The model emergent from the interpretation of narratives in this work will further the consolidation of theory and research to yield a richer picture of human experience under extreme persecution and abuse.

What we hope to discover in the narratives of the eighteen Holocaust survivors in the present work is this: How do humans help one another under extreme and crushing circumstances? How can they endure great suffering and yet remain whole and resilient? What do relational arrangements in coercion contexts accomplish for survivors? What is the nature of lived experience under extremity that gives survivors the courage to go on? The challenged identity model proposed in the final chapter of this work holds that survival involves social as well as physiological dynamics analyzable at the individual, interactional and collective levels. In this social approach to the study of survival, analysis turns to the role of discursive and symbolic factors. By examining other dimensions beyond the physiological, a fuller conceptualization of humanity confronting terrible odds can be developed. People confronted by forces of oppression and threat translate the imagery of terror into a vocabulary of motives and a rhetoric of action that guide them toward reachable goals associated with staying alive. This approach to the survival of extremity carefully honors the horror of both victims and survivors as they faced any part of the KZ system, or as they stood next in line to be shot at Ponary or Babi Yar. In proposing the Challenged Identity model I attempt to highlight the triumph of the human spirit and the renewing vitality of the social matrix that nourishes us all in some way, even at the furthest margin.

The rest of this book consists of the interpretation of survivor narratives (see also Methodological Appendices I and II) and the formal conceptualization of the model in Chapter 7. Each narrative is more than just an infinitely small part of an historical moment. Instead, it is a personal description of how individuals, ranging from children to young adults, endured the privations levelled against them during the Holocaust. The narratives are offered as part of sharing a rare communion, a chance given to us by survivors so that we might see through their eyes humanity confronting the ineffable. It is their memories that, in particular, this work acknowledges, treating the narratives as cherishable documents of the human heart centered on life as social process during a time of vicious persecution.

ENDNOTES
CHAPTER TWO

1. A qualification is in order here. The Holocaust was more than a genocide (see also Bauman 1989; Rosenfeld and Greenberg 1978). But it was at least a genocide in that it almost completely eliminated an ethnicity, religion and people (see also Porter 1982), that is, the European Jews. Fein (1976:3) wrote, "There was no word adequate to label and mentally assimilate the murder of two out of three European Jews in states occupied by and/or allied to Nazi Germany in World War II." It was more than a genocide in that it represented another assail against the People of the Word, one that with the technology and military precision available, almost eradicated the carriers of a tradition at the root of Western Civilization. In other words, the nihilism buried deep within our roots and not driven out, has within our times brought the defilement of our linguistic and cultural base. It spawned a self mutilation in which goodness itself is threatened and by which we are fatally altered.

    Hilberg (1985) offers a conservative estimate of the numbers of Jews killed in the 1939-45 period as a direct result of Nazi social policy and the KZ system (1991). It was an outgrowth of racism. Other works which explore the degree of damage and those affected by the Nazi system during this period include Dawidowicz (1975), Fein (1976) and Goldhagen (1996). A conservative estimate of civilians killed, not by war, but in the death chambers of the Nazi camps, is eleven million; six million of these were Jews. European Jewry was decimated. The extent of the genocide (see also Porter 1982) varied by nation with the greatest losses occurring in Austria, Croatia, Germany, Greece, Macedonia, Norway, Holland, Poland, Hungary, and occupied Russia.

2. Alice and Roy Eckhardt (1988) in an article titled "Studying the Holocaust's Impact Today: Some Dilemmas of Language and Method" pointed out that the word for final solution in the German was *die endlosung*. As it was used in 1942 at the January Nazi conference at Gross-Wannsee and anticipated by 1919 in Hitler's usage, the explicit and implicit meanings differ. The word references a centuries old

opposition to Jews, first as a religious minority, then as a competitive part of the rising classes as industrial capitalism arose, followed in the 1930s by a clear treatment of them in racial terms under the Nazis. A "final solution" to the Jewish question was in the early 1930s advocated as forced exile of German Jews. The effrontery of a modern government, even one that was proposed by a dictatorship which has become odious as we think of the Holocaust that followed, is enormous and startling. The proposition was tendered onto the public as rational logic--even science. Under Nazi practice, die endlosung was utterly villainous the terms in which it was first conceived to the murderous ways in which it was carried out. The Eckhardts tell us that it meant much more than just aktion or killing, but rather that everything (and anything) would be permitted in the process; "that any and every method [was] to be used in the struggle--indeed in the enjoying of the struggle--to obliterate" the Jews. They were maliciously labelled a *pestilence* that had to be eradicated. Endlosung was from this point of view part of "a physiological competition that makes one man's survival absolutely dependant upon the next man's extinction" (Eckhardt 1988: 432-33).

Within the shadow of the endlosung, Elie Wiesel (1968) points out that survivors also suffered greatly from the indifference of those they knew "would not weep"--the indifferent, the ignorant and the revisionists. Also within this shadow, however, is a different kind of cultural agency, one associated with healing and renewal, and committed to *tikkun olam*, a process of active outreach in our times that boldly embraces Holocaust survivors and seeks to develop wisdom that will save the future by repairing the past.

3. The term "wounded self" seemed an appropriate way to describe those who survived. Even when physical symptoms could be cured, memory seldom was. Lawrence Langer (1991) describes the wounding in his typology of memory for Holocaust survivors. The following are his concepts with my interpretations: 1) *deep memory*--the buried self, seeping out into the life from which it is walled off, altering the meanings the present could take on, 2) *anguished memory*--perception of self and life from within the wounded heart. The comparative backdrop for savoring reality includes a profound sense of suffering. To be part of what is ongoing in any present requires a separation from this self of the past, a dividing which could be painful and at

times is pathological, 3) *humiliated memory*--the self, alone within a diminishing past that is unwanted and rarely shareable. It is accompanied by an awareness of being completely violated, raped, having been powerless to change any of the conditions set by an oppressor who was both violent and exploitive. 4) *tainted memory*--the self remembered as having had to respond impromptu and in compromising ways to brutal exigencies in the camps or in hiding; and, overall, there is 5) *unheroic memory*--the irretrievably diminished self which could only stand by helplessly as homes, occupations and beloved others were taken away, emptying life of all that had been fulfilling.

4. To regain a sense of wholeness we turn to the survivors for healing, so that in our time we may in some symbolic sense join with them and, in the process, come to understand the nature of what has transfigured us. Elie Wiesel has helped the movement to remember, presenting us with vivid recollections of himself and his family in the concentration camps. He spent a lifetime sifting through memory, allowing us all to share. In 1970, in two essays, titled, "The Death of My Father" and "Snapshots," he tells himself and us, "surely it is impossible to invent suffering more naked, cruelty more refined." The smoke of the children burning (Wiesel 1969:44) maims our vision of the future.

5. Perhaps, in part, this is due to an interaction effect with other historical events. In the 1970s, in the wake of the war in southeast Asia, we identified post-traumatic stress disorder in the popular press, connecting it with combat liabilities. Attention turned from this to the human cost of surviving prolonged exposure to threat and pain under extreme condition. By the late 1980s, survivor syndrome became a more consumable cultural item, the start of a new trend in literature on surviving man-made and natural disasters. In this conceptualization, survival was a many dimensioned accomplishment (Hocking 1970). Research indicated that Holocaust survivors, prisoners of war, combat veterans, survivors of floods and earthquakes--that is, survivors of both man-made and natural disasters--all shared similar psychic displacement (Herman 1992) related to enduring trauma.

In light of these new "discoveries" we now understand that part of what we knew as survival trauma was influenced by the lack of response to the victims by the larger community. New concern regarding the sequelae of traumatic memory allowed for a critical assessment of the original medical position and ushered in a wide range of commentary embracing a more humanistic approach attuned to the victim as person. By then, tragically, most Holocaust survivors who had been twenty or thirty years of age at the time of their initial trauma had died without the hero's welcome they deserved from their community of liberation. While in the sections below the actual process of surviving prolonged extremity is separated from the interpretation of it by others, as cultural products they become intermeshed effects, especially in the aftermath of the conflagration.

6. Memories of what they had gone through were unwanted by survivors. There is a clear sense of this in Leitner's (1978) remarks when, having been liberated, she found herself glad to be part of a community life she wanted, but dragging a shadow self, an extra (injured and unwanted) person from another reality gladly departed.

7. The acronym refers to Konzentrationslager or concentration camp (see also Chalk and Jonassohn 1990) with not only its system of camps and subcamps, as at Auschwitz, but a system spanning many nations, geared to resettling target populations for elimination. The system also included ghettos of various size located at points where rail could be mobilized to transfer large numbers of civilians from one point to another. These were then exploited as slave labor or killed in the death camps. The camps in Poland were constructed primarily to carry out the genocide and secondarily to supply slave labor to the larger KZ system. Camps in Germany were in operation from 1933 and had been part of the "terror system" mentioned in Allen (1984) and Levin (1990). These also became killing centers later on, either by design or default (see also Gutman (1990).

8. This term refers to critical expression in a variety of fields but will be explored here in terms of the kind of material found in reviews of books, movies, political commentary and the like, material available to the wider public.

9. In the case of Deak's review of the survivor Rufelson in Tec's work, he is dealing with a most convoluted exemplar of survivor. Rufelson goes through a series of transformations that take him from victim through poseur, then to traitor, displaced person, and finally a Carmelite friar. He started out as a Jew, marginally involved in community life, and ended up as "Father Daniel" at a monastery in Haifa. When measured against some external criterion of consistency and logic, this unlikely progression in identity has an undignified look. Deak is reserved and cryptic in his comments, saying that this survivor's story sounds rather unlikely, almost theatrically contrived (Deak 1992b). Perhaps it is fair to consider Deak's own historical context and the prerogatives of the role of critic which leaves him speaking both to and from a generation surprised by the awkward way life fails to imitate art and comes out on the side of art. Whether or not this is fair or just, it is a position on surviving that may ignore the reality a survivor of Nazi persecution faced.

    Nazi persecution of Jews was not only cruel and arbitrary but found most people socially unprepared. They went overnight from acceptable, even prestigious social actors, to *tiermenschen* (see also Rubenstein and Roth 1987), that is, those unfit for life. "Decisions" were less choices than escapes from immediate danger. Rufelsen as a character is, understandably, not neatly packaged; then again, neither was the persecution he endured. What, then, may be the most telling feature of the critic's model has less to do with the survivor than the insufferable arrogance of those who presume to judge as though from an Archimedean point.

10. This is an unsympathetic approach to the survivor of prolonged extremity. Even the most optimistic survival literature described an anomic survivor with a small, extra, added-on existence at the margins of life (see also Ezrahi 1980; 1978). Ezrahi describes the protagonists in this kind of literature as appearing to be missing part of their humanity. They are emotionally numbed (Ezrahi 1980:93) e.g. Wallant's Nazerman in *The Pawnbroker* or Maria Langfus' *The Whole Land Brimstone*.

11. Symptoms ranged from headaches, impairment of memory and difficulty in concentration, to depression, disturbed sleep and chronic nightmares which typically manifested *after* the threat had passed.

Hocking (1970:23), who examined several kinds of trauma-generating conditions, concluded that when individuals were subjected to a prolonged threat to their survival, pre-existing personality characteristics were replaced by a universal and basic set of biological response patterns. The onset of symptoms which dated from liberation or shortly thereafter was not otherwise satisfactorily explained by factors antecedent to the trauma.

12. This refers to the theology of scholars such as Littell (1986), and, Littell and Locke (1974) for instance. There are many approaches to Jews even in post-Vatican II theology that might be seen as at least mildly anti-Semitic. Williamson (1993) examines some that still remain in fundamentalist Christian thought. He refers to this as Anti-Judaism.

13. This, of course, like any other generalization is never quite true for all cases. Tadeusz Borowski's (1959) "This Way to the Gas Ladies and Gentlemen" and "A Day at Hermenz" has about it the darker, bitter sensibility of life spent in the body pits of Auschwitz. He reserves special distaste for Jews and most of humanity who succumb to the disease of lusting for life over all else. His work is in the form of short stories; otherwise, it resembles Bettelheim's and the "expert" tradition in survivor models distinguished here. His biography reveals the torments he and his family suffered under various oppressors. He is a soul withered by pain and overwhelmed by the grotesquery of the life put before him. His suicide in 1951, when he was not yet thirty years of age, speaks for the suffering survivors continued to bear. He had spent three years in the concentration camp system, mostly at Auschwitz where he had been part of the Canada sonderkommando. His incarceration left unhealed wounds and scars no one might completely transcend.

14. Martin Gilbert, Winston Churchill's historian, is a writer whose works remind us that this trend was anticipated much earlier by some authors in their personal style. Collective tastes merely gave them more leeway to amplify what they understood. Gilbert's haunting records of what happened during the Holocaust were among the earliest made. In 1987, his work, *The Holocaust*, detailed for us with undiluted clarity the ravages of the persecution. In 1996, in the work *With the Boys*, he gives us yet another example of this style, one that is

embracing, even loving.

15. Danuta Czech recorded in her *Auschwitz Chronicle*, 1939-1945 descriptions of everyday life in Auschwitz (see also Pawelczynska 1979). She mentions the routine activities of the usual day along with the brilliantly courageous acts which occasionally broke their otherwise hopeless existence. She wrote of acts of witness great and small that survivors made both to history and for one another, anticipating a future which might affirm timeless truths and virtues.

16. While many would quickly say that sociologists have taken only a mild interest in publishing on the Holocaust, others would say that this is changing. The American Sociological Association meetings in 1996 sponsored roundtables and sessions dedicated specifically or indirectly to the Holocaust. There were others. Works like Goldhagen's *Hitler's Willing Executioners* (1996) are among the several that bring analysis of events connected with the Holocaust to the collective or systems level where mobilization of meaning is discussed in terms of social structures and dynamics. But they are not specifically associated with the field of sociology.

17. An exhaustive listing of such works would reveal some that are very notable. Helen Fein's *Genocide* (1976), Porter's *Genocide and Human Rights* (1982) or Nechama Tec's *When Light Pierced the Darkness* came immediately to mind here. But there is a general agreement that sociology has found its domain in subject areas distanced from topics like the Holocaust and surviving.

18. This was enhanced by the development of concern in the field for understanding domestic abuse and the victimage of women in gender cultural structures dominating everyday life. Many sociologists contributed to this area of discourse, including Caroline Ellis and John Johnson.

19. Hochschild's (1983) view of emotion is that sensations and other physiologically related elements of what we call feeling are articulated by the naming process started during socialization. Through language, meaning (and all of what we refer to as feeling and emotion) is no longer visceral or imagic but is responsive to wider cultural influences. In her analysis, emotion is socio-cultural as

well as physiological in nature. Emotion and feeling management are seen as part of situated self mobilization in which identity and motive structures play significant parts in any realm of society during good times and bad.

20. Perinbanayagam (1991) definitively conceptualizes the self in terms of discursive acts, clarifying the importance of language and the social nature of human reality.

21. Erikson's interpretation of survivors following the Buffalo Creek flood (Erikson 1976) exemplifies the interactionist approach. His position on surviving trauma construes it in terms of the disruption of relational networks. He deals with what is generally understood as survivor guilt in a variety of ways as he examines the firsthand accounts. The implication which I carry into my own treatment of survival is that the discursive self must reattach to a base of meanings with efficacy in the trauma context so as to revitalize itself and reconfigure ties to others in a way that allows for relative ease of transition back into social life after liberation.

22. Interactionists allow great flexibility and resilience to their conception of the self in ordinary contexts because of its source in social life. Streams of interpersonal life that spring fundamentally from culture are, during socialization, interpolated into subjective experience (see also Rochberg-Halton 1986) and set up boundaries which allow for selective affinities, tastes, and sensitivities. Through interaction, society is incorporated as part of the self, moving it toward certain choices. From this perspective, the self at any age or in any situation is shaped by interaction as much as by social forces, and what Mead (1934) refers to as the generalized other, or society incorporated within the self, continues to grow, guide interaction and suggest workable patterns for future interaction. This fusion between self and society may be made problematic by persecution and terror, leaving the self structure open to fragmentation. But by its very nature (discursive, interactive) the self may still manifest an ability to negotiate, to find the means to hold on and fight back against obliteration. Primordial tendencies toward sociation even under great threat have the capacity to keep the self functional and responsive to restoration as conditions improve.

23. The self under extremity manages feeling (Hochschild 1983:201-229) as part of being human. Socialization which spans childhood and the lifecourse, brings cultural components of language and meaning to the increasing refinement of feelings so that there is a growing synchrony between whatever social whole the individual is part of and the ability to translate it so as to engage purpose. This capacity involves managing feeling by naming it in response to others and has implications for conceptualizing survival. From the symbolic interactionist perspective, surviving has to involve the mobilization of self in informal social processes. Though much of this is out of awareness, the survival process is a socio-emotional one involving actions toward others which are responsive to the point of being at times altruistic, assessing the trauma context from multiple frames of reference, aligning past with present and future as points of reference for defining self and other.

24. Within each of us is a picture of the social order we are part of and were socialized to understand. Durkheim (1893) placed emphasis on social solidarity as a base for individual action. The moral order within the self (Gallant and Cross 1990) may be seriously helped or hampered by conditions in the immediate setting. Sociological social psychologists like Stone (1977) and Mead (1934) make this an important consideration in analyzing the construction of the act.

CHAPTER 3

THE CHILDREN

A few Jews had managed to hide in Buchenwald during the "evacuation" of April 8, 1945. One of them, Israel Lau, was only eight years old. He had been kept alive by the devotion and ingenuity of his elder brother, Naftali, aged nineteen. Three days after most of the Jews had been marched out of the camp, American forces arrived. One of the American officers, Rabbi Herschel Schechter, later recalled how he pulled a small, frightened boy from a pile of corpses. The rabbi burst into tears and then, hoping to reassure the child, began to laugh.
"How old are you?" he asked Israel Lau, in Yiddish.
"Older than you."
"How can you say that?" asked the rabbi, fearing the child deranged.
"You cry and you laugh like a little boy," Lau replied, "but I have not laughed for years and I don't cry any more. So tell me, who is older?"

(Gilbert, 1987:792)

INTRODUCTION

Children interpret the world differently from the rest of us. As beautiful as they are in their innocence, and as charming as they can be with their new combinations of familiar words, they have a specific point of view from which to judge and choose, that is, to act. They see the ordinary in ways that make sense to them. It is close enough to their parents' worlds of meaning to be interesting and for the most part comprehensible. In that region of their lives called childhood, they are learning to name what more completely socialized humans have come take for granted. Seen from the point of view of surviving extreme condition, childhood is not a categoric variable like gender or age, but it is a reality in its own right shaped by socialization.

In terms of what a child remembers and incorporates into adult narratives, the spontaneous and unguarded may filter into what is noticed and shared, the silent wholes indexed in gesture or choice of image (see also Terr 1990) much more than for the rest us. They lack discursive sophistication though they categorize the world with the words and meanings of their community of birth. Child survivors tend to retain their memories intact but holistically, that is primary memory and its imagic content dominates the structure of what is remembered. The content of memory may be locked into what was not yet reasoned into a rich array of concepts, categories and perspectives. This makes for a construal of the trauma landscape in the narratives that is different from that of adults.

In this chapter, the narratives of Holocaust survivors who were children when they were first exposed to Nazi persecution ranged in age from 6 to 12 years (see also table 2). Rene and Mariette were the youngest, Robbie just a little older, and Louise and Harry the eldest of the five. It is reasonable to assume that what might affect children in distress more than anything else is the state of their connection to parents and loved ones as the ordeal unfolds. Degree of isolation from parents and other family members influences how and what they experienced during trauma and the way in which they remember what occurred. Their narratives are studies in shadow and light, in the use of indexical expressions, glosses, and gestures as much as in clear statement of fact, of what they describe and what they omit, the emotions they show and those they leave unexplored. Their narratives are word portraits of the memories of a very young and fragile part of humanity living in fear and loneliness, under attack by what normally should have protected them.

Survivors mentioned in this chapter had some part of their childhood socialization interrupted by persecution and flight. They all had their families and home environment either seriously jeopardized or tragically transformed by events in the external community. They came from different countries and class backgrounds but shared being raised in urban contexts. Harry grew up in Prague in a wealthy family. Robbie came from Skarczysko. Mariette was born in exile as her family fled from Poland to Belgium. Rene's family were artisans of Polish extraction trying to settle in France near relatives. Louise was born in the wealthy section of Rotterdam and moved to Amsterdam just before the war broke out. In each of their accounts there is the anxiety of a child facing threat from a world they scarcely understand. Their words center on images of fear and loss in relational terms. The way they phrase things resembles that of ordinary children yet, what they speak of pertains to worlds most children never know. In their stories there is text and subtext, things they choose to tell or merely index with a gesture or pattern in the flow of ideas. They may signify terror as much by allusion as direct reference.

CHILDREN IN THE CAMPS
HARRY

Harry Groenen grew up in Czechoslovakia in a well-established family with roots in community that went back to the thirteenth century. His father had been a nationalist, university-educated and secular in orientation. His grandfather was observant and not part of public life. There were differences like these across the generations in their family. They were told that with the civil unrest in Czechoslovakia, they would be transported to a protected area. So he and members of his family were taken to Theresienstadt. Of the rest he remains silent. For Harry, the emotional scars are indexed under discursive patterns that suspend elaboration and bypass what might potentially pull him into despair.

By 1948, when he was fifteen, he was in an orphanage near Prague trying to finish high school. He, his sister and mother had survived Theresienstadt, although his mother died shortly after release. When he describes the past, he is chatty, perhaps breezy, repeating cliches or ritual phrase structure to give a sparse and fragmented description of his time under the Nazis. His earliest remarks, instead of being a simple description of events, tell how *lucky* he was.

> I was so lucky... never to be shipped out... seeing these transports of poor wretches coming in from the East and saying to myself that I would never survive this... and I somehow survived and I am still here... and that's probably the thing that's most imprinted in my mind. The rest of it is like a bad dream.

He provides few indications of his inner struggle as he was taken to Thersienstadt and provides little chronological organization to the remarks he does make. He might be describing a resort when he refers to the place where he spent most of the 1939-45 period. Theresienstadt was a fortress dedicated originally to the Austrian Empress Maria Theresa, a showpiece of the Nazis in which 135,000 Jews had been "resettled" from all over Europe. Only twelve percent survived. Toward the end of the onslaught, countless carloads of starving captives passed through this camp on the way to labor camps in Germany or on to their deaths in Auschwitz.

> What happened was Theresienstadt... the Red Cross did take it up. What

happened is a unique situation. The concentration camp commander in 1945, about April 15th made a decision that he was going to be turning the camp over to the Swiss Cross, which probably gave him a way out. The chap's name was R---. He was an SS and he eventually ended up in Switzerland, and that was the pay-off, that he turn the camp over in April '45, which was about the 15th of April, with that being about three weeks before the Red Army liberated Auschwitz... I mean Theresienstadt. We were one of the last places to be liberated... in the night of the 8th of May.

His elision of Auschwitz with Theresienstadt is telling. Harry says little of his own feelings but the pattern of avoidance references shock. Martin Gilbert, an historian records how another Holocaust survivor experienced the same transports and grapples with its meaning.

[May 6] "Sixteen more deaths and ten dying of cold and hunger." [May 8] "Our guards leave us to our fate and flee. We can't believe it's over! 175 out of 1,000 are alive. Red Cross truck appears--but can't take 175 men. We spend the night on the road--but in a dream. It's over." (Gilbert, 1987:810)

There is both elation and grief registered clearly in this rendering of the time. By contrast Harry does not directly confront the grim meaning of the dead and dying in the rail cars on the way out of Auschwitz but seems almost to be mumbling in something of a state of shock.

They were *shipping* them back to the hinterlands of Germany and parts of Czechoslovakia...

The 30th of November 1944 when they started coming back, it was dreadful. I mean these people were on a train and they opened up the doors to the... to the... cars and people were actually falling out... out of the... they were... they were without water and without food for four or five days. And wearing striped uniforms and they were *filthy dirty* and they were virtually human *skeletons*. And all of a sudden your eyes realized you know... looking at all of this... that... what the rest of the population of... went through.

And most of the people that were coming in were mostly young men, in other words, men between the ages of twenty and forty, and you very rarely ever saw very many women or very many older people.

There was a train, half the people were dead and half the people survived, and they were just grabbed and put back into the camp and eventually this created an epidemic of typhoid which was unbearable, you know. Like the Red Army finally set up a situation that sealed Theresienstadt completely and *you couldn't get out.*

The dead and dying represent the "not-me" of the pre-teen. Harry at this point had realized that what seemed beyond belief was in fact true. Jews and many others were dying shameful deaths in "resettlement" centers. Then, with the logic of a child, he simply felt lucky.

> Probably the most powerful memory that stays with me [of that time] would be the... the fact that I was so lucky. Never to be able... never to be shipped out. And seeing these transports of these poor wretches coming in from the East and saying to myself... I was about 12 or 13 then... that I would have never survived this. And I somehow survived and I am still here.

Like many other survivors, Harry used the concept of luck to account for the random and surprising accidents by which one was spared while others died. Beyond luck he acknowledged the importance of affiliations and collective identity as important features in the survival process.

> I think that most of us who survived the Holocaust are very strong individuals, sometimes very egotistical. But at least we know one thing, that it was a tough thing to survive. It [internment] certainly molded my personality. It taught me you as an individual cannot survive unless you're part and parcel of a group. Very difficult in this world to survive being individualistic.

> You always have to belong to something or some organization whether its political or religious or otherwise. Because as an individual, in a tough situation like the Holocaust, your chances are very good in a group situation. Your survival is much better. And that's what this world is based on. You always have a better survival in a group than you will have as individuals. Some very strong individuals didn't survive the Holocaust because they could not function in a group.

He is introspective more than descriptive, and while he notes the importance of the group and being able to identify with it or be nurtured by it, there is an even stronger sense of the importance of individualism, of being able to confront a tough situation and, if you were strong enough, you made it.

> I don't think that you ever thought that you're ever going to give up. You had in your mind one thing, you're going to outlive this thing and somehow you're going to return back to the... you know. It's like a story in a... in a story book and you're looking toward a good ending, or shall we say, you were in a tunnel and you were looking for light at the end of the tunnel and as long as you eventually saw light, you know, you knew already that the whole German Reich was collapsing. And it wasn't difficult to get the radios that were functioning... [it was a sanctionable offense however to be caught using one].

He started to construct this new life immediately on exiting the camp. He did not expect nor does he feel comfortable receiving the listener's sympathy. So much was lost and, relative to North American standards, the community he eventually joined, his childhood had been severely handicapped. The distance between these worlds, the then which might have been and the now that in fact was, is still important to him. His silence about these things carefully guards his self-pride. Education became his means of overcoming the dreariness of existence in the immediate post war period.

> I went to school after the war. My mother was still alive and we were living in my hometown and I went right back to the class that four years before I was kicked out of. -- My mother survived the war, but at that stage of the game, more or less, she was in very bad health and she passed away, 18 November 1945. My... my younger sister survived the war with me. She had some relatives in my Mum's hometown and they took her over, and I went to this particular orphanage situation in Prague and that's where I got my education in High School. --Lived through that.

> After that, you know, you lived the life. Very, very thin. It was group living for me til about nineteen.

They had been liberated on the 14th of May, 1945, and his mother died six months later. Even at this point he does not elaborate on what happened to his father the nationalist, the university educated, secular person who was the scion of the family before Theresienstadt. He does not discuss the fate of his relatives. He does not express his grief for his little family at liberation, reduced once more by his mother's death. The one reference to feelings he may have endured comes in his cryptic summary "lived through that." What might be seen in this pattern as individual style may also be understood in terms of gender ideals for self expression.

Survivors of prolonged extremity also speak of economies of emotion necessary for holding the self together in the face of immense threat. Huge tragedy could not be survived by indulging in self-pity or dwelling on the pain. Instead of exploring the pain of family lost, Harry focused on getting beyond the pain and shock and what this had involved. He was an enormously successful man, brilliant in the choices he made for his life. He was proud of becoming an accomplished military pilot, of being drawn to Israel after liberation but choosing to join the Royal Canadian Air Force. He had a fine command of many languages and was sought after as the Cold War started shaping up. There were drawbacks to being one of a kind, but he had learned to stand alone as a child in captivity.

> Physically, I survived very well and they [military colleagues] were amazed. And they always found out that I survived the war in a concentration camp [laughs]. I was always [laughs] a specimen that they always liked to study psychologically as well as physically... felt very uncomfortable. And they were absolutely amazed how easily I managed to survive it [internment]... because, on the basis... principle... I should never have been able to... able to physically and mentally cope with that sort of a... sort of a situation.
>
> I was the only Jewish flyer in active service in all of Canada. So I was the predecessor of all the things that in a nation that was blessed with... probably produced the first pilots in the war. It was probably the mix [he represented] that really made what it was [they were looking for].
>
> Normally it's very unnerving, you know, when you come out of these situations. But with a child, it doesn't go... the healing process... of the Holocaust. Survived.

He spoke next of his family by marriage. In his family of the past which was decimated by the Holocaust one generation would be more orthodox and traditional with the next more cosmopolitan and secular. Harry believed he was closer in personal style to his father than his grandfather. His children had chosen traditional Jewish schools growing up in North America and completed the pattern he saw recurring across the generations in his family, with every third generation repeating the cycle and renewing roots in Judaism. He was proud to speak of his son who is a rabbi in Israel and his grandchildren who are living there.

[Q: So, what about Israel? You mentioned it.]

I think of it.

[Q: But what does it mean to you as a survivor?]

To me? Well let's put it this way, I have two children who live there and seven grandchildren, the eighth one coming up. Seven of the eight will be...My oldest son [there] is a rabbi. The second [his daughter] is a judge. My son-in-law is an assistant dean of [ ] which is the academy dealing with the dregs of the world, and the worse... the children who have gone through the whole thing. So we're heavily involved.

He is reserved even when the subject gives him great joy. Then, without preparing the listener, he turns the narrative onto his eldest son who had not yet been mentioned specifically. Feeling is masked but homage is rendered.

And I just feel... my late son, my oldest, passed away. He was what you call a "bleeder."

Without him, half the kids that grew up around him, would never have done the things that they... if it wouldn't have been for my son Viktor. He had a tremendous daring. Fantastic waterskier, great snowskier, ...flying. Guess he burned himself out. By the time he got to be twenty-three, he's done it all. He was sent to XXX City and they told us very plainly, either he turns the corner or he won't. We thought he was turning the corner after nine months, but he didn't, so that was the sad part of it. The beauty of it is [coughs] that my younger son is... survived. Keen individual, that's very well adjusted.

His reference to his son lost to him is broken as were his remarks about his time in Theresienstadt. Where feelings remain unexpressed and deep, his pace is rapid. He does not want to linger long where hurt may pull him down. This space is his well of sorrows, and there memory of his son also rests.

At the end of his narrative, realizing he has chosen to say very little about what he had endured at Theresienstadt, he circumvents the issue by referring the listener for the first time to his chum Kurt.

If you want to see the other half of the story, get a hold of Kurt L---. He'll embellish on the other side... and his sister, Marianne. Kurt was interned in the same the same same... He was in 313. Three-thirteen has... has... has the worst reputation of the camp... has a very heavy [mortality]. We had a reputation for stiff... He doesn't ever mention the camp.

There is a sense of a stifled voice within that he must acknowledge if not gratify. He cannot say himself what Kurt might divulge but he knows what it has to contain. Only 100 of the 17,000 children who entered Theresienstadt survived (Levin 1990:90).

ROBBIE

Robbie Wymniewicz was eight years old when the Nazis entered his hometown of Skarczysko, Poland, near Warsaw. He had been born in 1931, the last child in a family of seven. He was six years younger than his nearest sibling.

> I remember only the happy times. We were a very, very close knit family. Maybe being the baby of the family had something to do with it. They catered to me. And [when] my older brothers went downtown, so to speak... to me it was sort of a mystery, they're going downtown... they're going out of town... I always look forward of them [putting] something under my pillow, maybe a chocolate bar or something that I didn't see on a usual basis. Or my older brother next to me, [who] was quite a fan of Tarzan... he's seen some of the movies and come home. Course I was too young to go to movies at that time, and he would tell me the stories. I looked forward to these things. It was a wonderful childhood.

Many relatives and neighbors gathered at his home on the Sabbath and his father's opinion was sought as anti-Semitism grew. He was both optimistic and practical. When in 1939 conditions began to worsen in terms of the Nazi threat, discussions at home and around town often turned to what might eventually happen.

> Talk was going around that Poland doesn't have the proper army and would probably be invaded. And there were also the pros and cons. There were also the aspect of how will we as Jews fit if there was an Occupation. And the grown-ups around me were talking about it and some were painting a very bleak picture and yet others would say, "No. The Germans are a very civilized nation and they will not... they might come and, because of Hitler, invade various countries, and maybe they'll invade Poland. It's a possibility..." But... [and] some were of the opinion that no good would come of it. My father used to say that there was nothing to worry about.

The consensus was based on the past--some hardship, some deaths, but not genocide. There was a sense, too, that the world was a forum, and that in moral and ethical terms, Hitler's Nazis would be bound, like everyone else, by universal reckonings of acceptability.

> My father I remember was arguing with some neighbors and he was saying "Well, if accidentally, say in our town, ten people die [pause]... fifteen..." he went as far as one hundred, "well that would be a world calamity" and people in the Free World would sit up and start complaining. -- You can't just go and kill people on a wholesale level without some people in other nations sitting up and taking notice and... and say, "Now just a minute. What are you doing here?" That was my father's theory. In that respect I wish that he would have been more alarmist and had done what some of the others had done. They just liquidated everything and tried to save themselves... got out of Poland. But that was not to be. Again, for the simple reason that he was a level-headed thinking man and thought that this wouldn't happen.

Robbie was a child sheltered by the all-embracing protection of his home. But fear had touched him personally in the sudden mood swings of friends, as religious hatred surged around them in the 1930's.

> I had two particularly wonderful [non-Jewish] friends. One was B--- and his sister H---, who were approximately my age. The girl was a little bit younger. They were my neighbors and my very best friends. I had sort of a devastating experience with them that might be sort of useful for our conversation. They were at my house where they were often sleeping over or I was at theirs. I was always fascinated when Christmas time came around. The tree... the dressing of the tree, and the lights and all the goodies that you would have on your tree, were wonderful things to me. And equally to them when they came to our festivals, Purim or so on. We sort of exchanged that kind of religious joyous occasion and everything. Fine. Except, must have been very close to the outbreak of the war, when Easter came around.

> I found myself a few blocks away from my home with my friends and some other Gentile friends. I was the only Jewish boy and I was surrounded and one of them threw a sort of a stick and he sort of laid it right down on my back. I looked back. I said, "Well, what was that for?" And I must have fell down and the others started in kicking and before I knew it I had a bloody nose and really beaten up badly. And, in the process of doing that, the accusation was, "You killed Jesus Christ and drank his blood and this is... this is... what this is for and we're gonna kill you and drink your blood." This... this kind of a thing. And

beforehand we were at my house, you know, and eating Matzoh, the unleavened bread and it... At that juncture I also heard one of them say that "We don't want your Matzo anymore because it's soaked in blood."

I made my way home and when I came home my mother just about fainted... took me to a clinic nearby to get me all patched up and nothing was broken. It was a devastating blow.

That was my first encounter with anti-Semitism as a child and I needed many-many explanations and the explanations weren't quite sufficient. I couldn't understand how my friends let me down to such a degree. I... after that, I couldn't quite reconcile our friendship to the same level. There was always some guard.

The battles of childhood, so deeply charged with conflicting feelings, now reflected the tormented illogic of superstition and racism as Hitler and the Nazis increasingly entered the collective imagination. Rhetoric the children used echoed sentiments that went beyond the simple world of their childhood and onto a world stage, giving their violent episode wider significance. That year, Poland was invaded and Skarczysko became a rail depot for the advancing German troops. First the area was bombed and then a week or two later, the Wehrmacht had moved through it.

I remember the planes coming low and bombing. In September 1939, a beautiful summer day, I was out playing. I think it was a Sunday. We were playing outside and these planes came really low over all the town and all of us ran, quite excited because we could see the little man sitting in the plane, you know. They bombed the railroad and they had some kind of a chemical. It was black smoke billowing out and [pause] we thought it was great fun looking at these planes but when the smoke and the noise of the bombs falling started to be so very prevalent, the parents of all the whole neighborhood started running -- including mine -- to get the kids. And we were all running. And what I recollect is my mother giving me a soaked towel, and "keep it on your face," because they all thought it was gas that they were dropping, which of course it was. So this was sort of the first... the first ... brush with war and bombs and what was to come.

It must have been maybe a week later that [the Germans] reached our town. The soldiers that arrived in Poland were fairly pleasant. Of course that was the Wehrmacht. And I remember one of them particularly came in once and asked for a cup of tea and which we told them to sit down and we brought some of his friends in and I remember my mother making some tea for them... showing them hospitality. They were the invaders nonetheless. I remember discussion ensued after they left. The talk was, "You see, they're not monsters. They don't have horns. They are human beings just like you or I." These [soldiers] were young boys and they were overwhelmed with the war as well and they tried to reassure us that they are here to free the country of whatever that meant at the time. They would make sure that Communism doesn't come, and this sort of thing. So it was very easy to rationalize at the time.

Gradually the population tried to adapt to invasion and defeat. Orientations toward tolerance were one-sided, and though Nazi social policy affected the intelligentsia, the military and public leaders, Jews became special targets for abuse. In each household, measures were taken to compromise and hold on through bleak times. The hope was that another force would destabilize the captors, but as family and neighbors were absorbed into a captive labor force, people were brought to new levels of fear.

I remember, what slowly happened was the Germans would need some work... something unloaded. So they would need workers. So. What they would do is hit the town in very rapid succession with trucks standing by and any able body on the street they would just grab and load on the truck and take away to work. I was sort of more or less free to go up and down the street because they didn't look for children at that particular time.

Things started going wrong when some of the people they were taking on the trucks disappeared. People started getting worried and concerned and anytime in the future when these people, these Germans, would come to find some people to do some work, they found it more and more difficult to find able bodied men because they [were] beginning to hide. And also, the odd time, when somebody ran away, they would shoot. So you started to see casualties here and there, not on a big scale but it... it ever so slowly started getting to a point where everybody would be just afraid to walk the streets. And then they would start sending people to different parts of the country and into work camps and so on.

Before long they issued cards... work permits. And when you got one of these work permits then you at least had some assurances you'd go to work... you'd do your day's work and then you would come home. [Pause] All my brothers had these work permits, okay. So they would come and go and there was a type of existence that was carved out and we were sort of waiting to get over the hump. And, again, [it was expected locally that] either Russia or America or England would come to the rescue and defeat the Germans and restore Poland and every other country.

Then word came that other places, bigger places, the Germans would ghettoize people and separate the Gentiles from the Jews and have the Jews in separate [housing areas]. And very soon this happened in our town. We were told to move from where we were and into the ghetto. So we had to pack up all our belongings and move out from our house and move into this ghetto which was designated as being the Jewish ghetto [deep breath]. We did that.

Each reduction in civil liberties brought families closer to unthinkable choices. It was becoming increasingly difficult to remain level-headed. The seriousness of the situation could no longer be denied, but still there were tales of things being worse somewhere else. For some, this was a sign of things to come; for others, it brought a sense that in Skarczysko things were still, relatively speaking, all right. This lack of consensus allowed for the generation of stories and the propounding of myths about what outcomes might in fact be at hand for them.

Rumors were coming back from other ghettoes -- bigger ones, that some of them were liquidated and the people from there... Again, we also heard rumors that they were separating the children from the able bodied people and... and that the... the children and the women were sent away to some special camps... to... and that it was all done for the betterment of the population. There wasn't enough food where they were, so they had to move into other parts of the country and those are the kind of rumors that I remember.

The times were full of shocking events and the realization that civilians, especially women and children, were being made specific targets by the German invaders inspired great fear. Rumor was made all the more potent. One evening a man who had escaped Treblinka had come to Robbie's home. Other towspeople had gathered there to talk with this man. No one was calm.

There was a real commotion going on and I tried to listen in to it and my Mom says, "You better go out and play. There's nothing here for you." When someone says that, my curiosity gets the better of me and I hid behind some curtains. I wanted to know what was going on [that] they didn't want me to hear. And, what I heard that particular day sent shivers down my spine. Because what was discussed was we're all going to be d... the plan is to annihilate the whole of the Jewish population. And what is happening...

Somebody... Apparently one of the conductors of one of the trains hid one of the Jews there and he brought him back and he was telling the stories that they were sent... that was the... Treblinka that he came back from... Said anybody that gets on those trains to be... what was the word... resettled... it's not true. They... they... killing all these people... the...the women and children!! And... and of course people were questioning him [to see] if that was true, and they wouldn't believe him and he said that it's absolutely true and... and... if you don't want to believe me, don't believe me. [Pause].

But I remember the panic then and there. It was just beyond description. And as a child I remember thinking to myself... being Jewish was... was really not the most wonderful thing in the world and being the Chosen, as sometimes we read in the Bible... I thought to myself, "There's something wrong."

This profound gap between the ideal and the real, the reasonable and the actual was paralyzing everyone as they struggled to deal with the situation. They decided in Robbie's family to get work permits for all but Robbie and his mother. Women and children traditionally had been the survivors of wars and it was unthinkable that it would be otherwise. Nevertheless, Robbie's father nested strategy within strategy to save his family. Finally he came up with a plan for Robbie's security.

One day my father came home and said "I've come...I've come up with the solution what we should... what we're gonna do with the baby" -- that's me. [Deep breath]. He told... so he told me very briefly, "We're going to pack up a little suitcase for you and I'm going to take you out to a farm. I've arranged it all. You're gonna be there with those people I know. You'll listen to them. Do what they ask you to do. And it's only going to be for a short while." -- Again with the same thing! "When it's all over, I'll come and get you and we will be reunited again." I says, "Fine. If that's what has to be done, it has to be done." So he put some of my clothes in a little briefcase... suitcase... and out I went. These people picked us up with a horse and buggy and out we went to this farm. We said our goodbyes. I said goodbye to my Mom. Don't forget it's all just for short while, so you don't make a big fuss, you know. You just hug and kiss and you say, "Well, I'll see you later..." this sort of thing.

For many who went into hiding, the pain of separation from family was compounded by a wariness about their immediate "protectors," who were under pressure to turn them in to the authorities. The situation was potentially abusive, and the fear felt by children at the thought of being separated left them inconsolable. Robbie was very unhappy in his new surroundings. He missed his family, but even more, he missed the center of nurturance in his world, his mother.

> So. Out I went to this farm. I was there, oh, less than a month. I was extremely close to my brothers and my mother. My father was the disciplinarian. He loved me very dearly but in a different way. He was more with discipline than affection. But my mother was very, very affectionate and not to... Anytime I would go to bed and not to have her to put my arms around her and to kiss her good night, was a very difficult time for me and I missed her terribly. I was there, oh, better than three weeks when I got very, very homesick and, oh, extremely uncomfortable around cows. Just couldn't get used to it. I put my suitcase back together again and ran home. It took me about a day to get home, but I walked all the way. -- Came home exhausted!

> When I got back into the house, first thing my father did... The only spanking I ever received was that time. And [sighs] while he was doing it he was screaming, "You know it cost me [pause] all kinds of trinkets of jewelry..." that he has given to this farmer to keep...

Hiding turned out not to be the solution it had at first seemed. This was true for more than Robbie. In Skarczysko, once the ghetto was liquidated the hunt for hidden children was upscaled by the device of rewarding those who would betray a child in hiding for a bag of sugar, or flour, or potatoes. In Robbie's recollection, without an exception, all these children were renounced and eventually transported or killed directly. Nevertheless, Robbie's return from hiding left the family with the same problem as before, that is, how to protect him should they be dispersed.

> Before the ghetto was liquidated my elder brother heard about it and he came about three o'clock in the morning and said, "Put your clothes on." [He] put me on a truck and covered me up with some potato sacks and smuggled me out of the ghetto. He... he was going in and out with this permit... these truckers...

> He put me up in a loft of hay on this farm and said "You stay here, and don't breathe! Nobody must find that you're here and I'll come back and get you." And I was there for about two days and two nights not knowing what was happening. And at night, I would come down and raid some of the gardens for food and go back up. I stayed there for two days and then afterwards he came and got me. And I says, "Well, are we going home?" He says, "No. There is no more home. The ghetto has been liquidated."

For a child of eight to remain in one hiding place, unattended and for two days be without food or water suggests a very disciplined character. Robbie disliked being a child at this time since in the traditional world of his parents a child did not make decisions for anyone. This ineffectuality was a form of victimization. As he obediently stayed in the hayloft his home had disappeared. But a greater grief than this was yet to come as he questioned his brother that night.

> I says, "Where is Mom?" He says, "She has been resettled."
> Of course I was hysterical. I didn't believe what was happening.
>
> So. My Mom was the only one who didn't have a [work] permit. So. She went to Treblinka.
>
> And, you know? The pain of her going to Treblinka wasn't [pause]... I knew about it... it was with me... I just didn't accept it.

It could not have been worse. As he hid behind the curtains of his family's parlor months before, he had heard the man who escaped from Treblinka tell of its horrors. The family had resolved to do everything to stay together, yet at this point its very heart was being "resettled" --gone forever. He was defenseless against the blow. His response to shock was to go blank, to make no specific response, to act as though the words he heard had not been uttered. This was a form of retreat from the specific part of the reality that had given him unbearable pain. It was not until over fifty years later, while viewing the movie *Shoah*, that the depiction of the rail journey to Treblinka jolted him out of this. Only then did the great well of grief flood past his reserve.

> It was haunting. It's only then that my pain has started and it's with me. Because that's the route that she took. And that's... that's where my Mom ended up. She went to Treblinka.

Robbie speaks out this memory with the innocence and simplicity of a child. When he first had to deal with the loss of his mother there had been no room for tears. The ghetto had been liquidated. There was nowhere to take a small boy, but his brother had a transport truck that he operated to take materials into and out of the camp where his father, sister and brothers, were in forced labor near Skarczysko. The ironic solution to the problem of how to protect Robbie was to take him *into* the camp.

> My brother smuggled me back into a camp and th-that's how I started my... It must have been 1942... 'forty-two to 'forty-five. I was in various work camps. I worked in a munitions factory. First I was in painting... They were painting the anti-aircraft shells. [He describes the detailed work he was doing] I painted 3,200 a day of those. I did them very fast.

Robbie was very young but worked well and at a prodigious rate, assuring his survival. Though his small size might have betrayed him in an adult work area where children were regularly selected for transport to their deaths, Robbie relied on his prodigious productivity to save him.

> I was revered and looked up to as being the wunder... wunderkind. That allowed me to live. That's the way you had to look at it. Anytime that there was some higher up from Gestapo people, they would come to take a look. They'd always bring them to my... to my table to show how quickly I was doing this [painting the "S" on anti-aircraft shells]. An adult wasn't able to keep these people [the ten other workers in his unit] supplied. And to see a young child do it.

> I didn't consider myself a child. You grow up very fast when you have to. I very quickly learned to walk tall and look twice the size that I was. My problem always arose going to the barracks and back to work because that was the danger of being spotted as maybe a weakling or maybe a young... a youngster and being packed out and sent away. *They were all being killed.*

Selections were the weak point in the plan for Robbie's survival since children were routinely sent to the gas. They created moments of havoc in lives that had already become chaotic, but his father remained determined to find ways to keep his remaining family alive and he spurred the ingenuity of his sons at least for a time. Once, at an early point in their incarceration, Robbie remembers being placed in a line with the older people and children.

> At that time I was already wise enough to know that this is not going to do me any good and I better get over with the healthy people, and particularly, with my father.

Robbie waited until the noise and confusion in the selection area increased to a frenzy and then went to the guard overseeing the operation and reported that he had been placed in the wrong line. He wanted to be put with the older people and the children! The ruse worked. The guard slapped him into the line with his father and the other workers. After this, in the time remaining before the next selection, his father began to work on a means to get his youngest son to the Polish Partisans. It involved an unlikely strategy of escape and return.

> My father... came to the barracks [after work one evening] and said, "We have a problem. I just found out that tomorrow there's going to be a selection." -- That's where you're lined up single file and the Gestapo man tells you left or right. And he says, "You will not be able to get through that selection and I must do something for you. Either to get you out of here or I have to hide you. We must at all costs avoid the selection." [Pause] He then tried to bribe a guard to see if I could get out of camp and I said, "Where will I go?" He says, "Well, go into the woods. Hide. Join the [Polish] Partisans. Do anything you want." Everything as far as my father is concerned is temporary. Nothing is going to last *forever*.

> He bribed a guard. My father had all kinds of little trinkets sewn in his garments. When he... when he bribed this guard I was told that in this particular place the wires are not going to be electrified this particular night and I was a small boy, I could get underneath, lift them [wires] up, put a little stick under. I was shown how to do this... and get out. I did that, made my way into the... said my goodbye to my father and he says. "Don't worry. Make yourself useful and you'll be fine. And... and I'll find you after this mess is over."

Once Robbie made contact with the Partisans, it seemed at last his father's plans had come together. They began to teach him how to handle a gun and would send him on simple errands. But neither Robbie nor his father had been aware of the conflicts that dominated the Polish Partisans when they had conceived their plan for him to join them.

> I got back to... I joined the [Polish] Partisans, I was with them for several weeks. Got shot at a few times *from them*. To make a long story short, I was the gopher, you know. They'd send me to do this and that

and to do various things. One of them was teaching me how to handle a gun. [But then] they wouldn't give me one! I was just unlucky. I had hooked up with the wrong group obviously. But after having bullets fly by and listening to -- ssst -- right by the ear, I think that one of these days they're not gonna swish by but just hit me and that will be the end of that. I was totally despised in that group because, again, because I was a Jew. In Poland it was very easy to distinguish a Jewish boy. Normally Poles were fair, at least in my experience, my town, they were very fair. I was quite dark. Much darker than you see me now. So I stood out. I realized very quickly that my chances of survival weren't very good and I looked for that same hole [he had used to escape] to get back into camp, because my chances of survival were better in the camp than they were outside.

The bitterness of this choice must not be underestimated. Great hopes had been placed on the success of his venture and once again it became unworkable. The draining fear which comes from being alone and surrounded by those who at best were indifferent to his well being, drove him back to the work camp where the dangers were more clearly defined and his father and brothers were nearer at hand.

Hundreds of such small camps were to dot the face of Nazi occupied Europe before the end of the 1939-40 period. Life was brutish and short for most who were held as captive laborers in them. He told of an experience with a co-worker who on seeing the holes in Robbie's shoes had given him a scrap of leather from the refuse piling up around the work area. Somehow the "gift-giving" was noted by the guards. Robbie watched in horror as the man was accused of "stealing from the Reich" and was summarily shot. At the time Robbie had been standing far enough back not to be noticed, but some of the bloody matter from the man's fatal wound splattered on him. He had nightmares about this episode ever since, and even today, he can still see the look on the victim's face.

Somehow Robbie managed to blame himself for the death of his would-be benefactor. Self recrimination was a luxury the terrorized prisoners at the time could not really afford. Claiming a moral stance against those with the guns, however, was a right they reserved. Others besides the captives held that claim. Robbie recognized this kind of human resistance in another kind of story about what happened early in his captivity.

> Every weekend we would load up a truck with these antiaircraft things and I was... [part of the work crew]. So they needed a bill of lading. So

on Saturday, they would send me because on [swallows] Saturday the Gentiles that worked with me wouldn't come to work. So I did odd jobs around the... the... munitions factory... did some stacking and everything else. And one of my jobs was to take a bill of lading to go with the information. Walk up to the office and there was a secretary there would do the bill of lading. Now I don't know if she was Polish or German or what but, because she never spoke to me. She wasn't allowed to speak to me. I would hand her the information and she would give me the bill of lading back. Underneath the bill of lading, I felt there was a little package of some sort and when I walked outside, I took a look and it was a sandwich! Two pieces of bread with butter and jam on it. Well that was... I can still taste it! I mean it was something absolutely fantastic. I mean you didn't see butter and marmalade [as a slave laborer].

That was a luxury of the highest order and I was so delighted that I wanted to share it with my sister who was in the women's barracks. -- Way out. And so at night I risked my life to take her half of that because I was so proud of having this and I knew how much she would appreciate it... because something like that would just sustain you for a week. And I would bring her... I would share half with her. To this day I just wonder at the marvels of how a piece of bread and butter and marmalade means [so much] and what it can do.

Now this lady, she risked her life in doing this. If somebody... if one of the SS men would say, "What are you doing there?" and he saw a piece of bread and butter... "Where did you get it?" she'd be shot. I looked forward [to this treat] on a weekly basis because she did this for weeks on end. Gave me her lunch. I don't know her name. To me she was one of the righteous ones.

This gesture by someone unknown to him gave him great relief from a drowning despair. For the first time in his account he uses words like "delight," "proud," "sustain," "appreciate," "risk," words of exhilaration and choosing. The precious joy had to be expressed in the best possible way. So he took a piece to his sister. That too involved risk, but it would give her something to break the dreariness and uplift them both.

In the years 1943-45, Robbie was moved to different camps away from Skarczysko. He focused almost entirely on work, taking this as his means of survival. However, conditions at these camps farther away from Skarczysko varied, and so did the personnel. The unpredictability of human sentiment, and the ravages of an even worse existence in these more temporary camps, eroded his balance.

For a child schooled in the Judaic tradition, love is the first commandment, and like most first principles of religion it was demanded of the practitioner regardless of time or place. The gift was for Robbie in the midst of his ordeal a sign of God-in-man. But the guard terrified him. As he measured the guard in terms of the small act of decency, comparing it to the bloodbath wrought around him, the contradictions in humanity left him reeling. Yet the story of the guard's apple gave him a memory on which to build wisdom and forbearance.

In this last anecdote Robbie was on his own; no other family member is mentioned. At a certain point in his captivity they seemed to all have disappeared. As Robbie's story unfolds, his father was the one visible sign Robbie had of his family and the longed-for past. His father was that and much more--rationalizer, protector, planner, nurturer. He cared for each one of them.

> I lost eight days [with typhoid]. Somebody covered me up with straw and I made it through the fever without any medication. My father apparently would come [every] twelve hours. I would be on my own, just covered up there [so as not to be seen and hauled away for extermination] and unconscious and when he would come he would cool me down because I would feel something on my forehead. It would come and go. That part is completely out of my [experience]... I don't know a damn thing. I remember that coming to and being extremely weak and my father telling me, "You just came through typhoid fever."
>
> When I started walking I needed some time to get back... [but] because I was very, very eager to get back to work... [I went before I was well]. I got spotted you know [and got put on a truck for elimination].
>
> I knew, when I got on the truck that I'm finished, that the same fate would be [mine] that my brother... [pause] We mounted the trucks and I was right at the edge and I remember seeing from the truck my father speaking to one of the guards and the next thing I knew is...

Robbie's father demanded that he commit to living. When Robbie fell into a slump during his recovery from typhoid it was his father's urgent ministrations that kept him alive. But Robbie had returned to life reluctantly; existence was too painful for him. He felt endlessly weak and tired of trying to be what others wanted. He felt more frustrated than glad at being "rescued" by his father. The contest between the world of adults and the expectations of a child gripped him. He was oblivious to certain changes in his father. Exploitive conditions and the threat to hims family had taken its toll on him.

> The last time I saw my father must have been in a few months after I regained my strength and worked at the factory. We would see each other on the weekend. On Sunday we didn't work, and I would renew with him on Sunday. I would be coming and he would be going to work. We... we just crossed each other and we would wave to one another. And very simply, one day I looked for him and he wasn't there. [Pause] He... he got moved to another part and that was the last I saw him.

> He knew much more than I gave him credit for and he kept it from me. Because at one point I was really mad with him, because there was a period just before we got separated [when] he gave up. He had a...a... had black hair, very, very full... head of black hair, and almost before your eyes he turned white, just completely white, and very despondent. He knew about his wife going to Treblinka. He knew my younger brother was already killed. He knew about another brother that I found out later that jumped the train on the way to Treblinka and with a... with another group got machined down [shot]. He probably looked at me and thought "There's no way he's gonna make it."

Robbie's only surviving relative from the camps was his sister. Yet he had seen only one of his brothers die while in captivity. After liberation he nurtured an illusive hope that he might still find members of his family alive. This hope stayed on as a scar that would not heal and this door on his past would not close with any finality. Even talking about it so many years later made him feel vulnerable; he had no devices to shield himself against the flood of feelings that it brought.

> Talking to you is very difficult. It comes... Saw my brother taken out and into the woods to be shot.
>
> [Q: This was your soldier brother?]
>
> No my soldier brother [Polish army], I don't know. But... but the brother next to me the brother... older... [who had saved him with his truck] his name was Abraham. His pain I feel. [Without warning, tears are coming; he is still]. I have to take a moment. [Voice is broken]. I'll be back. [He leaves the room and, shortly thereafter, returns more composed].

The Children

> The family that I was going to go back to had disappeared. I lost them all. In that little town [Skarczysko] that we lived, there were... [pause] there were about five thousand Jewish souls... fifteen hundred children... There's two of us that made it.

As the Russians advanced toward them from the east, the prisoners were taken on a forced march further west. Eventually Robbie ended up in Buchenwald, and it was there, with people like Elie Wiesel who were near his own age, that he was finally turned over to the Red Cross.

> We are four hundred and eighty children that survived... came out of Buchenwald and the surrounding area and we went to France, and when we realized in France that we've lost all our loved ones and there was no going home. The Red Cross came into Buchenwald -- "What would you like to do?" I says, "I'd like to go home." "We'll see about that." And a few days later, "There is no home to go home to." "The family that you're looking for, we don't know whether they're home. There's nobody there. We've looked." And the same story with everybody.
>
> During the Holocaust we didn't know, I didn't know of what had happened, that so many died. It took me months to come to terms with... with the enormity of it all. It took me years... it took me a year before I cried.

The children saved from Buchenwald were known afterwards as *les enfants terribles* and psychologists had only dire warnings and forebodings concerning them. They had lost everything but their own lives and verged on becoming nihilistic.

> The psychologists at the time had just written us off. They said that these kids are not redeemable. They have lost too much and they are absolutely lost to society. It... They are of no use to... They'll not make good members of society. They will always be outrageous.
>
> You see, we... we... I remember when we first arrived in France, we... they gave us this dormitory and we just broke it up and tried to set fire to it. We just went on the town and just terrorized everybody.
>
> It was just... I think what it was... we were mad. We were just mad... angry... and we just needed...

[Q: That was healthy].

That's right, but nobody could understand that and... So we wouldn't conform at all. And... but... ultimately we all settled down. Oh, one of us landed up in an asylum. He just couldn't cope.

Robbie favors "we" and "they" as referents here, moving away from the predominant use of "I" for his early work camp experiences. Adult inmates from Auschwitz and other death camps reverse this order in the use of pronouns, relying on "we" during their descriptions of internment and returning to "I" in their liberation accounts. At Buchenwald, other child survivors gave Robbie a social ground in which to meaningfully identify and he began to move out of his alienation and numbness. As he describes his life in North America his account shifts, becoming more relaxed and joyful. It was a time of growing and turning glaciers into rose gardens. He loved the new land of his refuge with a passion as intense as he loathed the land he had left.

You see Europe right after... was so devastating to us because it was so close to the... where all the tragedy occurred that we couldn't cope. When I realized of what had happened, you know... took about a year before I really had a good cry. And that was devastating. Coming in here, holidays were difficult, [because we had no family to share them] extreme sadness... and the sadness part was... it was because I didn't have my parents with me.

Having chosen a completely new place to start over, Robbie married. His wife was a North American by birth and had had no great trauma in her life.

My wife was born in [North America] and doesn't share the same kind of feelings [discrimination anxiety] as I do. It was sort of an education to get back into the lifestream and act like a human being again and be proud of... of your ancestry. That took me a long time... It took me a long time to come to grips with that.

In part, life had been urged upon him by his family and particularly, in the camps, by his father. In this new space, with children of his own, he felt he could positively reclaim his past.

When my kids were smaller--now they're adults--I relived my childhood because I didn't have a childhood. So I did... I skiied with them, I

The Children

> skated with them, I did everything possible with them. I took a lot of time with my children and I'm told that did me a lot of good. The childhood that I lost and was robbed of I recaptured with my children, and that was a wonderful feeling. It did me a lot of good, if you look at it in a selfish way, but it also did... it really made a wonderful relationship with my kids... We're [his wife and himself] friends as well as parents to them.

He began to relive the experience of family but from a new perspective, that of the father figure. His choice was to move toward closeness and away from a traditional father provider role. He and his wife had made a conscious choice to take this path. He loved now as deeply as in his childhood but with the complex profundity of an adult. It renewed in him his father's memory.

> With all the things that I've gone through, I wouldn't be able to take it [losing his wife and children], you know. In them I see the continuity of... of... my faith, my family. And, the reason for my survival maybe, hinges on the well being of my children. So I wouldn't be able to take it [to watch them be killed]. I would probably go to pieces. And so after all these years, I understand [my father]. But I didn't... I didn't, after the war. I didn't. .

> Within myself I had a conflict with [religion] because at the time I didn't understand and I wasn't able to reconcile the fact that all the suffering and all the persecution and the... the misery that we had to go through was because we were Jewish and we had this religion. So there were times when I questioned was it worth the accident of birth to lose your family and go through hell and lose your life for that purpose. And you reconcile those kind of things and come to terms with them.

Being very young, he had seen the larger philosophical debates in the starkly clear terms of acute personal loss. In France, with the other survivor children from Buchenwald, he had been part of a debate, the socialists versus the traditionalists. This had deepened his sense of the complexity of the issues involved in surviving the Holocaust. The socialists felt that the concept of God was an empty fantasy, while the traditionalists felt that living in a certain way brought the concept into being. Elie Wiesel represented the traditionalists.

> Elie Wiesel, his idea was, all right... God was always there but had a lapse somehow, somewhere, and I'm going to find out why and how

much and what happened with this lapse of... of righteousness. He [Wiesel] always thought there was a purpose for this [Holocaust] and that God in his wisdom did things in a mysterious way and he is trying to cope and is doing a marvelous job. I'm not as smart as he is...

With as much humor as humility, he acknowledged the problem he still has with religion and yet affirmed its social importance in general. There were still no comfortable answers for him to the questions that started with his betrayal by childhood friends in that first fistfight long ago--no final solutions.

CHILDREN IN HIDING
RENE

Rene Heusenberg was five years old when Germany invaded Poland. By the time Luxembourg was under Nazi Occupation he was ready to enter first grade. Both his parents had emigrated from Poland but at different times. Rene had been born in Luxembourg, and it was there his parents had started married life. But they had first come to France when they left Poland.

> My father first got to France when he was in his thirties. He had some people from his hometown who lived in Lyons, as well as relatives. But he was unable to stay, so he went down to Belgium, worked as a coal miner for a few months and... His profession... he was trained to be a tailor and then eventually he found a job as a tailor in Luxembourg. Then, on a trip to France, he met my mother who just came as a young girl to stay with her older sister who was a French citizen. So my parents got married and went to Luxembourg. So that's where I was born. [Pause].

His mother's French relatives were well established in French national life. One uncle in particular was highly decorated for his activities during the First World War. Another came to hold a position of prominence in the post-WWI government in France and was one of the first Jews to graduate as an engineer from L'Ecole Polytechnique. This extended family formed a protective network for each other as the Nazi Occupation progressed. Rene had wonderful memories of his early childhood and family life in Luxembourg.

> My memories... I think some of my fondest memories are Sunday mornings when my father would take me on a walk around the town. We were dressed in our Sunday best as was the custom in those days

The Children

and... Luxembourg was an old medieval city and the modern [part] was separated from the rest by a very deep ravine and there are some viaducts across the ravine and down deep in the ravine, the river, gardens, parks and so on. And in springtime, it was all these lilacs with all sorts of colors.

After the Nazi Occupation of Luxembourg, in the shelter of his family, things seemed more interesting than scary at first. The soldiers would parade through the city with marching bands and they would give children candies if they followed after them. He attended primary school where he started learning Flexabourgish and German. His parents were extremely wary, given their reading of the danger in the time, and were planning contingencies for any eventuality. It took great discipline and courage for them to be on the one hand planning flight and living out of suitcases, while on the other putting their son in school and taking him to music lessons, all with an apparent calm. They even had tried to interest him in accepting "adoptive" parents -- arranged through the Resistance. Rene absolutely refused to think of this. But things got worse at a steady pace.

At first things were normal... was very normal. But gradually I began to feel the effect that things were worsening steadily, that eventually the war was beginning to impinge... the Occupation.

I could see, you know, that my parents were worried. Also... at some point the order was given around that all Jews had to wear the Yellow Star on their outer clothing and... I remember the first time that I wore it. My mother had taken me to the cinema. There was a show for children and when I took off my coat... outercoat, and the star showed, then the kids who were sitting around were pointing their finger at me "Juif! Juif! Juif!" And so, I burst out in tears and ran out and somehow found my way home without waiting for my mother to come and pick me up.

Then the next thing, I remember seeing signs [while I was] going with my father... on the rocks... and seeing signs in the cinema saying "No admission to Jews and to Dogs." And, same thing in the parks when those signs went up. And eventually... I love theater... I was crazy about theater, and there was a certain theater which was a kind of variety theater. I... I went by myself... my parents let me go by myself. But eventually that stopped, they no longer let me go.

They were a loving family, new to their shared world and in love with life. An irrepressible contentment buoyed them until caution was no longer enough.

> [We set out as was our custom] on a Sunday to go to a park or a zoo and took the tram to the end of the line where the park was. We used to go every Sunday afternoon to... to... there were two or three large parks that were really beautiful, Bois de la Compte, Bois de la... and so on... very beautiful where there was a lake, some boats. My father [got] a row boat and we would sit down. --Our treat of the week. My mother and I had a lemonade and my father had a beer. That was like, together with a Sunday cake or Sunday pie, was our treat of the week. And so... I remember the tram, getting to that park and they had... the entrance to the park was um... some Germans... some German soldiers and a long line of Jews had been picked up. They were walking into I guess... because they didn't... whether they didn't wear the Star. What it was I don't remember. My mother promptly... They caught me by the hand and went right back on the tram and I went home on the street car straightaway.

Rene's voice remained quiet, reflecting his disappointment and astonishment at the dread in that adult world. Increasingly the family rehearsed and practiced how to behave in case of having to escape random stop and search points. While this rehearsal served him well, it brought new levels of anxiety to a child of five years.

> So we were walking outside on the street toward the next block or so [on Boulevard Carrie near his home]. There was a German officer stopping people at random for a check of identity. And so my mother squeezed me by the hand and says, "Cross the boulevard, to the other side. Walk straight ahead to that street over there. Do not turn around and look at me. And I'm going to walk this way." And she walked past. She wasn't stopped. But that was the kind of atmosphere. The fear was gradually sinking in.

Rene's parents were assessing their choices. One of these choices involved giving Rene into the care of a wealthy Belgian and his wife who had no children of their own and were willing to rescue Jewish children. There was a meeting between the two families but Rene could not be parted from his parents. In August, 1942, they decided to relocate to France, pretending to be tourists.

> I remember an afternoon. We were a fairly large group of people, about

twenty-five. There were these neighbors of ours and... crossed into Northern France, sometimes by train, sometimes by bus. On one occasion, there even were, somehow, mysteriously, bikes... on foot. It was really you know, I sometimes have chaotic memories of it.

Finally, we got to a small village. It's in the east, just near the Swiss... not far from Switzerland, and there was a demarcation line between the Occupied Zone and the sort of... called Free Zone... and stopped in a small village... for a night. And there was a passeur who came for us after sunset. I first remember we walked through fields of hops, things like that. Sometimes crouching right low and then the passeur would tell us to hide in a ditch or some other spot while he went ahead scouting. And he would come back for us. We had to be silent all the time.

I remember my father was carrying me on his shoulder sometimes and was whispering and we were in the ditch and he was whispering to me, "Don't worry. Tomorrow morning we will be in the Free Zone and then we'll go down to Marseilles and off to Montivideo." I remember my parents talking about Montivideo as our destination at the time.

The journey continued with the sense that while the Vichy government had enacted vicious anti-Semitic legislation, French Jews were protected from deportation to death camps. Since they had family in France it would be alright to stay there for a time. Working with these understandings, he and his parents arrived at Poligny. The next images Rene had were of a police station.

And anyway at... I remember we were at the police station in Poligny. Obviously they had recognized us or seen that the number of people in our group didn't speak French or didn't speak it well... had an accent. So that was... We were kept by the police and a police escort... taken to the town of Lons-le-Saunier in the same department, the Seurrat, and there assigned to residence in a small hotel. And that hotel was filled with Jewish refugees from Belgium, Holland, Luxembourg and... all detained in that hotel. And the rule was we had to reside in that hotel. We were free during the day to move around the city, but at night had to be in that hotel. So my parents reassured me saying, "No. We are going to live here normally. When we can afford, you will go to school here until the war is finished. We can live here."

I don't think we were more than two weeks there and this was in the second week, my mother began to tell me a different story... that she had written to my aunt, -- that's her oldest sister, who... She and her family, when the Germans invaded France, had moved to Limoges which was in the Free Zone... and that she had written to her sister to... to come and pick me up and... I remember protesting saying, "I don't want to be separated" and my mother explaining to me that it would be better for me to be with my aunt and uncle in Limoges. [Pause].

A couple of days after that conversation, one early morning, my father had gone out to buy the newspaper or whatever, the police came and rounded up everybody in the hotel. We were all marched across the city to the railway station to be put on a train [very quiet] that went to a camp, Rivesaltes, in the Pyrenees-Orientales, the Spanish border... built around 1938-39 to "welcome" the Spanish refugees that were fleeing at the time... And now, in addition to the Spaniards, they were putting foreign Jews into... So that's what they intended, they were taking our group.

So we were marched through the... the city and I remember it was a pretty awful experience. There was the police commissar... was a... was a very mean man with a big moustache. All the time shouting anti-Semitic insults and pushing and shoving us and when we arrived at the railway station, who should be watching out but my aunt! She had just come off the train from Limoges.

The quiet way in which tragedy stole into this small boy's world made it all the more frightening. Whatever was done had to be risked with a second's forethought and with little chance of success. The parents had clearly intended to save the boy at all costs and when things began to go wrong, had asked the Aunt to meet them at Poligny. Without any rehearsal, his aunt who has just emerged from the train herself, noticed her sister and Rene in this round-up and knew immediately what had to be done.

And she [his aunt] sees what's going on [excited whisper]. I still remember my mother saying, "Mon Dieu. Quel malheur!" And then that one moment she was standing on the side and when she noticed that the police commissar wasn't looking... and this policeman was sort of in front and I was in the back with my mother, she promptly grabbed me by the hand.

"Vien. Sauve-toi avec moi."

The miraculous timing with which his aunt arrived was due in part to the precautions his parents had taken. But events were moving too quickly. Suddenly, even his aunt appeared to be threatened. Rene did not understand what the adults were doing. He was focused on his mother and would not leave her.

> I wouldn't run. Of course after she [aunt] dragged me a few steps the police Commissar turned around and saw her dragging me away. So he ran after us! I'll never forget it.
>
> My aunt... was a woman in her middle years. She already had a grown up son and daughter.
>
> Big face [policeman]... He slapped my hand and he grabbed me by the hair and was holding me in his hands, running... Went to throw me into the train. I was kicking and screaming, and anyone could see a couple of policemen were dragging me to the railway station. There was bedlam in that station. People were screaming and yelling. Men, women, children were being shoved into that train and that was the French police. I'll never forget it.
>
> They put the regular police, the black uniforms... [to do the rounding up]. It wasn't the militia [in collaboration with the Gestapo]. Then something miraculous happened, you know. Two gendarmes in khaki uniforms arrived and they spoke. They walked up to the... to the Commissar and he handed me over to them. And they were kind. One of them just turned my head against his chest so he [reference is to himself] wouldn't see anymore what was going on. And after a while then he very kindly told me, "Now you can turn your head around and wave goodbye to your mother. She's there at the window." [Almost in a breathless whisper, half to himself, half to the room]. And that was the last I saw of her.

There was no question that without there being some divisiveness in the different sections of the French system, Rene would have shared the same fate as his mother. As it was, the gendarmes had been able to intervene. The "miracle" was a mixed blessing for Rene. He had gained his life but lost his mother.

By afternoon he was reunited with his father. Rene does not recount his feelings, just the images. By the time he and his aunt reached Limoges, he was seriously ill and had to spend a month in hospital. Later on during adulthood, on a visit to relatives in Limoges, they told him it was probably typhus he had contracted. There is no doubt, however, that the distress of his abrupt parting from his mother had affected him gravely. After he returned to health, he came back to his Aunt's house. But life was about to change again for him.

> After a few weeks at Limoges, I remember one night an unknown lady arrived at my place and very early in the morning, around five o'clock, she took me with her, waved goodbye to my aunt and uncle and... She took me to a children's home, a network, a series of... children's homes in central France run by a Jewish organization.
>
> I have never before been in a community of children. -- Didn't even have brothers and sisters. So, I have a terrible time in that place and I kept writing to my aunt, "Come and get me. I don't want to be here." And after a couple of weeks, my aunt sent a lady to take me out of there, then bring me back to Limoges. And shortly afterwards I was taken away and I travelled for several days with some other Jewish children. We were taken away to some village about forty kilometers from Chateauroux. So that really, we could not get a more French part of France. Right in the very center, a very conservative rural you know, deeply Catholic area. So I was in that village for about six months. At the time, it seemed like a very long time.

It was a precarious situation for Jewish refugee children. They were being hunted by Nazis for deportation to the concentration camps.

> In November of that year, 1942, the Germans took over the whole of France. Once the Germans invaded the South, they went there and they rounded up all the children. I had a second escape. Very few of these children survived.
>
> [Q: They were sent?]
>
> Into the death camps.

A child responds to danger with different points of reference than might an adult in the same situation. Rene was more afraid of the loss of family than an invisible enemy. He was determined not to be identified with children who had lost their access to family. He depicts himself as always going or coming from family and relatives to some kind of children's collective, and it is in this loss of family stability that he configures the danger. He is intellectually aware that children are being captured all around him, sold out to the Gestapo by collaborators. Hiding in orphanages or private schools, from this point until France was liberated, Rene consoles himself by plotting a series of escapes to reach his father.

> I couldn't be in a collectivity of children, a hundred or more children. I just couldn't get used to that life. And, my father was in Lyons. Every now and then, I got a letter from him. And you know, the interesting thing is, when I first arrived in that village in September or October, 1942, I still wrote. My father wrote in German and [I] wrote back to him in German. Three months later, his next letter, I couldn't understand it... I could no longer understand German [laughs]! I had completely switched to French mentally.

It may be true that a child can be more flexible than an adult in adapting to a new lifestyle, but Rene fought it at least for a time. Eventually, however, he became fairly involved in the life of the orphanage at Chateauroux, which he compared to the monastery school in the Louis Malle film, *Aurevoir mes Enfants*. He described arriving there.

> We arrived in the middle of the night and, all the nuns were waiting for us, and immediately the nuns gave each one of us a name, a French... really French sounding name and made us rehearse the new life story. So I was Rene Garnier, born in Chateauroux. I never set foot in Chateauroux. How do you expect me to know a life story about being born in Chateauroux [laughs].

> [When I saw the film] I thought I was watching an autobiographical... except that the boy in that film was several years older than I was at the time. In fact, I often reflect on that. How much more would I have suffered if I had been the age of Anne Frank or of that boy in the film. One thing in that movie that was amazing was those monks. They were quite easygoing! Our nuns were far stricter. We couldn't have had that sort of rough games as those boys had. And if anyone uttered so much as a foul word, such as "merde" -- that word! Punishment was swift [laughing]. Drastic!

His laughter now sympathetically embraced the child who would not be orphaned and preferred to be at odds with a world of well-meaning adults who were determined to see that he survived. The escapes that he plotted were the stuff of dreams; he pursued them as an obsession. Nevertheless, they were a compelling metaphor for what he truly desired, reunion with his father.

> Can you imagine us little kids thinking of escape?! There were... there was an older boy who was fourteen and he was sort of... you know... he was a big boy. We looked up to him. He was fourteen! He told us what we were going to do, and one afternoon... the afternoon walk... there was a farm... a certain farmhouse, we are going to straggle behind and quietly slip into that farm and hide in the haystacks and... then we were going to make our way to Chateauroux... to the railway station and get to...
>
> All of these things were being prepared and closer to the day I got scared all of a sudden. And then one afternoon, after class, one of the nuns walked up to me and summoned me quite roughly and saying, "Where are you thinking of escaping?!" And apparently, it was the big boy who chickened out, who revealed the... secret. And so we got a real sharp... very, very shortly... talking to from the nuns.

The joy was in planning escapes; he found some relief in having this particular one found out and stopped. When he revisited Chateauroux in adulthood, some of the same nuns were still living there, and they explained to him, "You would have been running straight into the arms of the Gestapo. You know we had to discourage you very energetically from ever thinking of escaping again!"

He relied on his caregivers, but not without spoofing them. It is the inalienable right of children to, in their play, reprise and even critique, the world of adults. They giggled among themselves at the innocence of their oversolicitous caregivers who were so unfamiliar with bomb drills that they emptied the whole school one day on a ruse.

Two years later, just as he had arrived in the company of "a woman who came for him," he finally got what he so yearned for--return to his father.

> Again a mysterious, unknown woman came for me... to take me to Lyons. This time it was unbelievable, really. I was taken to Lyons. I was overjoyed to see my father. He and my uncle and aunt and my oldest cousin, Linette... She was at the Elysee... she was seventeen at the time. They all lived in one tiny room which served as a kitchen, bedroom, everything. Very, very old building, #20 Rue Couteau in Lyons, on an uphill street with all steps... with hundreds and hundreds of steps up this hill.
>
> Strangely enough, during the day I was allowed out for brief periods. I could go out and play in the streets and wander around. I often walked down to my father's workshop and... and I remember that in the

evenings, I have fantastic memories of the evenings... the radio being sort of kept low and when you listen to the Voice of London... I remember the signal, [taps out the morse code] a few times like that and... "Ici Londres," and then give the news, the news of the Allies. And there were frequent air raids... sirens. Typically enough we'd hear the sirens and either it was a false alert and a few minutes later the siren would ring again saying the alert is off, or else it would be a real alert and after a certain number of minutes, it would be fifteen minutes maybe less, you would hear the bombs falling somewhere in the city. But we didn't dare go into the air raid shelter for fear that we would be recognized. We just stayed upstairs in the top of the flat, hoping that no bombs would fall on our part of the city.

After a particularly ferocious bombing through all of one night, a prison had gotten bombed, and many resistance people were killed while the intended target remained intact. At about the same time, several of the resistance had been caught and tortured by Klaus Barbie. The battle for France was mounting, and the safety of the children could not be assured if they remained in the city.

We were sent to farmers, farmers who had seven boys... from Lyons, hidden with them. We went to school in the morning then in the afternoon, [chores]. Whenever the peasants were talking among themselves and they didn't want us children to understand, they would speak in their local patois, but I understood when the old farm lady said to one of her neighbors, "The Americans are at Grenoble!"

It was only, you know, one hundred, one hundred and fifty kilometers away and so... And one morning suddenly somebody shouted, "The tanks!" On the roads, on the horizon, the German tanks of course. So we were all told, you know, to hide. And I was hiding and then someone suddenly shouted, "Those are not the Germans!" --They were the Americans! They were coming on! And oh, everybody went out on the road and the Americans had pitched up camp in the fields right around the village. Their guns... their artillery... and there were nets over their guns...

Shortly afterwards, there was combat for the liberation of Lyons. It was very severe fighting.

The long awaited joy had come upon them and everyone celebrated together. The boys were especially exultant, fascinated by the tanks and the guns and the soldiers. Rene soon translated the whole event in terms of finally being able to go home, that is, to be with his family again. Meanwhile, the enemy was being routed in hard fighting.

> The Germans fought for dear life. Before they left [Lyons] they blew up all the bridges, the five bridges on both rivers... blown up. The city was cut in three for several years afterwards. And I remember after the war seeing German prisoners of war being made to rebuild all of those bridges [laughs].

> [The fascist militia -- black uniforms] were absolutely loathed and feared. And there was one building where the militia... which was the headquarters for the militia... when the Resistance went for them, they let them run. I'll never forget. --They were determined they were going to get the militia, and [when] they [the militia] surrendered, they didn't let one of them live. They set fire to the building and those militia men were running out, being machine gunned as they were running out.

La Milice was a branch of the special French police formed to assist Nazi forces. The French Resistance became one of their special targets (Latour 1981:44). The Milice had organized the round-up of Jewish refugees at the railroad station where Rene's mother was captured. And so it was that what happened to the Milice during the Battle of France was of special significance to Rene and the Resistance. On the sixth of June 1944, Rene had a last visit with his father before the battle for the city of Lyons was engaged.

> I never forget. That morning when they announced on the radio the landing of the Allies in Normandy. And I was so... every night, when my father was able to be by my bedside I'd ask, "Daddy, when are the Allies going to land?" And he said, "Soon, soon, soon."

> [That morning] I ran out on the steps, quickly across streets and to my father's place and I announced... I ran in to say "The Allies have landed!" Everybody was overjoyed and the boss then took everybody out to the cafe for a drink. -- I got grape juice. They all got wine [laughs].

When the battle of Lyons had been won and it was safe for Rene to return there, his aunt came to the farm to pick him up. This was the day long awaited by Rene and he was excited for he knew at last he and his father and mother would be together. But when he arrived with his aunt, neither his father nor mother were there. He was shocked and hurt. His aunt told him that his father had joined the Free French Forces and was fighting in Germany, so Rene should expect no immediate reunion with his family. This masked the tragedy that had in fact occurred. Rene's father had been captured by the SS.

> My aunt didn't tell me what had really happened. And what had really happened was that exactly one month before the liberation of Lyons, fourth of August 1944, my father one day walked into the building where Pierre and his mother lived. And on the stairway, he found himself nose to nose with the Gestapo. They were not looking for him but for somebody else. They discovered he had false identity and who he actually was, and he was on the last train that left France for the death camps... the very last one! [Voice is soft, very hurt.] And you know... it was such agony, because they... I found out all the terrible details two years ago, at the time of the Barbie trial in Lyons. They were taken right away to Auschwitz.

The Resistance had been determined to prevent this train from leaving and blew up railway lines where it was expected to travel, but to no avail. The Nazis rerouted the train, anticipating the resistance effort, and succeeded in getting out of France. For the captives on board, the rail journey took twelve days. They had almost no food or drink and it was hot that August. Rene knew nothing of what was happening to his father. When knowledge of it did come much later in his life, it changed his understanding of so much of the past. It was telling that he inadvertently used "agony" for "irony" to make this early reference in his narrative to his father's final days. Both words were appropriate. Rene ended the war in a Jewish children's home near the Alps.

> Very beautiful there... lovely. [But] it was not a very well-run place, I must say, and I attempted to escape from there... with a couple of others. But we were caught and brought back, and I went to school there.

> And I remember [8 May 1945] the children from the schools were all being marched in lines to the city... to the town square in front of the loudspeakers they had hanging up. And then the broadcast and the speech... General de Gaulle [laughs]. I mean, everybody worshipped him then. He was the liberator of the nation. But I kept...the feasting over, I thought that my father will be back any day at least and what about my mother? -she would be back.

> And the days went by and every now and then, one father or one mother would come back to pick up one of the children. Nobody came for me.

Because of Rene's unhappiness his relatives had him brought back to Lyons and introduced him to a friend of his father's, who had been with the Resistance. He had suggested sending Rene to another Jewish orphanage affiliated with French socialists. Over the next five years he remained in three successive homes with this foster care system. He was a teenager and entering high school before the truth concerning his father was made clear to him.

> We were one hundred and twenty children in that place and the special ministry from the government was created to look after the war victims and the veterans affairs. We were all taken care of... we all got some kind of clothing, the same school smocks French children at one time used to wear. Usually the boys wore blue, and the girls pink, and there was a button on the side, and a button at the back.
>
> Almost every week, somebody would come [quiet again] to claim his child, the father or mother. And I kept waiting, waiting, week after week. And nobody came... and... you know, two years later, 1947, I had still not entirely lost hope that at least my father -- I had already given up hope for my mother -- survived.
>
> One day there came a lady from Lyons I remembered from 1944 and she told me the truth of how my father had been caught. She didn't know what happened to him afterwards.

The waiting was over, but it had cast a shadow over a great deal of his life. He still did not know the bitter details about how his father passed away. Until that happened and the sorrow could be dealt with, his self-conception and sense of meaning in life would suffer. He had been ten years old when he last saw his father during a trip to Lyons. Tears welled up in his eyes as he remembered.

> It [waiting] affected me very deeply because I very much missed my father and I often felt quite lonely. As I got older, I became lonelier.
>
> I was increasingly unhappy as I grew to be thirteen and fourteen. I remember being very gloomy and sort of aloof and not being able to blend in... into the life of the home and being very susceptible to being mocked by anyone and sort of withdrawing into my own shell.

Throughout the 1960's, while he started his career, he sought new information on the fate of his mother and father. More facts had been documented on the names of those brought to the camps and their fate. Increasingly, people who survived were willing to share the details of their experience under the Nazis. In that way, through third party ties, friends, and friends of friends, Rene found out what they knew of his father's last days.

> And here was a man. He had been with my father at Auschwitz, and both were tailors. The Germans treated them better because they needed the tailors for their uniforms. So they managed to... to live till the Russians arrived at Auschwitz. But then the Germans precipitously evacuated the survivors. They tried to erase all the evidence, the cremation and all that, and the survivors were placed on a forced march westward where anyone who could not go on walking was just shot down on the spot. My father and his friend survived the march. They got to Landsberg near Munich and there my father just died of exhaustion. He died in his friend's arms. It was just about a month and a half before the war... [Pause] [Q: ended?] [Rene: very quiet] Yes.
>
> It was in 1965 I found that out... and [also] two years ago... I found out the details about that trip, about that last train, something that my father's friend didn't want to tell me all those years because... tragic. -- Saw him every time I was in... This man died a few years ago. And I remember it was the time when Klaus Barbie had just been extradited to France and one of his last words to me was, "There's something I didn't want to tell you before, but I have to tell you... that your father went through Klaus Barbie's hands."

The lonely years, when as a boy "nobody came" to lift him back into the warmth of family life, had ended with this news which he received as a young man. It might be reasoned a cruelty to deny a child the truth about his parents and what had transpired in situations of crisis, but no one individual had been assigned responsibility for Rene, even though both family and friends cared for his well being.

> During vacations I went to my family and I went to Lyons. And one day, early in 1949, a brother of my father who survived the war turned up in France. He had been in DP camps for... He spent about a year trying to find me and he eventually did find me. He lived in Toulouse where he got remarried. Before the war, his first wife and two children were killed and he survived. He came to France as a DP and got married in Toulouse and then he found me.

He is the only person left in my parents' generation... family. And they wanted to adopt me, *to take me home* with them.

This couple wanted him to immigrate to North America with them. But too much and happened and his imagination was turning elsewhere. Yet it had pleased him that they had "come for him" in a sense. He eventually got a Ford Foundation scholarship which began his rise in the academic community.

I got a scholarship to study at Columbia University. New York was a way out of an insecure situation and still I was scared when I left for America. I don't know what my imagination was saying. However, once I arrived, I settled in quite beautifully, you know. In no time at all in New York, I was able to like it.

He had come full circle. He now was able to choose to leave what earlier he had felt moved to escape. He was now in a position to make decisions for himself, to build his own identity in ways not associated with the past. He was choosing to move forward, not out of feelings of fear or hate, but with a will to be constructive.

In his present life, as faculty member of a prestigious university, he visits family in North America and France on a regular basis. He is interested in human justice and has involved himself in Jewish community life there and in the Middle East. Recently he spent a sabbatical in Israel. He has a cosmopolitan's commitment to community and the future. His home is a simple, generous, space where many people. This is not to say he has fully escaped the past--nor would he necessarily want this, for his early childhood is part of that along with the loss, grief, and painful longing.

How it affected me in later life, you know.

For many years, memories of the war were not in my mind... and they are not generally in my mind, but every now and then, something comes back... out of nowhere... out of the blue... Like a dream one night of my mother and my father and then for four or five years I do not have such dreams. And then all of a sudden...

As recently as about three or four years ago, one night, I dreamt that I was at some railway station in Europe and I was about to board a train and suddenly they announced over the loudspeaker... my name was called over the loudspeaker... to go into the railway building and up to the fifth floor or something... My father was waiting for me there. I said, "My God! I have only fifteen minutes for the running of the train!" and I started running up those stairs. And of course, before I got up to the top, I woke up.

The stairs paralleled those at Rue Couteau near where his father encountered the Gestapo and had been taken in for questioning. In the dream he has to find his father, but there is so little time; he is on his way somewhere else. The train will leave, but he must reach his father because his father *is waiting for him*; there is no longer a sense of abandonment. The source souciant is the father image, and with it comes peace as well as stirring. He runs toward it still.

LOUISE

Louise Weinstein was born to an affluent Jewish family in Rotterdam. Though the grandparents were observant, her parents were not. Her father had moved to Holland from Vienna after the First World War, working initially with the stock market and then in his own business as a furrier. Her mother was Dutch, from a well-established family in the Dutch community. She was the youngest of two daughters. The family lived with the maternal grandparents.

> The house was built... it was built in the turn of the century by some millionaire grocer and... had all kinds of really elaborate pictures. This is alabaster [points to a lamp nearby]. I could describe my life in those days [1930's] as decidedly overprotected. I was not to play in the street. It was considered not only dangerous, but the children I might play with [pause] well, were considered perhaps not... not appropriate... for a socially climbing family.

They moved to Amsterdam in the mid-1930s and for Louise this felt very uncomfortable. There were many reasons.

> I recall many years later talking with my mother about the fact that I was actually very unhappy [at kindergarten]. I came in January, so mid-school year, and only experienced the last half, which means of course I was an outsider when I came in that kindergarten class and I mentioned to her at the time that I was quite... felt quite unaccepted... in fact maladjusted and that's... there was a kindergarten teacher and her helper that I found no solace or... or understanding from. Thereupon my mother commented, "They were anti-Semites."

The next year her family placed her in a Montessori school, and she began to adjust. Yet there was a sense of underlying tension marring their otherwise happy existence at the time.

> First of all, I would overhear my father listening to the radio and Hitler's speeches, and my father had a very high awareness of what was going on, I'd say greater than many Dutch Jewish families, because his mother and relatives still lived in Vienna and they were victims of the Anschluss when the Nazis invaded Austria and he... [sighs] he was instrumental in getting his mother, his sister, his brother-in-law... he brought them to Holland, unfortunately. He helped some of his nephews to go to Israel, and one nephew went to South America, and he's the only one who I still have contact with.
>
> So he was very aware of the impending threat and consequently I was aware, and there were the discussions at home and he made the decision to... to emigrate and... This was about 1939 after the actual... the... The Germans didn't invade the Netherlands til May 1940. September '39 they invaded Poland. So he... the minute... as far as I know... the minute they invaded Poland the second world war officially started, he made a decision to leave.

He shifted his assets to New York through a business contact there and then tried to get a visa to bring himself and his family over. Since he had been born in Berlin, he fell under the German quota which had been filled by that time, and so his visa petition was denied. He then determined to get the family on a ship to the Dutch West Indies, but the boat on which passage was booked sank. In the meantime, there was a problem closer at hand.

> My mother's mother, it turned out that she had breast cancer, and they knew that she didn't have long to live. It was spreading. And so... so they wouldn't leave because that... So, my mother's mother died in February 1940, and this was the big disaster in the family. She was only fifty-nine and... that was just the worst thing that struck the family. [With] hindsight you might say, well perhaps it was all for the better because my grandfather and my aunt and my uncle and his wife and daughter and my great grandfather and several of my mother's relatives were all gassed. So at least she... but at least the possibility of having been gassed was spared her.

> Anyway, so, here we were. Now after my grandmother died, the family was free to leave and so my father tried to book passage on a ship to Curacao, and it was filled. That's where luck and fate play a role, because that ship was called the Simon Bolivar. It was torpedoed and everybody drowned. So. [Pause] He booked passage on the next ship which would sail three weeks after the Simon Bolivar, and that was the third week of May, and the Germans invaded the tenth of May. So we never got out.

While the Dutch army were holding back the Germans at Rotterdam, many like the Weinsteins desperately tried to find passage across the Atlantic. Just before the ports were sealed, existing liners were filled to capacity and small fishing boats chartered by displaced ticket holders from cancelled sailings. When Louise's family got down to the docks there was no way out.

> I still remember us driving out of our driveway and... [pause] sounds so funny nowadays. We had a maid, a live-in maid. She was standing in the front door with our dog. And we drove to the harbor outside of Amsterdam. That was just around the time of the capitulation. I don't know whether it was the same night or the next day... it must have been the same night, and we were in a hotel and there were the families of my parents closest friends... several families. But one family that was among our closest friends, they were there too and when the news came of the capitulation and I remember everybody starting to cry and falling into each other's arms.

Being the youngest child meant feeling a little distanced from the adult world around her at this time. Control was already an important virtue for her then since otherwise she was all too easily dismissed as "the baby."

> We must have been all in that hotel or something. All I can remember is that I thought it was so ridiculous that all these grown-up people were standing there crying. I thought it was absolutely... although I understood it was bad, I felt they weren't in control of themselves. It must have been very important to me to be seen under control because I was always the youngest and I was considered the baby and I had to be strong, right? Because... because I... I was always as a "quantite negligeable."

> They were trying to charter fishing boats to sail over to England and

some people did. Some made it and some were shot down and drowned. But we never even got the fishing boat. We just went back along with some of the other families.

They settled back to life with the compromises they knew were inevitable. Observing what had happened to Jews in Austria and Poland, they began to prepare for confiscation of property, possible "resettlement" to some other part of the city, and rationing. They believed that refugees from Germany and other parts of Europe would be the most vulnerable population as the Nazis took over.

> Many of these refugees were probably not like ourselves, not even able to travel further, thinking they'd be safe in Holland and what happened was that [pause] whatever laws... whatever laws the Germans enacted, they were directed at those German refugees first. So, in the beginning we always knew what was up ahead because we knew what happened to them was going to happen to us. I can recall that a lot of Dutch Jews... Jewish families... settled Dutch Jewish families, probably including some of my mother's relatives, would say, "Oh dear, those poor dear German Jews. Look what's happening to them." It's human nature to think that bad things are not going to happen to you... always happen to other people, right? But my father had this raised awareness, and so he was a realist.

Louise remembers the Gestapo were going to affluent homes in the suburbs and confiscating property in the name of the State. Louise's family then decided to build their own defenses against the time when this would happen to them. Typically, someone would enter the house of someone known to be a Jew or a socialist or some other denounceable category, located in a politically or economically useful area "to take inventory," that is, enter a home in the name of the state and record its contents prior to confiscation. Louise's father thought that if you took what they were doing for what it was, all the rhetoric management by the Nazis was not just preposterous, it was hilarious.

> Oh, there were endless jokes, endless jokes, you know. How ridiculous, you know. Here come these stupid thieves, you know. I don't remember all the jokes, but there were all kinds of nicknames for these people [Nazis]. But I can remember... I still have here the fancy china dinnerware my parents... how my parents would hand over stacks and stacks of dinnerware across the fence to the non-Jewish neighbor, and the neighbors... some of the neighbors were very helpful, you know, and we would give all kinds of things that would be around to those near to

us. And in those days people had started to horde food, too, you know... bags of rice and flour and so on. That, too... gave it all to the next door neighbors.

We had a chesterfield suite that had cushions that were filled with eiderdown which was considered very precious and -- it [the story] has its own tragicomical angles to it. They... well, in those days you had specific people that you would deal with. This was an upholstered... that they had done work with before. He [father] had them pick up all the pillows and taken out the eiderdown and filled those pillows with the worse kind of filth and dust that you could ever imagine and everybody would laugh forever at the idea of how some German housewife in Berlin would forever try to clean those pillows when she got the furniture! Never to be able to *clean* them, you see!! [laughs heartily]. And that was very funny.

The tragic part of it was that the eiderdown was used... my parents had sleeping bags made out of it and the idea was... well, they were already starting to talk about work camps... I might be sent to work camps and you needed warm sleeping bags. So. I can still remember, they had this striped ticking that you use in hotel mattresses. I can still see them in front of me.

Anti-Semitic laws began to proliferate. Louise remembered all Jews had to wear a yellow star. All Jewish families had to register and receive identification papers. Those with jobs in the civil service were dismissed. Professionals were not allowed to practice outside the Jewish community, and most of their equipment was confiscated. Food had to be bought from Jewish grocers who were never adequately stocked by the State.

There were small islands of reprieve in this nightmare. Individuals made spontaneous gestures of good faith to one another, showing symbolic resistance. Louise took to the prescribed yellow star like a hairshirt, but wear it she did. She found unexpected allies.

Then came the stars. I remember the first day I went out we had blocked off streets and we would roller skate in the... and I would go out on my roller skates with my star on. The first person I encountered was an older man who lived somewhere down the street who would normally not even pay attention to me. And he saw me with this star and the first thing he did was he took off his hat and he bowed very deeply [illustrates] for me. And that made a very deep impression on me.

Finally the waiting game ended and they were "resettled" to a poor, inner city area. Her family had been processed through a quarantine area, stripped, searched for lice and venereal disease, then packed off to a set of rooms where a small stove gave them both heat and a means to cook whatever food they could get. Soon their business was confiscated.

> One day the gentleman turned up at my father's business. He would still... even though he had... he had sent some of his assets to the States to a former colleague of his who was in New York because we were emigrating, but his business was still there [Amsterdam] and he still went there. And one day this German turned up and said his name was Jaeger. Now jaeger in German means hunter and his name was YAHGER [she emphasizes] and, "You better turn over your business to me or I will shoot you," he said. So my father came home giggling and laughing because he says here comes a man who calls himself "hunter" and he said "I will shoot you!" [Laughs] And he thought it was just totally ridiculous. Of course he would laugh because he really didn't have too many assets left in... in his business in the first place, and this guy was just getting a lot of nothing.

While her parents eased the family into the restrictions and privations of their new life, Louise turned inward. She felt emotionally isolated. Her elder sister was six years her senior and had different friends than Louise. As "the baby" she was left out of discussions about what was happening and what they would do next. This gave her a sense of being insulated from what was happening but at the same time left her with a heavy sense of powerlessness. She had no one her own age with whom to sort through what was happening.

> I wasn't... well, I am putting it in context as an adult. I didn't totally reason that... [she had pure terror in the face of vulnerability], but the feeling was there. That was the awareness I had.

> [Q: Did you feel hostility?]

> [Sighs] No. I would say there was an awareness of fear and danger, certainly, absolutely, because you were at the mercy of somebody with total power over you. The knowledge that we were... that you had become a non-entity almost. Well, you know. In a deeper sense were less than a respected human being. I would pinpoint that as a moment of experience in raci... No, seeing that in our case a sheltered middle-

class family, you know... you could say that... that one was sort of protected from that sense of lack of power. But that's where it becomes very clear.

[Q: And so, what was your response?]

Withdrew. I didn't even talk about it with my family. You see I wasn't considered to understand anything about the human body at all at that stage. I was twelve. I... I didn't discuss things with my family because of the circumstances, even more so in that situation. So I wouldn't talk about my own concerns. No... I felt badly for them. I felt a mixture, I suppose, of unhappiness for them and fear and bafflement. It was a key moment in my awareness of-of the circumstances.

Her adaptation in her loneliness was to become her parents' protector and keep them from any sense of inadequacy in the new situation. In the ghetto she no longer lived near her school and much of the way was through bombed out neighborhoods. She made no complaints. Any problems with getting along with others she was determined to make a thing of the past, in keeping with her new resolve. But gradually, issues of surviving took preeminence over all others. Her friends and her sister's friends began to get notices that they were to appear at certain times and dates with a pack-sack and sleeping bag because, allegedly, they were going to be sent to work camps. Taking the notices at face value while fearing everything, families concerned themselves with getting the children what they might need.

I remember lots of energy and attention being put into the right kind of soap and the right kind of wrapper and this and that. Everything that would... and solid tubes... that would be so good for you to survive in a work camp. Everything that happened was focused on the best for survivability. My sister was called up along with a lot of young people.

Louise's sister had benefitted from her father's precautions. He had alerted her to the value of a work permit, which she got. She then was able to take a position with the Jewish community services. Work permits had some limited value in slowing down "resettlement." Louise felt that the contacts and information that her family had were directly related to their prestigious class standing.

> Where the split starts between those who had a better chance in terms of the society we lived in... between those who had a better chance of survival and others [deep breath]. That working class Jewish population in... in Amsterdam, being in very clearly defined neighborhoods and clearly defined industries, didn't have anywhere near the means to go in hiding or leave that the more affluent people with connections of various sorts would have. There were some very courageous Underground people and some very dedicated people who would help [all] Jews, and I am not saying any... casting any aspersions on those people. It was just the reality of the situation.

Her sister started working in the Jewish day care center and her mother got a position in the clothing depot, helping to sort clothes. Her father got a stamp saying that through his business he was "supplying the German army." By the second half of 1942, they felt reasonably sure that they might make it through the war unscathed. Then news came of their relatives in Rotterdam being "resettled." This included deporting a ninety-six year old great grandfather and five or six aunts and uncles and their families; they were all gassed at Sobibor or died at Westerbork on the way to the extermination camp. Of all these people only two survived. Louise and her family were in a state of shock because it meant that class standing would be no protection. If they were to survive they would have to take more radical measures.

Gestapo raids in their neighborhood increasingly threatened the family's balance. All they could do was watch as others were carted away. People were kept perpetually off guard and in constant fear. As the sirens sounded one night, Louise managed to peep through the black-out curtains.

> I remember looking out and seeing a little boy... young boy running down the street pursued by a green police (SIPO) and he was starting to outrun him and I remember seeing the green police taking... they were helmeted... that's why... another thing... they were not just wearing caps, they were wearing combat helmets... and him taking his helmet off and throwing it after the boy. I could see that helmet rolling across the... the cobblestones I guess they were... the way the pavement was sort of a brick pavement... and because of that it would bounce and sparks were flying off the helmet in all directions. I have that image of that happening as an image of pure terror.

By the fall of 1942, the adults started weighing the chances of hiding as an alternative measure. As long as the precautions they had already taken seemed to be working, Louise's father was against leaving. But her mother was determined to "not be lugged away like a sheep." She felt they must go into hiding whether or not it seemed relatively safe.

> And in the end, she won the argument and that was... She won the argument the day my father discovered that some of his colleagues were deported, despite the fact that their identifications were stamped as purveyor to the German army.

That having been decided, they had to locate someone to help them realize their plans. A myriad of details were involved in each step of the process. It required a wide network of contacts.

> They contacted a first cousin of my mother who herself was half Jewish to begin with and who was married to someone who was not Jewish. Not only that, but he was a very prominent person in Social Democratic circles and had a lot of contacts in the Underground. He agreed to help us get out of Amsterdam and find us addresses and false papers.

> You see, there are a number of things needed. First of all, it wasn't that easy to just leave Amsterdam because what it meant was taking the train. Nobody had cars of their own anymore. It wasn't legal to own cars for anybody. They were all taken by the German army, you know. There was no bicycles. There were, but you couldn't ride a bi... family on bicycles in the middle of winter for... for forty miles or so. But in order to ride a train, you couldn't wear a Star and, of course, in order to take your Stars off, you couldn't have identification papers that are stamped "J." So it was taking big risks. And then of course you have to have an address, people who were courageous enough to take people in hiding even though they didn't have too many material resources. [Going into hiding] meant that you didn't have food stamps. You'd have to buy food.

The decision to go into hiding had to be backed up by endless vigilance, ample resources, and a tireless capacity for detail. Even with that, by 1943, the number of hiding spots for refugees was shrinking. Members of the Dutch army and Allied personnel looking for refuge were turning up increasingly in the Dutch countryside. But this would be the last window of opportunity for the Weinsteins to go into hiding, and they took it. They ended up, finally, on a little farm in the west of Holland which had one cow, one pig, six chickens and half an acre of corn. Their sponsor was a fundamentalist known to the Underground through his ties with the

Dutch Reformed Church.

> They were so segregated [as a fundamentalist sect] that they didn't even have a minister. They just had Bible readings [laughs]. And they could never have afforded to hide us, but the Underground in that area was very solid. Strangely enough there were... there were two... two components to that Underground. The one was very devoutly fundamentalist Christian Reformed. -- The man who represented that group was our contact, and he was an exceedingly courageous person. The other component was a group of Communists. And... and they worked together. That was the interesting part. They... their common enemy was the Nazis, and they worked together. [Pause].
>
> But [the weak link] was this man, and he must have found this... this farmer, and quite frankly, although I must say about the man, certainly his life was at risk and he sheltered us and... and he never betrayed us. [Pause] Quite bluntly he needed us to... he needed our money.

The farmer had ten children from a previous marriage, and though he had promised not to tell that he was hiding Jews, all of the children knew about it. The man had been widowed and remarried, with the second marriage being fairly unstable. The house the couple lived in was owned by the wife as part of what she inherited at the death of her first husband. It was impossible to feel safe in the situation.

> This couple fought night and day, [like] cats and dogs. My father... our life depended on [them]... My father had to to be the arbiter for sixteen months between them, that couple, to make sure that this thing would hang together.

But this failsafe did not always work, and, at one point, the wife flew off in a fury to her sisters. This left Louise and her family in fear for their lives, since one word from her might betray them to an unknown source. Louise's father redoubled his efforts and at the same time placed more restrictions upon Louise and her mother. Since neighbors might drop in at any time, the father decided that it was a danger to have books lying around. So, no reading for Louise and no domestic tasks during the daylight hours. Once when Louise's mother had washed slippers and hung them to dry on the line, inquiries had been made by the neighbors, asking how the wife had come into such a bounty. It was tense.

No books! So you know what position that put me in, right? For months and months and months, seeing nobody, and sitting. I had actually been sitting for sixteen months in this room without books, no writing materials, absolutely total sensory... virtually total sensory deprivation. Not... never outside, except if it was very dark. We cooked late at night in the dark... occasionally take some fresh air.

It was a pot-bellied stove to heat the place. It was a little... see the... these houses they had a large sort of common room and then there was a smaller sort of Sunday room a few steps up that nobody would ever use other than for funerals or weddings. So that's where we were. And of course, in winter, you can't throw the coal on the stove because it would make a sound. If you had to cough you would put your head in a blanket or else they would hear you. They would sit there til an hour --two hours, having coffee and talking, because that's what's done in that community, right? Also you would look strange...

[Q: Everybody watching everything.]

Oh, yes. They would. Sure. This is farm country. Neighbors know each other intimately. And so they would scratch on the door and then we couldn't make a sound.

In the fall of 1944 things got worse. Raids were becoming successful in this rural area. Where she was hiding with a family of friends who had taken in twenty or so Jews, Louise's sister had almost been captured. There was fighting not far away and civilians were being billeted to their area. A family of three was assigned to the little farmhouse where the Weinsteins were hiding.

So in comes a family, a tailor and his wife and six year old daughter... billeted in our house! So the whole first day we were sitting there [pause] in utter panic. What should we do? Conclusion eventually was, there is just no alternative. In this house you can't... we have to take a chance. We have to tell them, you know. Who's to know if they're traitors or... or talkers or whatever. Well, as luck would have it, they totally accepted it. But we had to take a chance on the six year old girl, you know. She plays with other children and you never know what she says. Well, she may even have said... babbled something about people in her house. But probably nobody even paid much attention to it or maybe she was just not interested in talking about it. Nothing happened, anyway. This was from October til April of that winter. But, you know, it could just as well have been a total disaster.

Responsibility for the success of their hiding operation was assumed by her father but the onus for making it work in fact fell on each one of them. Her father, however, had been a soldier in the First World War in the German trenches, and knew the importance of discipline for survival. Unlike the trenches, however, the enemy was not tucked neatly behind a formally defined boundary and could be anywhere. Survival in hiding demanded a tolerance for endless hours of waiting for seemingly nothing to happen. There was no artillery to surmount, no enemy line to identify and take. It was a mental game that could easily sap the spirit and destroy the social unit. Small events like a dental emergency could become a looming tragedy.

Before she and her family went into hiding, Louise had left a tooth unattended. The dentist who started to work on it had been ghettoized. There were few of the usual tools dentist's have left at his disposal, and no anesthetic. She was delivered from her dilemma about what to do when the dentist and his wife disappeared and were never heard from again.

> Anyway, so that tooth had been sitting there untreated... half treated from early in '42 or late '41 and here we are in the winter of '44-'45 and it becomes very seriously impacted. Terrible tooth infection. And it hurts, of course, very much. So, what to do? The Underground contact... this man he came one night and he took me to a dentist, late at night, to get this tooth treated. Now, I don't know what he told the man, but he probably told the man that I was his daughter or relative and I had such a pain and I... I needed to definitely get this tooth treated.
>
> This man asked me where I lived. He asked for my address and I instantly knew that I never, of course, never ever was going to say where I was but I didn't know this place, you see. I had never lived there. I didn't know any addresses. So. But I happened to know one main street. So I blurted out to them, "Apfeldoorn Street," number so and so.
>
> Now, if... if you're on the good side of things and you know what's going on, you're not asking that question. So either he was just totally ignorant, or he wasn't, really, not very trustworthy. I don't know. I'll never know. But I remember that that was a very anxious moment.

Not knowing with any clarity who could be trusted and for how long meant being constantly on the defensive and, whether in praise or criticism, never feeling it was right to trust anyone. This gave a certain tentativeness to their relations even with those who were protecting them. Her father would not allow any of them to discuss matters pertaining to these years afterwards. It was his way of declaring it a space beyond the pale of normal reciprocity.

Liberation became a boundary between the desperate and the ordinary. It had gotten delayed while the Allies struggled to make a successful inroad. Waiting added excessive strain to the Weinstein's depleted personal resources. But now there were some armored vehicles in the fields near their hiding place.

> April '45. There w... first of all, some artillery, bombing, and we had a trench outside of the house covered with bales of straw. [Pause]. We went to hide in [it] because of the shooting. Only some cows were killed that time [laughs]. My father was so thrilled that they did this because the liberation was there, but... but my mother and I were absolutely petrified because of the shooting. And... he was snoring away! [he had fallen asleep] [laughing].

The tremendous tension her father had been under lifted enough for him to doze off as the Allies attacked. Not long after this he made the decision for them to move to the other side of the river, since, with the front shifting, he knew it was risky to remain in hiding where they were.

> We walked through an area, through a forest where there was an institute for mentally ill people there originally. And, at one point a lot of people went in hiding there. An awful lot of Jews went in there, pretended to be mentally ill, and then they were rounded up and lugged away. Every mentally ill person, Jewish or not--lugged them all out of there. And, when we were walking through that forest... that's a forested area and the SS were holed up in there, and the bullets were flying, [pause] whistling around our ears as we were walking, and we could very easily have been killed right then and there. Anyway, we... we weren't killed, and we got behind the lines.

> The first [Allied] soldier I saw, I'll never forget... as we walked through that forest, and at the end of the forest there was a main road with a lot of army vehicles, and then eventually we got a ride with some officers who got a jeep to go further. But the first... As we went round the bend, there was one army personnel standing there. Whether he was a soldier or an officer, I don't know but [deep breath] in my memory [laughing] he is the tallest guy I have ever seen in my life. He was a very tall Black man and... he was maybe 6 feet, I don't know, but [laughing] I'll never

forget that person.

They got back to Amsterdam eventually and moved in temporarily with the uncle whose daughter had been working with the Underground and was still in the concentration camps.

> You see he was... because his wife wasn't Jewish, even though they were religious Jews, he managed, you know. Somehow or other, he managed to continue living in his house. [Pause]. I really couldn't even tell you how that was possible, but he was. Course, he was in a terrible state because he didn't know about the fate of his only daughter at that point. Eventually she showed up, and incidentally that whole experience must have been too much for him. He died of a heart attack at quite a young age after the war. But that was where we went because he was the only close relative who still lived in a regular house that we could move into. And we did that for some months.

Shortly thereafter, another house was made available to them in the area where they had been living before the Occupation. Louise had no direct encounters with the Gestapo during their ordeal, but the other members of her family did. Nevertheless, they considered themselves very lucky. Close calls and near misses added to the anxiety and terror, but at last they had made it. They were the unusual cases. Of Holland's 130,000 Jews, Louise estimated that only around ten to fifteen percent survived. Nor were they welcomed unequivocally by all who witnessed their return.

> We did after the war come back [to the neighborhood in the suburbs] and sort of saying hello to people, and these were the people who... who when I showed up said, "Hey do you still live?" Th-that was clearly not a happy reception.

By fall of 1945, she was able to get back in school to try to regain lost time and missed grades. There were many others returning from abroad where they had waited out the conflict, and others who had survived the concentration camps. They, like her, had some catching up to do in terms of schooling. However, they were spread out, and though collectively there was an effort being made to accommodate the victims, for those like Louise who had survived in hiding, wounds had to be dealt with in a different kind of isolation than they had just escaped. Financially, in Louise's case, her father had a genius for landing on his feet.

As far as the business is concerned, well, every business... virtually every business was... especially in Western Holland, was dead. The country was plundered bare by the Nazis and... But his name and his know-how, plus the resources that he had been able to [recover, allowed him to] re-establish himself. It was quite remarkable of him, really. By then he was, maybe, fifty.

Louise was, in the meantime, struggling with her own personal problems. She felt isolated not just because of her unique experience but because, given her closed circle of ties, she had not needed to develop her social arts.

I basically didn't know how to make friends or relate to people and I felt very bad about myself. I tended to have a very bad self image. I thought that a lot of things I did were my own [fault], just... I did a lot of guilt complexes of various kinds and [after the "hunger winter" of '44-'45] the focus on food was enormous. At first there was still quite a bit of rationing and... and... lack of various things, but one would, you know... Suddenly I developed a very serious eating complex. Relationships with boys were just... I... because I didn't know how to handle them, they didn't exist, basically, you know. I would dream a lot, daydream a lot. There were lots of people, but I would only relate to them in a superficial level.

[Q: Did you find it hard to be involved in friendship relative to family?]

Well I simply wouldn't know how. I wouldn't have the skills and I focused a lot on academic work.

She knew she had to attempt to make some friends, but there were inconsistencies in people's conduct which spurred her confusion and discouragement. Anti-Semitism had not died with the Nazi defeat, though it was in retreat. She found an example of it near at hand. She had gone back to a school that had few facilities and was considered old fashioned. There she sought out a friend to walk with at recess who also seemed to be by herself. Louise had not questioned the girl's reticent manner. One day they attended an exhibition.

Anyway we went... There was some sort of a display somewhere... a war display. A lot of photos of traitors and we were standing there looking at it and one of them had a Jewish name and I said, "Look. A Jewish name." Just... you know, I quite... sort of naively, and... she said, "Yes, of course. Those Jews they will betray their mother and their father anytime." Something like this. I was totally frozen. I was totally incapable of responding, saying anything. She didn't know, obviously, I was Jewish. But I was absolutely incapable of saying anything in response, which then of course kept bothering me that I hadn't... But, just as an example of the kind of situation, after all, I mean, for several years I hadn't... [it was] as if one sits in a prison cell. There was no opportunity to relate.

Throughout their time in hiding, all her choices had been handled for her by loving parents. Unlike survivors of the concentration camps who had lost family, she had been lost *in* family. It was hard for her to heal the wounds of persecution without having the rhetoric of a larger political whole. She had endured pain, distress, torment, and fear because of racism but did not feel she could claim any special status.

I think we saw ourselves after the war as the lucky ones which in a sense we were. We had really experienced nothing compared to those people who were in the camps, and we saw ourselves... I saw myself... as someone who wasn't touched, which wasn't true. But it took a long time to realize that.

Of course the isolation and the fe... knowledge of being persecuted and of hiding and of the constant sense of danger for virtually... for three years, had a deep impact on me. But it's difficult to trace. It's only in a few respects that I can put my finger on it and say that's where I can see that it directly...

When we spoke, Louise had a family of five. Her husband was born in Denmark. During the interview he quietly entered the room with a magnificent pot of coffee which he served in the china cups Louise brought from her family in Holland. It was a symbol of strength and transcendence meant to reassure Louise, who, he knew, had sacrificed to make this return to the past. Later on, as the brilliant sunset burst into the room, he returned bringing what he and their son and daughter had gathered from their garden--cherries, sweet and rich, another sign to remind her of the love they shared as her family in the present.

Louise had actively tried to deal with any lingering threats to her emotional life in the present which derived from persecution in the past. She understood the concept of "survivor guilt" and through her community involvement turned what she knew of it into a constructive orientation.

I determined quite early in life that I have an obligation to the people that perished for having survived. Maybe I would feel that way regardless, but somehow or other I have the social obligation and so I have done a lot of things, but sort of related to social responsibility. Well, right now my job is related to fighting racism. I've done that for five years now.

I don't think you can understand discrimination in any form unless you've experienced it yourself. Women have it. Misuse of power is, in the ultimate analysis, what discrimination amounts to... to make someone less than yourself in order to gain power. I'm aware of this all the time.

MARIETTE

Marie Sorenson was born in 1935. By the time she was seven, her brothers were hiding her in orphanages. In 1942, her mother and many of their family of eleven were transported to Auschwitz. She remembered the trauma of those years from a child's point of view.

> My father died in... I was a year and a half old. I am the youngest of eleven children. There's eight of us alive. We found each other through research after the war. I found six of us. So my life with my father I can't tell you. With my mother... very religious woman, my worst memory of course was when I came home with this lady who was hiding me. It was my eighth birthday and I came home to celebrate my birthday and as I was walking down the street with this lady, I saw my mother and brother Albert... he died later in Auschwitz, being taken in a truck.

As the youngest, she had been born in Belgium. The rest of the family were born in Poland. They had tried to get away from there by moving westward as conditions worsened in the late 1930s. When the Nazis invaded Belgium and France, they were living in a tenement in Brussels when they were last together. The death of the father meant that the family had to survive on whatever resources the children could find. After the Nazi Occupation of Belgium, most of her family had joined the Resistance. One brother was hanged by the Nazis. Another was a victim of Auschwitz, as was her mother. Her brother Henri, six years her elder, became her protector, directing her activities, getting her in and out of hiding places, involving her as a courier for messages with the Resistance. Her memories of that period are sparse, dominated by single object symbolism and imagic rather than discursive memories.

> The only thing I can remember is my mother sewing a yellow star on all of us. I kept ripping it off as I ran down the stairs cause I didn't want to wear it, and my mother kept putting it back on my sweater.

She had a photographic memory as a child, and by nine years of age knew seven languages. This made her very valuable in her roles with the Resistance and capable of entering various kinds of situations in hiding.

> I was one of the children that... my family used in the French Underground. I happen to have had a photogenic memory and... which I didn't know, but I think we all had a gift, and I think when you're in stress, you fear. In everyday life-and-death situations, you call on resources that you didn't know you had.

> I used to be able to... be able to give them a message, to pass it until five years ago, I thought I'd forgotten the message. Five years ago, the message came back which I thought I'd buried, and that really scared me.

Not only was her childhood one of hiding and danger working with the Resistance, but she had been cautioned by her brother not to acknowledge anyone in their family when she might chance to see them, for fear of giving them away. She was taught to never completely trust anyone, and so she tried to keep mostly to herself. This meant that a pattern of social and emotional isolation became part of her self expression through a great deal of her childhood. Her memories now of that time flow out in bundles of inchoate images; they had not been reasoned into place by talk with peers or trusted others who might have helped her align her experiences with what others saw as happening. While, then, her memory for factual detail has proven itself correct over time, her feelings and understandings about the past have not been fully incorporated into her present. More than any of the other child survivors, she seemed tormented by her unexplored memories.

By her own estimate she lived with twenty families. Sometimes the hiding places were in Brussels, but others were in the surrounding area. She remembers speaking Dutch in two of them. One of her more harrowing experiences, which comes out in gasps more than in a straight story line, concerns living in a convent where she was the only Jewish child. She isn't sure about the exact length of time she was there. It may have been as much as a year.

I also lived in a convent for a year. I think it was a year... seemed like a year. One of the nuns sold me to the Germans. The Mother Superior put me in the sewers with all the rats [to hide her], and after she took me out, after the Germans left... the sister... one of the [other] sisters... anyway, I was caught.

I was taken on one of those trains they made stop somewhere, doors were open and there was a German officer standing there and I was lucky to be in front by the door, because I was very small and said in German which I spoke fluently, "What's my sister doing here?" He looked at me and I looked at him. But I spoke German and I started to rant and rave. I became a very good actress. [In fact she had seen her brother and, seizing the moment, she slipped away from her captors]. Anyway, that's how I never went to camp!

She had been betrayed, captured and taken away by the Nazi Gestapo, then on the train to interrogation, her brother Jean had somehow materialized and found a way to slip her through the crowds to safety. She depended on her brothers in almost every way and they were there for her.

Jean, my brother Jean, was the one who placed us... the rest of us children, in different homes.

[Q: What happened when he got you off the train?]

He... I went with him... took me to the car and dropped me off in Brussels. But where it was I can't tell you. And then I went to live with other people in a small town in... There's two... and I think I spoke Dutch in both places. It was on a farm... small town... Germans came... took everybody... Jewish... adults... They were all caught.

What it meant to have so many who were around her one way or another disappear, possibly to their deaths, can only be guessed. In the end, Jean, too, had been among those lost to her. Her days were full of terror, but feelings natural to this state had to be suppressed in order that she shoulder the next burden rationally. Her brother Henri became her protector after Jean was captured and killed.

Henri helped me to survive. He's the one that taught me to shoot, jump off a train, the Paris Express...the Brussels Express to Paris, whichever way you're going, taught me how to jump off a streetcar... [quiet] how to kill [pause]. You see?

He was... we call him "moustique," mosquito. He used to sting and leave. He was a kid that was never anywhere... never home. He was the one that taught me to steal food... not to cry whenever you wanted to... He is a real survivor.

Henri throughout the war, wherever I was hid, he'd find me and say, "Mariette, leave now," and I knew that the town would be taken by the Gestapo or the Germans. The youth army was very bad... the worst... the Nazi Youth Army.

The only one I ever trusted was my brother Henri. He seemed to always be there just when I had to escape or... He always seems to have known when the Germans were coming in the town or the city I was in. It seemed like he was always there. This brother is five years older than me, four and a half years older than me. But he was never a child.

While Mariette was on her own, she felt somehow protected, as if some unseen force were watching over her, balancing the current against her. She enters a very private world as she remembers her childhood, one for the most part not explored with others. She fights a tendency to retreat from those needing words to know what she does. As she speaks, her tendency is to speed along in a muted voice, casting the listener into the background, almost as though talking with herself. Solitude had been the companion of terror as she hid; she returned there as she confronted memory.

She had been in several orphanages as the war progressed and had gotten ill in one of them when, toward the end of the war, she got physically depleted and had to be hospitalized. At this point she referred to having had a friendship with another child there.

I was very ill. I had a sickness... it's a war sickness, a deficiency of vitamins. Your whole body is covered with... and you must scrape out the [lesions], and its a whole... You just cannot have a little [laughs]. It was scraped off and the blue skin... I was covered, and I was in the hospital section of the orphanage. And my girlfriend's oldest sister used to come and visit. She was in the bed beside me.

This little girl, after we got better, we were allowed to go and play in the woods which... This orphanage, there was a forest around it. [Sighs]. Anyway, the woman, the headmistress, whatever her name was, I hadn't made my bed and she says, "You gotta make your bed before you leave." And so my little girlfriend went out into the woods [ahead of her] and I said, "Wait for me there." [Sighs]. I guess I was gone... the headmistress and I never got along... I was rebellious. I didn't get there for over twenty... twenty-five minutes... and I went to the woods and found my girlfriend [voice is almost inaudible and breaking]. She had been raped a few... [Mariette is sobbing].

Her friend was murdered as she had waited for Mariette to come out and play. In listening to her narrative and watching her gestures, the movements of face and hands, the pauses and rushes in the flow of speech, the rises and falls in tonality, it is clear that the child Mariette had, in this episode, gone beyond what might be endured, proving the rule many survivors note about the danger of forming deep attachments during crisis. The unresolved shock of having found a playmate turned so unexpectedly into a victim had stayed with her throughout the rest of her life as unhealed trauma. Keeping the memories submerged in forgetting was important for her balance; remembering was viscerally painful. Marie signals the enormous misery of the child Mariette by shouting that she cannot go on with the interview; it is too hard.

She functions in her present life with friends and family and love and peace as Marie; from her past life of enemies, stealth, hate, and war, she refers to herself as Mariette. She believes these two aspects of who she is, Marie and Mariette, belong to worlds she must keep separate. She describes how Marie remembers the past through Mariette.

> I can only describe it as being like a blind person, like has senses, like they can feel an object that they can't see. They know the object is there but yet they've [never actually seen the whole of it].

In part "not seeing" past events is related to an incorporated fear of being hurt, but also it comes from her having been on her own then and not having been able to talk freely with others. However, Mariette had become Marie not by forgetting but in a very deliberate process. Though she had been a child deprived of tomorrows, counselled only to think for the moment, she managed emotions well and understood how to compromise in order to live with the burden of a violent past.

> Oh what you do is... what I say to myself... rebuild the... recovery, no matter what. *Close it* and live day by day. You do not have a future. You never have. -- With my husband, thank God, I learned there is a tomorrow.

> Firstly, I think is that you never think about tomorrow. You only live for the moment. [This brings on a] mental block, a very deep one. You close it, almost like a door. You won't open it. [Survivors] all closed doors. It's the only way.
>
> I became Marie, not Mariette... became two people. I call on Marie, like I'm doing now, but when I need Mariette's strength in life, I call on Mariette, and that strength is there.

The person Mariette became after the war was an achiever, one who could set goals and meet them. She continued to be as single-minded and disciplined as ever she had been, one who felt deeply but did not show it. She shares emotion cautiously even now, and with only a few well chosen people. For Mariette, who is Marie, intimacy is still a luxury.

She immigrated to North America with her four surviving siblings. She described them as accommodating, even doting, as families often are with the youngest child. But surviving prolonged persecution had placed an estranging structure on their interaction as a family. For three years they had been forced to live with vicious persecution and threat. Mariette had known isolation and estrangement throughout her early life; it was not easy for her to become a warm and cuddly "little sister."

> Your brothers and sisters are *not your friends*. This is the tragedy. You think sometimes that you've been as close. We tried. All right, we had family, we had children, everything else. I always [gathered] family for the Jewish holidays. Doesn't really work that way because we are four strangers with the same mother and father. You [appreciate] your sisters and brothers but you cannot really be friends.
>
> My sister Esther says to me, "Marie, please be my friend. I am good friends with everybody..." You could count my friends on one hand, and that's all I want. They're the only ones that I would allow past my [protective self system].

When she first arrived in North America, the remnant of her natural family was still with her, but they were all placed separately in different homes. She did not speak English, and the Yiddish she knew was not like that which her foster parents used. In the first year of her new life, her inner isolation was unrelieved. She tried running away from her foster parents many times. She was torn by contradiction; though she did not feel close to her brothers and sister, she still longed for the family she had lost. That ideal was the icon that had warmed her through her years of hiding, past the monsters in sewers, the traitors who denounced her, the indifferent strangers who did little to help. She could not at the whim of the moment throw that aside and replace it with what was unknown to her a year before so as to glibly suit others' expectation of contented adjustment.

> It had to be everything on my terms. My foster family had no children. It was very difficult for them. The first year I lived with them, I ran away twelve times [laughs]. The first month I think I ran away two times. My foster father--I called them uncle and aunt out of respect. Mr. Faslov always found me. He said something that really... After the twelfth time he sat me down. He says, "Mariette. No matter how far away you run, I will find you."
>
> You got to understand also that there was a language barrier. She [foster mother] spoke Russian and English. They were Russian Jews. I'm a Polish Jew. We spoke Yiddish... universal language... my Polish Yiddish and her Russian Yiddish did not mix! So the first three months [in that house] I could not speak with them. In the meantime, she pushed me on her husband to take me to school and even to the ladies wear to buy me clothes.

Without communication, tensions normal to family life became tragedies waiting to happen. Mariette still had a fear of men after her best friend's rape and murder, and with the estrangement between herself and her foster mother, suppressed emotions were creating their own walls. She truly believed that this couple, childless for thirty years, could not really take the burden she was bringing them. This translated into a sense that the woman did not want her in the house and saw her as a competitor for the husband's affection. In the meantime, Mariette had received no schooling before coming to her new home and as a teenager found herself with the dubious distinction of being in grade one. Her adjustment difficulties seemed enormous.

> [At school they only spoke English] I couldn't tell them I spoke nine languages. I was embarrassed to tell them I spoke nine languages because I couldn't speak English. I did grade one to grade six in one year.
>
> I was very lucky. I had a teacher, a Miss XXX. She was about three hundred pounds. She found a little French and English dictionary. She practiced this thing they call "show and tell." This teacher, she taught me classic comedy [using] comic books. I found the love of classics,

> music and literature, which I majored in [laughs]... But table--la table, window--la fenetre... She took the time in that first year [to help].
>
> They didn't know what to do with me... really didn't fit anywhere. Didn't make too many friends either. You really didn't fit anywhere. You tried to fit, but you were really... people made you stand out. And so [it has taken] thirty-five years to say, "Hey. I'm somebody." "Back off!" you know, if I don't like you, I'm going to tell you; I have no fear. "Back off!"

For the child who had been shoved in rat-infested sewers to escape apprehension, who could not acknowledge those whom she loved when she saw them for fear of giving them away, or who could not make noises lest her hiding place be jeopardized, being able to shout "Back off!" held a special kind of catharsis. Her past affected the way she took on issues in personal and public life, and what her style lacked in elegance it made up for in straightforwardness.

Her foster parents became her very generous benefactors. What they could not gain by familial intimacy they sought with material proof of caring.

> He was a very wonderful man. One day, I came home from school, he had a bicycle. [Another day] I had a new tennis racket, [then] a pair of roller skates. I think I was the only child that had a hundred dresses to wear and fifty pairs of shoes.

There were difficulties. Though the Faslovs united in trying to make Mariette feel a welcomed and important part of their life, she was in fact a stranger to them, and it would take a great deal of effort to build a sustaining trust that bridged their distances. Mariette noted that her foster mother conspicuously left things lying around as "tests" to see if she would steal, because it was believed that deprived children would not know how to handle generosity or abundance. "And it bothered me that she was testing me with all those things," Mariette reflected. Such ambiguities complicated the new problems she was having to face. Without sisters and brothers or any close peer group right at hand, there was no one to explain the minor mysteries of life to her as she came into puberty.

Mariette would never call her foster parents by the familiar terms used for her natural parents. On her deathbed, Mariette's foster mother asked her to call her mother, and amidst tearful protestations and proclamations about the depth of their bond and its meaning to her, Mariette refused. She needed that part of her past to remain inviolable. In part, this maintenance of the division between the self past and the self present heightened the need for rules of conduct she followed to reflect deeply-held conviction. It was critical that Mariette never be merged with Marie, that "then" never become "now." But to manipulate the self as an object is not the same as having insight into that self. Mariette is very much a puzzle to Marie, and surviving is something she did, although she doesn't quite know how. The past must be respectfully contained.

> There are certain things that are there I have not opened. But I've lived with it before. It's just like doors should be shut. [Pause]. When something happens to a person... they should have... be able to close that door... let the mind rest. You know what I'm saying? Let the evil or tragedies or everything [stay there]... as an escape. But then eventually if you are healthy, your mind starts scraping at it, scratching away.
>
> But a lot of people that are sick today, I would say [pause] it's because they have not opened... opened... that door. To face oneself, I tell you, is a pretty rough time. To face... face-to-face with death. Because it [pause] really is [pause] almost like death. You are killing yourself when you open that door.
>
> [Q: That's the first time I've heard it put that way.]
>
> I can only see it that way, see. When you are two people [voice is full of controlled emotion, but soft]... safeguard you.
>
> When you have no parents, you have no friends, you have only got the survivor... that survivor, I got to tell you, is [capable of anything].

Her husband and children are her oasis of renewal and fulfillment. She is, with all her being, wife and mother; childhood and adolescence cannot claim her fully anymore. With her family she can be angry or gentle, intense or calm; she is accepted as she is. She defends her right to be both a survivor and a mother.

> When I saw my daughter when she was twelve or thirteen and looked and I think I travelled half the world by her age... they have the weakness [of affluent life] and they have the... everything else that's supposed to be... [pause]. But I think things must rub off on your children.

> I've tried to [learn more about] effects on the second generation.
>
> They're not strangers [but] like my friends would tell you today, "What you see is what you get." And that's the way it is. I don't try to change you; don't try to change me.
>
> But I've got a future in my children. My daughter's pregnant [laughing]. I'm going to be a grandmother. They all got married within a year and a half of each other [she has three daughters].
>
> [Q: Happy?]
>
> It's happy. I live for tomorrow.

She speaks of autonomy, fulfillment, and self-assertion in this passage which ends with a reference to her children. Her family--husband and children--is a rich source of healing which invests her in the present. It seemed appropriate at that point to question the role of meaning in her life and the extent to which religion mattered for her both then, during the war, and now.

> [Q: What part has religion played in your life throughout the Holocaust and now?]
>
> None at all. In the Holocaust... I hated... I hated [even my own religion] for [in a sense] making me an orphan. [Pause]. Like all Jewish people I'm the same, "Why me?" I was fortunate, I think. When I [go now] to the synagogue I enjoy being there. But [I had to forgive the past to be there]. Now I would say I'm a real proud Jew. I believe in God. I thank God for all my children. Life is a miracle.

In explaining the concept of God to her children she defined God as "Being," represented in all of life. "Everything you see and touch, that's God. You are part of God; I am part of God. So you do not have to go anywhere [specifically] to find Him." When asked if this way of seeing things squared with all she had been through, she replied, "This was Marie talking to her daughter! [Laughs] This was not Mariette! I was very careful." For her children, she would sacrifice even the past.

There are whole sections of her self presentation that can only be called Marie--North American, upper middle class, comfortable, untouched by the grotesque in any guise. And then, suddenly, the reality of Mariette asserts itself. She is a survivor of what was incontestably the most vicious assault on a human group in recorded history. There are

The Children

scars. For instance, she decided to return to Europe after a twenty year absence to show her part of it to her husband. Also with them were Henri, her brother, his wife, and their granddaughter.

> I wanted to show Sidney the church where I hid... Paris, where I was hiding. Now I took him... he wanted to see the concentration camp. There was a concentration camp outside of Brussels and my brother took us there. I didn't want to go inside [pause] because I remember the place. But [pause] I had my grandniece... my brother's granddaughter. Natascha [was at the time] four years old and it was raining that day and she says, "I have to go to the bathroom. You have to take me." Anyway I went into this building to go to the bathroom... concrete building... I wish they'd tear [it] down. While she was in the bathroom, I was standing outside in the hallway, and I looked at this picture of this man standing with a child. *Turns out to be the man who sold my mother to the Germans.* [She is dissolving into tears]. He was a friend of my father who brought him out from Poland to Brussels. Jews sold Jews at that time. But that picture... And I said, "I know that man!" and I started to yell. And my brother... [Henri overhears the distress and comes to her aid].

Contradictions of this kind are startling and painful for her, but she has an elemental energy which is strong and in the past could be violent. To Mariette the oppressor and survivor are opposing, self-conserving, violent forces best kept separate and suspended in the back regions of memory.

But the prejudice and discrimination that was so dominant in the past must be fought in the present. What threatened her with death in the past must be negotiated out of the present. She fights with all her strength what she sees as the dormant human monster of racism and hate, wherever it appears. When the children were quite young and she and her husband were just starting their business, a neighbor who had been very dependent on them found out they were Jews and felt it was correct to respond with distance. Mariette engaged in a battle and kept her friend, but it was hard.

> Her little daughter and my daughter were friends, and one day she came over and said... said to me, she says, "That g-d Jew, the druggist, charged me [more than she expected to pay]." I looked at her and said, "Ruth, what has the g-d Jew got to do with it?" She says, "Well, he's a g-d Jew." I said, "You're talking to one. You have for over a year." She thought I was a Mormon because I didn't have Christmas lights. She told my child that [pause] she [the child] killed... Jesus Christ. I mean,

my kid came home and said, "I killed Jesus Christ!" And I said, "You did what?!" And I jumped over the fence and went over to Ruth and I said, "You ignoramus!" I said, "How dare you say that?" She says, "Well, our children could never be friends." And I said, "Ruth, your name is a biblical name. A Jewish name. What are you talking about? All of a sudden, from yesterday, your child can't play with my child anymore. What happened from yesterday? -- My taking you to the hospital to have your son? -- I looked after Lyn while you were in hospital. Because I am a Jew!!!"

To make a long story short, my daughter was the maid of honor at their wedding [laughs]. -- My daughter with her daughter all these years.

Mariette learned early that life sometimes asks a vigorous fight from one who would live by their principles. She has fought back against the insidious. For her, subtle misjudgment, stigma, and bitter discrimination that filters into ordinary life as anti-Semitism or religious hatred were a tyranny to be confronted and rooted out. Whether the fracas had turned out the way it did, or whether she had lost the friendship, her identity was established in terms of being able to respond decisively and vitally, to secure a better world for her family and a home for Marie.

DISCUSSION

Each of the five narratives in this chapter--Harry's, Louise's, Robbie's, Rene's and Mariette's, is about transcendance--confronting ordeal, surviving it, and living with the memory of it. Together they indicate how the few Jewish children who survived the Holocaust dealt with its horrors either in hiding, with the Resistance or in the concentration camps.

They vary in many ways, each reflecting different personal styles, a range of social backgrounds, different countries of origin, as well as different survival contexts. They differed in age. Some were older, some were younger as children confronting Nazi oppression. Some remained with their families throughout the persecution; others lived variously separated from their families. The variation may account for some of the differences in narrative style and content. What joins them together is that they describe the past in words and paragraphs, with gulps of emotion even now not completely managed, straining to people its scenes and delineate trajectories that make sense of what must have seemed incomprehensible both to their parents and themselves as they experience unfolded. In the present they live in worlds shaped by forces associated with their liberation and the vanquishing of their enemy. But their inner worlds of hurt and pain remain. In their narratives these child survivors provide a rich strain of insights on which to construct a socially dimensioned picture of surviving persecution and genocide.

CHAPTER 4

THE ADOLESCENTS

> Boredom and cold; it is bleak outside and in my heart. Vita's brother left for some place afar, and I do not know where. Uncle and aunt are somewhere in a desolate land, and I am here alone, a stranger. O God what a burden it is to be solitary among aliens, fatherless and motherless. There is no one to whom you can run for solace, to embrace or kiss.
>
> Tamarah Lazerson, survivor of the Kovno ghetto, 14 January 1945. In Laurel Holliday, <u>Children in the Holocaust and World War II; their Secret Diaries</u>. 1995:133-134.

INTRODUCTION

Klara, Michel, Leo, Peter and Serge ranged in age from twelve through eighteen years, with Serge being the youngest. All but Serge went through Auschwitz and a string of smaller camps. Leo was a Mengele twin and Klara, Peter and Michel were captive labor, selected for work rather than the gas, living under the most primitive conditions. Peter's confinement was the longest, extending from just after the invasion of Belgium until the Allies took Bavaria. Serge lived with his parents as they hid from 1941-1944. Survival for him involved a different set of hurdles than those caught up in the KZ system. But though the trauma experience may have been far more intense in the concentration camps than in other contexts, regardless of the condition of their persecution, all had lost the gentle innocence of childhood to a ferocious, all-consuming force.

Under normal conditions, teenage years are a time when the young deal with their "raging hormones," learn to manage changes in their relationships and handle emotion as they take on new statuses and identities. Appearance concerns them greatly. They expect the world to open up before them. So was it for the survivors who shared their narratives in this chapter. Coming from intact families as they did, with long roots in their local areas, they would have been carefully sponsored into the lifestyle and roles of adulthood in community. But within the contexts of terror and death which the Nazis orchestrated, the rises and falls of ordinary life escaped their grasp, their lives counted as worthless. As the narratives will show, the crises which marked their days in persecution and captivity required unimagined struggles and frightful possibilities. Transcendence processes would be focused less on fitting in than its opposite--that is, holding courageously to what they learned from family life in the past, and, with every small act, standing *against* the devouring current of organized life.

ADOLESCENTS IN THE CAMPS
LEO

Leo Lerner was born in Ruthenian Hungary in 1928. He was shipped to Birkenau from Beregova in April of 1944 with his twin sister and the rest of his family. The two children were immediately identified as twins at the Auschwitz railway siding. Both became part of Mengele's experiments.

The family had been transported to Auschwitz from a makeshift "ghetto" in a brick factory where they had been sheltered badly for three weeks during March of 1944. By that time the family had been stripped of everything they owned, and terrorized.

> They loaded us on [like cargo] [deep sigh]. I... you know... I don't even want to think about it, but we were like sardines, and the doors to the freight cars were not opened. And they... they closed it on us [hermetically sealed]... and they had little windows in each cattle car measuring about... well, just a little bigger than that picture frame there. That was the only daylight that we had coming in and the [deep breath] crying and the moaning, because we had babies, we had elderly in the same car... world... and the stench, the smell. Its just...

> [Pause] The train... I don't recall the train stopping ever in between... In other words, it pulled out and the train just kept on going. It may have made one stop in all the two... two and a half days. It was non-stop, day and night. I still have nightmares about that wayward clack, wayward clack, you know. The sound of the train...

His father had been a simple tradesman. Both his mother and father had moved to Beregova from a village in the region, met, married and started their family. As the children grew, they would take the train for summer excursions to visit relatives. A trip by train to visit grandparents in this way became for Leo a romantic adventure. Now the train was the vehicle of their undoing. It took the family two and a half days to get to Auschwitz-Birkenau. The sounds from that fateful journey remained an agony for him throughout his life.

He prepared documents and newspaper clippings, photos and other items to formalize his remarks for the narrative. His style was subdued. As he spoke, he had just had heart surgery and was worried about his sister who has been in and out of hospital ever since the camps. Unlike him, she had been taken on the last of the infamous death marches out of Auschwitz and into Germany. Leo had hidden. He had been among the few inmates still at the camp when the Russian soldiers arrived. His sister had travelled with her sisters and helplessly watched them die from exposure on the way.

The bitter journey to what for them was an unknown destination had ended with a great commotion as soldiers with their dogs unlocked the doors of each car and routed the hapless passengers onto the railroad platform. He and his sister were small in stature and at age fifteen looked younger than their years.

> There were some soldiers running around with dogs looking for freaks of nature. And they considered twins experimental material for their purposes. A neighbor from my hometown hollered out that these two are twins. So they just pulled us out of the line and hauled us in a wagon.

Suddenly the family was separated. They who had never been apart were never to be together again. Over the next few days someone eventually pointed to the smokestack, the crematorium chimney looming over them, saying something he could hardly believe. From that point onward, he could not get the offensive smell out of his mind. Even so, he could not let go of the idea that someone from that brick factory ghetto must still be alive. As he pressed for more information from whomever he met, he found a few of them. The sight of what they had become added to his terror.

> They were skeletons. They... they... they weighed 60 or 70 pounds, and I'd give them my ration and I'd ask them whether they'd seen anybody... my relatives, family, you know, that I know [deep breath]. And they could barely talk, they were so weak. And when I went the following morning, they were out on the [body] heap. They... they had a pile as high as 15 feet, 12 feet, 16 feet, you know, just arms and legs sticking out and you... you wouldn't have been able to recognize them because you didn't see their faces. They were just thrown one on top of the other.

He was being kept in a separate block for twins. Experimental subjects fell under Mengele's protection and it meant that they were not beaten or malnourished by camp wardens. It was a dubious privilege. The "hospital" where he was kept "was spotless," "looked like some fancy park or garden for visitors to see and [bring] flowers". It was a lab specializing in racial experiments right in the middle of a death factory. There were reminders of the ghoulish side of the human experiments taking place.

> I [talked with] a young man there who was castrated. And he was telling us his story and I just can't forget the conversation with him, you know [sighs]. We had a family with us...some of them are still alive today in Israel. They were midgets; a total of five: three women and two men. And then we had some dwarfs. It was like a circus, you know. We had some twins that were so identical we couldn't tell them apart. They were like two eggs.
>
> There were experiments performed constantly on us. Matching eyes and nails--in my case was not [fraternal twins]. They were working on identical twins, you know... made a difference for them. But still they wanted to know how twins were conceived, what differences are between them so they could increase the German population and... [Sighs].
>
> I really don't know what to tell you except that I've been reliving my experiences and have got every little bit of scrap paper on Birkenau itself and the doctors that performed these experiments on us. I can't recall them being painful, with regards to the experiments themselves. But not knowing what they were going to do was a torture in itself because we saw the various instruments and tests and... And you know, after seeing those corpses in the morning, we knew that it could be any hour, any day, we... That they will take me or my sister or one of us and just... Never see them again. [Pause]. I don't know what else to tell you.

There is no flood of tears, just his staring quietly into the middle distance as he says "I don't know what to tell you." Looking into the faces and broken bodies of those images held in memory, he cannot find the right words to connect the worlds of then and now. He had endured what the listener in a normal lifetime would never have encountered, yet he does not try to be emphatic.

Part of the terror in situations like this is that it represents for the self the complete reversal of the taken for granted assumptions of everyday life. Twins and other experimental subjects were not just *tiermenschen*, life unworthy of life, but could be exploited with impunity, unless someone more powerful might be offended or irritated by it. It was an awkward irony for Leo to discover that by invoking the identity "twin," he could claim protection in some situations.

> [At the start], just to get out from the environment I was in, we went out on a work crew and we ran into some drunk SS soldiers, and they took us into an empty room. There was four of us, and they started beating us one at a time. As they were beating us with their canes, I, always being the smallest, I try

to sort of go to be the last one. And they hit the first one, and then they hit the second one and then they hit the third one, for a considerable length of time. Then when it came to me--it had to be a miracle because, I just blurted out the word "Twin... Mengele." And these two soldiers just froze in their tracks and they hollered, "Out!" and they never touched me. They knew that if they harmed us they would be in trouble themselves.

Wanting to go on living in this context itself humiliated the captives. In the case of being an experimental subject, continuing to live meant in some sense giving up something to captors using them for unknown ends. There were in fact few words to assess the nature of their pain as the experiments continued. They themselves, lacking standards valid at such an extreme, harshly assessed their feelings within their camp ward existence, misjudging themselves as "selfish" for coveting food when they were starving, or trying to save themselves in a moment of terror.

> Everybody was for themselves. We were selfish. We were guarding our rations. We were afraid to put it down, see. The guy next to you might steal it. I don't know how the day went [other than] it went in fear. Everything [else] was secondary. All we were doing was wanting to live and survive. We were just like zombies.

> [Q: What do you think kept you going?]

> Well, hope. Hope, you know. I mean we witnessed situations of people being marched in and not come out. We knew what to look for and we were just wondering when we'd be next. We hoped that, you know, something will happen. There's no way of explaining it. What kept me going [was] just the instinct of wanting to live. And there was nothing we could do about it. It was constant terror.

The trauma context, based as it was not on compassion but coercion, threatened the anchorages on which reason itself was pegged. Yet, as fear and despair threatened equanimity, survivors felt driven rather than inspired. They watched helplessly as each new transport unloaded its human cargo.

> I was in the camp where things were starting to happen to the people that they brought in with the trains... the cars. This was the central point of the distribution center. So when they brought them there, they got off the trains, they eliminated the ones they didn't want, and the rest of them were just brought in for a couple of days, and within two days, they were dispersed to various areas by trucks or trains in the various work camps. The

place that I was in was strictly a death camp.

In 1944, the Jews of Hungary had become the main targets of the Nazi killing machinery still in operation at Auschwitz-Birkenau. As many as one thousand people a day were gassed and cremated there. Resistance activities, or "organizing" of any kind, was less likely for those isolated in the "hospital" area where Leo was. He became taciturn and reflective. It was his way of displacing his rage and sense of impotence. As an experimental subject, he became somewhat detached from others and began to disidentify with the prisoner collective.

> How shall I describe the Jew of that era? We didn't feel equal. Always on the defensive even in his own home village or hometown, okay? Now here [in the camps] he's faced with the situation somebody has a gun and a uniform and he's seen the... the... the deaths. How could he rebel?. [Pause] They were like sheep when they were led to the slaughterhouse, you know. [Pause] The likes that you would describe of an Israeli soldier of today, you know, the chutzpah and the forcefulness, being a human being and feeling you have rights...

The captives breathed diminishment in the smoke by day, and by night, slept with it in their dreams. But, there was a small reprieve for Leo in that, just across the barbed wire he knew he could find his sisters. These remnants of family were comforted by the sight of one another.

Between 1944 and 1945, forced marches took many of those selected for work out of Auschwitz and into Germany. When the order came for Leo to march, he had already decided with a buddy to find a hiding place. This decision was a turning point for him; he referred to it as "a miracle." He could not see himself as an ingenious risk-taker, but he was credible as a vigilant and cautious person. Hiding could be risked.

> Well, what happened... Auschwitz was a huge place with buildings... huge buildings, and they all had basements. These buildings, with stairs leading down... And what has happened--I didn't do it by myself, there was about four or five of us. We did not go on the march. We decided... We went down into one of the dark basements. Now this [shows drawings] these were the doors to the basement, okay. The doors opened like this [folding upwards], and there was two doors. These doors were about thirty inches [wide]. I opened these doors and put a board up on top of them, like that [shows how]. And I was sitting on this board and before the march started, German soldiers with flashlights came in and they... they searched the basement. And I was sitting above. [Deep breath].

By morning [sighs] the hollering subsided and it was quiet and we started coming out slowly, eighty-five or one hundred people, who did similar things... who did not go.

Those who stayed behind in the camp eventually started breaking into the stores left behind. Suddenly, a jeep with several Nazi soldiers in a convoy of about six trucks drove into the camp and started rounding up the able-bodied prisoners. These they made carry sick prisoners into the large compound.

And this was January and it was very cold... lot of snow... and they had soldiers with machine guns standing around, guarding us. We spent, oh, an hour or so standing there, and we felt that we would be machine-gunned down [sighs] when all of a sudden from a distance we saw two headlights with a small vehicle approaching and they gave some orders to these soldiers that were guarding us. And these soldiers jumped on the trucks and they gave us instructions not to move, then took off. [Pause] We stood there for maybe another hour or so and that's all we could take. We decided that whether we get killed or not, there's no way that we can continue staying there because we'd freeze to death. So we ignored instructions and we went back into the buildings, shaking and crying.

Much later, soldiers draped in white camouflage gear approached. The survivors were terrified until they discovered it was Russian troops. One of the soldiers was Jewish and Leo struck up a conversation with him. He advised Leo to find a way home, since the front was unstable and could collapse or be won at any time. If their line broke, they would be unable to protect the camp. Leo made it home on the 19th of April by hitching rides on Russian army vehicles. It had taken him only two days to return.

With most of his immediate family gone and whatever the family owned taken away, his homecoming was full of sorrow. Leo had been through a destructive self journey; the return brought him little respite. He no longer felt joined to community as he once had, nor could he identify with much in it anymore. He was treated with indifference or disregard, like something of a non-person, by those he met.

[Q: Couldn't you go to the neighbors for help?]

Well, [sighs] they were just as bad or they were worse.

And it really boiled down to... [having no place to call home]. The homes...

the people living in them, they would not even let you in.

He managed to stay with some cousins whose families had gotten "Gentile papers" and fell in with about twenty men whose families had been "resettled." Now that the war was past and the Nazi occupation a memory, they anticipated their relatives' return. Leo had seen too much to offer them much hope and they refused to believe what he said had happened.

> They [friends] felt that I should be given medical treatment [for concocting such stories of death and bodies and abuse]. Not long after, others started trickling in and they told the same story and so...

When his sister returned home in the middle of May, he knew no others would be coming after; they had all perished. For he and his sister, he was determined to find a better way to live. Seeing several of their friends strike out for Israel suggested new possibilities to them. When Leo looked into going to Israel he found out through an arm of the United Nations in Prague that there might be increased opportunity in Vienna. So they went westward, and there they were put in displaced persons camps. Eventually the chance to go to North America came their way with the whole operation funded by the Jewish Congress of Canada and the Jewish Defense League of the United States. There were one hundred of them in the group who left Vienna. Their journey now was tinged with hope and new discovery. They made the most of small joys.

> When we got on the boat in Italy, the Jewish Congress gave each of us $5.00, and we got on the boat and we were all smoking. Cigarettes in Italy were a dollar a package in those days. Very expensive. And we got on the boat, it was .20 cents a package. So we took this money and we each grabbed a carton of cigarettes, [chocolate] bars for the rest. --It was .05 cents a chocolate bar, you know. And there were all the chocolates and cigarettes [you'd want]. It was just out of this world. And so... It was a Greek liner with poor refrigeration and... bobbing around the Atlantic that time of the year... [it] was pretty rough crossing. A lot of us took sick, couldn't eat the food.

They knew nothing of North America and found its hugeness baffling as they headed westward out of Halifax by train. Though the place names were unfamiliar and the distances between cities huge, they felt excited and glad to be moving away from everything that symbolized what had brought them to the camps.

It took us three weeks by boat to come from Italy and then it took us another day from XX- to XXX- and then when we said, "Where's that?" [another city] and they said five days by train!! [Laughing].

We just couldn't visualize the vastness, [the size of] the world; to be able to do all that travelling to get some place! And sure enough, they put us on a train at XXX- and [it] took five days to get here and that train had a dining car, like you know some of these fancy cars in Europe. And we would get three meals in that dining car, and we were treated royally, you know, by these waiters.

[The bread]...about six slices, neatly put on a silver tray at each table [went in a flash as everyone reached at once]. He [waiter] hasn't turned around yet and the arms reached out and we cleaned it! Turned around, you know... we didn't speak English...so he brought another [tray of bread]. It was still in mid-air and the arms came up for it! This guy made four or five trips with the silver tray and then finally, he brought two loaves of bread [laughs] and put it on the table.

They felt welcomed by a warm hearted steward, the open and generous sharing of food, the camaraderie. For these young people, from whom so much had been taken, it felt a little like falling in love, but with everyone and life itself. At the appointed destination, he was adopted by a local family. They had a son his age, and for Leo, a room all his own. Now he felt lucky to have survived. His adoptive family treated him as their son. He still looked like a teenager but he took perspective as an adult. When they encouraged him to go back to school and complete his education, he felt that he had experienced too much and "could not visualize himself starting to read and memorize again." His sister was adopted by a different family. They both went to night school to learn to speak English and then on to jobs that at that point did not pay very well. But, his adoptive family let him save all his earnings so that by the 1950s, he owned a harberdashery shop. It was in that shop that he sat to tell his memories of a terrifying past.

He married a soft spoken, loving woman who knew little about wars, or death camps, or hatred that could send millions to slaughter. They had a family of three sons. One of them had married and had two children, his first grandchildren. When he started the interview he took strength from mementoes of them all around his office. These were the touchstones of his joy, the fulfillment of his longings. From so long ago, in the mirk of Auschwitz where he had struggled to keep his courage, he had lingering effects of trauma; but from his new life, he knew unforetold blessing. Even so, traumatic memory did not go away. Even the transformative emotions of love and contentment do not dislodge it. Leo spoke of how it breaks in upon everyday life, cued into full awareness by the simplest trifle.

> I happen to be living right now in XXX and unfortunately for me, about two and a half miles away there's some tracks and a locomotive will every once in a while whistle, you know, and I come to work and cross these tracks and will go home and there might be 75 to 100 railway cars going by with Japanese cars on. But... I really have to control myself not to break down.
>
> When I sit at XX- highway with the ramp down and I see these cars going by clank clank clank clank clank. Even though you see the cars... the vehicles... the red and the yellow and the green cars on it... But just the sound of the... of the train itself is very traumatic.
>
> [The pattern of his thoughts focuses on the question: could things have been done differently? He has been imagining through all these years how they might have escaped, restaging the sequence of events.]
>
> No. There was no way. [Quieter, almost whispering] There was no way. Nope. There was no way [voice trembles]. Where to go... Where to go...

PETER

Peter Estevan was eleven years old when he and members of his family fled in the wake of the Anschluss, March 12, 1938, when Nazi troops crossed the Austrian border and annexed Austria. They had been living in Vienna. The family had consisted of his mother and grandmother, his sister and himself when they reached Belgium. His father had been born just across the border from Vienna, in Czechoslovakia in a small town about fifty kilometers away. His mother and father had divorced. Peter was, in the wake of this severance, the nominal head of the family, its symbolic protector and keeper.

Somehow the family found a place to stay in Brussels where his mother attempted to get a work visa for England. Her plan was to cross the Channel into England ahead of the others, and within a few months find the resources to get them all safely to what would by 1940 prove to be the only place of refuge from the Nazis left in Western Europe. Her timing was off by a few weeks. She did get the visa she wanted by August of 1939 and began to put in motion the first part of her plan. Belgium had been neutral during WWI, and she expected her children to be relatively safe there until she could send for them. But by September, Britain had declared war on Germany. Belgium remained neutral. The papers she sent her children so that they could join her did finally arrive. Peter and his sister booked passage for a crossing on May 17, 1940. On May 10, Germany invaded Belgium. Ports were closed. Peter elaborated:

> So we got stuck there. Unfortunate. My sister and myself stayed with my grandmother who the proceeding winter died. She had an accident. She was half blind and she fell down the steps. Terrible conditions with being emigrants.
>
> We didn't have any money, so... [pause]. My sister and myself--I was thirteen, my sister was fourteen, were more or less left to our own devices.

In Peter's world at that time, there was little room for dwelling on what might have been. "Unfortunate" summed up the tragedy for him. Peter tried at the time to remain calm, looking neither too far ahead nor too far back. In Vienna, where his mother's family were well established they had enjoyed prosperity. In Brussels, they lived a hand to mouth existence. Unable to leave, Peter and his sister grew used to a tough regimen, fending for themselves, working with few resources and trying to remain in school despite the repressive laws against Jews and refugees. They gave their address as a vacant attic and slept wherever they could find shelter. A few months after the start of Nazi Occupation, Peter was denied the right to attend school because he did not have documents to prove he was neither a foreigner nor a Jew.

> For the next three years, 1940-1943, my sister and I survived as best we could, starving a lot, you know. Very little to eat. You got ration cards but, unless you had money for... on the black market, you can't get anything for it. So we really had a very rough time, but somehow we survived and became ind... streetwise, you know. We learned to beg, steal, or whatever it took to survive.

It was not safe to be found together or to register with the local authorities. Each day they took reasonable precautions to avoid being noticed. Remaining invisible while authorities were actively hunting down Jews required a highly finessed skill at hiding, as well as a strong determination and plenty of information on actual Gestapo patterns. Though they were growing better at covering their tracks and remained grimly determined, the third resource was more elusive. Peter knew he could easily "pass" as a Belgian, but his sister could not. He developed a plan to follow should they be spotted by the omnipresent Gestapo. He almost got it to work.

Peter rendered the details in a controlled, quiet voice, almost a monotone. "We weren't smart enough" is how he analyzed getting caught. As he saw it, they had not sufficiently second-guessed the enemy. His metaphor compares the deadly interface with the Gestapo to a game. It was far from this.

> When they arrested me, they asked me where I lived... or first they asked me who was the girl I was talking to. -- I knew right away it was the Gestapo when he stopped me. I say, "What girl?" [The agent retorted], "I saw you talking to that girl." I said, "I don't know. I just asked her for the time."
>
> My sister had enough sense to walk on and not turn around. She also knew what it was. So she kept her cool and walked on. So. They forgot about that and took me to the address... upstairs. And I'm... No clothes, nothing. So, [they say], "What do you mean you live here?" You know, "Where are your clothes, in the first place?" and one stuck a... on my temple... a knife on my throat and then when they talked to me... first spoke in German. I said, "Sorry I don't speak German I... I speak French." So they spoke to me in French, you see. And when I... when I was there at the attic of course I was scared because... So he spoke at me in German, "Where does your father live?" and I answered in French. [They replied], "You said you didn't understand German. How come you answered me?" Ach! More or less, game over.

He spoke now at an amazing pace, hardly taking time to breathe or vary the tone and timbre of his speech. The logic of his game metaphor denied the degree of control his captor actually had. Powerlessness and terror are not what the human spirit either accepts or chooses. In memory, silence or a false bravado is much more likely for the terrorized captive (see also Terr 1990). But with the player identity, he remains autonomous in his own eyes and holds on to some dignity. With this comes the possibility of "luck." Peter needed all of these devices in the hours following his capture.

> Took me to Gestapo headquarters. Now how do they get things out of people? By torturing them, [using] whatever means. And [I was wondering] whether I'll be able to resist to tell them the real address where my sister was living. That really worried me. And they put us in a cellar. Anybody who was picked up during the day was put down in the cellar and then they would interrogate them in their time. Now, as it happened, they caught a Partisan, a very important Partisan they were looking for... for a while. So they were busy with interrogating him and as my luck was... [Aside, to himself] *Luck!*

The Adolescents

> The next day the truck came to pick up all the people over there to their assembly camp which was nearly twenty kilometers from Brussels. There was an old barracks where they gathered all the people they picked up and waited until there were 4000 people. Got transferred to Auschwitz with 4000 people.

His intellect kept ahead of his fear as long as he reckoned in terms of strategies, and "me vs. them." He was imprisoned but he had met his goal to protect his sister and family at all cost. If he were to "break" under capture it would have meant their freedom. He did this and even managed to hold some hope of release until a few weeks further on. He measured good luck in such terms, and with this point of focus he was well served. He had no sense until much later of what it would mean to be "sent east." As he entered this part of his narrative, for the first time he inadvertently replaces "I" with "we" or "they" as the subject of his sentences. The metaphor of the game is no longer salient. He now focuses on the betrayal of hope.

> So all people--babies, young, everybody, was put in those barracks and there it was, from the first week in July til the first week in September, until they got the 4000 people. And they were told... I think it was the 9th of September... outside the barracks were railway lines... to get ready and we were going to be sent to work in camps in Eastern Europe.
>
> Now there was all kind of rumors, [about] people being gassed and so on, and... grown up people saying it was true, and everything else. When you are young, fifteen... sixteen, you are a lot more optimistic about... We wouldn't believe the gar... no human being would. And we really didn't believe; it will be a work camp, and so on.
>
> So they put us on these wagons, ninety people with all our luggage. They encouraged people to "send their relatives" all kinds of clothes. To the East. To the East, it's cold in winters and the long warm stuff... They wanted them [captives] to get as much stuff as possible... so they could have it for... for... the... for German people afterwards.
>
> So. With all the suitcases... some people with three or four, and ninety of us in a... in a railway wagon, not that... cattle car. It was probably as long as this thing and half the size [indicates a small space]. You did not have room to lie down anywhere. Some were sitting, some were standing. They put us in there... they put... in... [Pause] I think it was a ten liter bucket and a small pail of water and locked the doors.
>
> Now ninety people in there, doesn't take long for a bucket to fill up. Didn't take long for the water to be used. And from then on, if you had call of

nature you just... It was terrible, you know... [pause]. Old people suffocating. And after a while you start, you know... you want everyone to sleep. So some are starting to find... to lie down, sit up, taking turns. It was five days it took us to get to... One morning we saw... well, we're going to Auschwitz.

The line length has a sobbing rhythm which Peter's face does not betray. "They put us in there... they put... in... [Pause]." "Some are starting to find... to lie down, sit up, taking turns." This is the section of the narrative filled with his deepest grief.

Guards lined up with their dogs and every one [in the cars] had to get out.

"Out! Leave your luggage. Leave your stuff here. That's going into the camps with the trucks." And, "Everybody line up, women, children, old people."

Everybody lined up, five in a row. And then the camp commander, camp doctor, whoever he was... impeccably dressed, shining jackboots, perfect uniform and... real, real arrogant SS man, staff on his arm [gestures pointing to right and left]... selection, you know. Three hundred young men, able-bodied men, were put to one side. All the old people, women and children to the other side.

Now there's a bunch of German army Red Cross trucks there, and we were told, all the old people, young people, young kids, and so on, who were going into camp by truck, *they* don't have to walk. *Us* three hundred we can walk into the camp. Now, there were some kids that were there with their families. They were on one side, their parents over there. We didn't know what was what. So the... and... they didn't know they were going to their death.

They... we started to march, the three hundred. About three quarters of an hour... half an hour, we come to a place. --It was Birkenau [Auschwitz II], and there was a big arch, and it says "Arbeit macht Frei," which means "work will free you". [Pause].

We got in the camp and... the old striped uniform... and there was something eerie about it. I couldn't explain what it was. A mummy got in there. The people, they looked like zombies... were walking about. Nobody could look you in the eye... but walked about... you know, a dumb face... and the only... The Kommandoes, the prisoners at the station that took all our suitcases, they were well fed and we thought, "Oh! they look all right." But they were what was called your Canada [kommando]. Their charge was to take all our goods and then prepare them for... Some of them said as we got to the camp, "Your family... you had family over with the Red Cross?" And we said, "Yes. My children... My wife..." He said... he says, "You see that chimney there coming out? --They're just going up in smoke!" I said, "That's a cruel joke to play!" I couldn't believe it. I was too guilty [for being alive].

As I say, I couldn't find out what that eerie feeling was, and then I realized afterwards it was a stench of burning... burning bodies that came out. It was a kind of sweet burning flesh, and it hasn't left me. And when we barbecue, anything like that, its something that I just can't... [pause] can't... get out of my mind. And this has been with me all the time in camp. Never left.

The collective referent is very evident in this part of the narrative. Peter sees himself among the "we" and "they." But the strength which came from his will to protect and provide for those around him had no inner preparation for Auschwitz. Hearing of the others sent to the gas, as he did during his first night, gave him guilt--not joy. His heart was with the children, the parents and grandparents; he was in agony.

His experience of that first night at Auschwitz-Birkenau had many layers. The first related to the physical details of setting, the second to the divisions made at the selection, the third to implicit but unclear hierarchies among the prisoners, the fourth to what could not be named and fell beyond belief. Finally, there were self-feelings of pain, and discomfort. He was being treated as an expendable object by his guards in the degradation rituals which were about to fit him for existence in this total institution.

So when we got in the camp, the first thing... [Pause]. We were put in a barracks [pause] with bugs, dirt floor, stone walls, about four times the size of that room [points to his living room], a long barracks, and were told to take all our clothes off, tie the shoes, neatly fold everything... in the morning we would have a shower. So we collect all the clothes, make sure people didn't hide anything... had to bend down and they would go up with a stick in the rectum to see any jewelry or diamonds hidden in there, and were left... locked the door.

So, here we were three hundred of us, stripped naked. It was about the second week in September, and in... it was... in Poland, it gets pretty cool at night... nothing to lie on... so standing together... everybody naked... embarrassment. *We didn't really get decivilized yet.* So it was embarrassing and... and I lied down and you're trying to lie on top of each other to get a little bit of heat. So we didn't sleep much that night.

> So. In the morning we were told, "We are going to delouse you." They ran us about two kilometers right through the mud. Mud was cold, it was drizzly... to some cold showers and then back again. I was standing there, no clothes on. First thing they did [shows the tattooed number on his arm]... and we were told from that day on there's no more name. You are 151535. That's all. There's no John, Peter... no more particulars.

Peter's narrative is stark. He makes no bid for understanding. He just reveals a picture which he cannot stop, but yet, still being in it himself, must withstand. "So" is a repeated feature of this section of the style. This particular area of his narrative is well travelled in reflection; it stands for deeper parts, less clear, to which numbing had been a survival device. Survivors speak of camp life as numbing them to their former sensibilities, desires and tastes. But Peter means more than this. He wants to condemn what was done to himself and the others, to get beyond the numbing. His first hours at Auschwitz ended with the almost complete exhaustion of all his inner resourcefulness.

> The first night I came in the camp... was my worse night because I... that night... I... [coughs] *I cried my soul out.* I blamed God, I blamed my mother for... for... I blamed everybody. It was, why me? Why me?

> By the time morning came and I had no more tears left. I was dried out. I made a resolution. I am going to try and survive as much as I can. They might be able to get me down physically but they'll not get my mind. [Pause] Somehow, consciously, it [this resolution] stood with me.

The significance of this time and the desperate realization that he might not make it out alive troubled him greatly. Survival in such a space would require more than a passing thought. Being with others who shared the same orientation helped, if only to confirm that what was happening could indeed be defined as "atrocity." "We," "you" and "they" rather than "I" predominate in his description.

> The next two weeks were called quarantine, and we went through all kinds of meaner tasks just to get you down to... scientific way of getting you down from a serious person to a grovelling "criminal."

> And we all got sores. We fell down, we got kicked. Some of us got kicked to death. One of the things they did was... heap of heavy dirt on the one side, and, one hundred yards away, another heap of heavy dirt on the other side of the wooden trough... old wooden trough... handles, two in front and two in back, and they were heavy themselves [when] empty. Had to run at the

The Adolescents

double... empty it out. They went from there to there, never ending. Useless. Totally. And, as you were going, [if] you fell, you got kicked, and... all day long. That was "conditioning," you know. Perhaps one day we would get a bowl of very salt soup. Then, no water for two days. Everything they could do to... to... to... really... Make us stand for hours... for appel [roll call]... for hours and hours. Wake you up at 3:00 in the morning... Stand at attention. No reason. Go inside and out again. It was a designed, scientific way to get you down to animal level, and, believe me, by the time the three weeks were over, that's where we were.

Now out of the three hundred that got in the camp, after the two weeks, there were left 170. Some were kicked to death, some shot, some died of dysentery, some died because, you know, they... they got cold and pneumonia. Now a lot of kids my age that come in there, came from good homes, from well-to-do parents that were always looked after, never had to do anything for themselves. The saddest thing for them was psychological shock, you know, and you just couldn't take it. I was very independent. I had learned the rare parts of survival in the streets, so. It was worse than what... It wasn't as hard for me, so I had already become a survivor in a way.

The first days killed many who entered the work camps. Peter knew he had limited physical strength. As savvy as he had become about surviving during those days on the streets of Brussels, Peter knew he had limited physical strength to make it here. As soon as he could find the smallest easement, he took it.

Two weeks in Auschwitz, I heard they were forming a... a... they were sending a group to Warsaw where the ghetto had been burned down in the Spring. They were making a work camp there for... All the shells that... apartments, homes... they were all burned down. There were just shells left of brick and they wanted to use the bricks for... They needed people to work on the forced labor units. Two and a half weeks. And they [buildings] were swaying in the wind... [the wind] was blowing. There was no more officer corps [to properly supervise]. And [the work assignment was] to go up there and just throw down the bricks and then clean them for the war effort.

Now, we didn't know what at the time a work party was. I volunteered. There was a golden rule in the camp. You were never to volunteer for anything because... But in this case, I figure out, nothing can be worse than this death camp. If I'm unlucky, I'm just changing one death camp for another one. But if it's only ten percent better, then I have a chance.

Peter had taken a calculated risk. "Volunteers" had to climb four-story buildings in all kinds of weather. Some of the men fell to their deaths. Wearing only wooden clogs, they slipped on the icy surfaces. Others who were only injured in falling went to their deaths anyway because they would not be able to work, and what passed for camp hospital facilities were way stations for the grave. Without something more propitious opening up, his fate would have been sealed.

> One of the kids got sick and I got in the potato peelers, all young kids there. What we had to do was sit the whole day and we had to peel ten buckets of potatoes a day. [Coughs] Potato peeler... and... your hand was formed to take a potato. You had to do it.

> It [the new work spot] did two things. It kept me... Winter was coming on... it kept me out of the elements and inside. So you got a little bit warmer. Also, you managed to steal a potato every now and then, and even though it was raw, you find some way of trading it in. And every now and then the guy from the kitchen give you half a bowl of soup. So you managed to augment your food. That helped a little bit to keep me [pause] above starvation level.

There had been no way for the prisoners to wash in the primitive camp near the destroyed Warsaw ghetto, and lice, which carry typhus, overran it. Peter got placed on sanitation duty. Performing the range of functions associated with that task included bringing refuse to the latrine. With an epidemic underway, first the prisoners got infected, then the guards, and then the camp was sealed off. Two weeks into the epidemic Peter noticed he had a fever.

> People are coming down left, right, and center. I withstood it for a few... All of a sudden I got high temperature and that was a sign... [Pause]. [Coughs] They put you in a... a barracks is called quarantine barracks, and you got put in there with everyone else who had typhus. I was in a bunk with three other people, and one died the first day I got there. The second died the day after. We were lying there for about four of five days. I was getting hotter and hotter, burning up, and all you want is to drink water. I didn't get enough water and I got into a coma, and we started getting delirious and I was dreaming like all kind of wa... all kind of things. No medication. Nothing.

> After the third day my temperature broke. My constitution... I don't know what it was... I started going down. But that's... A week I was in there. Couldn't eat because of the burning up. Not getting enough water to drink, I was down. Really, I was very weak. And finally, when they let us out, the ones that had... we were sk[eletons].

Meanwhile, they were building... now they were building... showers because they realized they don't do it, they themselves couldn't...

So weak. It was time to go back to the kitchen and I was so weak, I couldn't even lift potatoes out. It was a question that every day for about four weeks I didn't know whether it was my last day... whether I would wake up the next morning or... It was terrible. And I started coughing... started coughing and... Every time I went from hot to cold, I got the coughing attacks. That's when I got TB. Nothing was done. That was in 1944.

As he describes the onset of typhus, his narrative is peppered with signs of discomfort--deeper breaths, pauses, and more pronounced coughing. By spring their camp commander had them digging "a swimming pool." They had taken the term to be a reference to their own untimely end once "the pool" was complete. Since there were thousands of Hungarian Jews being brought into Auschwitz at that point, there was plenty of new manpower. Those worn out by abuse could be easily replaced. However, as they were digging the "shallow end" of the commander's "pool," the sound of fighting on the horizon led to a change of plans. With the Russian front collapsing to the east, prisoners were put into units of one hundred and marched westward. By this time, Peter had a buddy who was older and more experienced than he, higher up in the inmate pecking order, a "prominenz." He sought him out as the march got under way. This man had determined that the safest spot was at the front of the column since this position sets the pace for the rest. Eventually, having started the unit out, not too fast, not too slow, they ran into other kinds of problems.

The repetitions of phrases "when you're thirsty," "with thirst," "thirsty and thirstier" together with the reference to moisture increase through this part of the account. Tiredness or exhaustion is reflected as well in his choice of terms, e.g., "stopped us," "and we were stopped," "we were just about dead." During this time of heightened crisis in the time remembered, Peter slips from "I" to "he" in reference to himself, e.g., "as he went, he kept filling up with moisture." This practice shows the survivor putting the willing self apart from the experiencing or suffering body; reason was used to buy endurance. Such a split is inadvertent; Peter seems unaware of the practice as he re-enters the memory frame. The split allows action to continue well beyond what the person in awareness would have guessed was his own capacity to keep going.

Peter recalled that by the third day of the march they had reached the demarcation line between Poland and Germany and were put on trains.

The men had still been given no water or food and many were begging the retreating soldiers at the siding for something to drink. One soldier filled his helmet with water and gave it to the prisoners, but they fell upon each other trying to reach it. Some of them were hit as the soldier pulled himself back and used his gun as a club. The train went on, this time into countryside that, despite his misery, Peter found very beautiful. They were moving through a mountainous area. He believed they were in the Bavarian Alps and the air would have a healing effect on him. He was showing signs of having, in addition to exhaustion and weariness, a coughing that did not go away. En route they were confronted by Allied combat planes and bombers. The anti-aircraft gun mounted on one of their rail cars drew fire. Their train got hit and the soldiers ran for cover, leaving the prisoners in the open, by the track. With a break in the gunfire, some prisoners seeing less danger from the air than from their own starvation, tried to leave the rail track to forage for food. Guards hiding nearby opened fire on them. Getting back on the rail cars with the others, Peter got hit with the butt of a gun and almost passed out from the pain and shock. At the end of this episode, prisoners and corpses were piled in together and the train went on again.

> A lot of people that had survived the camp four or five years got killed the day before we got liberated. [Quiet]. The next day, finally made it...

Their eventual destination had been Dachau. Peter's head wound was messy.

> I must have had all caked blood on me... and... and... when I got into the camp and... Dachau was an assemblement camp. They needed everybody for the war effort because they needed Germans to fight. So any able-bodied... they could have. It was a camp where they wanted to "recycle" the people, so they had to get them working again. So they had a first aid station. Somebody grabbed me... an orderly grabbed me and washed me, dressed me up, put a dressing on the... and dressed my head. For two days we were left to sit and we were fed [pause] normal food, something left. After two days they started making small groups for camps.

He feared at first that his having a head wound would set him back with the diseased and injured who were judged unfit to work. It was important for him that he ally himself with those who were healthy. He sought out the "prominenz," a prisoner who fared somewhat better than Peter had.

The Adolescents

[Dachau] was a major camp with work sites. The little camp, it was in upper Bavaria, and they needed the workers for these camps. Well, again, I wanted to be with that guy ["prominenz"]. So, I watched out. He went to one camp... and I went there. Of course, with my head all bandaged, [he said], "No kid. You wait couple days. You're not too good." So, I stepped back in the barracks, took off the bandage, just left a little gauze. Happened to be another guy was there. He didn't notice me. I went through there. Needless to say, that thing had festered the whole time I was in the camp. It never cured because I didn't have enough in me.

Anyway, we were sent to this camp. It was in upper Bavaria near the Austrian border near Rosenheim... high in the forest... a small camp... there was maybe [pause] a thousand of us there... all Nissen huts, prefabricated huts. And they were [pause] working on this major construction, and we had to go out, and what we would do is... They had a human chain of cement workers. They had these huge cement mixers. They had this huge hanger. Apparently they were working on the A-bomb and needed to have the work. They had three meter thick reinforced concrete and we had to feed those huge mixers. It was like a chicken ladder... continuous feed. It was in the height of summer.

Now the narrative style stumbles over the concept of "work camp." The story line is burdened by many references to the new focus for his struggle. His choice of terminology reflects the subjugation and debasement he felt but could not indulge and yet survive. Nor does he openly discuss his feelings about that time now as he stoically relates the details. Surviving meant being ready for the next ordeal.

Conditions at the western camps were as bad as any he had known before this in the east. With the heat of day, cement would cake on the workers' skin and seep into their perspiration, causing itching and discomfort. In addition, hard labor in the summer heat was depleting. Peter found a way to get on the night shift. Here he could snatch a few extra hours sleep without getting caught. He was determined to regain lost strength, and he believed he was getting better--he was, at least, coughing less. Meanwhile, overhead, American planes were flying, bombing the railroad repair operations and leaving craters in the railway lines that the prisoners had been brought in to fix. In itself, road repair was hazardous duty and physically demanding, but in addition to that, sometimes passers-by would stop to look, often the same people. One day while they worked, they noticed a little girl watching them as she nibbled on an apple. They asked her if she would share it, since on other days it seemed her habit to eat only half and then discard the rest. She looked at them horrified and said "no." They asked her why, and she replied, "Because you're Jews."

Peter balances this memory against a different one.

> Another time, [it was carpentry work]. I went off with a saw and a hammer. But we were sent somewhere that was near a convent. They needed somebody down underneath... a work party. [He saw a pear tree not far away] And I had a pear tree! So I managed to steal a couple of pears and then, as we were working, and we were always working, a couple of nuns went by and put out a pot of soup. So the guard turned around and says, "You get out of here or you're gonna join them!" So, they ran away. They were scared. They tried to help us. –Always something. But they were determined. We managed to get some people who were working forced labor... [to approach the nuns for them and soon they had a loaf of bread to share].

Their ordeal ended abruptly as suddenly, one day, tanks emblazoned with a white star appeared out of nowhere. Liberation did not come in a torrent of violence and gunfire, but with Allied soldiers and support personnel pouring out caring and compassion as best they could.

> We looked, and here we see cars coming, and comes closer, and closer, and we see those khaki... what looked like tanks with their guns down; tanks, you know, and they stopped. Hopped in... American! Asked if anyone spoke English.

The place where the survivors were eventually housed ironically had been a Hitler Youth camp the week before. Too physically abused to absorb even the plain army rations of the troops, the prisoners were given a gruel, something which Peter called "oatmeal soup." Survivors now moved about as they pleased with the Allied soldiers sharing what they had with them, unaware of the danger. The cheese or chocolate which seemed so benign, cost some exhausted victims their lives.

> You know, the way your system was... your digestive system, it would die... because your digestive system just couldn't take it. The ones that had enough discipline... within a week, we got better food. And the first day we sat at a table, and we got a proper meal; it was really fine. It was a long table [at this] holiday camp.

> [They couldn't bring themselves to leave the table area.] Nobody believed that tomorrow we would have another [meal]. Food! They couldn't understand... didn't have anything. So finally they [American soldiers] caught on. Finally they said, "You're going to get fed tomorrow. Don't worry." -- It takes an awful long time to get back.

They were still living within the shadow of the terror just past. Prisoners' bodies would take months, sometimes years, to accommodate normal amounts of food. Starvation had removed from them many aspects of correct bodily function. Table manners and toilet habits had also to be carefully regained.

> [Even a year later] I could not lie in a bed. I finally got to England. I [slept] on the floor. For one year, I could not go to a movie. I couldn't go... myself go... in a bus or in a street car. I would fall asleep. My mother couldn't understand it. It took me quite a while to be able to associate with other people. You feel like a... a wild animal.

> The day we got liberated, at the age of nineteen, I weighed seventy-two pounds. I hadn't grown an inch since we got in the camp. At nineteen you usually have a beard, you got pubic hair. Nothing! I had nothing. I had stopped growing. I had stopped...

He had come back from the dead in many ways, and felt like some of the clay was still upon him. All his teeth were rotten and needed dental work. He was malnourished and dangerously underweight, his heart was enlarged, he had sores from the body lice, his lungs were scarred, and he was susceptible to colds as never before. It was hard for him to trust authorities and his "not remembering" got him diagnosed as having "partial amnesia." He still would tell no one the addresses of his sister and his other contacts. Therefore, when he returned to Brussels, authorities had no known address to inform relatives that he was alive. He did his own reconnaissance when he was well enough.

> I went to the grocer I used to work for and he had remembered my sister. He had heard of my sister who was working on... for the canteens. I went there. She wasn't there. And, "Yes, there was a girl working there..." So I left a message and then I was also told that she... that my aunt... that she... So I went there to the address. My aunt's mother-in-law was there and the poor old lady was so much... She started... She thought she saw a ghost. She nearly had a heart attack when she saw [he was alive]. Everybody felt, well... nobody comes back from there. Nobody thought I was coming back. I had no way of letting anybody know. I sent... of course I sent a notice, but it hadn't... hadn't gotten there.

Brussels had been liberated since 1944, months before he arrived. When his sister found out that Peter had been sent to Auschwitz, the family gave up hope of ever seeing him again. It was with considerable elation that she wired good news to their mother in Glasgow. His mother responded immediately.

He was the only one in their family to have experienced the camps. No one completely understood his responses, though he was given great latitude for idiosyncracy. In fact, at this point he little understood himself.

> Whatever you have heard or seen is not as bad as it was in the camps, because feeling... the utter feeling of frustration, of helplessness, and the devastating smell and the atmosphere. You cannot show that on a movie. You cannot show that in films. I mean... You can get a picture but you can't... you can't... unless you have been there, you can't realize what it is.
>
> I used to get a lot of nightmares for the first ten years. [Pause] But it has been getting less and less and less.

He felt degraded to a level he had never known and searched for insight that might guide him back to wholeness. He needed to understand why he had survived. In part it seemed to be a result of simply wanting to, of being driven by some force inside himself. But as memories kept flooding back, they were peopled. Others had helped him.

> It was just survive. In general you had to live the jungle law and fend for yourself. Your death was my life so to speak. I've seen fathers and sons sell each other for a slice of bread. [Quiet] And I have seen completely strong people...
>
> *I was helped*. After I had typhus, the selection was made for me. I was on that list, because I was so skinny. And, the kid who commanded... who was in charge of the block was a young Slovakian and he kind of took a liking to me and he went and spoke to the old guy who was also... who was not taken, but who was not... who was going to die anyway and spoke to him. [Subdued] He [blockalteste] came over and he said, "This guy is going to take your number." I couldn't understand, but, he [the prisoner] came over and said, "Look, I'm an old man. I'm not going to make it. You have a chance." I was... *He died for me.*

Suffering he believed brought either the best or the worst out in people; it was the crucible, the one true test of nobility of spirit, he felt. But of course this was not a straightforward association, nor was it safe to assume that social status and moral worth were directly related.

Eventually he allowed luck to account for his survival; something fairly random but yet tied uniquely to individuality. Nor could he decide why some people had helped and others had not, but he had a romantic's vision of goodness as being heroic and rare, rather than situated and socially influenced.

He married and had a daughter. His wife was of a higher social status than he. Her family had gotten out of Vienna before the Anschluss and had not lost everything. They had moved to Scotland where they once again started up a business.

As he spoke, he had gone through two marriages and was on a third. He had met his third wife later in life when he had a solidly established reputation as a successful businessman, vice-president of production for a moderate-sized firm. When they met, they were both smarting from marital break-ups. Peter mostly blamed himself for what had happened in his intimacies.

> It's [this aggressive style which is] hard on other people. A rabbi once told me of my first marriage--I spoke to him. Obviously he realized my way of thinking. He said, "You know, when I listen to you, and you have every right to talk, but you could be mistaken as being arrogant [by] other people." I say, "What do you mean?" He says, "Well you paint everything black and white." I say, "That's the way I see it." He says, "Well you've got to watch for that." And he didn't really realize that [was the heart of the problem].

This first marriage did not last beyond his daughter's earliest years. His second marriage also foundered. He thinks the third one is solid since they have similar expectations of one another. Peter's friendships struck a contrasting pattern to his marriages. In these relationships he had known strong, reciprocated bonds from the start. They afforded him a place for renewal without excessive demands and responsibilities.

He had come from a family where there were mixed sentiments about the importance of religion. His grandfather was an observant Jew, but his father rejected all religious ritual. As Peter phrased it, half of his family were religious and half were Viennese. He had experienced anti-Semitism as a boy and genocide as a teenager, but he was determined not to develop what he referred to as a "ghetto" mentality -- a tendency to shun outsiders. He believed survivors learned their fierce optimism through their response to persecution.

> All survivors I have met, they all [have] the same optimism and zest for life. Now, there's a Catch 22.
> Did it come because we were in the camps or did you have to have it in the

first place to be able to survive? It's got to be a bit of both. I was a fighter to start off with, because as a kid I was left to my own devices. I learned from a very small person to protect myself.

Peter believed in his own resourcefulness. He never relied on formal education in getting ahead. In a competitive world, he did what seemed logical rather than tactful. He was innovative, and he found a way to show it to advantage. He is now officially retired but continues to work as a consultant. He remains active and vital in all aspects of his life, skiing, volunteering, travelling.

> I love the outdoors. I think I would have loved it anyway, but because of camp, a lot more. So it's... well, I think it's a bit of everything. But, zest for life... you have to live every day. You're never dead til you're dead.

> [In the camps] you live from day to day. -- It's another day, you know. We had no hope to get out. We never thought we would get out alive because we figured they could always set up machine guns at the last moment, and they did--never get out alive. We did!

MICHEL

Michel Nielski grew up near Bialystock in the border region between Russia and Poland. He had relatives in both countries. He was fourteen when he and his family of four were put in the Bialystock ghetto which was formed August 1, 1941, and, in the following year, December 1942, he was transported to Birkenau with his family. As The Holocaust Chronicle (2000:517; Levin 1990:73-74) notes, the last 25,000 people still in the ghetto were murdered at Treblinka by August 1943. Michel's narrative may be roughly divided into descriptions of what he experienced first at Auschwitz-Birkenau, and then at Nordhausen. At that camp's liberation in 1945, he could by anyone's measure be seen as a veteran survivor of the Nazi KZ system and the sonderbehandlung. His story was a torrent of ideas and words by which he attempted to relate what few others ever knew of him.

> I was born into a family of two children on the 17th of March [1927]. My father was a hard-working person and he respected all nationalities and religions. I was brought up to be kind to other people no matter what their race or religion. So I had a very good upbringing which helped me later on to cope with a lot of other nationalities in the concentration camp. My mother spent her lifetime helping other people. So I have a completely

different attitude for my life. I respect other people and feel sorry for the underdog.

I had a good childhood, but that doesn't mean I didn't suffer a lot. One reason or another, children in school are not kind to those of Jewish nationality. We're supposed to be brothers. Every time they had religious lesson, they were very... throwing stones and things like that. So I experienced in the early years what it means to be different. Like, we don't want to have anything to do with you. I knew at a very early age how tough it is to be Jewish. You have to be strong and no matter how kind you are, you have to expect that not always other people will be good to you, unfortunately.

He experienced both acceptance and betrayal from his neighbors and childhood peers. While polite middle class frameworks held, there was an aura of acceptance. With Nazi ideas spreading through the 1930s, this began to change. Rancor and division were glorified. By 1941, the Nazis invaded Bialystock and the mopping up activities associated with Operation Reinhard brought a massive reorganization of local authorities under the direction of Einsatzgruppen A, one of five spearheads following the regular army with orders to implement genocide. Jews in occupied areas were officially denied civil and human rights. They were separately registered, forbidden to work, and their property confiscated. Then they were rounded up and wither taken to killing pits in the forest to be shot or corralled into ghettos. When ghettos were liquidated, those who had not already died from starvation or disease were taken to concentration camps and either gassed or put into forced labor. They became non-persons, treated by former peers as socially "dead." As he watched, "friends" came not to grieve but to strip the casket.

I was betrayed many times. I had good friends, Christian boys. I took things seriously, like the ten commandments--"Thou shalt not kill." As a child I could fix electrical things, make some money. So I had a camera, a good pair of skis. And the day when the war broke out and the Germans came in, all my friends came in too, and I said, "Oh, its so nice [you] came," because nobody wanted to have anything to do with the Jews. They came and just helped themselves to everything I had. The camera, sleigh, my skates. They took it [and] said, "You won't need it anyway."

It's very easy to hate. It's very hard to love. You know we... we went through a lot in the concentration camps, and I wear my tight shoes. I understand what it means when someone else is wearing tight shoes and somebody else is in pain. So I... I have no right to be otherwise. I have to

> be strong and be able to guide and help other people to get out from the stress... stress of losing a family...
>
> [Q: Would you tell more about your earliest memories of family life?]
>
> To tell you the truth, it is a very difficult thing to tell something where a person missed it. Because, I went [almost at once] from a child to manhood. I never had a teenage happiness because as a teenager I was in the concentration camps.

Such experiences made him withdraw from others even before he reached Auschwitz-Birkenau. As he spoke now, he wanted to linger in generalities and platitudes, just at the edge of his pool of specific memories, each with its own emotional eddies.

> They made the people [go] to a small portion of the city to transport to the concentration camps. They don't give you what to eat, and they treat you like dirt, and within one year or so, you become like a nobody, you are afraid to go out. You are afraid to do [anything]. You are afraid to... you can't go and provide. The strongest person is usually the provider for the family, he's handicapped. He's going to jump the fence and go somewhere, get a few potatoes. He'll be shot... shot, for just trying to feed the family. You go through a year of two of a ghetto, and if you stay there for a while, no food, people dying from hunger. You became an old person, and all your will to fight... goes.

In his teen years, he watched people starve and young men grow old trying to provide for their families. Having started his description in this way, he then became more detailed, speaking his soul poem.

> It was easy for them to bring everybody together to the trains and then ship them to the concentration camps. They shipped people to the concentration camps in wagons [in which, typically] you ship coal or cattle. And pushing in about one hundred people... You couldn't take nothing only if you wanted to take more shirts on yourself... two jackets, a pair of heavy boots. They... they said they were bringing you to certain camps. You would be working for the Reich.

He uses "they" frequently at this point, trying to imagine the strategic thinking of the perpetrators. The victims were trapped, and did as they were ordered to do. People like Michel's mother still thought well of Germans. She had worked with German companies in the post WWI period when Jews in Russia were still experiencing pogroms. Such contradictions allowed them to hope that the misery of the ghetto might have been due to the strains of war. Gradually elements of resistance sprang up in the Bialystock ghetto, but at the start, there was still doubt, ambivalence and denial.

> [Many said] the German people were very good people. They used to be the safest in the first world war to Jewish people. And the Jewish people could never believe... they're going to take us. [But] finally they bring you to the concentration camps where on the trains we were arriving late at night-- all the people in the train were all dead.
>
> It was 7 or 8 days or sometimes a week or two in the trains. You went in the trains and you couldn't stretch out. The way you went in was the way you were for the rest... five, seven, or ten days. And whatever you had for food that was it. You couldn't go out. It was really like in a [pause] bad dream.

At Auschwitz, there was a brutal efficiency. People were forced to jump out of the cars, the sick and weak just like the strongest. Selections began immediately.

> And you came to the concentration camp that's at Birkenau and they... right away they screamed, "Out, out of the wagons." And we had to form lines, five [to a line] and then... there... Mengele, of course. He was the one who did all the selections.
>
> They were taking ten percent. Young people in their health were the ones they were taking to the concentration camps. The older ones they were taking to the... They told them they were going to a place to have a shower. It was all well prepared. They had the shower heads [fitted for gas instead of water] and so on. I guess when the people [selected to die] start to come in from both sides [of the large shower area, one from the women's dressing area and the other from the men's] and they were all naked, men and women, that's... They must have realized that this was the end. I experienced these lines, but I was taken with my brother to the... the side where you go to walk [into] the concentration camp.
>
> My father noticed that [the family was being separated] and so he went after us. The SS man threw a stick on his neck and he pushed him back, you know. "You get back! Jew! Go back there." And this was the last time I saw my father.

That night he lost all that remained of his past life. The smoke flumes rising from the crematoria were all that remained of his loved ones.

> When we arrive we are told there by the people who operate the concentration

camp that your parents you will never see again because they are already in flames.

So they took us in and they shaved us everywhere and then you got some clothing which... a tall person got short pants you know... exchange. It was a horrible experience. Cold. No blankets the first night. And then they build more and more. When I arrived they started building the concentration camp. They have only two small crematoriums at this time, and my parents... I guessed they were burned in what was called the Brizinski [crematorium]. They were building up piles of wood and piles of corpses. They gassed them in a very big... like a horse stable.

He was in the concentration camps from the end of December 1942 until 1945. During the early part of his internment he dug the pits for the crematoria smokestacks at Auschwitz.

The first few days [at Auschwitz] I thought I won't survive. We were digging... digging the big holes for the chimneys... for the crematorium, the modern ones. And one fellow slipped in... was a side that collapsed... and the SS man said not to let him out. He's going to be one of the first ones that experienced this crematorium. They were not ashamed to tell us what is going on. Said, "Here. This is where we are going to finish all your people." They... they... So. But, somehow, somebody pulled this SS man over, another SS man, and got him out of there.

But many times they could bury people alive. They were very, very sadistic. There were a few Germans [who were] worse than animals.

While he did the menial, pointless tasks assigned him without complaint and at the double, his physique could not bear long stretches of heavy physical work in all kinds of weather. He kept watching for some means to get on less destructive work details. Then an opportunity arose, and he ended up making pillows and blankets for his next work stint. Getting on this work detail protected him from what he could no longer withstand, but the operation was closed down within a year and he got transferred to the Birkenau Canada kommando, the work unit appointed to strip the gassed remains, stripping them of any still useable items and bringing them to the crematorium. To do this, the bodies had to be disentangled. Death by gassing was, Michel discovered, violent; he could not get the ghoulish imagery of the bodies out of his mind. Working this close to the killing operations left him with few illusions.

We had to make an assortment. One time, the first time, I remember we come and they [the victims] were just gassed and I saw this open door... Open the door and they [inmate attendants] ventilate all the place before they take out the bodies, and I saw this big pyramid of people... dead ones. This was awful to see. The...the...the people that died, these people with children, [were] one on top of the other. Many times, they were all tied in like this [meshed together]; you'd have to tear them apart. People who worked in the crematorium, they had to hack off fingers, take off the gold and take off pellets from the dentist [tooth fillings], shave the heads and [take] everything from the bodies.

I knew people who were working in the crematorium. [One of them] said in the beginning it was horrible [for him] to see because when you put in the body, the heat grabs it and all the... the man comes like he is standing up and it's a horrible... You put in the corpse and the corpse slowly from the heat rises up like this... all the ligaments and everything... And he says how many people recognize their fiance or their own family [going into the ovens]. It was something of a... I don't think that... ever... ever...

What is humane about when... when it was a rainy day... the zyklon gas you... absorbing humidity... and it... it wasn't that a person was choked from... from that. It took a half an hour. It was a horrible death. Dry, it did it in about ten minutes. But if it was a humid day, it took a good half hour before the people... And they were screaming... and you... you... bring in gas. It's a horrible... horrible... The obersturmfuhrer, the commander from the camps, he could look through the little window watching this. They enjoyed it, how these people are suffering, how people are dying.

He was half crying, half screaming these words *soto voce* because his wife was just inside the house and could hear any disturbance coming from the garden where he sat. Captive workers could grimly estimate the origination points of the transports by the density and color of the smoke as the bodies burned; the thicker the smoke the better fed the corpse had been. Their focus of awareness seemed to be somewhere near the perimeter of the ovens.

So many people burning. So much time. And let's say in twenty-four hours, burning maybe twelve thousand people. So we knew when we start finding out where the people... you knew this is a ghetto brought from France, from Belgium, from Holland. But they have still better, Poland. The Polish ghettos were already half [pause] dead... dying from hunger. The people... the... people which were still full bodied was going through flames of three or four meters high; and the people which have only bones, it was a very small... sort of yellowish type... up from the bones. We knew from that alone where the transports are coming. It was... And the smell of this burned flesh was horrible.

The bizarre and the macabre were commonplace complements of the ordinary day in death camps where the major work involved handling bodies, either preparing them for labor or plundering them after they were gassed and before they were burned. To accompany this there was music.

> You went in, you learned to... to leave your dismay. And the orchestra... I had a friend, a Christian friend, he was in Auschwitz. He was taken as a youngster. I never knew why. He just died a couple of months ago. Nikki W—. He [later] had a restaurant in XX- theater. He was playing in the orchestra. They had this orchestra playing! People were [coming from] the transports straight to the crematorium. Those poor people, they don't know where they are going. One hour [later] it will all be over. I was lucky.

If he could find a way to unobtrusively help others he did. When one of their unit fell ill and there was no medicine available, Michel hid some gold from the plunder of the bodies to obtain the needed treatment using the camp's blackmarket. To be caught holding anything back would bring swift death to the culprit.

> I find once twenty-five pieces of gold in a blanket and we were seventy people and we split it among ourselves and one of them needed medicine because he had typhoid. We saved him with that. You could pay a gold piece and get bread from the Polish people who are coming into the camp. There was... So a lot of people in the surrounding area got very rich. I don't know if the money... it doesn't stay for long anyways. But I don't envy you the money like that. It... it... it was horrible you know.

> All the clothing from the burned people... the dead people, coming to us and we making assortment. There was all SS around us. We were opening up... and anything we were finding, gold or diamonds, watches, was all going to German banks. And when there were big diamonds or big pieces, expensive, this went straight to the obersturmfuhrer which was the chief officer... and there was a... once a week, there was a man coming with a motorcycle and he had a big leather pouch and he would... This was going straight to Switzerland. Everyone of them, they made their own fortunes, and some of them became very rich.

That quiet slip, "It was horrible, you know" revealed the depth of his pain so important for him to hide anyway he could in the camps. He went to immense lengths to never blame unnecessarily, to never become like his enemy. Endless inner discipline was his strong reserve.

Michel defined his survival in terms of gradually learning what to do. His view was that survival was processual and incremental; the longer you lived, the more survival skills you learned. This notwithstanding, those who did stay alive more than a few months were considered rare events. But Michel was a practical young man and given to a necessary optimism.

> The Germans they like strong people, and if somebody is not very strong, he [German] beats him up. He falls. He starts crying. The guard is kicking him to death. But if I would be kicked, I would stand up [stiffly] and salute and just say, "Yavul!" and right away they were stopping. So I knew the mentality of the Germans. They were strong people and I did anything to wash myself to keep clean and to lay on my pants, not to sleep in them so they're always pressed out and to do anything not to be... look neglected. And I would always try to appear that I work hard.

Michel had thought of ways to minimize damage to himself. Appearance he felt was as important then as ever it would be. In this he showed astuteness in role-taking from the guards' perspective. Demeaning stereotypes of his captors might have fit his mood more than his survival needs. Instead he mobilized his energies with "the Germans are strong people," and hence, the Germans like strong people; therefore, stand smartly at attention when you have been slapped; never cower or whine. When in doubt, act so as to claim respect from the captor. Such was his code of conduct in the realm of appearances.

While the Kanada kommando was a manageable work situation for him, the substance of what he was doing filled him with revulsion. Emotionally it was an extremely risky work detail. The piles of corpses associated with the crematorium were thereafter for him the stuff of nightmares. Michel displaced his profound disgust by focusing on the people with whom he worked. They represented all kinds of persons and backgrounds, who, though kept from easy communication, had a common bond in suffering, deprivation and a will to withstand. They became for him a company of heroes.

> We were all living together and very close. This was my brother, that survivor. No matter what nationality, he feels a brother to his fellow man. I think that when a person goes through a bad time, it gives him a chance to become a better person, because he realizes what life is all about.

Even more than luck, or the successful management of appearances, Michel valued the care and compassion of his fellows. But given the kind of stress the inmates were under, this could vary quite a bit and be unstable when it did occur. It was precious to find some expression of tenderness and virtue where brutalization of life was the norm. As rare as it might be to find it, Michel reckoned his survival was due to his being "adopted" by several of the Russian POWs in his work detail. While his felt identity--that by which he knew himself best and most authentically, was with the Jewish prisoners, they helped him pass as one of them.

> We were moved around constantly, and they changed camps. [One involved electrical work.] It was a better [work] camp. I was with a few Russian officers from the Russian army that was prisoners of war, and they transport us... [We were] making synthetic methanol and rubber. I worked as an electrician. It was very primitive work. We were digging holes, making holes in the walls for the electrical wiring going through.

> This [camp] belonged to IGA which is a German company still today. When the Russians approached me, [the Nazis had] started to bring people more to Germany and there was [a lot of] disarray. There were a few of us [who got to know each other, and they said] "Tear off your number," and, "they won't know that you're Jewish. Come with us." So I did. And they shipped us as a group to Nordhausen.

From this point on, Michel "passed" as a Russian. Coming from Bialystock, he was familiar with Russian ways and spoke the language. The support of this work group became all important to him. At Nordhausen conditions were as precarious as ever for inmates.

> [Nordhausen] was a concentration camp deep in Germany where they were making Messerschmit motors and they made the V-1, V-2 rockets. And they took a group of young people and they taught us welding, and we were working on the V-1, V-2 rockets doing certain welding things like that. Of course, you did only a certain thing, what you were taught, and, God forbid somebody fell asleep... working fourteen hours... fell asleep. This was considered sabotage! In the night, people were hanged. [Quiet] So you have to do anything not to fall asleep. In the night they were hanging between sixteen people [at] a time with those big electrical cranes, the ones that were attaching the rockets to bring out. It was underground. It was a horrible thing to see all the time the people hanging.

Michel narrowly missed death by hanging--not for falling asleep, but for trying to make a container for some of his barrack mates so that they could claim an extra bit of soup when food was distributed. He could do this because at that time he was working in the aluminum tubing part

The Adolescents

of the camp. As the guard who caught him passed by, he was just ready to weld the base on one end of the tubing he had found and complete his "mug". He could not disguise what he was doing as part of his work. Utilizing camp materials in unspecified ways was referred to by the SS as "sabotage," an offense which in practice was punishable by death.

> I couldn't hide. It [the container] was too big. He [SS officer] says [to] me... [trails off]. He gave me such a beating and I was put in an area for being hanged because this was "sabotage." But I was lucky. Somehow they had some victory [that day], so we were pardoned. We were supposed to get twenty-five lashes on the behind. This was done.

> It was a Sunday; everybody is staying in [day off]. A very primitive table... wood. You put in your two feet sideways and then you straighten them out and you can pull it out and it's your waist and you're laid down and I received... [trails off again]. The first five I felt. It was... And then I fainted. But they give you twenty-five. And, lucky, my... [trails off]. Usually, the meat [muscle] was beaten up and detached itself from the bones. Then you were finished. You get gangrene and die. And I... I... I... survived that. So I got twenty-five instead of being hanged. Thank God. *I was helped.*

> Then [as a scab forms over the deep cut marks] whatever you had for skin, it shrink in after and it's so tight that you can't stretch it out. You walk like this [illustrates]. I was walking like this for three weeks and you can't go to hospital because you are punished. But somehow a Swiss doctor knew about it and he gave me something to smear to soften up the things. He risked his life to... By the way, this fellow saved... he saved our whole camp in Bergen-Belsen [by refusing to distribute 20,000 loaves of poisoned bread to the prisoners before liberation]. But they did poison the women's camp in Belsen, with typhoid.

Recalling the pain, Michel starts to tell something, then drops the thought and turns on to something else. Eventually some of the story line holds. He highlighted luck rather than the bitterness of false justice. He focused on the Swiss doctor rather than the guard who did the whipping. Despite what he went through, Nordhausen became for Michel a way of surviving. Nevertheless, he was passing under an assumed identity and facing extreme conditions. By the time he arrived at Bergen-Belsen, the cumulative physical and emotional stress was beginning to show.

> The end of the war, they pushed in so many people... it was so tight you know. They were sleeping... For one person it was really tight. You sleep like a sardine. And it was a very bad experience. The first time in my life...

> I once found a piece of mirror. *I took a look of me.* I saw myself... thousands of little things from fleas, going in the night in the ears... [while] you slept.

Just as his childhood had been marred by watching the strongest and the best lose their lives to protect others, so in the camps he watched helplessly as his body became a collection of bones loosely held together. The mirror captured his young life's tragedy. The flea marks spoke out his helplessness. He was being ravaged.

In adolescence, authenticity and uniqueness are important issues. If in the wasteland of the camps they could be dismissed as irrelevant trifles, character still mattered. Survival forced certain priorities on survivors, and a thin line marked the margin between holding some level of equanimity or being pushed to some primitive extreme which some at least knew to avoid.

> I'm very thankful to the blockalteste. He was the leader from the whole block, and he knew I am Jewish, and I had a few conversations with him. They... you know, right away... he was Polish... Polish prisoner. See, the Germans, when they went into Poland... four years of Occupation... they took all of the Polish intelligentsia, which is the lawyers and doctors and priests, and they took them all in the concentration camp. So we were with these people and they... they understood us [Jewish prisoners] very well, but they couldn't [change anything either]. They were themselves in a mess. The only difference was that they could have to die from a... a natural death or, for certain reasons, shot. But they [did not have to fear] the crematorium... to be gassed. This was reserved only for the Jews, the crematorium [deep breath].

> And what I want to mention is, we were given out every Friday a double portion of bread, a piece of black salami made from blood. It's... And so, you eat a little bit and the rest you keep. You hide it in a piece of cotton wrapped around [you] and then you had your pants wrapped around that and you slept in this. A man stole it from me. So I jumped at him. He start screaming and the whole block woke up and then the... the... blockalteste--he was a former priest, he said to me, [calls out to him using the Polish endearment of the name Michel]." He started saying to me the ten commandments. "In your religion, thou shalt not kill..." He persuaded me. He said, "Leave it to me. Believe me, you're going to kill him, you're going to get hanged tomorrow. You won't gain anything." And he persuaded me and I left it. He [the priest] really punished him after that, that *vladimir.*

> You know, I think all the time of this priest, the blockalteste. [Maybe he

is] still alive somewhere. He should rest in peace if he's not. But he saved me to be [from being] a murderer.

While Michel accepted that, under the extreme conditions of the camps, hunger might press a person to take a certain license, that license-taking was not part of how he ordinarily saw himself. He believed there could be no dilution of principles. The blockalteste correctly understood this of him and also that for Michel to kill on impulse would have marked his life permanently. Michel reasonably saw that night as a victory of the human spirit over the oppression.

> You know, you go through a certain extended length to do things with people who [don't appreciate it], but [who]... are primitive in a way... and they don't know about religion, the ten commandments, and humanity. Some people were killing for stealing. It was... If they [Nazis] took away from you all the dignity and all your strength and all your moral thinking, and the only thing you've got is that bread... get as much as you can... and also water...

At first the enormity of what was happening to them as people invited denial and a defensive turning against old values. Many were led to question the assumptions on which the earlier social order of childhood rested. Once trusted implicitly, where starvation and abuse gripped them daily, scions of a beautiful life could easily fall into disuse. Trauma and powerlessness had brought everyone a crisis in meaning, however it was resolved.

> I was fourteen [and] in the ghetto, one year in the ghetto. No education. And then when I am fifteen, I'm exposed to a... a holocaust, to a situation where people are being... being by the thousands... the hundreds of thousands... put to death. Those were good people. People... poor people, rich people. People. Just because they happened to be born Jewish. It's... it's... it's... was a, you know... We... It was a moment... If there is a God, I'm sure he wouldn't let do... You stop believe in God.

> Some people prayed in the camps. We... It was like a... a... You go through certain stages. In the beginning you're upset. If there is a God, you're upset about him. Why he let this thing happen? And then you start thinking of [others who also suffered]. There were in the concentration camps philosophers and lawyers, gangsters and homosexuals. In 1936, when the Nuremburg Law came out, that they all had to divorce their Jewish wives, some of them did not, and they went to concentration camps. I met a lot of German people, their wives were Jewish and a lot of people that were religious people from different nationalities. They... they... they [Nazis] didn't

> make any segregation. Anybody that didn't suit them, they just sent to the concentration camp.

> God gave us all [as humans] the liberty to do what we want with ourselves and our fellow man. [At first you] forget that. But later on, you come to that... this is beyond what is controlled. We are free people. We can do good, we can do bad-- this was the choice. To do bad... the Nazis did it!

It was very difficult for him to deal with admitting that his faith had been sorely tested. The Job-like tussle with the question of why a just man should suffer consumed a great deal of Michel's solitude. As much as this involved an unfamiliar spiritual rebellion of sorts, the dialogue was with a wisdom that held efficacy in all places. It was a means of symbolically entering a space beyond the grip of tyranny where the oppressors themselves might be judged. And so it was that regardless of what stage in the questioning process Michel and other Jews might have attained, they celebrated Yom Kippur. "No matter how hungry we were, and for sympathy and solidarity with our people, and poor people that were lost, we didn't eat on the day of Yom Kippur".

Bergen-Belsen was where he ended up by 1945. The British army's arrival at that camp is formally documented and with it their moral outrage at what had been done to the victims and those who were still alive. The soldiers and medics were heroes to the survivors, bringing food, healing, compassion--salve for many different kinds of wounds. Starved and abused as they were, the prisoners still felt no sense of celebration, however.

> We were liberated in Bergen-Belsen [yet] we were closed in. The British army didn't want us to run out and [grab food. Some did anyway]. Now, they had a good reason [for this but] it was for us miserable to see that we were liberated and things remained the same. Our stomachs [were reduced to such an extreme] that they were giving us porridge and all kind of things there in order to let the stomach loosen up and... But a lot of people who did jump out and run away to the peasants, they died. They became so ill from... the... The stomach couldn't digest the food. People surviving... already being liberated... [and dying]! It's a horrible thing.

Liberation also meant separation from the noble company of allies he had won in the camps and being cast back into the society that had betrayed him so bitterly a few years before. There were other contradictions that constituted personal disaster for many. It was difficult to absorb the shocks hidden in these contradictions, to bear the same hatred and apathy from the general population when they returned as they had left when they were taken to the camps. The "home"-coming was bitter.

> It was hard to go back. I... I came from the concentration camp to Poland, and it was very bad to see that still they hate us, and of course they took away the business and they had the houses and apartments and... A few times there were situations where people went to the country to claim a house or factory, like a couple that I know that survived. They got murdered *after* the war. Came to claim the... and both shot in the head in a little village. And nobody said anything about it.

The neighbors who had watched as Jews had been led away to the ghettoes and eventually the transports, had wanted their own lives to go on as usual when the victims returned. Sometimes these same "neighbors" were living in the houses or running the businesses the Nazis had confiscated from the Jews. It was to this kind of rancorous situation that the survivors returned. There was less than a welcome for the dispossessed. Most of their families had been murdered in the sonderbehandlung. Michel describes the loneliness.

> I used to have a bit of vodka after the war and have a meal... once a week I got a good meal... paid for it... [with] a lady who survived, too, and she was cooking for a few people. Survivors. Bread and all that. And one time... [trails off]. There was nobody to look after [me]. I was getting a depression. She [the woman who cooked for them] said, "Go and lie down in my little room." I used to cry. I just couldn't take it. It was horrible. *There is nobody to listen to you.* They [were] still shooting at Jews. They couldn't care less, and the world couldn't care less.

The key phrases symbolizing that time were "nobody to look after..." "I used to cry" "nobody to listen to you" and no one to care. He was not released from his emptiness. The reasons he left eastern Europe after liberation are not otherwise specified in the entire three hour interview. His deep anguish was unabated; it was another wounding rather than a healing which liberation had brought.

> I came out with eighteen years and three months... with no family, with no profession. I had to make... become a person, a human being... *on my own*. No psychiatrist. Nobody to help. You had to do it by yourself. I...

The "I" which rose like the phoenix from the ashes of the "we" in the concentration camp left for Paris. It was there that he began to build a new life with new friends and a career in the fashion industry. There that he met the woman he eventually married. She was also a survivor of Auschwitz who had lost her family.

> She was ten years old [when] her mother was taken away and when she was twelve, her father was in the camps. He was taken hostage. He had to dig his own grave. Every ten people went out and [got] shot. She stays completely [away] from meetings [of survivors]. She can't go through it. She wants to go on with life. She can't live on that.

> She was in Auschwitz. She has a number. I am married from a concentration camp.

They were wed in 1949 and shortly thereafter had a son, followed a few years later by a daughter. They decided to leave Europe behind and immigrated to North America. He believes that of the two hundred and fifty thousand Jews from Bialystock and its surrounds in 1941, only around thirty five of them survived. Though he finally escaped from the space where so many atrocities had occurred, it is still important for him to believe that those who perished must not be forgotten. Holocaust deniers give Michel a sense that the world not only did not learn from the survivors' sufferings but is unwilling to do so. To these he points out,

> The Germans are very organized, and everyone who was burned has a name and a number. If you want to find out about a certain village in Poland, they will tell you. I have my own experience when I wanted to find out something. They had a way of putting everything on paper. You want to find out something, go to the German consul. Find out how many Jewish people were in this city, where are they now. They will guide you, they will tell you what is true. It's absolutely unbelievable that people will come up today and what do they want to do? Prove that the Holocaust never happened!

> [The survivor] must tell people the truth. But it hurts when, you know, you lost your parents. My mother wasn't even forty years old. My father was forty-five. What did they have from their lives?

Facts recorded in an archive cannot relay the depth of sorrow in the human heart which also documents, but in a different way, the progression of a tragedy. Traumatic experience cannot be integrated into an ordinary lifetime, but there are small balms to ease pain, and for him this involved helping others make a future free from hatred and repression.

You know, we are born with hate and with love. Why is it easier for us to hate than love? It's... you can get a lot of pleasure of giving... making people presents, seeing how they open them up. They love it. It's a pleasure to give. You have to teach yourself. People are expecting a lot from the world. [Instead], give to the world.

There was so much he wanted to forget, to turn into a private issue and find a personal balance for while moving on to new things. But with waking up in the middle of the night, sweating, staring out of a raw nightmare that put him back again in the terror of the camps, he felt the experience had become part of his skin. He said, "It's like glue. It's attached to you. Try to scratch it off and you can't. You can't get rid of it." Where he said this was also important--his garden, full of afternoon sunlight with the songs rising from little birds flickering through his hedges and trees. It was a modest upper middle class house in an unassuming but comfortable neighborhood. Through the windows of their kitchen his wife and a few of their friends were chatting, out of earshot. These were the sights and sounds of his transcendence.

KLARA

Klara Raikauff was born in Hungary in 1928. Her family had lived in what had then been Hungary for six generations. She remembers living in fear from 1939 onwards. Conditions worsened in 1943 with new anti-Semitic legislation. They were virtually under house arrest. Her father had been forced by the vicious turn in public policy toward Jews to put his import-export business under an associate's name. This man assumed ownership and denied the family any income or profits from the turnover. Klara attempted to continue her high school training at home. On a morning like any other, a knock came at their door. Police gave them twenty minutes to get their belongings and come into the street. At that time, Klara was sixteen years old. She and her family were shipped by cattle car to Auschwitz-Birkenau. She spent one year in captivity from 16 April, 1944, to 15 April, 1945. When she was liberated by the British, she was the lone survivor in her family of five.

We had never heard of Auschwitz. Never. We didn't know what happened to the Polish Jews. We didn't even know what happened next door. So when they came to take us, when it was... The Germans came in, the Germans marched into Hungary March 19th, 1944. Of course that was the time when we were really like prisoners in our house. We didn't dare to leave the house, and we didn't know anything about deportation and Polish camps or anything. But when they came to get us, and this was the Hungarian police, not the Germans -- even

> though the Germans were all over the place, it was Sunday morning, 5:00 am, when everybody was asleep, you know. The whole town was quiet and they came and just knocked on the door, and my father opened it, and there was the police with a handgun pointing at my father and saying, "Get ready. You have twenty minutes."
>
> So my father probably tried to ask why. We were all in bed, of course. We were asleep. They said, "Don't ask any questions. Get ready and get some of your belongings. Twenty minutes you have and then we go." "Where?" –"Don't ask. Just get ready." And, you know--with the gun at his head... The door stayed open, police stayed right at the door, and we just got a few of our belongings and they took us to... to a school and we stayed there overnight. Next morning, we were put on a train, and that was it.

She had not at that time heard of Auschwitz, since they had been forbidden the use of radios. Secrecy, force and political lies had plotted the direction of their lives for the past few years. Severe restrictions had been preceded by milder ones, and control over emotions like fear seemed strategically more important than considering radical alternatives. Round-ups of minorities and political undesirables, confiscation of property, and severe restriction of all social activity led up to that early morning knock on the door. Her description of events was evenly paced, her voice was balanced, but with a strained tone. She spoke of the train leaving one rail station and proceeding to another. There were the five of them: mother, father, one son and two daughters. At the second stop, the SS were evident as they were not before, and there were now many others gathered there for transport.

> The SS were there and they said, "Look. There is a war..." They were very polite, very nice. "There is a war and you have to understand. You are going to work on a farm, in Hungary, of course, and when the war is over you will come back, and families will stay together." And we believed it. We believed it because we didn't know anything.
>
> [Soon] we knew something was wrong because we had no water or food or provision for toilet or anything. They just locked us in and they closed this... this door from the outside. And we were practically suffocating because, for eighty-four people, there was a little window like this [points to a small window high in the wall of the room] and it was a very long ride.

They were being treated as though they were already dead. She had been used to a life of privilege in her upper middle class world. The house they left behind was a prize for plunderers who sealed it and stripped it of even its door knobs. On returning two years later, she tried to find even a photograph to ward off her desperate loneliness then, but nothing was left, and neighbors said they were "so sorry."

As time went by and the train drove relentlessly onward, the misery of passengers and the secrecy of the journey claimed everyone's attention. They had been told they would be kept in Hungary by the officials as they left the first collection point, but all indications as the train moved relentlessly onward seemed to deny this.

> We looked out the little window and knew that it was night and then it was day and then it was night again, and we knew that we can't be in Hungary. And it was getting very cold, too, and that time in Hungary it's very pleasant. It was very cold. And then we arrived at Birkenau, and we didn't know where we were, and... all the barbed wires... It was at night, a Friday night, we arrived. And there was Mengele.
>
> The men and women were separated right away, and I was very young, very, very shattered [drifting, fading] and... and... this whole... really cruel, sadistic scene there at... at...
>
> When we arrived there at Birkenau was something that I don't think I will ever be able to forget. And when I have nightmares, I have that scene. I dream about it all the... [Sighs. She is controlled but at the edge of tears.]
>
> The people were getting out... pushed out of the cattle cars. The Germans, the SS, came up. They just jumped up and pushed people down. But the platform was way down. So it was high. But we were so cramped in that place [cattle car] that after two days we could barely move. And there were these old people who couldn't move at all and so they just fell, everybody on top of each other, and the small children and the babies and these young mothers holding their babies. And everybody was screaming and everybody was just terrified. They were asking for water... and, of course, there was none. All of a sudden we were surrounded with dogs, you know, the German shepherds. The SS always came with German shepherds. They never walked without a dog.

Klara's careful control over her speech and expression strikes a direct contrast with the scene being described in which there was mayhem, pain and terrifying betrayal. The crowd, though more numerous than the guards, were disoriented and weaponless. They were civilians who had been told that all would be well. How unprepared they were for the concept of selection. Her voice was full of tears.

Before we knew, my father and my brother were gone. I never said goodbye to them. I never said goodbye to them. I never had enough time to... to... to look and see what was going on. And then I found myself in front of Mengele. I didn't know who he was at the time. I learned it after.

My mother... We were walking and my mother was in the middle and I was on one side and my sister on the other. He was there, standing, and he just put his arm between my mother and myself, and I went the other way and [deep breath, her words are coming very fast in run-on sentences] they went the other way and that was it. And I didn't I... I... And again, with the dogs barking and that blinding light there... because there were hundreds of light bulbs and it was night and it was terribly cold and everything happened so fast.

It was so frightening, because of all the screaming, and people were shouting to one another. And so, by the time I looked what was happening, when... when Mengele put his arm in between my mother, sister and myself, they were... they were lost in the crowd [soft, more tearful voice; the room is dimly lit and her face across the room does not show the change her voice does. She doesn't move. Finally she starts to speak once again]. I looked, but by the time I looked, I couldn't see them anymore. And so, this is how [swallows painfully]... this is how it happened.

She and the other women were standing all that night, waiting in the icy rain to be processed. Shaved of all body hair in the presence of a bevy of SS men who treated the women's modesty and embarrassment with indifference, they were in shock.

My first... you know... we were taken to... to a disinfectant bath and everything was taken from us, clothes everything. And when we were taken from the bath we were shaven with a machine. And I... everybody got a piece of clothes... whatever I... It so happened that I got summer clothes... was about four or five sizes too big for me, so it was just hanging, and [deep breath] no underwear, no socks, and a pair of wooden shoes. And as I said before, it was very cold. So we got out of the bath and with my shaved head which was bleeding because they were terribly, terribly rough, and there was no time to just gracefully and gently shave our heads off. So we got out and I had a short sleeved sort of a little summer dress down to the ground and... and no underwear and I was *freezing* [stresses this]. And it was pouring outside, a very icy rain and we got out and had to line up!

Probably the worse part of it [stripping and shaving] was the SS were all around us--men! And we had to get undressed. And... They looked over while we were shaved everywhere. And we were completely naked and, you know, for a sixteen year old girl to stand there in front of... of men and to be shaved and... and my head... I had long hair, heavy, wavy hair, and I... [Gives up trying to find the right words]. This was something then.

Tall and willowy, Klara has a peaceful appearance. She is quiet, gracious, compassionate. She kept a rapid pace as she spoke the images she still saw. "And" draws the phrases into strings of word sounds that slap against the sensibilities we share as she tries to express what was done to the women and what it was like for her on that first night. She is not declamatory in her style; her sparse description is sufficient judgement against her tormentors. These women had been selected to be captive labor rather than gassed. At this point in the Nazi war effort, women as well as men were chosen as slave laborers. Their barracks were shoddy, having been constructed the previous winter by other abused workers. The guide to their bunks that night had been in the work crews who erected them. In the sub-zero temperatures and without shelter themselves the guide's hands and feet had been frozen.

Klara remembers there was one blanket for twelve women that first night in Birkenau. They squeezed, twelve to each of the three levels of the bunk beds, all strangers to one another, trying to rest. The women had hardly slept when a command was given to reassemble outdoors. Her first appel was about to be etched upon her memory.

> So, we lined up. It was [still] pouring. We were waiting for the SS to come and count us. This was my first morning in Birkenau and my first experience, and this was enough for me for... for... for the rest of my life.
>
> The SS came with a dog and a whip. With his whip he would point at "You..." "You..." "You..." and so on. And whoever he pointed at had to come out and get up on the truck. We didn't know what was going on, but, as he came close to me, [sighs deeply] he pointed at a girl who would have to come out. But [she was with] her mother, and the mother came out too and was holding on to her daughter. We didn't know that... it was a "no-no," that we should never let them know that there were sisters, or mother-daughters, or even close friends, because they... they made sure that they would be separated.
>
> So, the mother was kicked by the SS man [swallows] and was told that she had to get back into the line and the girl had to get up on the truck. But the mother wouldn't go. And so he kicked her again and she fell, and there was-- it was raining, and there was a big puddle. She spoke German, the woman, and asked the SS to... to let her [daughter] go with her. She said, "This is my daughter and I-I want to go with her." And he started to... to beat her with the whip and kick her and then finally the dog... he was holding the dog on a leash and he gave the order to the dog, and the dog just took her... just

> tore her apart... right in front of us... in front of her daughter.
>
> The girl had to get up on the truck. By now the mother... I don't know if she was dead by the time we were allowed to go into the building. She was there... she was left there in the puddle. And we were all splattered with blood.

All through this description, only the images are depicted; there is no commentary on how they all were feeling, or how dreary the weather might have been, or what new dimensions terror took on for each of them watching. What would have been unthinkable before this time, that is leaving a suffering and helpless woman lie in a puddle of her own blood is simply accepted as the women turn to leave. This scene symbolized the passing of a boundary between ordinary life and a coercion context. In such a space, trauma was to be the norm and death its logical catharsis. But to survive, Klara had to take back control by finding some area of existence in which to exercise judgement, and live by it. In part she did this by managing her intake of the food allotment; she was determined not to let hunger force her into uncritical dependence.

> You got a piece of bread in the morning and some kind of soup in the evening. But the first day I tasted it [soup], it was so horrible that there was absolutely no nutrition in it. *So I decided that I wouldn't eat it.* So all I had was this one piece of bread in the morning. I guess that this was partly the reason that I survived the four months in Birkenau because the... the people who ate that so... that kind of soup or whatever they called it developed diarrhoea, practically the first day or the second day. And because there was no food and because it was terrible, I saw... there were twenty-eight girls my age--sixteen. We knew each other. I saw one after the other either [deep breath] taken in the morning--selected for the gas chamber, [or] just dropped dead.

It seemed apparent that no part of this abusive context could be trusted. Her decision not to eat was a carefully reasoned, self confirming act which served her well in the course of events to follow. The physical deprivation she felt was of her own choosing and as such was a luxury that sated her at a different level. In many ways, the decision to carefully select what and when to eat proved to be wisdom many times over.

None of Klara's group had been given identification numbers at the start. That meant that when any of them were killed or taken to be gassed, there would be no record. For several months they just waited with nothing to do in full view of the towering crematoria.

> The Polish girl [who led them from that first night] told us that the truck [slows her speech] is going to the gas chamber and every morning at random people will be selected to be taken to the gas. And [pause] the girl told us the truck would take the girls to a gas chamber and then of course...
>
> I was in Camp C, and the next camp was a road next to us beyond this barbed wire, and after the road was another barbed wire, and in that camp was the gas chambers and the crematorium. And we could... we could see the flames coming out of the chimneys. We were very close. And the smell was so bad.
>
> This was when the Hungarian Jews came. [Big sigh]. I... I... there were thousands... thousands of people killed everyday because this was the end of... We could hear the transports when they came, you know. All the shouting and the crying and the screaming and... and then...
>
> We could see the trucks... open trucks... coming, you know, with young mothers holding their babies. They were put on a truck. They didn't have to walk. And... and we could see all these small children and babies with their mothers and... holding their teddy bear or ball. And then an hour or two later we could see the same truck going back, piled up with toys but no children anymore. And I saw this day after day after day.

Her voice is full of grief and fatigue, soft, but resonant. Even doubt was denied them as a comfort. They knew where the children were and what had happened. In all likelihood it would happen shortly to them. But what they said to one another made little direct reference to this fate. Habits of caring and good taste rendered discursively would not endorse the obvious.

> We said, well yes we could see the chimneys, we could see the flames and we could smell the... this terrible burned flesh, but still we... we just didn't want to believe it. I... I guess you... if... I guess it kept us going. We didn't want to believe that...
>
> My... she [the Polish blockalteste] said that those who went to the left went straight to the gas chamber. My mother and my sister went to the left. I... I didn't know what happened to my father and my brother. I was hoping that they were together. I didn't... I didn't want to believe it [that they were dead]. And then... this was... and after this first morning, you know. [Sighs].
>
> I... I don't know how I got through the days.

Within Klara's camp the women eventually started helping one another by gesturing or symbolizing caring. For instance, when volunteers were requested for an industrial operation, the older women counselled the younger ones to hold back. Some women they knew of had been turned into prostitutes.

> We were told... There were women in the building who were around thirty-five, forty, who to me were "old" women -- I was sixteen. And they said, "Don't go. Just hide. Don't go." Because they were sure that we would be selected to... for prostitutes... which was [in retrospect] really insane because you can't imagine what we looked like. We looked terrible. We were just skin and bones.

Reminding each other to resist any dubious form of "work" kommando that might, in fact, turn out to be a form of prostitution was important where there were no supports against base subjugation. More than that, the women's vigilance served to acknowledge at the same time the ceremonial status of women as bearers of life and the keepers of virtue across the generations. This kind of caring was also expressed in other ways among the women. Klara found examples of it after making friends with five others who slept in her barracks, whom she had known from grade school.

> So there were five of us in... in Birkenau who were always together, and somehow we kept each other going. Little things. We had absolutely nothing to give to each other because we didn't have anything. We had no food to... to share. We all had the same amount, but we could do little things. For instance, it was so terribly cold in the morning and five had to stand in line. Each morning we took turns, always another person was standing in the middle. You see... the one in the middle at least she was a bit warmed by the two bodies [standing] next to her. And then the next morning [it would be someone else's turn].

They shared what little body heat they could offer like they kept each other's confidences. There was no special art or reason for their bonds other than natural receptivity to one another in such desperate times. The stories told to cheer each other as well as the words used to phrase them held familiar keys to meaning which had the power to uplift the spirit. So also these gestures which could not protect them physically against the violence in camp life were used to make each other feel a little stronger or warmer, even with a stormtrooper looking on. These simple strategies could not turn the tide of events, but like the stories some would tell, they gave hope that things might change for the better again and just as quickly.

> The day to day life in Birkenau was possible because there were older people who came up with all kinds of unbelievable stories that we would be liberated soon, because they knew. They didn't know! We had no [news]paper and we had no contact at all with outsiders, but they... they lied to keep us going and they said, "You will see the Americans coming because this happened and that happened..." and they didn't know anything. *But we believed...*

The belief that something good was coming, that they would be saved, eased their fear, soothed their aching hearts. They needed to believe that they would be released from their misery. But it was difficult to anticipate the cruelty of the guards.

> In camp we were taken to a disinfectant bath after... I don't know... a month, and one of the SS women thought it was a great joke. I... I was small and I looked like a twelve year old little boy and she held me back when we were standing in line to get... after the bath... to get a piece of clothes. She held me back. And by the time I got to the table, there was no clothes. So she laughed and she said it was all right. The next bath was four weeks after that! You will be, you know... without clothes. I was *stark naked*. So they took us back to the camp, because this was outside the camp, the bath, and I... *I was naked*. Can you imagine? At sixteen? For four weeks. Not just the men... the SS came, but even the people around me, the women.

> [Q: You remained without...]

> I didn't have a stitch! [Pause]. [She lowers her head].

> And so, when we had to stand in line to [swallows] to be counted, the... the woman who was in charge of the building would come and throw a blanket over me.

> But other than that, I didn't have anything. So the girls, these four girls I was with, they would just tear a piece, you know... We didn't have anything. We didn't have a knife, didn't have a scissor, we didn't have anything at all. We had this one piece of clothing and they would tear a piece of their... their skirt or a sleeve or something so that at least I had a little bit that would cover me. And for four weeks [pause]... I would stand in the middle... for four weeks... because I didn't have shoes or anything. At least they had a pair of wooden shoes. I didn't have that either.

Klara felt the nakedness as a wounding. She could not control her appearance now even in the most meager of ways. In the ironic illogic of such moments, it is the innocent who feel the smart of powerlessness as shame. To know that another woman would specifically target her for humiliation made the suffering keener. Without the symbolic embrace of those around her, she may have perished. Her barracks mates, with no extra fabric or cutting tools, had improvised a symbolic dress, a cloth of caring, in which she could think of herself as standing at each appel or when they sat together.

> I think that you would hear it from every survivor that to be alone or on your own in a camp was impossible. People who were on their own, who didn't have friends who didn't create a little family so to speak around them, didn't survive. Because you couldn't survive in Birkenau, or even in... in a labor camp, all alone.
>
> People needed people, because without them there was no survival. We had to [swallows] somehow encourage each other that it will be... that our par... "I am sure our parents are young and strong and they are working somewhere and our brothers and sisters and so on..." "We will be liberated and be together again."
>
> And we told stories about... we were [fictive] cooking all the time and because we were so terribly hungry and we had "gourmet dinners" and we were... were sitting all day. We were not allowed to move outside of the... in between the two buildings, and we were not allowed to speak to people who came from another building.

The talk relaxed them a little in their hunger and temporarily pushed back the gnawing anxieties spurred by their existence at the edge of the crematoria. It externalized pressing needs and collectivized the misery. By September, she had been selected to go to a work camp making parts for aircraft. Three hundred of the women were selected. They were taken again in cattle cars, this time westward into Germany, without food or water for three days. At the end of this journey they could not walk and had to be carried off the cars.

> So we arrived into a small place called XXX and we worked in an airplane factory. I... worked in a factory with a magnifying glass and... making tiny little... they call it "armitur." I don't know exactly... know what it was... an airplane factory. This tiny thing that was put together out of thirty-six pieces, we needed a magnifying glass and a little welding... electric welding machine [to assemble it]. This is what I did. And then the... this was getting on... it was winter and... and then they [moved the women to another camp in Germany].

At these work camps where she was doing precision work connected with arms and aircraft manufacture, she had been existing on the same reduced diet as at Birkenau: a potato and margarine on Sunday, bread and liquid in small amounts throughout the week. Some of them would each day save a scrap of bread for the day off on Sunday. Then, with the bits of bread saved, the potato and bit of margarine, it felt like they had a feast. They would imagine what it would be like to see the Allies coming and thought of how they would celebrate. They phrased their gladness in terms of having all the potato and margarine they could eat. Finally, five days before they were liberated, their work group was marched to Bergen-Belsen. Klara said little about this time, though it deeply affected her, since she was so weak.

> From XXX [the second work camp site] to Bergen-Belsen is... was a march and it was... I... not very many... I don't know how I felt. I don't know why I could go on and... and... still be able to walk. And we arrived in Bergen-Belsen. There was already a typhus epidemic, and, of course, I had it right away, and I was going from [pause] [sighs] one... [sigh] fainting to the next.
>
> In Bergen-Belsen [swallows] I think the... Most of the SS, by the time we arrived there, fled. And we were put into a building that had no beds at all. So we were on the floor... the first night we... we went into the building, we laid down and it was terribly crowded, terribly. There was no room. We were practically on top of each other, and in the morning when I woke up, I seemed to be the only one alive. There were... everybody dead... all around me. I woke up and I had these very heavy legs and arms all over me and all stiff. [Pause.] And I...
>
> Bergen-Belsen was the place where at liberation the dead were piled up like mountains. They... the SS... When the British came in, they caught the SS, whoever stayed, and they were put to work, and they would have to put their very long ladder to this mountain of corpses, and they would carry up the corpses and put one on top of... it was like in the... in the forest... wood. And then later on they had a mass grave... fifteen thousand in one grave-- this is the German's [own records], thousand in another grave. These were all mass buried and... I... I don't remember after that what happened. I was taken to hospital by the British.

Hearing this section of the narrative the listener is struck by the pauses and delays in Klara's speech. She is inadvertently conveying the overwhelming reality she knew. Everything else that happened she saw through this fatigue, and then the typhus took hold. While in the other camps she had gotten temporary fevers or sore throat, but at Bergen-Belsen infection became full blown. She remained in hospital for two months and then was listed on a children's transfer to America but refused to go. She had to face what was left; she had to know what happened to her family. She wanted to see with her own eyes that, in fact, not one remained but herself.

In her decision, there was the contending of different kinds of longing. Klara wanted to find a future in which she could belong, and, on the other hand, to somehow recover what she could of the past. There was also a tension between facts and hopes. Somehow she needed permission to accept life as an adult by finding a fitting symbolic closure for her earlier life.

> I just wanted to go back and go to my parents' home and just have something. [Deep breath]. I knew that I was alone because there were people coming out of Hungary, and there were some childhood friends, one or two, who came, who had already been back to... to our town and who came and told me that nobody was there. And I still wanted to go. I just wanted a photograph. I wanted something.

Hungary was, after the war, configured in the Russian zone. Unlike Czechoslovakia, it did little to make the concentration camp victims welcome. Almost immediately it became a police state under the socialist regime installed to turn the country into a Soviet satellite. Klara's family had been without a doubt capitalist, and whatever records still existed showed that. She was treated as a class enemy and was not permitted to attend university nor be employed. With no one to help her start out, life was not just unbearably lonely, but depressing, and there were unanticipated difficulties. Though her home had been stripped, she was its sole owner. Estate taxes were owed on the property. Unable to meet the mounting bills, she was almost jailed for unpaid debts.

> This was my welcome back to Hungary. I went around the neighborhood [where she had lived] and said, "I don't want anything back. I'm not interested in furniture or anything. I just want a... a photograph of my... my parents and my family." But no. I didn't... I didn't get anything. [Very quiet]. [Pause]

> I didn't belong to anybody. Nobody cared whether I lived or died. And nobody asked, "What are you going to eat?" "What is going to happen to you?" I... I had a terribly, terribly hard time. And then I found one or two girls who

survived. They were put in other camps in Germany, and we moved into a house that belonged to one of the... of the parents of one of the girls, and we stayed there for a while.

She watched the friends she made get on with their lives but could not seem to revitalize her own. She was withdrawn. Eventually she met someone her own age who also was a survivor and they married. This finally helped her turn things around.

I didn't want to go anywhere, I didn't want to do anything. Some of the girls tried to make up for the lost years. You know, they were trying to... those who went back to school, finished school, couldn't go to university, got a job. And maybe they had something to live on. I don't know. But they were trying to go to theater and to dance. We were young. I didn't go.

I got married in 1953 and... it was a... a... I think my husband was quite brave. I was so depressed. Even after... after... eight years, I was so depressed [voice is full of tears] and I didn't... very introverted. My husband helped me gradually to... to gain a bit of self confidence. I was terribly insecure and terribly lonely and terribly depressed and... It took him quite a few years.

Her husband and his parents had been sent directly to a work camp in Austria. Someone had helped them circumvent the typical route through Auschwitz and the selections. It had meant their survival as an intact family unit. Later he returned to Hungary and was one of the very few Jews who was admitted to university. He got a doctorate in law. After their marriage, his family became her family and, in 1955, despite being warned that what had happened in the camps might mean she could never have children, she had a daughter. In 1957, with the baby still in diapers, they fled Hungary with what few items they could carry by hand.

I always wanted to get out of Hungary. I never wanted to stay. Only we didn't have a chance. And then the uprising came and the borders were more or less open, and so we fled with nothing but thirty-six diapers! [She is genuinely sounding happy now]. A peasant took us across the border in December, and we arrived in Vienna. [From there they went on to North America].

Her husband had practiced law in Hungary but had to take whatever work he could get in their new home. The transition between the old world and the new was demanding in many ways. Since he was not used to rough labor, he broke his hand at a dockyard job after only two days. Oddly enough, the accident proved a boon. With worker's compensation, he could get new training for a job he wanted. He returned to university, eventually, and obtained undergraduate standing for his doctorate in Law. With that he took a Master's in Latin and French and now teaches languages. Klara also came into a new sense of fulfillment.

> I was always a very... very... too reserved, too retiring, too quiet. But I think I have changed since my daughter got married and I have the grandchildren [deep breath].

When her grandson was born she drank in his loveliness and wondered how children could be beaten to death in the camps. She could remember one night in Birkenau after the women had told them that the Americans were coming, hearing strange noises and thinking something might be happening. Perhaps, in fact, she thought the Americans were at the gates. Instead it had been the cries of a woman in labor. Afterward someone had quietly placed something near her bunk. It was a tiny corpse. It had to be hidden until morning when it could be disposed of as unobtrusively as possible. To have signs of a newborn baby around would have meant death for someone.

> My grandson is three and a half... very blond curly hair, and he looks like a little angel. [Laughs.] He is quite a handful. I look at him and I think, "How could... how could people [pause] hurt these... these beautiful innocent children?" [Pause.]

> However... life goes on and I... I don't... dwell on it. [Almost in the same breath she continues with this statement's contradiction]. I... I don't think I have had a day since I was liberated or since I was... was deported that I... For some reason, I don't exactly know why, but something always reminds me of... of Auschwitz or Bergen-Belsen or, you know. Just a sound or a smell, or I see a face and I think, "Oh. I saw this person." Or maybe her mother or his... mother or something that reminds me of camp. And I still have nightmares.

She does not catch the contradiction in her comments, "I don't dwell on it," "I don't think I have a day... something always reminds me." Both are true. Klara intends to be forward looking and cheery, but the memory of the camp clings to her, a shadow upon her joy. The memories might more easily be compartmentalized except that the experience took away her family and forever separated her from the ordinary, a world untouched by the betrayal of life she had known.

> We enjoy our little family because this is all we have. My daughter never knew what a relative is. She doesn't know what a cousin or an uncle... We have some distant relatives in California who came out long before the war, but to understand a survivor... a person who was in concentration camp... someone who lived... [is beyond the North American's compass]. You know, their little problems to me are just so meaningless, so trivial, and they make a big issue of it. And... I don't even try to explain.

The sudden truncation of the family line by systematic murder meant there would be no uncles or aunts or cousins. The sense of being "the *only* one" in this case left her feeling less lucky than extremely lonely.

> I am the only survivor. My grandparents and uncle, aunts and cousins and everybody... large family... in those days there were lots of children... both my parents from large families. My father... was a businessman in Hungary and my grandparents, great-great-great-great-great grandparents were all Hungarian. They... we... Not only that, we... they... were all Hungarians, but they lived in the... the very same small city I lived... [where] I was born. We lived in a house that belonged to my parents and my grandparents and from far back, I don't know how many generations. My father was in the war, the First World War... fought for Hungary, for his country. He was... he was an officer. We had lots... we knew lots of the... we... I knew everybody in the town we lived in.

She stumbles over the words that would share what she felt. Having just barely survived the Nazi genocide of her people, she had to endure a life withered by it. Even with the happiness her family brings her now, some part of her grieves for the family that might have been. Her small shoot was all that was left of a family tree that had been full of generations. She longed for what might have been, cherished what she still had.

ADOLESCENTS IN HIDING
SERGE

Serge Noviski spent the war years in hiding with his extended family. They were untouched during the slaughter of Jews that followed the Nazi occupation of Romania, June 22, 1941. By June 29th, the Nazis took over Iasi where his family were then living. That date had additional meaning for him since it was also the day of his Bar Mitzvah.

> I was supposed to go up to the synagogue... read a chapter from the Old Testament and be confirmed as a man, assuming my own responsibilities for my own sins. We got up at six o'clock in the morning trying to get ready and,

all of a sudden, we heard all kinds of noises.

> Now, we happened to be renting [sighs] an apartment in a very good district [not far from his father's business and across the street from a bank] in a fortress-like building. Downstairs there were stores, businesses. Upstairs people were living. We were in the house. We started looking around to see what was happening, because we were hearing shooting, screaming, yelling, running, and we didn't know what was happening on the streets. So we started going from one place to the other to see in every direction facing the street.

> What did we see? We saw people running and people being followed by their youngsters. Sticks in the hand, bayonets, rifle butts, all the time running after the Jews. Wearing the Star of David... people were going to the market... weekend market... which had a central location... they were being shot. They were beaten, they were dragged... abused. Dead in the street, butchered on the street... clothes torn... dragging the dead and dragging those who were still alive... taking them somewhere.

There is fright still in his voice, though it is controlled. He is now a successful businessman. He says it is hard for him to speak about the past. As we talk about these deeply troubling images, he says he will not be able to sleep that night. During the worst of these times his family had somehow managed to remain intact. One and a half years later when the Russians took back the region, the family moved to Bucharest.

> My family... my mother, my father, my sister, were very close to me. First of all, the family was scattered. Some of it was in Bucharest, some was in Iasi, some of it was in Polonoj, some of it was where my father was born, so we didn't see much of the [extended] family. The only ones that I remember very closely in the young years as a kid was my grandfather, my mother's sister, and her children. Her children were as old as my parents.

> We never suffered from hunger really, but it was always the fear for tomorrow. We had the money; we were able to buy on the black market anything that we wanted, and our cellar had enough food.

He had been born in Polonoj, one of the small towns near Iasi, twelve years before the Nazis arrived. When he was two years old the family moved from Polonoj to another town within thirty kilometers of Iasi. In Iasi, June 29 1941, 4000 Jews were rounded up and put into sealed railway cars. After several days (Levin 1990:108-109) according to Romanian police reports, 2,530 of these had died of suffocation and thirst.

While the Romanian government under Ion Antonescu had been convinced by influential Jewish leaders, especially Dr. Wilhelm Filderman, that the economy could not sustain the loss of the Jewish component of its business sector, Jews were used opportunistically. Nevertheless, between 1938 and 1942, eighty-nine anti-Jewish laws were enacted. Hitler had been the architect of these enactments, having personally handed Antonescu a manual, titled *Instructions for the Treatment of the Jewish Question (Richtlinien fur die Behandlung der Judenfrage)*, outlining policies being followed wherever the Nazis were in control. Romania's virulent anti-Semitism of the late 1930s and the war years had earlier precursors in the patterns of prejudice and discrimination which were evident before that. Serge reflected on this in his earliest remarks.

> Our family came from Germany originally. We go back in Romania since 1700s.
>
> The good part of my life I lived in Polonoj. Now, I went to an elementary school there [sighs]. I don't remember too much except that I was pointed out to be a Jew. A Jew is call "Jedon" in Romanian, "dirty Jew." I don't know from where [this term originated], but there is an expression which I don't even know how it's called in English,--some people have pus around the eyes-- and it became "Jedon pukinah," Jew with those things in the eye.
>
> So I'm talking about 1930s. Now, I know that this was the era of Nazi Germany, Revolutions, Iron Guard, formation of the Nazi movement in Austria.

He grew up with a sense of being embattled, being caught up in the nasty give and take of barbed speech and malicious conduct in this relatively rural area. His growing up was dominated by ethnic hatred. Religious differences marked ethnic boundaries.

> So I recall from school the occasional beatings from these almighty boys who in a group felt they could do anything with those little Jewish boys.
>
> Basically [he has decided now to make some coffee and moves about as he speaks]. I remember the teachers very vividly. My being Jewish... we were exempt from taking religion as a course. And we had the freedom to either take a course with a Rabbi or whoever it was, or just... I remember the priest coming into the classroom talking about the funny customs that the Jews have. For example, Jews are not supposed to drive on Sabbath because... [He tells the joke]. These type of remarks, you know, do not necessarily create good relationships and understandings.

From 1919 and the Paris Peace Conference through the interwar period, Romania was considered one of the most virulently anti-Semitic countries in Europe (Levin 1990:107). But even before this, institutional leadership distanced one group from another and created a difficult setting for good will, one person to another, across ethnic lines. Romania was an Axis power for most of WWII, but it had started ghettoizing Jews and confiscating their property as early as 1938. Serge's parents had considered emigrating to Palestine. But his father felt that they would do better to stay where they had personal ties to people they knew who might help them if things grew worse.

> My father was a druggist. He had a wholesale [business], imported drugs. He put his business under two people that we knew, two Romanian people who happened to be of Italian descent... very fine right to the end. He made them partners, put the business in their name, gave everything under their name. Actually, anytime they wanted to be nasty they could say, "Walk out," and they had everything! This didn't happen. So my father ran the business and they were home reaping profits from it... which is fine. As long as he was left alone, we were left alone.

Convenient compromises made during times of upheaval hold a bitter edge in memory when the danger is past. His family had been forced to jeopardize everything, carefully judging each step taken in terms of its necessity for survival.

After the Nazis actually entered Romania, a reign of terror descended upon the Jews (Levin 1990:109) who were specifically identified as suspicious persons, saboteurs and spies. Many Jews were detained and tortured by local police working under them. In Serge's area, local authorities, rather than using bullets to slay those who were rounded up, placed large numbers of people in sealed railway cars and left them to suffocate in the summer heat. Serge heard about a great deal of this from relatives who lived through it.

> June the 29th and the beginning of July the temperature is anywhere between twenty-eight to thirty-six Celsius. It's the height of summer... very dry summer. And those doors of the cars were closed. One hundred and fifty people in each car... And they were dragged a distance, no food, no air, no water. No nothing. Just back and forth. A result was, as I was told by my uncle [a veteran of the First World War, decorated for bravery] who was in the same boxcar with his son--his son perished, that from one hundred and fifty people that were in each boxcar, two to three came out alive, dragged themselves out of that boxcar onto the station pavement, trying to gasp for air or licking

their wounds. And then the German tanks came through, and whoever was not able to move was squashed to death... by the tanks.

Serge cannot fathom how his own family were not discovered and killed. Perhaps they were overlooked, or somehow, someone with influence protected them, he reasoned. In any case, they remained relatively untouched throughout the onslaught.

> I cannot tell you by what miracle we escaped, except possibly the fact that we were in [a fortress-like housing complex] and we kept quiet. I lost a cousin the same age as mine... as my own... a brilliant student who died. Where we saw how close we were to death... we literally lived [for] each other throughout the war.

Three days before the Russians took back Iasi from the Nazi forces, on the 23rd of August, 1944, his mother was wounded in the market square when she arrived there at dawn. She had gone out to wait in line for food when the area had come under bombardment. By that time, Allied bombing had become something everyone in the town had learned to expect and cellars became a common living space for those who had them. The confinement was especially difficult for the older people and for growing children with a desire to be more active and unconstrained. He configured his loss in personal terms. He had seen too much to hold on to innocence, and his schooling had been interrupted. He had come to hate, even kill, by the end of this period. But he had helped his own family and protected his kin who also shared their cellar shelter.

> We were almost for a year... a year and a half under constant bombardment either at night or by cannon, you know, during the day. So our lives... and the most of the time really, was -- particularly in 1943-44, was in the cellar.

> I remember myself at the beginning of the war, picking up after bombardment, limbs of people scattered all over the place. Sometimes you couldn't even recognize more than body [parts]. Anything else was crushed by the force of a shell against it. And all you had to do was pick up pieces. Now you didn't do those things voluntarily. You happened to be caught on the street because you were going to get some food, and soldiers came in and they picked you up and you had to do it.

> I've seen atrocities by the Russian soldiers, cutting fingers because they wanted that... that... ring or because... cutting an arm because they wanted the watch. They weren't exactly kind, the soldiers. Neither were the Germans

or the Romanians. And that's how it was...a survival.

Romania as an Axis country had proven itself more opportunistic than ideologically faithful in all matters. The country had been "occupied" by the Nazis as they moved their eastern front into Russia in 1941. By 1943, Allies were bombing the Ploesti oil fields and Bucharest. The American forces had attempted in the months following that to get Romania out of the war. All Germans were ordered to leave, and five thousand Jewish children waited to be moved to Palestine. Romania was pulled in many directions by August of 1944, when the Russian army broke through the Romanian-German lines in Bessarabia and Moldavia. Serge's reference to soldiers indicated how the population felt about any soldiers whatsoever by this time. With the food shortages accompanying the war, those living in their cellars or the streets never felt free from fear. When there was no sound of guns or bombs, life did not return to normal. That would take years to effect. Serge's own family could not trust even the passersby to be friends rather than thieves or collaborators. Whether war was raging or a quiet had descended, Jews still alive and still living in their own communities feared being discovered, robbed and murdered by bands of itinerants or locals. Under Antonescu and the Nazis, their lives did not fall under protection by the law. Quite the opposite.

> You didn't know when you had ventured outside of that gate [to the apartments]... you didn't know what to expect. You didn't know what is going to happen next hour, next five minutes, what orders and what changes may come down to the soldiers, to the army, or to the Germans, and what's going to happen with you. So whenever you got out of that compound, okay, it was a chance that you took, and every one [with you] had to take that chance. [Pause]. [You had to act] so as not to endanger everybody.

The family's refuge became a prison of sorts. For a teenager, full of suppressed vitality, it was that much more oppressive than for adults. The fictive aggression of the childhood games he might have played indoors at another age could have mimicked combat and become a means of displacing the anger and vulnerability he felt. As a teenager, he needed peer interaction to achieve the same catharsis. Toward the end of the occupation, more avenues for self-expression opened up. Games of violence, often with real weapons, made it easier for him in one instance to aim a real machine gun at two Nazi soldiers. He fired from the roof of his house when the time seemed right. It worked. "A gun for me was a... was a toy that I knew quite well." Afterwards, at school he chose boxing as an outlet.

> Friendships at that age [early teens] were not very important. The friends that I remember more are the later friends who I associated with in the Jewish School where we started boxing. And these are the friends that I remember very much. Of course they were all Jewish because there were no contacts between Jews [and] non-Jews at that time.
>
> The concerns of the war were so great, we didn't have a fine youth. Our games were cops and robbers or always with machine guns or with swords. There were no games that could be played in the home. Very few sports that you could do in the open areas.
>
> [Because of all that had passed] I was very rebellious, very, very rebellious. And probably because of that I don't think I had a heck of a lot of friends. I always wanted to pay back somebody. Really. For losing the time [youth]. Really. For not being able to enjoy things. Even at school, when I was travelling from [commuting]... most of the times I had to be there [school] at five in the morning and take the three o'clock train because I [used to] fight with all the kids. As a punishment I had to be there at five and in detention. And my parents were always called in, at least my father was -- "What's-a-matter with him? what's-a-matter, what's-a-matter. He's very bad. Give him more freedom at home so he will not be a savage here in the school!" I just could not take authority [pause] ...not the authority of the teacher, [nor] the authority of those who were a little older than I am who were trying to prove their will upon me.
>
> I was very small for my... I was [nevertheless] a powerful machine. I was champ for many years, six, seven years. In one minute I destroyed people three times my size, that's how... What a fighting machine I was. There was never hate in it. Never hate. It was just a question. I had to dominate because I didn't dominate. It was my way of asserting myself... that I am equal to everybody else. And they recognized that. They recognized that because they became my best friends.
>
> I remember a fellow that was--Badyjak, his name was--about a six footer. I was maybe four foot eight inches. He came one day, very arrogant teasing me in my nose, "You dirty Jew." And I says, "Badyjak, leave me alone." He says, "You dirty Jew." Before he said anoth... a third time, I just punch him in the stomach and punch him in the nose. He became my best friend after that! And he fought many fights for me... with me... against other people. Says, "This guy [Serge] has got principles!!"

Boxing became his medium for banging back at a world that mistreated and stigmatized him. Strangely enough, amongst his age peers facing many of the same emotions, it won him their respect. Locked in the rigid structures of small society, Serge became an example of Camus' (1956) rebel. Always an outsider, he fought his own causes, imbuing his battles with nobility and purpose they may not on their own merits have claimed.

After the war was over and his high school years completed, Serge expanded his philosophy of survival to other spheres. With the Nazis gone, his father was satisfied to trust the turn of events, but Serge was not. Romania had fought with the Russians against the Nazis in August, 1944, and in a few weeks had destroyed 26 German divisions. The new government made contact with the previously outlawed Communist Party in Romania, and a new Communist regime took over under the auspices of the Soviet Union. Serge began to search out information to emigrate. In the end, he just took his chances and left.

> I had to assert myself. I had to fight for every possible thing in order to survive, to be the best -- and I was the best. Thank God, I was. Because I was able to cross all these borders being the best. I crossed the borders in record time. All of them were illegally crossed in the sense that I wanted to run away from the Communists. I could not wait for the [sighs] for the Hagganah, which was involved in transporting Jews from one camp to the other. It was with... I had to do it by my own way. I was caught many times by soldiers. Turned back--to snow, to mud, to anything. My flight to Italy was [sighs] [pause] was under a tarp... in a truck, under a tarp, loaded with stones on top. That's how I crossed the Italian-Austrian border. You had to fight to get to...

In November, 1947, he entered Hungary and made it to Budapest. There the classic contradictions of the romantic rebel character surfaced, as they usually did for Serge in his manhood when crisis threatened. He had been part of the postwar blackmarket trade and known by the border authorities wherever he went. For his own sense of worth, he found himself identifying with the violated and vulnerable, helping refugees and protecting others in flight from corrupt officials or marauding bands of thieves. In one of his adventures he brought to justice some bandits who, in the hungry, chaotic years just after the war, had been robbing travellers and burying some of them alive. In Budapest he affiliated with a joint relief committee, part of an international refugee organization, and was himself in a final convoy of refugees from Budapest before the Communists closed the border. His fighting spirit served him well.

> We were the last convoy to get out of Budapest. There were over two thousand

> of us. We reached by truck the Hungarian-Austrian border, and we were supposed to get through. [But] the orders came in and they wouldn't let us through. So we were camped right at the border, maybe a mile inside the Hungarian border, over two thousand of us. Well the soldiers and party members came around, says, "Look, we cannot take you this way. We have to make papers for you. Take you back to Budapest and then we'll put you on trains and we'll send you to Vienna in trains, legally." There's no way! [What they said did not ring true].
>
> And there was a tremendous dissension at that particular time. The older people [among the refugees] looking at the [younger] people. The older people wanted to say its okay. So we [the young group] organized and there were a hundred odd people, Romanian, young like me, got our sticks, got knives. [They were told eventually] "Anybody that defies the order to stay put is going to be killed."
>
> I was ready to kill anyone who would move, because my life was in danger the same way. I had already killed, didn't matter anymore. [Pause] And we kept... day and night... it was a drizzle... was December... for three days and three nights... no food, no shelter, nothing. We stayed there, over two thousand of us, because a hundred men, young kids like me, decided that we're either going to die there or go to Austria!
>
> Finally they let us go through. They saw they were... they could not cope anymore, and they let us through, and it was salvation! Really. Because anybody else that was caught [sighs] in Hungary after [that] date was turned back to Romania and they're probably still rotting in jail. So you had to do it that way because you couldn't survive otherwise.

History books might not acknowledge what he achieved at that border crossing, but he understood it as a personal victory. After his days in hiding, action became his philosophy. He grew to be self-reliant, savvy, knew people, could judge character and how much to risk in a given situation.

> So. It's a question of choice, really. You can be bogged down or beaten by circumstances. Okay, regardless of what they do to me, I'm going to win or die. [You are taught], "Look, winning is not the most important thing. Living is the most important thing!!" I think that ultimately... probably unwittingly... I said all along in my life, living is the most important thing. And it must have been!
>
> [Q: Did religion contribute to this valuing of life and this kind of bravery?]

> To a great extent. But I am not a blind believer. [Pause]. I believe very sincerely there is a God. I believe that I have a destiny in the sense that I survived. But I also feel that somewhere in my religion it says that God will help you if you will help yourself--I help myself. I think this was always there [in my understanding]. I pray that I should be in a position *to be able to do things*.

Serge had been fighting against something or other all his life. He could hold and wait or move as he judged best because he knew he had that inner strength which formed the first line of defense against oppression, whatever form it took. He could be flexible. He knew how to work hard and think on his feet. He had immense energy and would get what he went after. Eventually that brought him to North America.

> September 5th, 1950, [I came] to [North America] via Nassau and Bermuda. It had to be done all by myself. I was still young. I look at my kids. Now, when they were 18-19 they were "babies." [At that age] I was working eighty hours a week. Six months after I came here, I [had] no money and nothing. I didn't even have heavy clothes to wear because I came from Cuba [in winter]. I had to work to eat--a bowl of spaghetti because it was twenty cents, once a day... and twenty-five cents to go to three movies in a row in order to learn the language--that's how I learned English. After three months, I spoke English enough to take a job as a shipper at $17.50 a week. My room was costing me almost that much. I appreciated everything that I grabbed, and I am very thankful.

Eventually, when he had settled and begun to raise his three sons, his father and mother came to live with them. He referred to his daughter in a special way, mentioning her public-mindedness, her dare-and-do orientation. With his son the rabbi, he spoke of attachment to tradition. In 1978 he moved again and now owns and operates a Jewish delicatessen. Across the street from his business is a synagogue; down the street is a Jewish bookstore. He is an impassioned humanist.

He will not sacrifice his principles to gain acceptance. He would fight to protect the rights of others, but he must first secure a space from which to hold his ground. From his experience came his promise to himself.

> If any of my life or my children's lives is going to be threatened again... No Holocaust is going to happen to me again! I can look after myself today and tomorrow, and nobody is going to take my life again or threaten my life again or consider me as a second class citizen. And I'm not saying this with hate,

because I hate no one. I love every human... decent human beings. But nobody's going to threaten me again. Nobody.

I think that nothing will ever wipe out the memories of seeing people killed. I saw people killed for nothing. It [the good life] cannot erase out of my mind the fact that there was really no reason for any of this. This stays in my mind. It was a well determined will to destroy people. They were just people, Jews, Gypsies... for no reason at all.

DISCUSSION

These narratives of teenagers facing brutal threat and complete disruption of life as they knew it, afford us a study in the humanistic management of terror. Klara, Peter, Michel, Leo and Serge gave vivid descriptions of what they experienced in the KZ camps and in hiding. Above all they show us the inner landscape of young people living through unwanted, threatening day-to-day exigencies. Each variously explored the self journey from shock, through degradation and then to inner struggle, as they attempt to salvage the self and the past from obliteration. Finally they showed us something of what they were thinking and feeling after release into conventional life. As their narratives moved toward the present, they confirm how well-placed values and practical reasoning in the presence of strong family and community life can help rebuild functional levels of trust and good faith after traumatic abuse.

The five teenagers in these narratives acted in age-appropriate ways in their survival contexts, showing individual imagination and courage as they perdured. Affiliations formed during thise time of crisis were also important to them. Like adolescents in conventional contexts they mobilized appearance, worked on identity issues and were carried along in daily currents of interpersonal interaction, albeit as captives in a time of genocide. The implications of this realization are as staggering as the human suffering the narratives depict. While ties to others framed under the duress of surviving have an urgency and intensity that might be absent from normal lifecourse interaction, yet there are continuities; the reality these Holocaust survivors returned to find in memory was heavily peopled as they recounted their trials and dilemmas. These narratives, in addition to providing details of the genocidal process as it unfolded in Europe 1933-1945, also show us how the survival process each individual experienced was socially dimensioned.

CHAPTER 5
ADULTS--THE YOUNG WOMEN

> Most of us walked in silence. Some were praying and hoping. Some were still overpowered with the tragedies they had left behind in Auschwitz; they walked quietly with their heads down.
>
> The guards were few and old. Their guns over their shoulders, they marched alongside us in silence. Here and there a human being stared at us through the window of his house, or from the back of it, as if frightened to face us or frightened of us.
>
> Close to a barn stood a woman holding her two children close to her skirts; their big eyes looked at me with fear. A smile curved my lips, but the children only hid their faces in their mother's skirts.
>
> My heart tightened... Mother, where are you now? How I long to be near you, you will never know. How I need to be near you for just one breath, for just one second of your warmth, your love, your understanding. How I need to belong to someone, nobody will ever know.
>
> Erna F. Rubinstein, *The Survivor in Us All; Four Young Sisters in the Holocaust.* 1983:150

INTRODUCTION

The young women discussed in this chapter are Bertha, Elsie, Vera, Polla and Ruth. They each encountered Nazi persecution in different situations and at different ages. Bertha was put in a ghetto, then shipped to Auschwitz-Birkenau from Hungary in 1944. Elsie was already married when, in 1939, the Nazis took Poland. She was later put in the Krakow ghetto and worked at a factory run by Oscar Schindler. Vera grew up in Hungary, in the Budapest area, and was just finishing high school when the Nazis rounded up her family for transport. Ruth had graduated from high school and had been politically active in Germany when she got her chance to leave; she lived in exile from September of 1939 until 1945. She had witnessed the growth of Nazism in the 1920s and its racist violence during the 1930s. Polla, the second oldest of the group, lived in Warsaw with her family. She had just been accepted into university when the Nazis invaded Poland. She decided to flee eastward into exile. She ended up in the Russian gulag system. The difference in the ages of these young women was no more than seven years, and, beyond being a way of thinking about how each of them is unique, the difference in age matters little. The implications of being a woman in a genocide are not as easily dismissed.

At a time in their lives when most women expect to be having families or preparing to start them, Bertha, Elsie, Vera, Polla and Ruth faced stigma, exclusion, starvation and the sense that they might never live to have children or a happy life. Surviving under different conditions, each in her own way stood between two worlds--the one known since childhood and the other generated by persecution. All but Polla lost over ninety percent of their families in the 1939-1945 period. Whatever represented organized life to them was compromised or went missing. Property their families owned was confiscated or made unrecoverable. They varied in terms of class background (see table 3), country of origin, age (see tables 1 and 2), and the dreams they had for the future, but they shared respect for others, love of family, awareness of heritage and a worldview that honored the spiritual dimensions of everyday life. They were each in their own way possessed of strong character, energetic, vital, responsive and discerning.

WOMEN IN THE CAMPS
BERTHA

Bertha Remanski was born in Czechoslovakia in 1926. She was the second oldest child in a family of five girls and two boys. When she was nine years old, the family moved to Hodmezovasarhely, a small city near the Hungarian border with Romania.

> We were a happy family because we had lots of love. Love. The sisters and brothers. We loved one another and we cared very much for one another. Like for instance before the war, a year before the war, they took [father] away. My mother was very sick, and I was the second [eldest] child. My older sister... the two of us took care of my mother, and my father was already in... in Belgium in a camp. And then after that they took him to Auschwitz. Mother was very sick. So me and my sister had to take care of my mother. That's how it started out when it started being bad.

As she spoke about her beginnings her voice struck something of a monotone as of one in pain who has held back great distress for a very long time. Even with the sorrow showing she was intuitive, lively, and caring.

By 1943, the Jews of Hungary were in grave danger; a year later they were being transported to death camps. Bertha and her family were among them. A year later, the German army invaded Hungary. By March

19, 1944, Action Commando Eichman was put in place under the direction of Adolf Eichman. By July 7, 1944, 437,000 Hungarian Jews had been deported to Auschwitz (Levin 1990: 114-115; 318). As conditions around the family worsened, their sole comfort was in each other. Her happiest memories were of family celebrating the Sabbath.

> Well, the happy times was ... We were religious. [Pause]. And [in] Europe, the people were very religious and [sighs] no matter how poor a person was [pause] there was always enough food for Saturday and always happiness on Saturdays, especially with big families.
>
> We would sit [deep breath] at the table. Our dinners would last two, three hours and we were singing religious songs. We had a whole week of hardship... working hard. We missed lots of things. Not the best food... we had just once a week meat. But we were always waiting for this Sabbath. That was our happy...

They had left a larger network of family and friends in Czechoslovakia when she was nine years old. Aunts, uncles, cousins and the like were effectively lost to them. The bolstering effect of the generations was lost and the situation only got worse. Bertha talks about the 1939-45 period with the phrase "and then the hardship came." She never found these relatives or her family again after the camps.

> We had aunties, uncles--my mother's sisters, my father's sisters and brothers. They were left in Czechoslovakia. We... when I was a young girl... child, we would make an effort to see [them] at least once a year. But then the hardship came and we didn't see them, and after the war I was searching and looking everywhere if somebody came back, but I never found anybody... back from the camps. [She is crying].

There had been five girls and two boys in her family. They lived in a mixed ethnic neighborhood just before the war. The loneliness they felt was exacerbated by intensification of the hostility around them as pro-Nazi sentiment and anti-Semitism rose.

> I played with Gentile kids. But the problem was there with the neighbors [who] could be very friendly, and the neighbors [pause] I mean... we got along beautiful but, if it [was a religious holiday, they turned bitter].

Even in the warmest bonds there was always the threat of surliness not far beneath the surface of interaction. Jews were a small part of the regional population and felt as though they were on display. They had to think of their personal acts in political terms since whatever they did as individuals could be used against the Jewish community.

> And then, like most of our... of my Jewish friends, we tried to be exceptional good, not to hurt anybody because we always thought, "I'm not allowed to make a mistake because then they'll blame every Jewish person for it." And that bothered me.

She could not afford to go to high school and took whatever small jobs she could to help the family. It singled her out from others not pressed as hard economically. Since the family saw this as part of putting down roots in a new place, she bore the sacrifice without complaint. But when Nazi racial laws were enacted, Jews had to wear yellow stars as a sign of exclusion. She tried to be larger than the situation, to salvage whatever good it yet might have.

> We were not supposed to go downtown. I had to carry my birth certificate and if they saw on my birth certificate that I am Jewish, then they would give me a hard time. I mean it depended on who it was. If some good person would check me, then they would let me go.
>
> It depended just who the person was. I mean, that time was already... Hungarians did that. They didn't... I mean they were under the German Occupation, but they didn't have to do the extra mean things... like lots of terrible things. I'm not saying too many [were this way]. But like the Health Inspector, he was extremely mean to Jewish people. Not like, "Close the shop!" but privately, I mean, take you... just claim you're dirty... or take you and the gypsies to be disinfected.
>
> That happened on the whole street... on our street... the whole neighborhood. It was just terribly painful... terrible. Because, at home, maybe we were poor, but we were clean. We cleaned, thoroughly always, the houses. [By contrast] there was... we had lice in the concentration camp.

She felt undermined by a social system that did not honor personal worth and individual goodness. Nor was group loyalty rewarded.

> My mother and father, they would always tell us to be good citizens and... telling stories, how good... once upon a time in Hungary there was... I don't know... used to be a king, and he was so good to the Jewish people. My mother always told me this story with love. And it was built into us to be good [pause] and like, for instance, we... when we go to the synagogue, we have a

prayer for the country, always. Our belief is in the country where we live. We have to be... that's our country... do the best we can for the country. This is how we were raised at home. Especially religious people, they built it in their children to be good.

She had come of age when Nazism had intensified religious differences, turning Jews into a defiled racial category. The base of people who could be scapegoated widened. Among Bertha's affiliations, even Jews who had been Christian converts for several generations, were set up for abuse. We-they distinctions which once might be tolerated were now promoted.

> There were Jews who were religious people and there were also those who hardly believed in Jewishness. [Pause]. They were mixed, you know. [Some] were converted. They were Christians really [breath] and... [struggling for the words]. They were already for two generations *Christians* and they were still counted as *Jewish*. And that, I mean... It bothers me terrible, more than even [pause] the concentration camp I was in. [There] I couldn't think anymore, I was numb. But in Hungary... it was... I could still think, and it was... [pause] [deep breath] It's injustice.

No one came to their defense. Rather the majority of the population seemed to be in complicity with the Nazis. It was the failure of human goodness that eroded her confidence in life. Nothing that had seemed right before could be accepted at face value anymore. The fracture in her tie to community went deep.

In 1944, they were placed in a ghetto with the other Jews in their town. It lasted four weeks and then it was liquidated. Those within it were rounded up and sent to Auschwitz. Her first statement at the start of the interview showed she was still wrestling with powerlessness and the anger it provoked in her. "When they dragged me out of the house, I was eighteen," she said.

> My mother was sick. They took her [with the] sick people. We had to leave her at the... She was just forty-five years old, my mother, but she was so sick, they couldn't line her up. We were lined up and the police took us to the... to the trains. [But] my mother couldn't walk so they... we left her at the... we had to leave her at the fence, you know, beside the ghetto... not beside our house, because we were taken out from the houses. And my youngest sister was five years old.

While some camp survivors mention the physical hardship of the transport in cattle trains, Bertha was transfixed by grief at the parting and could only focus on this. Her anguish was followed by numbness and disarray as the fateful selections at Auschwitz replaced the grim realities of the ghetto. They had been pushed into unimaginable extreme at this point, but there was worse to come.

> We got off the train in Auschwitz. Suddenly I didn't see nobody. Not my older sister, not my little sisters, nobody. I was left alone.

That was the end of life as she had known it. From that point on her memories were measured in terms of the emptiness she felt. Within this pain she noticed other things that were sentinels; iconic imagery indexes her fateful first night at Auschwitz.

> That Mengele was standing... he was sort of greeting us. I mean that's how he called it. He was standing there, you know, watching us come and go from the train. And I told him I have to go look for my sisters and my brothers. I... And he said, "Don't worry. You'll see them tomorrow." But [later, inmates] told me where they went. They went to the crematorium.
>
> I didn't think... couldn't think there [pause]. It was just like being dead. [Pause]. I mean like... I don't know... just like walking like a skeleton.

She summed up her horror in one phrase, "I was cut off." In her suffocating pain, she felt outside of life itself. She was the eldest and felt responsible for the others in her family. In a moment, they were gone from her forever. She alone survived. Had she not been noticed by a friend from the past, she might have forgotten to breathe.

> [For the longest while] *I didn't have a friend*. Nobody. But luckily there... when they took me to cut my hair off, they brought me in... in the barrack. From far away I saw a girl familiar to me. And this girl recognized me. In Czechoslovakia... I was nine years old when we moved from there, and suddenly they... and there she was. She recognized me. *She called out my name*. So I became close with her and [deep breath]... We used to play together in Czechoslovakia. I mean, it was just my luck that I had somebody from... whom I used to love when I was a small girl.

Her childhood friend encouraged her, understood her reserve and introduced her to others she knew. This friendship had in many ways been crucial to Bertha's survival. The personalizing of her immediate context made it possible for her to summon identity to revitalize her being.

Adults--The Young Women 169

> This girl always tried to work on me. Because she was... maybe she coped better than I did. She tried. And eventually, I mean, [deep breath] I started... to develop some kind of way to be able to cope at that time.

Even with the solace of a childhood friend, conditions in Auschwitz went beyond being oppressive; it was torture. Each small part of experience was planned in some insidious way to bring privation and misery.

> So I was in Auschwitz. The food was so... I mean, you could just survive. There was a soup... a bowl of soup and there was a little potato floating and... But, the food didn't even... didn't bother me even so much. I just... This meanness, like with the whip, a gun, and with the dogs... shepherds, German shepherd dogs.
>
> And always slow, slow [prisoners]. So like hurry, hurry, hurry [guards]. And we could hardly walk. And always hurry, hurry, hurry.

Cruelty was not the sole domain of the guards. Her simple code of ethics directed her to expect consistencies, like "good people" do good things, and victims--who themselves were suffering as she was--do not knowingly cause others to suffer. This left her emotionally vulnerable and feeble in her own defenses.

> There were on each bunk ten girls and we would sleep like herring. I mean, we wouldn't move. Sometimes I would just lay on one side maybe for a whole night because I couldn't move and then I wouldn't say to my friend, because I didn't want to disturb...
>
> [Eventually] somebody took away my blanket [camp issue] and I didn't have a blanket. I couldn't speak up. This was my problem. I would lose my voice, my... just... I wanted to talk but I couldn't.

She felt swallowed up by the enormity of it all. Her fright and sorrow gripped her so completely that she had to struggle to make her voice work.

The contradictions in camp life could bring the inmate to despair and death; it was a gift to be able to generate sustaining insights out of the ongoing trammel. While she was aware of having done nothing wrong, she suddenly found herself being singled out for punishment.

> I'm sure I didn't do such a terrible thing. An SS put me... For a whole

> night, I had to kneel on the road. [Instead] this Slovak, she was our blockalteste, and she told the SS that she's going to beat me up. She's going to "take care" of me. The SS left. The [Slovak woman] took it over but she didn't [carry out the punishment]. She said, "Just go and have a good sleep and don't worry about it." So from then on, I'm always thinking about those blockaltestes, because everybody says they're so mean.
>
> That blockalteste, she wasn't a mean person. Like for instance, the Hungarians... [some] were so naive. They... if an SS came in the morning and said, "Who is sick?" in the barrack, they would come out and say, "I'm sick." And then that blockalteste, she would get really, really mad at them. And then I caught on. She is not mean. She didn't want them [to get killed by being taken to the "hospital"], because they would have taken them to the crematorium [from there]. And she would give them with slaps on the face, "You are not sick!" So then I didn't think she did it for meanness. And I'm thinking always about that Slovak girl. After the war they put them in jail. I would have saved her. She was so good.

Bertha saw others through a unique kind of lens, drawn from her attachment to the Jewish tradition and her early childhood experiences. In the distrusted Slovak guard she had been able to discern a determination to help others. With the clumsy English she had come to late in life, Bertha who had been so let down by people and events in her pre-captivity world, spoke from her heart of finding goodness in humanity.

When she entered Birkenau, Bertha had been a woman of deep faith and used prayer to help herself cope. She saw her survival as being based on help from others, physical strength, and spiritual commitment.

> I was maybe strong and I have this faith, too. I have lots of faith.
>
> [Q: Were there any things that you did on a day to day basis that helped you survive the camps?]
>
> No. I wasn't doing much. We were just sitting, praying and... I mean, actually I wasn't really... maybe I wasn't even thinking. Sometimes I didn't want to think. Most of the time, I didn't want to think. [Pause]. But people caring [was so important]. Like, if somebody was working in the kitchen, they would give me a little extra food so they gave me so I could survive. So, if they cared about me, then I mean, I should care about myself.

She was sustained in finding her own ability to love echoed in the chance kindness of someone else. Her family had treasured personal kindness not just as civility but as an expression of moral being. Even in Auschwitz such a view was still part of her framework of taken-for-granted understandings. She was shocked when on a work detail she chanced to see a ritual of endearment divested of the element of compassion. She saw the base objectification as a form of violence. The object was a captive child.

> There was this SS woman. She was a beauty and I always thought of her, "Well, how can she... She's such a... she's a beauty. How can she be so mean? -- Have a beautiful face like her and such a bad heart... such ugly heart." That's what I thought of her always [deep breath]. [Pause]. This woman, she would... When I had to...
>
> When a transfer of families would arrive, they would pick out the most beautiful child, two or three years [of age], and keep her there for themselves to play with. Because the SS, [pause] maybe some of them had... but most of them didn't have... so they had to have a little child to play... just for a little plaything, like a dog or something. And then... after they had their fun with her, they would take them to the crematorium.

Stephen Katz (1996), comparing the treatment of children at Auschwitz and those in the gulag underscores the abyss between the two. Reports of the brutalization of children under the Nazis join what Bertha acknowledged here. What she witnessed violated the very foundations of her sense of how reality must be ordered. Woman, traditionally associated with the nurturance of children, with love and beauty, as an SS officer perverted this relationship, using children as things. Bertha watched the smashing betrayal of life and goodness on a daily basis. The objectification of the child in this anecdote referenced the unthinkable for her--the uncontested murder of the innocent. She began to suffer a change in her faith.

> Eventually, [deep breath] I started to develop some kind of way to be able to cope at that time. So, I didn't want to be religious anymore because I thought if... what happened... God let this happen... why be religious, especially when my parents and everybody... and I was... everybody was religious.
>
> [But] I still needed something. So I said "All that matters [is] just to be good. [Be] the best you can be. That's [what's] important in life. [Pause] Things... what happened to us... it's because people are bad. If people wouldn't have been so bad, we would be... I would have been with my parents, with my sister [deep breath]. So I built this up as a religion and stop this

tradition, doing praying. This was my religion, *being* good.

Before the Nazi sonderbehandlung, religion had integrated experience into a single cloth for many Jews, Bertha included. There were no problematics about ultimate truths, only the practical aspects of making a living and holding with tradition. Religion brought joy and meaning to a life of material limitation. Now she had to carefully reconstruct a philosophy of life to fit the new reality. When asked if she and the other inmates shared religious occasions as part of their survival she said there was variation.

> Well, I didn't fast, but my... People who were not religious, they started to be religious there. I was religious and I didn't want to be religious. [In the old country] people were religious because they had to. Because they were religious they had a happy life. If they wouldn't have been religious, their lives would not have been happy. They had a clean, nice, life, always studying the Torah, and that occupied their mind. Now I think about it, then they were very smart.

In the concentration camps, she had passed through a collapse of social worlds and, in what remained, found an inversion of life as she had known it. No longer was experience for her integrated in terms of a religious philosophy. Yet she could not imagine living without embracing some aspect of the religious tenets of her childhood, for those were based unquestionably on love, and that emotion still meant a great deal to her.

> I mean, first of all, in our religion, in Jewishness, I mean, there are still a few things I never gave up believing. A person is not supposed to commit suicide. You have to go on living, no matter how hard it is. You have to live. If I have to live, then I have to look for kind of... base to live, to make my life easier. Not easier, bearable.

She determined that, firstly, the evil of the Holocaust was human in nature. The God of goodness and steadfast love did intervene in history, but only occasionally. The basis for such intervention she left unquestioned. Bertha walked carefully where only angels tread; modesty, not blasphemy, was her forte.

> Some people will say that... God did it to us. I don't believe it that God did it to us. It's people who did it.
>
> That upsets me because I mean we give... In my mind, I mean, we take off the

guilty ones from what they did. We put it on God. It's not... I don't believe God did it. He saved us.

But when we went out of the concentration camps [were liberated] then I thought, well why did God let us [suffer]. If there is a God, why?

She believed and so she questioned. Her G-d was greater than history. But she reserved the human right to reason. When she was transported from Auschwitz to a small work camp in Sudetenland, her questioning did not stop. And if she could not provide any ultimate answers about where G-d was in the Holocaust or why good people should suffer, she was determined to notice when even one person stood against the encompassing evil.

When they took us from Auschwitz to the work camp, an SS drove us with the truck to a work camp. It was very cold 'cause we didn't [have warm clothes]. It was very early [frost that Fall, and by] November it was very cold there in Auschwitz... was very cold. Sudeten, too, is very cold already in the Fall. And this SS [functionary] he had a blanket. He covered us. He gave us a blanket and he... and the tears came of his eyes.

At the work camp there were other signs of this kind--contradictions on which her spirit feasted as the end approached. The approach of the Allies was bringing other kinds of concerns forward, this time for the SS who were running the camps. They were now gingerly tendering contingencies related to an unexpected reversal of fortune.

The kommanderfuhrer who is... she is an SS. Once she put us in the line, and she asked us if we would be liberated tomorrow and would see her on the street, what would we do with her. Would we tell on her? And I mean, she asked me, too. I didn't know what to do. And I say I would just keep quiet. I wouldn't say nothing. I mean I couldn't. They [people] wouldn't believe me if I would say. They wouldn't believe me anyway.

Bertha imagined then that she could re-enter ordinary life and not demand some kind of justice for what happened for the victims. The painfulness of other's indifference to the injustice to herself and other Jews was not yet a thought. What she feared most was losing the only people she was close to in the dismembered world she then inhabited. The first to go was her best friend who was moved to another camp.

She told me to go with her because she was *watching over* me. My friend...

> I... we shared. I mean, she was considerate, and that was a good feeling for me. But this friend, she went to another camp [gulps].

Other women watching this understood what such partings meant. Survival hung in the balance created by the meager interpersonal bonds they shared. Some of them had been friends of her friend and quickly embraced Bertha as one of them.

> These Czech girls, they were two sisters and a cousin, they felt so sorry for me, and they said, "From today on you are my sister. You are our sister." So I stayed with them.

> Up 'til the end, I was... [protected by] those... [by her three Czech friends]. But they went back to Czechoslovakia and I went back to Hungary. So we had to part and I never heard from them again [near tears] because the mail wouldn't go and I couldn't write to them.

Tears still welled up as she remembered all this. The bereftness signified the profound loss she had known in a relatively short time, as her world was stripped of all she treasured. Bertha had spent nine months in Auschwitz and then been sent to a work camp in Sudeten. It was from there she was liberated. She had no family and her only friends were those she had made in the camps. Without someone to stand for you and with you, the hatred of Jews which was still very strong in the general population became a serious threat. Even among the camp guards there were those who were determined to pick up where the war left off.

> An SS man came to tell us we are liberated. That was in 1945, in April. [Pause] So suddenly, I was happy, but, on the other hand, I was sad, because I was afraid of being alone... not to find anybody. [Pause]

> We were all over... running out on the street. [But] the man... SS man, came and he says, "I'm still going to get you and kill you."

Being liberated in Czechoslovakia was good luck for Bertha because she found them as a people to be so refreshingly different; they were compassionate, kind, and willing to help survivors of the camps. In the weeks ahead, while the KZ system was being dismantled, Bertha and some of the other women were placed with a Czech family. This interlude restored her in many ways, even with the reduced amounts of food available.

> In this month, [between liberation and the return home], in the Sudeten, there were Czechs... the population were Czechs, and we stayed in a Czech family, and they were so good to us. They fed us. We slept there--two, three girls. They didn't have much, but... the Czech people are special nice people. I always remember them since I was a child, that they were very good people. They were mad at the Germans, too. See?

When she got back to her home on the Hungarian-Romanian border, she was placed in a hospital for one month. After that, the Joint Distribution Committee allotted her two weeks of food if she needed it. She immediately entered a home for women and found herself a job with someone who was starting up a knitting industry.

> Before the war, I used to knit sweaters on knitting machines and I found the man who I used to work for. Came back and he went to the same business, and he called me to work for him. So I made money... not much, but it was enough to keep myself going.

Her independence spurred up as she left the closed and vicious world of the camps. But the community to which she returned continued to ostracize Jews. Old enemies had not learned a new compassion; former friends had compromised themselves in their terror of the Nazis. Countless crimes of the heart had left her estranged from neighbors. She felt bitterly disappointed with their hardness of heart; because of it she had lost her whole world.

> It was very hard you know to live. Where we lived, the lady was a Hungarian, and I thought probably those people learned by this [time] how they are going to be good people. And I would talk to them. They would hardly answer me. Or they would call... they would say, "DPs!!" you know. It wasn't Jews anymore. It was DPs. That was the nickname. But this didn't bother me. I mean, so "DPs." I mean that wasn't the worst. The name wasn't the worst. The worst was that my family didn't come back and what they did to us.

As she got on her feet, she began to come to a realization that if her larger community would not recognize its failure of responsibility to the victims, she, at least, would honor the victims and, in particular, her dead family. Only this would bring her the peace to get on fully with her life.

> I couldn't really... I didn't have the love anymore for... [my homeland] because I was thinking, if I can't love this country, then I don't want to live there. I just didn't want to live in a country what I can't love.

> I mean, how to... Like, right away I didn't want to stay mad. I wanted to make [a new life]. If I have to go on living, I have to live a normal life. Can't stay mad. So I had to figure out how not to be mad.
>
> If I would think about my sister, brothers, how they died and how they suffered, I couldn't go on working. I couldn't go on living like this, you know. I... [pause] It would have been hard for me to mingle with the Hungarians or...
>
> But then I chose to, every morning when I got up, I would count out my sisters' and brothers' names, my parents'. Thinking a little bit the way it was in the happy days, and that gave me something like a prayer. Then I could go on and cope with the day. Because, not to think of them... it... it... I felt terribly guilty. I didn't want to get them out of my memory. I wanted to have them everyday. But to have them on my memory, it was hard. But this was my cure.

She was caught between two worlds, needing to honor them both but pulled in opposite directions as she did. She let the wisdom of her heart lead her to what made her feel more alive. First she helped start a local Zionist association. Israel was a warm and brave ideal that was very attractive to her, a means of displacing the loss she felt. Friends in this group generated their own purposeful atmosphere. They sang and danced together, but after it was over she still felt empty. Meeting the man she would eventually marry helped resolve this emotional knot. Her husband's experience of the 1939-45 period had been different from hers.

> He was in the war as a soldier. Those Hungarians were very good to him. He helped Jewish boys. He took food to the camps. I mean, they knew it. They wouldn't put him in troubles because they were just good. [One of his] high ranking officers [was honored by Yad Vashem]. We were at the gathering in Israel, and they named a street after him because he saved lots of Jews. His son came with his wife and daughter to Israel to take the award for him.

Eventually she married, and seven years later, having lived in barracks waiting for emigration first from Hungary and then from Germany, her husband's brother sponsored their immigration to North America. They now live near each other. Bertha, in the meantime, found that she was one of the camp survivors who could not have children. She was not forthcoming about how this happened. Instead she spoke of how much she loved children. They adopted two sons. The eldest was, as we spoke, dating someone he would likely marry, and Bertha was looking forward to having grandchildren. She and her husband had made a family despite the obstacles. They worried as they helped their sons get established that they might have spoiled them with their doting.

> We are worried a little bit that... that everything comes so easy for them. But then I think my parents gave me more--my thinking gets like that. My parents gave me more than I'm giving my children even.
>
> No matter how much I'm giving them, my mother would take things from herself. And me, no matter how much I'm giving, I'm still not short of anything. My mother wouldn't eat meat so we would have... I don't [take anything] from myself really. My parents just worked so hard. Never... they didn't see us [grow and prosper]. Nothing.

Her song of generations was filled with mourning and joy. As her sons grew up, she did not discuss her experience of the Holocaust with them. Though she and her husband kept their bonds with other survivors and mentioned close ties to religion, they did not ask the children to feel what they felt or know as they knew.

> I was afraid they [the boys] would hate everybody, you know. Hate Germans, hate Hungarians, and what for?--I mean, it's a new generation. If I hate somebody, I know myself how to hate. I know where to put my [feelings]. I could love. But if I will tell my kids [what happened] they will hate everybody.

Now that they are both young men, she has gotten them involved in Holocaust memorials. Through some of her community activities, like speaking at local high schools around the time of Yom Hashoah each year, she has shared some of her past with them. She had her parents' names and the names of her brothers and sisters inscribed on a new memorial for Holocaust victims where her family now lives. So she has integrated some of the past with the present and future in positive ways. She decided to become a citizen of the new land she so loved and wanted to include in her excitement the other women working with her as seamstresses. She told them why she would be taking time off from work the next day. When she returned from being sworn in at the courthouse, they had a bouquet of carnations for her; she brought wine and cake.

> It's a very, very good country. Too good country. When you don't speak English, everybody will encourage you, "Oh, you speak Hungarian. I understand." If you would go to Hungary maybe--not so much now but before the war--and you would say something wrong in Hungarian, they would laugh, you

know. But here people are so tolerant.

She was glad to be in a place where she could resonate with local values. In the last few years, she had even felt secure enough to speak to students about the Holocaust. Working with a group of survivors who were viewing a documentary of the camps one evening, it suddenly dawned on her that it was affecting her as it usually did others. She had crossed a threshold and could now find tears welling up as she watched. This was new for her.

> [At a certain point in the documentary] I turned my face away, didn't want to watch it. I am asking my... [neighbor, a fellow survivor] "Gee, it's funny. Why can't I watch it? What they did to us, shouldn't I be able to watch it?" And then I realized something, "I'm happy. Maybe [her response] meant I am human! We are human again!" And so we were dancing and we were happy! When we left the camps, *we still felt unhuman.*

VERA

As the Nazis swept over Eastern Europe, Vera Weiss was attending Gymnasium near Budapest. Her family had lived in the region for generations. Their neighbors were from mixed religious backgrounds, and everyone seemed to get along well. They owned a textile factory and ran a farm. They had begun to raise cattle just before the war broke out. One of Vera's childhood victories involved "Susan," the pedigreed cow, taking first prize at the county fair. Stories that filled her childhood home were of overcoming obstacles and staying the course. Atrocities were unheard of; religious persecution was something from a tale of distant lands.

She had a happy upbringing in which family members lived to fortunate old age. They feared the violence in Germany, but Vera could not be convinced it was of any importance to her as she entered High School. The Munich Pact signed in 1938 and the Anschluss that followed in the same year, fateful as they were for history, held little interest for her. When the Nazis took the Sudeten from Czechoslovakia it did bother her, but then, these border areas had been a point of contention between Germany, France and Czechoslovakia for centuries. When the Nazi war machine had taken not just Poland but also western Russia in 1941, her main focus was getting "a first" for graduation. Her plans for the future still seemed bright. She would become a surgeon specializing in the human hand. Nevertheless, the *numerus clausus* rule was in effect and her report card was marked "Israelite."

It was especially painful, therefore, for her to recount how she and her family had been forced to leave the land of her childhood memories. They went from well off to pauper status in a small part of one day. All their property was confiscated. They were left with nothing. She remembers "seeing people peeping through their... their windows as we were leaving town with our bare minimums. Nobody, nobody moved til we got on the trains and away we went."

The family was first placed in a ghetto. Her father, acting in what he thought was Vera's best interest, arranged for a policeman to hide her with the pastor of a Methodist church. She remained in hiding only for a short time, since she could not bear the solitariness of it and asked to be reunited with her family. By the time their ghetto was cleared in 1944, and its population transported to Auschwitz, her father had been taken to a camp in Germany near Dachau. She and her mother were later taken to Auschwitz-Birkenau by cattle wagons. They stayed together throughout their internment, and, though her mother, who was a tall woman, was reduced in weight to eighty pounds, Vera says that she brought them both back alive to Czechoslovakia. Her father perished, having been separated from them to be used as a translator at one of the camps in Germany.

Vera recounts that after ghettoization in Budapest, she and her mother had been transported to Auschwitz, then to Krakow and the Plaszow concentration camp, then back to Auschwitz and on to Leipzig. Finally, on a death march within Germany as the Allies were winning the war, she and her mother had escaped and wandered back toward the camp. It was in Leipzig that they were liberated by the Americans and eventually the Czech government "sent little trucks--it was the farmers," she remembers lovingly, to pick them up at the border.

Vera talked of hunger and thirst as reducing the human capacity for emotion and inducing lethargy. All through the interview, which began with coffee, she nibbled and sipped almost as a way of balancing against her memories of privation. She maintained an indefatigable cheerfulness, regardless of the story being told, but repeatedly returned to themes which were focused not on physical privation, but humiliation, vulnerability, and shame at the hands of others. For instance, of Auschwitz and her first experiences there she recounted:

> First of all they kept us naked for two days before the crematorium, you know. They don't examine you, they just pass by and look. If you happen to have a little pimple, it's enough to put you in the crematorium. They don't

examine you, they just stand there for hours and hours and hours. Two days we stood in front of the crematorium...

Loss of attractiveness was painful for her and unbearable for her mother to witness. Shaving of body hair by others was a boundary point between the self of the past and the conquered self. The aftermath of delousing, branding, and shaving left them both stunned.

We were shaven off, and mother was standing next to me and she kept calling out to me my name. So I said, "Mom, its me!" She looked at me. She looked up... away. She totally refused to acknowledge me. She kept calling. Finally, I convinced her; she was hysterical. Momma was a very beautiful woman and she really took it very badly. When your children suffer, its much more weighty than for yourself.

They recovered from this and eventually were shipped to Plaszow where they helped build the barracks in which they were sheltered. The camp was on a hill at the outskirts of Krakow near a Jewish cemetery. The woman commandant was cruel. Vera talked of the few months she spent there.

It was called Plaszow. It is quite well known now. It was on the outskirts of Krakow. It's an old Jewish cemetery, and there I have a terrible recollection because it was upon a hill. And Krakow has terrible windstorms. And the worst part was that those nights you know... First of all, the wind was very, very severe and it was blowing and you looked around you and it was all... all... cemetery and all old... old names. You were around those stones and there was this woman Kommandant. She was absolutely cruel. She would ride a white horse, and whoever was in her vicinity... she had a whip and would whip people for no reason at all. In Auschwitz [it was] more structured. Here she had... she could do whatever she wanted, she could shoot you when she wanted. There were no... no rules that she had to live by.

In the past, woman had symbolized for them nurturance, love, innocence, and life. This woman symbolized power and ruthlessness, perverting the imagery of renewal associated with a woman on a white horse. The whip and gun, not light and flowers, were her tools. She brought sadistic violence, not wisdom, to her domain. As each of them stood before her, shorn of hair, dressed in flimsy rags, they were to her mere objects to her and completely vulnerable.

Vera and her mother remained at Plaszow for three months, and at the end of the period the Russians were advancing toward them. All were put on railway wagons and hauled back to Auschwitz. Vera relates with a certain cynicism that there are few people who can say they went twice to Auschwitz. The second time was beyond any misery she had endured before, and, in fact, most of those loaded onto the cattle cars were already so reduced by the conditions at Plaszow that only a few survived.

> We were five thousand. Five thousand in that camp, five thousand... women... men... and we had to go to Auschwitz. I think not even ten percent made it past the selection. That's how abused we were in those two months.

At Plaszow, she took responsibility for her mother's life and this pushed her farther to the limits of her reserves. She volunteered for extra duty to get into town where she could ask for food from the locals. She led a group of twenty women and with them organized an expanded base of opportunity.

> I was always lucky... luckier than most people. I had a job. I had to go into Krakow to bring supplies, twenty of us. So with the supplies, we got some shoes... we could have been shot for it... and a little bit of bread. So that in Krakow, you know, I was able to get some food from the outside world for mother and I. We didn't look too bad. We kept ourselves. But this was a fluke. Nobody realized. Nobody watched us, you know. But I realized after that I took a tremendous risk. As a consequence I built myself up, because you walked... it was about four kilometers everyday... and I still got a little food there. Better than that, [some days] I ate with the prisoners of war... that was a little better than our food."

Vera helped organize a fast for Yom Kippur that went from sundown to sundown. She greatly admired the women at Auschwitz who led the prisoner "symposiums," where discussions ranged anywhere from how to bake very delicious (if imaginary) cakes, to lofty discussions of philosophy and ethics. Later, at Leipzig, women organized the same kind of forum.

> I had the job of serving "the tea" in the morning. You stood two hours outside. Then you took off to work. You got home at night after a twelve-hour shift. A piece of bread, that was our dinner. [Pause]. [Sighs].
>
> So what we used to have [at the Leipzig camp, part of an aeroplane factory] is get togethers. We had a professor. We used to call her 'old lady.' She was thirty-seven, thirty-eight, and she was... gave us lectures in philosophy and Judaism and ethical behavior. She was marvelous and kept us going, really. And we had a lady who was one of the finest bakers. She would

bake imaginary cakes. So we did that at night. Then you went to sleep, because you were dead tired. [Or they spent time] talking, discussing schooling... what we will do when we get home, what clothes we going to buy... planning for the future. Was wonderful.

She does not speak of her hunger nor describe what her mother did while she was on a work detail. And though she felt a camaraderie with the other women, she learned early on that to grow dependent on close bonds could turn out to be devastating where conditions were rough. When asked if friendships had been important to her in the camps, she said that she and her mother were very friendly with everybody, but they had only become close friends with two others, another mother-daughter pair.

> There was a doctor. She was a doctor, the lady. She was my mother's age and, young lady was her daughter, my age. She had the same tattoo as we did--not the same, but the number after. And we went to Plaszow. We became very close friends and... she had pimple [very quiet now]. She was taken away. She didn't make it on the second selection. So that was three months friendship that was finished. And then you were afraid to become close. You never knew when, see? It [selections] came at night, and if you not getting... losing a lot of weight, they took you away.

The shock of losing someone with whom you identified closely was overwhelming, even with murder all around. Vera translated her hurt into new goals for organizing her energies: get food, look smart, hide any sign of weakness. While intimacies like close friendship might be seen as too emotionally risky, general solidarity with fellow captives was essential. Vera was celebrated for helping keep group spirits high. The women survivors sharing her barracks acknowledged how much she meant to them on one occasion--her "nicest birthday."

> Let me tell you what somebody did for me. It's easy to buy presents now when you... everybody can afford a little present. But there you got a piece of bread. That was our dinner. And for my birthday, they all got together and saved up bread and made a little "cake" from that and the margarine--we used to get a piece of margarine about that size [about a half an inch] here. So people gave up their last piece of mouthful of eating to make that cake. I never forgot it. That was my nicest birthday.

> [Q: Did you sing?]

> Yes, and I have a terrible voice. My children used to cry whenever I sang! [Laughs].

Adults--The Young Women 183

[Q: And jokes?]

Very much so. We told German jokes!

The gift of their esteem stayed with her all her days. They shared the last days of the camps together, knowing the Nazis were doomed. Vera recounts that many of the women were very aware of how the war was progressing. The Allies were on the continent, advancing on Germany from several fronts. They searched out any signs of coming liberation. Allied bombers overhead delivering their loads all around them were inspiring-- especially so to Vera.

> I was cocky. You know when you're seventeen and you believe... We used to... The most wonderful sounds in February already -- January-February, came from the artillery... was pounding constantly. And they [Germans] were like zombies. They [Allies] were working the Germans. We knew it was getting closer, and closer, and closer. We knew Hitler is losing the war. And we knew--the Red Cross came in, they told us, you know, very, very quietly, that the gas chambers have been eliminated.
>
> [Later in Leipzig] I had mother with me, which helped. She did all the fearing! I gave her warning... and many times she refused to go down into the underground because they bombed very heavily. But they knew that our places... where we are... so, they didn't bomb [there] ever. And the Germans kept running *to our place* [underground shelter] you know.
>
> Ah, but I would sleep in the barracks [during those raids]!! That was the time to sleep when they bombed, you know! I always believed that the [Americans] know where we are and they're not going to bomb us.

Vera was quite sure that if the Allies had bombed any of the prisoner areas there would have been needless carnage. She still believed in these bomber pilots as her heroes. Given the Allied policy of bombing only strategic targets, it was Vera's sense that each bomb brought the exhausted captives that much closer to some kind of vindication.

She continued to actively develop an other-focus, to be friendly with fellow captives, helpful, and wherever possible, lead. She worried about keeping others alive and fussed with them when they appeared taciturn. This is illustrated in her anecdote of Ejlie. They shared the same barrack. Ejlie was a very petite woman of her own age who, like many, during the winter was not wont to go into the bitter sub-zero temperatures at daybreak to take a cold shower. Vera considered it essential, since the camps were infested with body lice which carried typhus. Eventually the situation became serious.

> She was nicknamed "the lousy Ejlie." In Hungarian it comes out different [laughs]. She always felt so bad about being called "lousy Ejlie" but she was full of lice! And I said to her, "Don't feel bad. It's a nice nickname." Anyway, she didn't like it. So what happened was--she was very sweet and very nice, I threw them out for her [helped her get rid of them]. I never gave up. I used to practically drag her to wash her, you know. I was scared that the lice would give her away and she will be taken away.

Many of them, including Vera, her mother, and Ejlie were sent on from Auschwitz to Leipzig where eventually they were put on a death march. As Vera tells it, she considered this a most unfortunate turn of events with the Allies so near at hand. So she decided to escape.

> I couldn't go on the death march because my mother was falling off her feet. So. About five or six kilometers after we left our camp, we escaped from it. When the bombs came... laid low... because they shot anybody who escaped, you know. Hitler's last hurrah. Final solution was to take everybody to Theresienstadt and then blow up the camp. So we didn't go. I escaped from... [it].

Her indomitable sense of humor comes through in her choice of remarks. She says with mock matter-of-factness, "So we didn't go..." It almost sounds as though she were declining an evening out with friends, but she is at the same time quite serious. Survivors report being able to venture risky choices while under extreme duress, choices they would not under normal circumstances consider. With bold inscrutability, Vera and her mother escaped the death march and returned to the Leipzig barracks to wait for the Nazi surrender. The maneuver did not fail them, for soon American forces appeared on the scene.

They were cared for by Allied support units. Eventually they were told that her father had perished in a camp near Dachau just months before liberation. Her mother was placed in a sanitarium to recover her health. Vera said nothing about her own health, just expressed exuberance at being free once more.

> I had wonderful experiences after the war. I got to Prague. First of all, Czechs are so wonderful. They sent me... See the Polish Jews had a horrible time because they had pogroms. The Czech Jews... the Czechs who came for us... sent in little trucks to take us home. I got to the border, and they

> brought us all kinds of food. It was just Czechs who came and who waited for us... and they give you the last piece of... They were farmers' children... and there was very little food, but they split it with us. To give you an idea, the first anniversary of the end of the war, the Czechs set up... you know, we had trolleys... no buses, but trolleys... they set up an orchestra. They were dancing in the street.

Joyful as the times may have been, Vera was, in a sense, at something of a loose end. She had been uprooted from her birthplace. Contacts made in the camps had been dispersed in all directions. Many sought a certain kind of homecoming, a reuniting with those who had shared their ordeal. Such meetings helped salve survivors' sense of lostness. Vera spoke of this.

> I was poor [now]. I had nobody come home for me, you know. Everything was gone. Confiscated. All properties. And the Communists took over everything. So after the camps, that was the situation for many people who were in Budapest.

> She came from a very wealthy family, this Ejlie, and went back to living in her gorgeous home. And I remember going shopping. Shopping!! I went to *look* at how the rich live in that part of Budapest. And, I was sitting there watching this beautiful girl come in with two poodles and this... all dressed up and she looks at me. She starts crying! She says my name! "Vera. It's you!" And she starts hugging me. I said, "Who are you?!" I had no inkling. She must have been a good customer because... She just broke down. She says, "I'm lousy Ejlie!" [laughing]. She took me home and dressed me.

According to Vera, Ejlie's family was three generations "not-Jewish." In the camps it had been Vera who had more of the resources in the economy of survival. Ejlie could not forget Vera's good faith and care. The bonds of simple intimacy formed in the camps were not necessarily lost afterwards.

Vera eventually got a grant to study medicine through the government of Czechoslovakia. She was given a tiny apartment she could afford on her student's stipend and brought her mother up to Prague with her. Vera, too, began to heal emotional wounds. She was determined to move away from what she saw as a siege mentality in many who survived the camps.

> We thought that this war would eliminate every other war and there would never be another. So there was a tremendous outpouring of hope and love. Even though people didn't have food--everything was rationed... but you make

do with... the farmers worked double. All the students, I was a medical student... it was in summer time... we went to work on the land to help out. So there was this camaraderie.

These were the images on which her spirit was nurtured back to wholeness. Central to the rebuilding of her life was meeting and marrying "the kindest man in this world." He "took care" of her and while they were waiting for their son to be born, they fled Stalin's military and political grip on the region, making it to Salzberg just ahead of imminent arrest in Prague. Eventually they sought and were given refugee status in Montreal. From that point on they made North America their home. Fifty years later, Vera has become well placed in community but is still fighting the ghost of the camps, trying to live her life so as to avoid what has happened to other survivors.

> So what I'm saying to you... I still have not got this paranoia. I don't look over my shoulder. I taught my children not to [hate] because I have no bitterness. And that's why I'm surviving.

She is proud of the autonomy she feels in having friends both at home and in the international Jewish community. Having been born Jewish in a time of genocide, she felt it was important to not turn away as she nursed her own deep wounds. She reaches out to vitalize new bonds in as many diverse groups as possible. She mentioned being somewhat inspired by the character Scarlet O'Hara in the epic novel, *Gone with the Wind*.

Vera is a generous benefactor. "Some people become so afraid to share their wealth, even when they make a little money." She is aware that it was her religious faith which got her through the camps. She used it and the Jewish tradition's focus on humanism to continually inspire others around her in the camps. Today, her son is a Rabbi in Israel. She has a daughter who, as a scholar and academic, writes articles on the Holocaust from time to time. In all of her commitments she has tried to surmount the past and transform the future.

ELSIE

Elsie Sziemanski was born in Krakow, a city in southern Poland which from the Middle Ages was an outstanding center of Jewish learning and culture (Gutman, 1990). In 1939, there were 60,000 Jews in a population of a quarter million people living in Krakow (Gutman, 1990:830). The Krakow ghetto was sealed March 3, 1941. A wall and barbed wire fence that the Jews had been forced to build set the ghetto apart from the city beyond. The final liquidation of the ghetto took place in March, 1943. That month, 2000 Jews were transferred to the nearby Plaszow work camp, and 2300 more were deported to Auschwitz.

In terms of Elsie's part within this larger story, by the time the Nazis took Poland, September 6, 1939, she had completed high school and was just starting out as a new wife. In March, 1943, she was part of the transport of people from the Krakow ghetto to Auschwitz. During the time in between, Nazi industrialists ran several factories using captive Jewish labor to produce goods for the Reich. Among them was Oscar Schindler who Elsie credits with the survival of herself and more than a thousand Jews in the city (see also Keneally 1984).

Elsie mentions very little about living conditions in the ghetto. For her the Holocaust was about the deaths of family and relatives, and she disciplined herself to honor the personal in her choice of focus. The time she spoke about was just after the Polish government had capitulated to the Nazis, and the largest administrative unit of the German Occupation of eastern Europe had moved to Krakow. Just before the ghetto was sealed, workers began taking whatever equipment they could call their own inside. Schindler took advantage of the cheap labor, but he subsequently came to know those who he continued to employ and spent a considerable fortune protecting them as the full brunt of Nazi plans for genocide took hold. Schindler had used his position in the Nazi system to do business with the Third Reich (see also Keneally 1982; Gutman 1990: 1331-2) The list of these workers became through his efforts a protected category, justified as a necessary reichindustry even when what they made were pots and pans. In this way he came to be their rescuer.

Ghetto workers were given work permits and told this gave them standing within the Nazi wartime economy. Elsie got permits for her mother and mother-in-law and equipment to use in the factory Schindler ran, which was outside the ghetto. She felt reasonably sure that, with just a little effort, her mother could find a hiding place with someone on the outside, or at least she could stay away on the days the transports were being organized. By the time of the first selections for transport, her plan fell apart.

> One day there was the gossip that there will be a transport going to... So I said to my mother, "Don't come here. Don't come back [to the ghetto]. [You have close friends] Gentile friends in Krakow. Go there [after work]." You know, we thought to go there and stay there, wherever she was before, and-- "but don't come back [emphasized] until things quiet down. Then you can come back."

What shall I tell you? [Pause]. My mother went out [of the ghetto] but she came back! And when she came back I was just furious. Why she came back? you know. Money to stay and everything. But she worried about me because it just so happened that at that time... swollen, my face [Elsie had contracted mumps]. And she worried what would happen to me and she came back. [Pause]. What shall I tell you? Next day, they closed the ghetto. She couldn't get out anymore. She went to... They took her... this transport. *That's how they took my mother.*

Such pain comes through in this single sentence, *that's how they took my mother.* Her mother-in-law was taken from them in a similar way. Elsie and her husband lived in a fairly substantial middle class neighborhood before the Nazi invasion of Poland. When they were forced into the ghetto their house was confiscated. Hope slipped away with each round-up as rumor became the main source of information for those still alive. Elsie conveyed a complex set of messages in her anecdotal style. With it she personalized her window on history on survivors and victims. She masked her sorrow with a lilting, joking, manner; she had finessed a special kind of nurturance in her storytelling during captivity, and it came through in the way she chose to tell what happened. The themes and anecdotes she chooses all end eventually in symbolic vindication for those worn by tragedy. At certain points, when she can no longer contain her feelings or the topic is too emotionally charged for her even now, she dissolves into silence. Analyzing the various clusters and themes of her anecdotes reveals much more than story line, but that is grim.

By May, 1942, in the deportations from the Krakow ghetto (Gutman 1990), there was mayhem. Hundreds were shot. The ghetto size had diminished by 6,300 people by the end of the first roundup. The ghetto perimeter was halved, and crowding was worse than ever. By late October there was another roundup, and seven thousand ghetto inhabitants were taken with six hundred of these shot on the spot and the rest sent on to Auschwitz. Institutions like the hospital, the orphanage, and the home for the aged were wiped out and the ghetto area reduced again. The remaining area was divided into a working section and a non-working section. The workers were taken to Plaszow on 13 March, 1943. On the following day, what was left of the ghetto was shipped directly to Auschwitz.

Being one of those transported to Auschwitz, Elsie spoke about what happened to the children of the Krakow ghetto. One of the children belonged to her brother. When the round-ups first started, her sister-in-law was in hospital with typhoid. She was eventually taken with all the other sick people and shot. The father also was killed. Elsie had full care of her niece and great horror when the children were taken. She never saw her again.

> And she [sister-in-law] had left behind... she left... left behind a child, a little girl, and I looked after that girl.
>
> [Q: Did that little girl survive?]
>
> No. No. Again, they took the children away from us and put them in a barrack there for children, and there they will "teach us"... they will have that. And there, you know, because we work and we are not... And she had her father... the father was still there. And when we had al... the most of the kids together, they did the same thing. Took them.
>
> And when we came to Auschwitz our first question and the mothers' question was "where are our children?" We were still hoping the children are there because they said, "There is a good big camp for children, and there they have schooling. There they w..." And we were all hoping that, you know, we *see* the children. So when we came to Auschwitz the first thing the mothers ask, "Where are our children?" And they [guards] laughed and say, "You were asking where your children are? Well, I think you know! Show you to the smoking chimneys. [Elsie is overwhelmed and seems about to stop the interview. Long silence].

The women workers in the Schindler factory were not supposed to have been removed. Schindler had paid for their safety. The children were taken from them by stealth in the general chaos at the liquidation of the ghetto. This moment in time was still an emotional minefield for Elsie and she had to carefully negotiate her entry to it. Instead of simply telling what happened once they got to Auschwitz, describing the routine elements of a day, or the specifics of their subjugation, she composed stories of the people which contained transcendence themes. In the mosaic of episodes she recounted, a choice word or a phrase disconnected from the rest gave evidence of what she found too upsetting to reclaim. Thematic apostrophe emphasizes the emotional distance still required for her to balance.

> In Auschwitz, you see, it was getting worse and worse, and they didn't feed us properly and, you know, you were afraid to go to the latrine and, you know, you never knew if you would come back. Those were terrible circumstances there, you see, and... especially my cousin.

> My cousin... my cousin, she was always [Aside to her husband, as she searched between languages for the right word, "'not pessimistic'?"] --She was pessimistic! I was optimistic.
>
> And there she told me, "Elsie. This is impossible. How can we stand it? We can't survive. How can we under these circumstances?" But I was always optimistic. I always thought... looking for a hole somewhere, a mouse hole where I could hide maybe, or something like that. And the evening again she started out, "That's impossible..." because she had already developed a temperature [with typhus]. It was October or November, I don't know now. The winters were... shocking there.
>
> What shall I tell you? The next morning [after the sharing of fears] I wake up [quiet; pause] and I don't know... did I wake up on account of my dream, or did I wake up because the horn was blowing there? [for appel]. And I wake up and I say to her, "Don't worry. Don't worry"--Trishka was her name, "Don't worry. We'll get out of here." --I had a dream, and I rarely have a dream. But, I had a dream there. I saw my parents' home. I saw the table set for Friday evening, because we were observant. My grandmother was very religious... observed the Friday evening. And the candles were there... were lit and everything was new with the white tablecloth and everything, and I saw my mother. My father comes in. My father reaches for his overcoat and his hat, and he wants to go out. And my mother starts to cry and says, "Where are you going?" He was the head of the family, you know. We wouldn't sit down for Friday evening without him at the table. And, "Where are you going?" she says, "everything's ready for Friday." And he turns around and he says, "Don't you worry. Everything is fine. I'll be back in time. You don't need to worry. Everything is... is fine."
>
> And that woke me, and I said to her, "We'll be all right. My parents are watching me and we will be all right." [About that time the] horn was blowing and they got us up in the appelplatz and called out our names. And the same day we were in [Schindler's work camp] !!

Within the general framework of a particular survival story like this one, the horrifying event is briefly delineated with the main idea being the elaboration of the transcendence theme. Another anecdote from this time period highlights corruption and personal profiteering among the Nazis. Jews are being victimized, the situation is complicated, and she renders the details with a characteristic humor.

> That German [officer], there wasn't a day that he wouldn't shoot two, three or four people, you know, when he walked in the camp. And he was... Anyhow, he hit on two young... two young couples, Jewish couples whom he picked out

and... "assistants," like the police... [Pause]. They didn't have to wear the thing, the Star. And so on the day... They did whatever he wanted. So what did they do?

The Red Cross was sending so much food for every person. See, we were supposed to get... What did this good German do? He sold that by the dozens, because there were five thousand people in the [camp at any given time]... sold it from the truck. But he didn't do it [himself]. He let the Jews do the dirty jobs. He sent them down to sell [the Red Cross packages].

So. What shall I tell you? With time, there came a young... a German guy, SS guy, and he was everywhere. He wanted to be everywhere. What shall I tell you? He found towels that this guy was selling [she laughs] with [Red Cross] food. And he reported it to Berlin! He reported it to Berlin! [More laughter.]

And, [the corrupt officer] got scared. He found out about it so he was afraid about the Jews that they will give him up or something. What did he do? He sent some other German [to the Jews who were assisting him, convincing them] that... that [it] is a good opportunity to leave the camp and go to Hungary, that he will help them to get out because...and he will help them to get out and will give them papers and everything.

And they really took him for real [trusted him]. And they [Jewish couple] got all ready to go out and they never checked, you see. When they [were ready] to go, there were police [waiting for them]. There was an SS man [at the gate] who checked them and he... and found that they [intended] to leave the camp. That's how they arrested them, you see. You see, with everything they arrested them and they were shot. [Pause]. They were shot. Five people. I remember that. They were five. And they were put down, and the whole camp was... was... had to go out and we had to pass by and see them lying there... Threatened that if we will try to go, that's what's going to happen to us.

Her profound sorrow quietly brings reverence to the victims. At once her story underscores the importance of keeping faith with your own community while clarifying the twisted perfidy of the Nazis. As her story witnesses and mourns, the community is always a silent and dignified presence, remaining whole and timeless, unscathed by oppression. She eventually achieves a lift in mood and timbre by turning the story against the antagonist, whose position she pretends to try and understand as she lands her punch,

So I don't really know why [but] it didn't help him [corrupt officer] anyhow, because it... it... There was an investigation and... and he was demoted. He was demoted. Demoted! [Mock chagrin].

And did anyone care for the sorry plight of the greedy blockalteste? Among the Jews, the community to whom she addresses her humor--clearly not, for obvious reasons. But the story goes on; for Elsie mere vindication is much too crude an emotion, so she ends it another way. Not only was the Nazi officer demoted but his replacement increased the food ration. Elsie triumphs with, "There was more to eat! [Laughs]. There was *more to eat*! See?!" In Elsie's world, evil could not stand long; because of its very nature it must collapse. Her humor also captured with mock seriousness how, in the Nazi system, bureaucracy and efficiency were legitimators for simple graft, greed, sadism and murder.

Interesting twists of fate were always attractive focal points in her rendering of what happened around her. Her next story told of low characters operating to undo Schindler on his own turf in the Sudetenland. It had happened before to him, but sometimes friends of his in the Abwehr in Berlin came to his assistance, and other times, as Elsie tells it, the assistance came by chance from an unknown quarter.

[Laughs.] He [corrupt officer]... was a very close friend of Mr. Schindler, see. They were very good friends. So when we were in the Czechoslovakian camp, in the ammunition camp, you know... in the West, what did they do? Because, you see, during the war, if they didn't put people in jail anymore, the Germans, what they did, they sent them to the front. But Mr. Schindler was not such a good soldier. He was good to serve the people and do these things [such as run factories], but he didn't want to go to the front! So he was on the run. *He* was on the run!

So one fine day, we were all upset. People start telling that this [corrupt] lagerfuhrer is there. But when Mr. Schindler brought him into the factory, there where we work, when we saw him, we knew we had nothing to fear anymore. He looked like he was... [He used to be] handsome, tall and fat with many medals. But now, nothing! No uniform. You know? [Laughing].

And he came and he wanted that Schindler should keep him, you know. But Schindler said, "I'm sorry. There's no room for you." And he had to go out. And he was one of the first Poles... I don't know how, but he got... he was sent to Krakow. He was sentenced there. He was hung. Poor man. In fact, this story [is about] a "good German" [laughing]. You see, that was our trouble too. We never thought that Germany [would do vicious things]. Like in school... in schooling, you know... [Germany was associated with] the nicer things... And there, *you couldn't believe it*. You couldn't believe it, you see, what [Germans] were doing.

Elsie beautifully interprets the material so that the villain becomes the victim, betrayed by those he foolishly emulated. Such is the fate of those who cast aside ethics and principle for material gain. The pathos was that the fate of Jews was often completely in the hands of such unfortunates who, during the Nazi years, were catapulted into authority positions. There are suspicious parallels with the story of Amon Goeth who at the end of the war was hanged by his own side. But there were so many corrupt officials and violent Nazis who fell by their own hand that the story Elsie tells need only sketch the archetype. Another story of hers highlights the last days of Nazi power.

> Of course we were just praying that Hitler should go, you know. If only Hitler would go. And there came the rumor at night [after she had fallen asleep]... we got the rumor that Hitler... what is it? [turns to her husband] committed...
>
> [Q: "Suicide?"]
>
> Yah! [Elsie doesn't like to speak the word]
>
> And of course [gulps] the whole camp was, you know, full of the noise and everything. Eleven... twelve o'clock at night, you know, and everybody was... Because... How did we get it [the news]? The Czechs came there [to the camp], the Czechs that worked there, and through them we got the news. See? And that's how we got the news of Hitler.
>
> So I say to her [cousin who woke her with the news], "Now, was that so important that you had to wake me up!! Go to sleep." [Laughing].
>
> Would you believe it?! My favorite story!

Elsie firmly believed that the wisdom locked into religious tradition provided clear insight into what ideals to honor and what commitments were meaningful, even during the ordeal of transport and internment, so much so that when she was asked if religion helped her in the camps, at first she was caught off guard.

> [Q: Did religion help you?]
>
> [A little irritated] Yes, of course. I was brought up in justice... in doing things right and not wrong. And we believed it. He [Hitler] won't last and we... we didn't know. We were... Everybody was just praying, you know... to

live up to... OF COURSE IT HELPED [her emphasis].

[Q: Some people say they prayed all the time, even while they worked in the camps].

Well, I didn't. I wouldn't say I prayed. I hoped.

For Elsie, religion was as much a fact of life as breathing. Under Nazi social policy, Jews were forbidden to celebrate their religion, and this especially applied in the ghettos, at Auschwitz and the work camps. With Elsie's group, as for many, religious practice while under coercion was a viable form of passive resistance and one most meaningful to them.

> There were leaders, but [also] there were religious people who observed, you know. They observed the holidays, and they got together in one barrack, and in the front there were two people watching. If a German comes the [codeword] was given. When they called s--- [the codeword] we knew the Germans were coming. So then they started to work.

> But for instance, for Passover, they went in the kitchen, you know. The ones who wanted to observe, they went to the kitchen and of course all the Jewish group were working there. So they let him [the leader] clean, you know. There's special... for Passover, special things that... They let them clean up and they can... [make] acceptable for Passover and they would give them just beets, no barley or whatever. Soups that they could observe with, and then they had Matzo. There were no stores, but in the canteen, you know, there was a stove like where I worked in the lumber mill. So they would come, and there they would make the Matzos themselves, these... Whoever wanted to observe could observe.

And so it was important for her to tell the story of the Jewish boy, to acknowledge an ideal and in the process describe an archetype of heroic martyrdom. This story clearly associates the heroic with keeping the Jewish faith. With certain words on his lips the people's hero dies, and seizes truth and inspiration out of pathos and tragedy. The words in this story are borrowed from thousands of years of Jewish history; the details happened at Auschwitz.

> There was a boy tried... tried to... runaway. Young guy. And [with others] tried to run away from the camp there and got caught and hung and we had... again, we had to watch it. But he told the lagerfuhrer that, "Today you are doing it to me. Tomorrow it will happen to you, because it is not... The unjustice won't last." [Pause]. That's what he said, and he recited the

Adults--The Young Women

Shemah Israel--it is our prayer, most important prayer where it says, "Hear, oh Israel, I am your God, just one." And with these words on his lips [very quiet] they took him.

Their factory was close to the demarcation zone between the Allies and they were not sure whether the Americans or the Russians would make it to their camp first. Schindler, though revered by the prisoner workers he had protected, would undoubtedly be apprehended by Allied troops as a Nazi collaborator were he not to make a move. His workers were determined to save him.

> And the... he took two trucks with... He had no children... just his wife and another couple's child. They went in two trucks. They took whatever they wanted, and two boys and a girl assisted them so that they should get into the American zone.

The prisoners remained, waiting with apprehension, for even now, those who came to "liberate" the camp might be marauders. Finally some Russians arrived.

> When Schindler left, and the Russians came--we didn't trust the Russians. They made with... a group of people handled the whole thing, you see, and they decided, that to be on the safe side, we better... Whatever they had in the warehouse, we should get it, or the Russians would get it, [laughing] and at night, they started to distribute the stuff. So everybody... when the Russians came, when we were liberated, we had three yards of material for suits--police navy blue, and three yards [of a heavier fabric] for a coat, and... At the time, you didn't buy readywear... thread to sew. What else did I get? Things like that and everybody got. When we walked out, we had something to go and sell.

They each might choose to sell or otherwise put to practical use the material, but in any case they each at least left with something. During the first two or three weeks of liberation, she had to travel home again. She took great joy in savoring even the smallest details of ordinary life.

> I decided I'd live it up! I went straight to Prague. We had paper that we were former inmates... that we were concentration camp inmates, you see, and so we could go free. No tickets. So we went. I went to Prague and there they were wonderful, the Czechs. They always were. So anyhow. Everything... there were schools... there were dormitories... there for women and for men, you know, and... where we could sleep... And then they had the Red Cross there, kitchens, and, oh, they make so good dumplings! They were delicious.

> They are known for their dumplings. And of course...
>
> So we went to Prague and this is what I told you, the material. So there at this time it was in style to have long jackets like three quarter length jacket was the newest, you see. So I was on a street in Prague waiting for a car or bus and there was a lady standing there, and she had that modern jacket. So I said to her, "Would you be good enough to tell me where... who made the [jacket you are wearing]. I am from the concentration camp and I would like to get a suit like that. I have material." And she gave me the address and it wasn't far from where I was. So you know, I can stay, but I want to go home and [the tailor] makes it in a few days. I ask him how much I have to pay him and he said, "Nothing." And that's how I got my suit.
>
> Anyhow. So I wanted to have shoes now. I wanted to buy shoes and I wanted to have the money. The stores were not open yet in Prague, see. Most stores were closed. So I couldn't find anything. But the B-- store was open. They had no shoes, but they had the pedicure. They made pedicure!

A dream of Elsie's in captivity had been to have a manicure. Now it seemed all she could get was a pedicure and some sandals. She took it! Appearance, which had been a symbol of their deprivation in the camps, became the focus of her healing activities after liberation. She went shopping in Prague. At this point in the interview she moved away from the "we" referent and towards "I" as she approached the end of this story. Liberation at the very least meant, for Elsie, dressing in nice, new clothes. Feeling good about herself was something the Czechs helped her accomplish. But Elsie was on her way to Krakow.

> I went. Not many went home. See, it was really behind the Iron Curtain; it was Poland. But I wanted to go home. I wanted to see. I was still hoping, you know. [She needed to find out] who survived. So I went home. [Pause] [She is lost in her thoughts. Twice the interviewer addressed her to no avail].
>
> I didn't have time to feel sorry for myself [laughs] you know because you had to do things, you see.

Her return to Krakow was bitter, rough and empty. To claim any property that had been her family's, she had to confront those who were given it by the Nazis. This was most unpleasant all around.

> And I became... The first night... the first night [pause] I slept at the train station in my hometown where I was born because there was still, I think, curfew, and I didn't know where to go. I didn't know who to stay with.

> So I slept on the floor. In town--I went into [town] to look around, when I came to our house, there where I was born, there was a woman and she didn't... She was *disappointed* to see me. She didn't want to let me in.

Elsie's mother had owned her house and had registered it in Elsie's name. This proved to be of some value eventually, because when the person living in the house went to City Hall with Elsie, hoping to secure her holdings against Elsie's claim, she was not entirely vindicated. Authorities then being the communists, expected both women to share what before 1939 had belonged only to Elsie. In the end, neither of the women felt justice had been served.

> She thought that, you know, that she... she lived in the house and she [had rights over it] and she... she went to the City Hall. And it happened that this house... My mother bought the house, and she put it right away in my name. I had the right to it.

> And so they went and they said that I had the right to *one room*. She had to give me one room and use of the kitchen. So then I found out that one of my cousins--she was like my oldest sister. She survived in Russia, see, so I waited for her to come. Then we stayed a while until we got papers to go to [North America].

Elsie has managed to omit directly telling that her entire family perished. She will not mention her first husband and his fate. She merely starts to describe life alone in Krakow after the war and leaves the rest to imagination. Eventually she married another survivor whom she had met at a Jewish community function. He had practiced law in Warsaw prior to 1939 and had been deported to Auschwitz at the liquidation of the Warsaw Ghetto. She and her present husband have a family, a daughter and a son. By their daughter, they also have two grandchildren. It took a great deal of emotional and social grappling to generate this little family. Elsie had not wanted to commit herself to having children after the Holocaust years. Her husband did.

> He never gave up. He will never give... never give up. It was only because... I was nervous because I felt we Jews shouldn't have any children after what we went through and what happened to our children... I think [then] we shouldn't have children.

> But I got the good doctor, and he was very positive, and he said to me, "Young woman, you are going to have children."

With children, their lives took on a whole different tone. They now have a living room wall full of mementoes that memorialize those who died as well as those who are still with them. Their children went to Jewish schools and their daughter is Orthodox. They had accomplished more than they dared hope for from the wasteland of the KZ system. Elsie had not wanted to conquer the world, just simply to have the right to live in it as she chose. That right was now hers.

WOMEN IN EXILE
POLLA

Polla Frisch was born May 15, 1919. She lived most of her life in Warsaw. In September 1939, when Poland was taken by the Nazis, preparations were started immediately for the formation of a ghetto. By November 15, 1940, the ghetto was sealed. In those intervening months, Jews in Warsaw had been registered, their property confiscated, and 80,000 non-Jewish Poles already in the area cleared out and settled elsewhere. Polla's family, who were Russian Jews and immigrants to Poland, had one son in the Polish army and were living in a mixed ethnoreligious neighborhood.

The Nazis initially carried out several round-ups looking for laborers. Polla's father was caught up in one of these and sent on a hazardous work detail during the course of which his hands were injured. In the end, her father was taken to Maidanek, and her brother in the military went missing in action. By the time the ghetto walls were sealed, Polla had already fled the city. Her mother was saved by neighbors who kept her hidden in their attic until the Nazis were forced out of Warsaw.

Trying to save whatever family she could find, Polla had returned to Warsaw within a few months of establishing a safe haven further east. She made it safely to Warsaw despite the danger. On the return eastward, confused by the new boundaries defined under the Nazi-Soviet agreement of 1939, she was captured and held by the Russian authorities as a spy. She was jailed immediately, awaiting trial. Eventually she was sent into the Russian gulag system. It was here that she survived the Nazi genocide of the Jews in Poland.

Her life until 1939 had been sheltered by her family's growing good fortune. When she was six weeks old, her parents had moved to Warsaw from their small town near the Polish border with Russia. Her father. knowing there would be more jobs available in the city, moved there with his wife and started his own roofing business. The family grew up in a mixed ethnic district and holding on to a Jewish way of life.

> In Warsaw there were different districts. It was a specific Jewish district. We lived among Polish people. [Pause] My father was a sheet metal worker. My mother was a housewife. In the family we had three children--I had two brothers.
>
> It was quite difficult economically. There was lack of employment. My father couldn't get a job in any factory or big undertaking because, you know, he was Jewish. So he had to work for himself.

The family lived in a fairly humble space in the early days where their living area served also as a workshop and store. As business prospered they moved again to one of four apartments built around a central courtyard. Their final move was to a space on the same street where the family lived over the store. She was then in grade five.

> We moved to another place on the same street. We had the store in front, again, because it was easier to get work being in front. My father was a sheet metal worker so they used to bring all kinds of repairs to the store. Pots and pans. They used to get a hole in it, my father used to fix it. Also he used to do sheet metal work on roofs because mostly the houses in Warsaw were covered with sheet metal. That was a profitable trade. There wasn't a lot of competition from the Polish population. So my father used to have quite a few clients, and the landlords, they used to hire him.

Polla grew up with a keen awareness of anti-Jewish hostility. If there was a quarrel in her play groups, it did not take much before epithets and ethnic slurs were hurled at her. She and her siblings were sent to Hebrew school for their religious studies. The family celebrated the Sabbath, keeping the store closed on Saturdays and going to synagogue for Sabbath services. Later, as things got better for the family, in the late 1920s and early 1930s, they invested even more efforts in maintaining their involvement in Jewish tradition.

> When I was about twelve years old they sent me to a Jewish evening school where I used to learn Hebrew and Yiddish literature, the language. At home they used to talk Yiddish. [But] with my friends [we used to talk] Polish. Also at school, Polish. Outside, Polish. Everywhere, Polish. But at home, the family, we used to talk Yiddish.

The family was very close knit. Her brothers were taught their father's trade so as to contribute to the family business and were also encouraged to be creative in many ways.

> My older brother was very creative. He used to play a flute. He was tops. He taught himself. Anything, he could play. Whatever you could sing [he could play]. He was very capable mechanically. He used to make all kinds of inventions, and the last one I remember, it was about two years before the Second World War, he invented a machine to bind sheet metal for roofing. And my father and he... they rented a special shop and they used to produce these machines to others. Two years before the war, our economical condition was much better.

In summer, the family would visit Polla's grandparents and they in turn provided hospitality for relatives visiting Warsaw.

> We used to have a lot of visitors from that small town. Somebody needed a doctor, a specialist. Somebody need to find a job, our home was the place to come! [Laughs] Because otherwise, nothing was available to them unless they paid. They were all poor people, but my mother used to help them out in this way. There was a lot of love.

When the National Socialists came into power in Germany, Polla was just finishing elementary school. The situation deteriorated economically from 1933-35. In 1933, when she had just turned fourteen, she had just finished elementary school. The outlook seemed bleak for her. Despite that, because she was a good student, she was offered a scholarship to one of the city's high schools. By working as a messenger she made up the difference in cost that the scholarship did not cover and by 1938 found herself struggling with entrance exams for university. None of her battles could be taken for granted, and all were approached with determination.

> The influence of the Nazis and the internal situation in Poland made it impossible for Jews to enter certain faculties like medicine or engineering. Law, they could enter, and humanities, at the university. So I put my papers in and [was accepted] in the humanities... languages. Then the war came about.

All her documents remained at the university during the war years, and, while there was some danger of records being damaged or burnt, hers had remained intact. After the war she pulled herself together and finally, when she was thirty-seven years old, got her master's degree in languages. In the meantime, during the year in which she first prepared to enter university, Germany made plans to invade Poland. The Munich Pact was followed by the Anschluss in 1938, and German Jews who had been born in Poland before 1919 were being sent back. They were aware of Krystalnacht, November 9-10, 1938. Polla and her friends were in dread of what might happen next and could do little more than watch as things got worse.

> We had groups usually talking about it. What could we do? It's hard [for you] to imagine. You... you fear things. Not because you're a human being, but also because you're a Jew. It's worse than for anybody else.

> All we could do was discuss, argue, discuss... that this would be better or that things would be better. But you couldn't do anything substantial to change... All our... we tried to work out our frustration by discussing things and seeing what kind of solutions there would be. Things were getting worse and worse. We couldn't go out of it. We couldn't leave the country; we couldn't go nowhere. We had no means of quieting down what was going on around. It was getting worse and worse for us. We felt trapped. [Pause]

Feelings of being trapped and helpless permeated her choice of words. As she spoke, the panic was still there beneath a well-controlled rhythm of speech, and phrases like "couldn't do anything," "couldn't leave," "couldn't go," "can't find" were thematic.

> And then the annexation of Czechoslovakia by the Nazis... the Germans, and the war was coming closer. After Hitler annexed Austria, Czechoslovakia, the so called "corridor" -- it was always a quarrel between Poland and Germany about ownership of this little corridor [to the free port of Danzig]. Then suddenly Warsaw started to hear the bombs. The siege of Warsaw took a few days, then the Germans came in.

> They were greeted on the streets by Poles. I can't find the words.

She spoke softly of the folly that overtakes the conquered. What followed for Jews and the Polish intelligentsia was wholesale persecution and killing. There was delegitimizing of the intelligentsia and outright persecution of Jews. Slaughter was companion to coercion.

> Round up Jews... force them to clean up the streets after bombing. Force them to do all kinds of menial and very degrading jobs. They caught my father once in a group like that, and they took him to the... a place not far from us on the outskirts of Warsaw [to a coal works]. From coal they produce gas,

> heating gas. This is a good thing in the city. So they rounded up groups of people. They took them there to clean up that place and they didn't... they didn't give them any tools or anything and the coals were hot--burning, and they used to do it. They forced them to... to clean up with their hands. And my father was away for about twenty-four hours. When he came back, he was terrible. Blisters. They did that to him. They used to catch Jews with beards and cut one side, regardless if it's to the skin. Left them bleeding... faces. So in this situation we felt terrible, and about then we [she and her husband] decided to go... to run away, and we did.

Her father, the successful tradesman, the innovative tinsmith, the patient provider, who endured bitter ethnic prejudice to earn a decent living for his family, was made to handle hot coals as a captive laborer. All they had worked to build for so many years was reduced to nothing in a matter of weeks. Family and relatives were rounded up and killed.

> They perished. They perished in Maidanek. So did my father [her voice is broken]. My mother survived. She was kept hidden. My... Some of our Polish friends, a Polish family, they took her out from the ghetto. They kept her hidden there in their attic, and she survived.

Polla now had to play her part in the family's effort to survive. She and her husband had choices forced on them by the war. Marriage had been one of these. If they were to act on their plans to flee Warsaw, they would have to marry. They determined to move further east where she had relatives, since with Germany, to the west, this was the only real alternative for a flight of reasonable duration.

> We went illegally. We didn't have any papers. Couldn't, because in case we were searched by the Germans or something, we could face the [voice wavers] you know... shot anyways. It was a risk.

> We had to marry in order to... Such a situation! [In] such circumstances... to get married was a terrible thing. It was a very simple celebration, as simple as possible, and so we took off our stars to go and went by train to that little town where I was born, on the border between Russia and Poland [then Greater Germany]. The river [Bug] was the dividing line between them. The town was right on the [river border]... the town I know the best, and I had still relatives there.

> We said to our parents, when we'd leave they should go with us, because the situation is terrible. But my parents... [sighs] older people... they were in their fifties... Well, it was hard for them to leave everything. And they

said they lived through the First World War with the Germans and the Germans were very nice people. Maybe there is a Hitler there, but, privately [individual Germans] are nice people. So they wouldn't think that something drastic could happen. My parents thought they can get along with [the Germans] and they stay and wait for us to come back. Who would think that the world would take such a turn and go on for years and destroy so much? So we went without our parents.

Difficult choices were coupled with heavy risks. Nevertheless, they did make it to the little town where her relatives still lived. Refugees from all over Poland were gathering there. Locals were acting as guides for those wanting to head farther east.

> It was a lucrative enterprise for some. In this kind of time, some people are gaining this way, and money is a very important thing. Also... you had to see to it that the Russian border guard didn't catch you. These peasants had already some agreements with the peasants of the other side to pick them up and take them [refugees] to the towns. As long as you didn't pile into the Russian border guard, or the German border guard... And so it had to be done at night when it was really dark.

She knew this area best because she and her family had stayed with her grandparents during summer vacations when she was a child. Some of her cousins still lived there. In another village, about five kilometers away, an uncle, her father's brother, and his family lived. Both of these villages were near Brest, which is where she and her husband obtained work.

> We went to a big town, Brest, and there I had relatives where we stayed with them and we started--I need five hours to tell this story [laughs] and then we got jobs. My husband got a job at the railway station, and I got a job at the railway station, too. And I [also] got a job in the Red Cross. There's a lot of people were coming there, and I got this because, before the war, right before the war, they were prepared in Poland for something, so, they used to take people for special courses, Red Cross courses, and I finished a... I don't remember, it was a six weeks nursing course. So when I came with this to Brest, I told them that I had my little education in the Red Cross and so, they took me in, and I got a job there. I was to work 24 hours and 48 hours off.

As newlyweds they had set out with more courage than material resources. Getting some work and locating relatives was a beginning. They had big hopes but small means.

> We didn't have nothing. We didn't take with us nothing, no documents--nothing, because in case they catch us or something. So one day, being there [sighs] I decided to go back to that little village... in through this little village... go back to this little shtetl... this little town, through the river, and back to Warsaw. I told my husband my plans. He was terrible upset. I said, "Sure I have to do it because we are with nothing." It was impossible to buy anything even for bread. You had to line up at that time already, and winter was coming. We had only summer clothes on and he was shivering. So I said, "I'll go." And he said, "Don't go. Because it's war time and we will not see each other any more." And it was true.

She stumbles over the words "little village." Flight had forced upon them the sacrifice of intellectual life that was part of urban complexity and university life in Warsaw. The village where they sought refuge had been a sometime holiday spot for her parents because they still had family there to visit. To remain for any length of time they would need documents and other resources to plan their next move. Then, too, though she says nothing about her concern for her father and mother, her thoughts could hardly have been far from them. They had been in a terrible plight when she fled. Being strong-willed, she believed that a brief return to Warsaw must be attempted immediately or be forsaken entirely. As she looked back upon that time, however, she seemed to favor her misgivings.

> I went [applying firmness to her voice]... not listen to him [husband]... I went back to Warsaw. Anyway, somehow I managed all by myself, and I came to my parents' to pick up a few [voice becomes subdued] packs of clothes. I picked up his mother. She was alone there. So she went with me, and we went both back the same way to the border, and it was already January. [Mood worsens].

> It was cold. The river was frozen and we made arrangements just to walk through the river from a certain place where the German guard wasn't there. And we started to walk and it took us about two hours to cross the river on ice with our luggage and we came to the other side of the border. They... the Russian guard was there and they intercepted us, and that was it. I didn't see his mother any more. I was put in jail. I was sentenced to jail for being a spy, because that's what they usually accused you of when you crossed illegally, and I was pregnant at the time already.

She does not mention her anguish. She speaks without demanding the listener's sympathy. Her own tragedy was referenced in a few simple phrases like, "the guard was there," "they intercepted us" and "that was it..." After her capture, she was jailed, tried, imprisoned in a work camp deep inside Russia, and then, twenty months later, released to a collective farm in the Black Sea area. As a tribute to the well of emotions eclipsed by her style, she said she had to stop her narrative and she temporarily left the room, saying once more that it was impossible to tell this story in a short period of time. In a while she returned, composed.

> I had terrible experiences and in Russia [very quiet]. [Pause]. I couldn't fight with them. Whatever they said, they were right and you couldn't say... You see, even when they had this court and sentencing us for this... being accused of crossing illegally, the court was in Moscow. We were in the jail. I wasn't the only one. There were a lot of people like me in jail. So the court was in Moscow, and we couldn't even defend ourselves. And they came to the jail to read us the court's verdict. Three years in jail... so on, so on, so on. So what could you do?

Despair followed frustration and disappointment. She felt the smart of hopes dashed. Conditions in the prison were bleak but adequate for bare survival. Interaction with the other prisoners was minimal and relegated at first to a system of gestures. Through these they offered each other sympathy.

> I was with the group of other women in the same cells. We were trying the best to be nice to each other. I'll give you an example. They took us each morning out... ten o'clock in the morning for a half an hour. Twenty women. There weren't the bowl toilets. You had to stand on your feet... it was a hole. They took us for half an hour. Twenty women.

> They were so considerate, all of them [women], that they went to one side [double-sided arrangement of the toilet holes] and let me stay [in relative privacy on the other]. You cooperate. You try to do the best for your neighbor... compensate for the tragedy you're going through.

Being pregnant put an added strain on her and the other women tried to help. Her prison mates were Russians, Jews and Poles, all sharing a similar fate.

> In a situation like this, how you get so close to each other... and... and... you don't feel any differences. Only... our common enemy was the guard... the jail guard.

These bonds, formed by chance, provided her with the inspiration she needed to maintain her faith in life. Even the staff joined in this ministry of little gifts.

> They used to bring me little bits of carrot or something which they wouldn't get in jail but... They felt sorry for me. [She is laughing a little] And for the baby they used to bring me some things sometimes. It's unbelievable how people get when you are in a situation like this. There are people still in the world who can feel with you, who can relate to you and be nice to you. That makes a difference.
>
> I always remember the old nurse who just came once to me and she said, "Here's a carrot--don't tell anybody--I brought you from jail." I still have her face before me. You knew she had no interest in doing it, but she still did it because she felt that... how much injustice is done to people like me, and, in a way, she wanted to help. She would be in such trouble, you know, if they would find out. Terrible.

Polla was allowed some minimal communication by letter with her husband once she had been transferred to the work camp from the jail. He thought of moving farther into Russia to be near her, but she saw Russia as a temporary situation and believed there would be no long-term gain in making such a move.

> In jail, when I was in jail, for a time being, they wouldn't let him know where I was. But then I... finally, when I was transferred to the labor camp, they gave him my address. I received the first letter. I used to receive all the time. I was allowed to write once a month.
>
> Actually I remember in one of the letters, he didn't work anymore in that station in Brest, but he got a job as a teacher because he also had some education as a teacher, there, you know, in that village. And he used to write to me and send me parcels.
>
> One letter, he said to me that since I am there he wouldn't mind... he wants to come over and live on the free... but near, so he could be... So I wrote to him, "Never do it!" Because, this would commit us to stay there all our lives. I didn't think it will be forever. Maybe another half year or something. I hated that place.
>
> So he didn't come. [Subdued] I made a mistake. Such a mistake. But how many mistakes do you make in a life?

The agony of their separation was heightened by its representing the machinations of political "justice." Having done nothing worse than travel without a visa, she was sentenced to prison on some trumped up charge of "spying." The intensity of her distress comes out in the uncharacteristic frankness of her phrase, "I hated that place." Unfortunately, she once again had not thought things through from her husband's point of view. Her decisional framework was based on the assumption that the war would be over shortly; anything could be endured for a short period of time. Near the time for her delivery, she was transferred to another prison.

> They transferred me from this little town with many, many things. My husband came, and they got to know... [she is sad]. They didn't let him in to see me. I saw him on the yard walking.
>
> So I didn't see him since then. That's it. We were cut off.

Only later did she know that her view from that prison yard was the last time she would see her husband alive. She was transferred from Brest on the border with Poland to Gomel, well inside Byelorussia on the Dnepr. There she had her daughter.

> I had my baby, Laura. She is with me [now] here. [Laughs] Survived. When I was ready to have the baby I had contractions already, they took me to the city hospital to have the baby because they didn't have the facilities in jail for it. But I made a lot of friends in hospital. I made a lot of friends among the guards and the nurses in jail.

She was protected from the worse conditions by a diffuse network of supporters and the urgency which love for her child pressed upon her. At Gomel, she placed the baby in the camp nursery while she worked. She was given time out to care for the child. Her most powerful experience during this period related to a strong character she met in the work camp north of Moscow.

> Because of me having to be with her [Laura] every three hours, breast feed her, they couldn't send me out to work far away. I had to be inside this small enclosure of the camp where they kept... used to keep children and mothers only, and there was a hospital. So this... there was a doctor there who... a woman doctor there. She was jailed in 1933-34 for being against the government. It was an awful time for a lot of people who were innocent entirely. Sometimes they said a word and they sent them to jail because they thought that they were against the government.
>
> So this doctor was a very nice lady. So I got to be friends with her and she took me as a nurse to this hospital, and she taught me all kinds of things.

> As a matter of fact, because of this, when I [immigrated to North America] in 1958, I got a job [with a major hospital].

The meeting had an impact on the rest of her life. But it was her own awareness and understanding which altered who she was in such a desperate environment, and how she saw life from that time forward. As she moved through this imprisonment, her experience of others in it with her allowed her to transform herself.

> Anyways, she [woman doctor] took me in the hospital; I worked with her there. So my own condition... attitude changed. I was entirely different. It felt like [being] a person. Doing something, worth something because it was a hospital for children. It was a camp for mothers with children.

In the presence of this very strong professional person, Polla had felt whole again. She could then take pride in what she could do for others. Her woodenness began to alter: "I was entirely different." Acting as the doctor's assistant meant she did not endure the most gruelling conditions and activities. It also meant that her focus could change. She was allowed to be a mother. She lived for her child, but she understood this as a gift made possible by others.

> There were different situations in jail and in camp, but somehow I tried always to make friends, to have support. I always tried to keep others' feelings up... and hope. I'm alive, and I see to it that the other people feel good... have hope. Things will get better. It was important to hope.

Reaching out to others, her child and various others around her, provided a self-confirming identity for her. It was not a small accomplishment. To not only survive injustice and disruption of one's life, but to accept and work within the limitations of internment while raising a child took great stamina.

> It's your spirits keep you up, your hopes for a betterment, and, in part, it's your own behavior, too. The way you relate to others. The way... I think the way I relate to others, the way I try to help people... And there was... when you see friendliness among cruelty, your hopes are growing. Your spirits are growing... that something could happen... people could be better. It gives you strength.

She was a woman of very tiny stature and unassuming ways who showed a surprising acuity in her observations. At this happy juncture in the narrative it seemed alright to ask if there had been any time during her period of internment when she thought she would not be able to make it through. She said quietly,

> Probably not once only. Because life was very hard, very hard. Degrading. The conditions... it wasn't easy. But still, the baby kept me.

It would be hard for anyone to endure extreme circumstance with only a sense of infinite regression as a standard for interpretation. But, with so little information and so much need for hope rather than fact, errors in the timing of events were inevitable. The war continued for three more years after her sentencing. This was much longer than either she or her husband had anticipated.

> When they let us go from labor camp, the war was already on with the Germans. And the part my husband was in was taken the first day by the Germans when they started to invade Russia.
>
> [Q: Did you hear about that right away?]
>
> Not [very quiet] right away. [Pensive] Also I met people who were with him. He was killed.
>
> [Q: Killed. Where?]
>
> [Angry] There!
>
> [Q: Shot?]
>
> Yes. By the Germans [very quiet].
>
> [Q: How did you get information?]
>
> Okay. There wasn't possible to find out right away. There was such a chaos that you couldn't do anything until things calmed down and until the end of the war. I started to look for him through the Red Cross.

It took two more years to officially confirm what she then knew. In the meantime, she was contending with the everyday regimen of life in a Russian work camp in the far north. Temperatures there in winter went down to eighty degrees below zero, Fahrenheit. Laborers working outdoors in the extreme cold of a Russian winter suffered most bitterly.

There's so many people died there, especially men. They used to send them to the forest to cut trees without any clothes. So many perished in that same camp. It was from cold, undernourishment and... You see, the difference between a concentration camp or a work camp, and Russia was, the... in the work camp, you didn't fear for your life. You could live there... a meager [existence]. And that's where I ended up until 1942.

Under an agreement between the Russian and the Polish government in exile, those like her, imprisoned due to the war, were released in specific areas after their sentences were served.

They only gave you [sighs] an opportunity to live in places, not in big cities, just in certain cities far away from the battle front, because at that time already, they fought the Germans. So we were "freed," and I went with Laura to a little town in Russia on the... not far from the Black Sea... not far from Stalingrad. And we had to run away. We lived in a collective farm, and we had to run away. I can't talk about it.

Despite the obvious risk, she escaped with her baby and headed back into German territory. But this time, the Nazis were on the defensive; the fortunes of war had begun to change. She returned to the little Russian village in the region near Brest and found her husband's mother, her companion on that fateful river crossing, still alive. When the Nazis retreated, they went back to Poland together. She eventually found her mother alive in Warsaw in the care of the Polish family.

[Q: How did you feel?]

How did I feel? --Delighted. [She laughs.] At least mother was alive. I couldn't believe it.

See, my closest family--both my brothers survived, myself and my mother... which was a unique thing. Generally, families were wiped out altogether without anybody surviving, or one person or two. But my... our family... except for my father, survived. We were strong, durable. We went through in our lives enough from the beginning, from childhood. It wasn't [easy]; it was a struggle, and maybe that made us strong. Also when you... when I had my daughter, that gave me strength to survive, because I had to take care of her.

Despite the loss and destruction and because of what she had learned along the way, she did not turn inward or isolate herself. She set up household with her mother-in-law. Later she married again.

He had two children [sighs] and it was the... the excitement of meeting each other, having the same background and the longing for our past, the peaceful, considerate past [to make up for] what happened to us during the war, that we got together and got married.

She blossomed overnight into a mother of many children. In addition to the three children they brought with them into the marriage, they had two more. Eventually they all went to live in Warsaw.

We lived in Poland because the situation changed [after the war]. It was a different government. They were pro-Jewish, the government, and we didn't have any problems as Jews. And, second, I grew up in the culture. There were my roots. So it was good to be there after the war. But in 1955-56, the government [showed] racial discrimination and the Polish people showed their real face, and anti-Semitism grew up again, and for fear of our future, we had to run again. So we did. And we were lucky. My brother was here [North America]. He came in 1946, and we corresponded [sighs], and he sent us papers to Poland and we came in 1958.

In the new country, she got a job she liked, bought a lovely house, and began to enjoy her life. She and her brother established a foundation in honor of her first husband. She now has four grandchildren. She continued to actively work upon the past. Part of that involved, recently, taking her granddaughter to Poland with her as a graduation gift. To Polla, the journey was deeply meaningful.

So we went there, and I showed her all the places I loved. I [also] showed her Auschwitz, and she was terrible upset and she went through Auschwitz. She said, "Why do you take me there?" I said, "It's important that you know something like this existed." And, you saw it yourself. If K--[a local Holocaust denier] comes around and tells you that it never happened, you can openly say that "I saw it with my own eyes."

And I took her to [their old apartment building], in Poland. It's now a warehouse... big warehouse... not warehouse, department store, and I took her there one morning. She didn't... I have a cousin there, so we stayed with her. She didn't know where I take her. We ordered a taxi and I took her there and I took her in the middle of the main floor, and I said [voice wavers] "Here! Here did you mother grow up! This place!" It was an experience. [Laughs]

With this journey she had come full circle and marked it with exuberance. In the year following the interview, she planned to go again to Poland and take her grandson with her. Despite the exultant tone on which she was ending, there was something left unsaid. In response to the question about whether or not there was any lingering pain associated with the past, something that went beyond simply having had a tough time for a few years, she became tearful and replied,

> When I speak to you, my heart is breaking, you know. Sometimes I break down, but you can't help it. You live with it every day in your life. You try to forget, but you can't.

RUTH

Ruth Kirsch was born in Germany in 1916. She lived there with her family until September 1, 1939, when she sailed to America on one of the last ships out of Rotterdam before the ports were sealed. The rest of her family remained. All but the nephew who she convinced her brother to send into hiding in Sweden, and her father who died in hospital in Berlin the day after she sailed, perished in the extermination camps in Poland.

She grew up in Bad Freienwalde on the Oder river. It was a small town of 35-40,000 people, thirty-five miles from Berlin. Her father was a merchant. He owned two stores and was for many years the mayor of Bad Freienwald.

> Freienwalde. "Freien" means free and "walde" means wood. I don't know where it originated. Very pretty little city. In those days there wasn't much transportation. We didn't have cars. In fact, when I was little, we had cobblestones. Then they slowly paved the streets. There were no cars. Europeans didn't have automobiles. My father had an official car, and the doctor had a car. We took the train to Berlin. From Freienwalde to Berlin was about a two-hour ride. It stopped in all the little villages.

Growing up, she attended Hebrew school once a week on Saturday but otherwise did not feel the weight of tradition and religion pressing upon the family lifestyle. They were Germans and believed in the goodness of those around them. Unlike many who grew up as Jews in Eastern Europe, Ruth felt no particular degree of community prejudice against either herself or her family.

> I grew up in Freienwalde. I went to school there. Our schools, the German schools, were very strict. No comparison to American schools. We went to school six days a week. We couldn't play very much, and boys and girls did not go to school together. We went to the elementary school until eleven years

of age, then high school. In my days they were private. You had to take a test. If you passed it, you could afford it, then you went to high school. Those children whose parents could not afford didn't go to high school.

I went to high school when I was eleven and there were only about twelve girls in my class. I had six years of French, three years of English, and one year of Latin. In my senior year I carried twelve subjects. We were pushed. And if you failed, you were out. You couldn't... you had to pass. By 1933, I was in my sixth year, my last year in High School. I was sixteen or seventeen then.

I can't say that I suffered a lot of anti-Semitism. That wouldn't be true in my case. My father was well known, and my family was well known. The children accepted me like one of them, and I didn't have any problem. Not until Hitler came to power or somewhat before that. In fact, in the last year in school, our class went on a trip and I didn't want to go. The teacher said, "Yes, you are coming with us." And I went. I am still corresponding with some of the girls I went to school with.

German institutional life had been anti-Jewish throughout its history, but there were opposing currents. Throughout the 1800s, these currents became more pronounced, and Jews were given full citizenship. In Ruth's Bad Freienwalde, she is describing a pocket of life in which Goethe's Germany may still have held sway. After 1929 and the fall of the Weimar Republic, Nazi extremism became increasingly typical of public life, and racist anti-Semitism was a significant component of national ideology (see also Allen 1984).

I met an awful lot of well-known people when I was very little, and I loved it. I loved that very much. I like politics. But unfortunately, now, my father was so German, we were all so German, he never believed that anything could happen. That's why they didn't survive. I was a rebel, yes. I was always a rebel. That's why I'm here.

As a student, she hoped to become a physician. She felt very close to her father in manners and predilections and knew she could master the rises and falls of public life. They were equally stubborn when they disagreed. A continuing tug of war sprang up between them over the interpretation of events between 1932 and 1939.

In 1932 I read *Mein Kampf* [a book by Hitler] and I believed every word he said. I did. And that was the year I decided I was not going to live in Germany. I wanted to get out. But of course I was in school. I had to finish school.

[Q: How did you feel as you read it?]

I was upset. Terribly upset. I believed it when he said he was going to kill the Jews. I believed every word of that because this man was crazy. Vicious. A murderer.

Even in 1932-33, life went on, and people like Ruth's father continued to hope that the economy would get better and Hitler would remain an unfortunate but inconsequential shadow upon the twentieth century in their country. But the First World War had left the population shaken and vulnerable. Ruth thought a different policy toward Germany in defeat might have changed what happened there in the 1933-45 period. In any case, she and her family were Jews, and Ruth saw trouble coming with the rising popularity of National Socialism. Nazi marching songs were bloody and violently anti-Semitic.

The family reluctantly acknowledged that there were dangerous trends but, disattending Ruth's insights, they moved to Berlin. She persisted in her belief that the only correct move was to emigrate and at least got herself prepared to do this.

Right after I finished school, my parents decided they were going to leave for Berlin, which I thought was a terrible mistake. I think we would have been much better off in a small town where we knew people well. We moved to Berlin and I made up my mind to get out. I begged and pleaded with my parents, "Please. We can still all get out. We can go to Holland. We can go to South Africa. Let's all go together." They said, "You are an emotional child. Nothing is going to happen. Foreign nations won't allow it."

Though her words had no consequence, her conduct showed great determination to pursue the path she believed correct. She spent 1935 in Holland with relatives and went to the American consulate to apply for visa status. While she was waiting, she also applied to enter Britain.

I had an aunt and cousin in Holland, and I spent one year there. I just lived with my aunt and cousin, helped them with their store. He was a photographer. In the meantime, I found my relatives in America, distant relatives, and they sent me an affidavit, and it took me til 1939 to get a visa. And I like to mention that I had to deal with the American consulate.

Now I wasn't going to stay in Germany anyhow. I had already gotten a permit to go to England. My friend... she and I grew up together, she had a permit to England. We were going together, but then my visa came through and she went [alone] to England and spent the war in England.

By 1936, it was clear that the difficulties her family had started to feel in 1933 were not abating. But these were not people to give in easily, nor to throw away the beliefs of a lifetime because things got tough. They were as determined as Ruth was to get through the times, but not by leaving. Germany had been their home for centuries.

> Life in Berlin was pretty bad. [Pause] They used to march down the street, young Germans, the Hitler youths. They marched down the street voicing songs. I'll translate this one: "When Jewish blood drips from our knives, then life will be good." This went on day after day after day.
>
> [Q: And your father still didn't believe that they meant it?]
>
> 1938 was Krystalnacht. I was there. And we had then an apartment. We had to get rid of our house and our money and we were sitting in the dark on the floor and I said to my father, "Why do you sit here on the floor? Why don't we fight back?" He said, "We don't make waves."
>
> My father was a very liberal man. He did listen to his children, even though he was German [laughs]. I explained to him how I felt, and I told him that I was going to get out one way or another, and he didn't stop me. He didn't stop me. He said, "If that's how you feel, I'm against it, but I won't stop you, and I think it's all wrong." We were two of a kind. Strong willed.

Ruth had been working on ways to protect herself and her family throughout the 1930s. She had information on who to contact in connection with rescue. Her brother was seventeen years old when he married and had a son. The son was born in 1934, and before she finally left Germany, Ruth had managed to impress upon the couple that they should put their son in hiding. Events of 1938 helped convince them.

> He was five years old. When he was four years old, I talked to them and told them that children can get transported out of Germany to the Norwegian countryside. But they just had to let... and it was a terrible struggle. I told them what was going to happen. Very few German Jews believed this. Finally, they did. They let him go and took him to the train, and they didn't speak to me for four months. He went to Sweden and he lived with a farmer's family in Gustafson, Northern Sweden, and they treated him like their own. He grew up, and he lived through it.

Of the family of nine--her parents, a sister and her husband, her unmarried younger sister, her brother, sister-in-law and nephew, only she and her nephew survived. As they took the child to the train, no one could be sure they were doing the right thing, and the parents were in agony about the parting.

> They lived near the Alsace-Lorraine border. They came to Berlin with him so that he could leave. But they came before that so they could talk it over... a year or two before they did anything. It was my sister-in-law, of course, the mother, who didn't want to let him go. Who wants to let a child go? a five-year-old child? But she did. But then they were upset. Terribly upset.

The parents were eventually transported to southern France to a concentration camp there and thereafter to Auschwitz. Her last correspondence with her mother and sisters was from Warsaw in 1942 as they were being taken to one of the Polish extermination camps. When she left Europe, her father was ill.

> He was in the hospital. He died the day after I left. And I told them I would stay, I would not leave them. They said, "Oh yes. You must." Then he made me go, because I wasn't going to go. He was dying. And he said, "Yes, you have to go now." He told me I had to go.

Somehow she seemed to need her father's blessing to make this break with the past, leaving her family and country with not much more than principled conviction to support the move. It was early September, 1939, when she made reservations for travel with the Holland America line out of Rotterdam. Seas at that time of year would at best be choppy. As luck would have it, Germany had just invaded Poland when the ship was due to leave port. It would, in fact, be the last sailing of commercial vessels out of Rotterdam for some years. Fortunate, too, that this particular ship on which she booked passage did not turn back when war was declared; others had.

> I was first going to be on the Isle de France [which canceled its sailing when war was announced]. But then the last minute we changed to the Holland America line, and I went from Rotterdam. And a few days later, Hitler was in Poland. There was a discussion about turning back. The Isle de France and many other ships turned back and those Jews who... those refugees who were on the Isle de France, they just jumped off the ship into the Atlantic. But people don't know this. It was never made public. I was lucky.

> And all the American tourists tried to get on the ship. Eight or twelve hundred people on the ship. So we had to double up the cabins, and there was a honeymoon couple, a teacher, and her husband was also a teacher, and they put her in the cabin with me, because they didn't have cabins just for husbands and wives. We had the stormiest voyage because we had to take the northern route, and of course it was horrible. I didn't want to stay in the cabin because everyone was seasick. This poor lady in my cabin was so seasick. I finally made her go upstairs. I can still remember walking her back and forth in the fresh air. I never went back in the cabin. I slept in a lifeboat.

"I stuck to it," "I was lucky," "I never went back," these are the rhetorical pillars of the pluck and bravado by which she identified herself. She would outwit the attacker and surmount the difficulties. Ruth was a small knot of courage and energy. Her voyage lasted eleven days, and they all finally arrived in New York. Members of a contact organization met her at the dock and brought her to a German hotel.

> So they put me in that hotel. They told me not to go out, not to do anything, til they picked me up in the morning and put me on a train. But I knew there was a World's Fair in New York. [But she had been allowed to immigrate with four reichsmarks in her possession] That's all I was allowed to take out [of Germany]. Four marks. [Pause]. After they left, I took fifty cents and I knew enough English to get myself through. So I found the subway. I think it was a nickel, and I went to the World's Fair, and I spent another ten or fifteen cents there, and I went to the Florida Pavilion because I was [heading for Florida]. I went all over! I stayed until eleven o'clock, then I took the subway home... back to the hotel.

She relieved any lingering anxiety she had about her new social space by getting out and moving around in it. She felt it was important to signal to herself that a boundary into a new life had been passed and that harm was behind her. Claiming the freedom to stay out as long as she wanted that evening did that. She was not only self reliant, but now was master of her own vessel.

> The next morning they picked me up and told me what a good girl I was. But I didn't say anything. They put me on the train. I think it was a good two days... took the train down to P--. I was homesick. But I was so lucky.

Her distant relatives had a nine-year-old daughter. The husband was a physician. She became part of their family. She still lives in this town which meant renewal and safety for her then. As the town changed, bits of her earliest memories got shifted around, but the meaning of this family's embrace carried her across the years.

> Dr. H-- was in the old medical building on C-- Street. He was one of the founders. He greeted me, and then we went to their home on 20th Avenue, then a dirt street, not E-- [where she lives now]. From then on my life was just beautiful. They treated me like a princess. Always they couldn't have been any more wonderful to me. I was so lucky. I couldn't study medicine. I wouldn't have expected them to give that. So I went into nurse's training in New Orleans, Tulane Infirmary. And here, after I went to New Orleans, I came home on vacation and met Jack, my husband. And oh... we liked each other. He came to see me a couple of times, and then it was close to Pearl Harbor, 1941. He had a commission [in the military] to college. So we decided to get married, and that was just before I graduated. I felt we had to be together. So we were married in July of '41.

She felt secure and welcomed in that gentle space, but this made the label "enemy alien," formally assigned her by the State Department inasmuch as she was a German national, an even more painful anachronism. She fought it.

> I finally wrote a letter to President Roosevelt. I was furious. Why would I be an enemy alien? And they wrote back and said they couldn't do a thing about it. I was still a German citizen in 1943.

Her husband rose to prominence in the Navy and moved around during the war, working on bases near home. They had a son in the first few years of their marriage, but with no word from her family since 1942, as the war continued, her doubts about their well-being grew. Right after her husband returned at war's end, she began searching for them. She located her nephew.

> The organizations helped us. They found him in northern Sweden. By then he was twelve or thirteen, so we asked if he would like to come, and we brought him over. He is now in Miami with two grown sons, and he is an engineer. Graduated from XXU. Top of his class.

> [Q: You must feel good about that.]

> Yes. Of course. My husband, too. And he didn't have anything when he came back from the service. When my son was born in 1942 [laughs] we lived on Navy Point. He [nephew] was the valedictorian of his class in high school. Then went on into the service for a year or two under the GI Bill and went to XXU

and became an electrical engineer.

This symbolized some measure of transcendence for her. However, the loss of her family in Europe was painful. She held little hope of finding any of them.

> I never expected them to be alive. I would have heard from them. They never got out. My sister never got out. [Pause] I just don't have a good feeling.

As her husband neared retirement, they visited Europe and were invited by the German government to join a national celebration. They were with a larger group who were similarly honored. She was reluctant to accept this distinction, but the invitation had been directed at her American-born husband.

> They wined and dined us and... It didn't please me. I just didn't want any part of it. I still don't. But we spoke to a lot of Germans as we drove through Germany and went to Dachau. I wish I hadn't. I was sick for five days after that. It was a terrible experience.

They had made their own itinerary as a concession to her misgivings about joining in the celebration. Even at that time she was still trying to get information on her family, though it was decades after the war. She understood that new sources of information had become available.

> All these years I tried to find out what happened to my mother and my sisters and what happened to my brother. I didn't know which concentration camp, so. We couldn't get information from the Germans. So when we went to Berlin, to the man was in charge of this visit, I told him my problem. He said, "Well, I can help you," and he sent us to the place where they keep all the books and papers--the archives in Berlin, and we told them what we wanted and they weren't very happy about it. So I told them that Mr.--- told us that they would help us. So they said, "Okay" [laughs]. So a man came downstairs, thrilled to death. He was in a prisoner of war camp in [America] and he loved this country so much [sarcasm; she is not convinced]. And I said, "Well that's wonderful but in the meantime, I'd like to hear about my family." "Well, just a minute." And he came back five minutes [later] beside himself with joy. He said, "I found everything." I said "You did!" He said, "Yes, I have it here." They were deported in 1942 on an eastern transport, and it was signed by that Nazi, with a swastika. I said, "Well, that is something, but..." It only said "east," it did not say which concentration camp. But he was so thrilled that he found it. And I have my papers. So. It was from Warsaw they got taken.

She and her husband went back to Germany a second time in the mid-1980s, again by invitation. There were contradictions in what they saw of the German people's response to the disruption and suffering they caused during the 1933-45 period. With regard to the Holocaust, there were those people who felt the damage could never be recovered but were determined to help; there were also those who denied anything had happened. Those who were of the first sort she saw when they visited Dachau.

> I noticed quite a few young people with their leader, a guide. And when I had a chance I asked him and he said, "This is my life now. I'm trying to atone for the sins of my parents. That's all I do is teach these young people what went on."

> In the meantime, I heard from everybody, from people who live around there during the Holocaust, and when I asked them, they said they didn't know anything about it. How can you live around buildings with ovens and not know about it?

> [Q: How close were they?]

> Across the street. "Oh," they said, "they saw some political prisoners around there." So I asked this teacher. He said "Lady, don't believe anything they say. They're all lying."

To her, the heartless inurement of those living near the more than three hundred German camps, and the larger death camps in Poland, could not be overlooked.

> I can't forgive that. I can't do that. Maybe forgive but not forget. So I have... kind of distanced myself from everything that happened in Germany. I just have no more feeling for it.

She was further estranged from the way the past was being handled in Germany by the general public who they ran into on their visits.

> The German children know nothing about that [the Holocaust]. 'Til that movie, that tacky movie, what was the name of that?

> [Q: Shoah?]

> Yah. 'Til they made that, and they saw it in Germany. That's the first time

a lot of Germans even knew what was going on.

> On the plane [over to Germany], one German student was sitting next to my husband, and they got into a conversation, and she said she was studying for one year before she went back to teach. How they got to history I don't know. And then he said, "We hope that as a teacher you will let the children know what really happened." And she said, "What happened?" My husband said "Well, you're talking about the Holocaust now, about Hitler invading all those countries." She said, "Hitler invaded Poland to help the Poles because they were in such bad shape. He had to help them." This is what they believe, and that's a teacher. What can you do about that?

Her sense of alarm was not relieved by what she saw on these visits. A belligerent chauvinism was not uncommon, reminding her of what she had fled fifty years before.

> We were in Russia last year, and the last stop was Berlin again. This was the second time, and a person [German] got to talking with them, and we were talking about the war [WW-II], and several people said to me, "You just wait. When that wall [in Berlin] comes down and we're unified, we'll get strong, and we'll take our territory back!"

For those like Ruth who had been lucky enough to escape and then return, there was a sense of dread, of watching something ominous unfold once again that no one seemed to notice; of shouting alarm and hearing only silence.

> Even when Hitler marched into the Rhineland, everybody knew that if they had fought him, he would have drawn back. He said so. But nobody did anything. Nobody.

Her father had served in the German cavalry in WW-I. She had two uncles who were in that war who had been hailed as heroes. All became, in the 1933-45 period, "lousy Jews." Though she was happy about her life in America since 1939, she is angry about the past in Germany, wary for the future. Some part of the grief is always with her.

> There isn't a day that I don't remember. Once you have lost somebody and you were lucky enough to escape, you can't ever get over that.

DISCUSSION
For women survivors in this chapter--Bertha, Vera, Elsie, Polla and Ruth, took strength from the relationships that sprang up during their

ordeal. They configured their daily existence less in terms of the physiological deprivation which threatened to overwhelm them at any time, than in describing what was happening in terms of patterns of interaction with those around them. These patterns were influenced by values celebrated in their family life of the past which they extended to embrace one another in community. Their cooperation and caring were informed by a belief in goodness and truth. Identity that for them supported the self under extreme threat was based on the limited interactional involvements from which the survival metaphor could grow.

Looking at survival in terms of developing a self sustaining identity, each of the narratives contribute something to the idea of constructing the self by way of meeting the challenge of the moment. Bertha learned immense compassion during captivity and to extend to an ever more inclusive range of others. Using inner discursive strategies which maximized values from the past, she determined to not grow cynical; nor would she allow herself the hate so evident in that camp context. When she was released, despite the aching pain that went with loneliness and grieving for the family murdered, she carried on, got a job, formed a Zionist group, and made her beliefs constructively reshape a bleak external reality. The child weeping for her mother on the way to Birkenau was transformed into a woman acting for her people. Vera also developed a strong pattern of identity under challenge which suddenly showed itself, seemingly without prior elaboration, at Plaszow as she worked energetically to help not just herself and her mother but the community of women survivors around her. Elsie was the optimist and humorist who found stories to bolster others and inspire a limited solidarity with those around her. Modestly, but with grace and sophistication, she analyzed a situation bereft of all but tragedy, and turned it into manna for the wounded soul. Polla by helping and working with the other prisoners in the Russian camps underwent a personal transformation. While at the start of her lifestory Polla showed herself to be headstrong, independent, and idealistic, in the Russian prison camp system she became a careful mother, nurse, and friend, one who could listen to others. She could take risks, could follow as well as lead, bear doubt and sorrow as well as gladness. Ruth formed a challenged identity as she tried to deal with the upheaval in her personal life brought on by Nazism in Germany of the 1920s and 30s. She used reason and critical insight to take the stance of "rebel" against a sociopolitical reality she knew was primed for genocide. She worked with a natural tendency to confront problems. Full of fiery insight uncontaminated by illusion, she managed to save her nephew and herself.

All of these women became, in the process of surviving, transformers of reality, growing beyond their limitations to new depths of wisdom, inner strength and courage.

CHAPTER 6

ADULTS--THE YOUNG MEN

> In the sick bay of the Lager at Buna-Monowitz eight hundred of us remained. Of these about five hundred died from illness, cold and hunger before the Russians arrived...
>
> The first Russian patrol came in sight of the camp about midday on 27 January 1945...
>
> They were four young soldiers on horseback, who advanced along the road that marked the limits of the camp, cautiously holding their sten-guns...
>
> They did not greet us, nor did they smile; they seemed oppressed not only by compassion but by a confused restraint, which sealed their lips and bound their eyes to the funereal scene. It was the shame we knew so well, the shame that drowned us after the selections, and every time we had to watch or submit to some outrage: the shame... that the just man experiences at another man's crime...
>
> Primo Levi, *The Reawakening*, 1965:1-2)

INTRODUCTION

At a time in the lifecourse when young men expect to be invested in corporate status and gain the social resources to act as protectors and providers for families, actual or potential, the survivors in this next chapter were stripped of everything. Family property was confiscated, citizenship was withdrawn, depth of lineage in community was treated with indifference, and they were publicly humiliated. Perhaps for these survivors who share their narratives with us here, the contexts of war and genocide became the ashes from which they grew to new strength, but they tell of friends and family who instead were swallowed up in ignominy and terror. Nor was it a safe and easy journey for each of them. David survived Auschwitz and ended up in Bergen-Belsen, Chaim survived the salt mines of Mauthausen, while Leon trained and served as a Partisan under the supervision of the Russian military. They ranged in age from sixteen to eighteen years at the start of their ordeal. David came from Transylvania, Chaim from Hungary, and Leon from Lithuania. Each was torn suddenly from the arms of normal family life in happy times to become objects of derision. Under the Nazis these survivors were the subjugated and exploited elements of the Third Reich--*tiermenschen*, life unworthy of life. Regardless of the obstacles confronting them in their ordeal, their narratives are about survival and transcendence.

MEN IN THE CAMPS
DAVID

David Leitner was born in Transylvania. He was thirteen years of age when the war broke out in 1939. By 1943, his area was exposed to the full brunt of German racist policy; by 1944, David and his family were being transported to Auschwitz. The round-up started in the early morning.

> Eichman came down in '43 and that's when they started rounding Jews up. January, February... and we were deported in the spring of 1944, in April. There was a knock on the door one Wednesday morning. I slept in the kitchen. European homes, they're very large homes. There's a back room and three bedrooms. Nine of us were living in this three-bedroom house, and there was a bed in the kitchen also. About six o'clock [in the morning] there was a knock on the door, and I see three bayonets, you know. There [was] a French door and it had drapes, curtains about this high [illustrates]. So I see the three bayonets--two Hungarian officers and one German. I don't remember their rank... doesn't matter. And they said to me, "I want you to go and get the whole family to the kitchen." And I did that. Mother, father, younger brother, older brother, grandmother, an aunt... We got to the kitchen, he made a short speech. He simply said, "Pack. You are allowed thirty pounds per person, and you have to be on the street within a half an hour."
>
> First we didn't know what to take. The kids got panicky. I didn't know whether I should take my soccer ball, my younger brother, whether he should take his games that he had. Women are always the practical ones. Mother said, "We have to eat, to sleep. We need food, clothes." So we get out all the food in the house, and we get out blankets and pillows that we had. And we went outside.

The officer had simply said "pack" and with this the end of their lives as a family began. The new laws of 1943 had meant months of social hardship for Jews. They were not allowed to take public transportation, and Jewish children were excluded from schools. But David's family felt they could endure these hardships and survive. In less than an hour this definition of the situation was nullified.

> The whole street was blocked because they did this simultaneously. Every door was knocked at in the morning. They did it so people didn't tip off

their neighbors. I lived in a city of twenty thousand people of which six or seven thousand were Jews.

The ghettoization process had begun. It was the first stage in what we now know as the Nazi *sonderbehandlung* in this Jewish neighborhood. But for those who were assembled, nothing was explained. Lies and euphemisms were used by the captors for purposes of crowd control. Mostly those rounded up were simply told what to do next--walk, get in trucks, stay in line--whatever it took to get that many frightened people into an orderly dispersement. Even with knowing so little, small ironies formed the puzzling contradictions that heightened their anxiety.

> They took us all to the synagogue. We used to play in that field behind it. We used to play soccer. That was the first time I was scared because I saw that [pause] there was something wrong with that scene. I saw old people, young people, disabled people, blind people, doctors, lawyers, postmen... It was scary. And everybody with long faces, dressed in black, some. You put on a lot of clothes, you know, because that did not get included in the thirty pounds.

The next stage was to get them to a farm where the entire population could be kept as a unit. It was offensive to be treated this way, but they acted as unarmed civilians often do in the face of violence and deadly threat--cautiously. They were many together facing the unknown, but not in disarray. They organized themselves almost immediately to take care of their many needs.

> They put us there. There was no provision for sanitation, no food, no kitchen. Nothing! They dumped us there.

> So we had to get organized. They pooled all the food. Everybody had to hand in their food so that it is shared. The doctors took the farmhouse and used it for a hospital. Nurses volunteered immediately. We had a population of seven thousand. They put up a police force so there was no looting and they dug ditches for sanitary purposes. And they set up a kitchen.

> Old people were allowed to sleep in the barn. Although it wasn't totally closed in, at least they had a roof over their heads. April you can get showers. It was raining continuously for the first two or three weeks of the gathering. And we slept outdoors. Everybody slept outdoors on the ground. Some people made tents with their blankets. It was hell. We were there for about four weeks. But at least you saw your relatives and your friends and you begin to say to yourself, "So what can they do to us?"

There was a false sense of safety in numbers. The community had been concentrated for ease of loading when the boxcars were available to ship them to selection points like Auschwitz.

> Finally the trains came. The Germans were on the Russian front... and the railroads were really busy. And they were not cattle trains because, as you know, cattle is transported in trains that has some air in it. You know, you cannot transport cattle to market in closed cars--nor turkeys. Some humane laws say it is unfit to put a turkey in that... *We were sent in closed cars.* There was just a little window with some barbed wire and each car had one of them for ventilation. There was no air, no food, no information. We didn't know which direction [we were going in], whether east, south, north. Then there was all the people who died--crying.

When they arrived at the unknown destination, the doors were thrown open, and suddenly a burst of light flooded in on them. The Nazis in polished boots and tailored uniforms were waiting with their dogs and whips on the platform outside the cars. Those inside were standing in the debris of their frightening journey, their vulnerability striking an unfavorable contrast.

> So finally we got to Auschwitz. You didn't see too many German officers. I saw maybe two or three. They walked around with a leather whip like you see in these movies... supermen from outer space almost.
>
> Most of the work was done by little... by inmates, by those who came before us, you know--French, Jews, Ukrainians, political prisoners and what not. So we were asked to get off and step in a line and that's where the selection took place. Those who were capable of work, they were in [one line] and the others were gassed and they were burnt.
>
> My Dad was a young man, only forty-one years old. He was put in the gas chambers. My youngest brother went with Mother to his death. I surv... I was only sixteen at the time... I survived. So I was told by prisoners, "Say goodbye to your mother." I said, "Why? I'm going to see them tomorrow." They said, "Oh no." So I said, "What are you saying that for?" Someone answers, "Well, see those chimneys? Right this very minute she went to the shower. They're being gassed and burned now."
>
> I thought at first, you know, that they spoke lies. They had been there four or five years and we had just got there. But it was obvious pretty soon that it was a death factory. You could smell the burning flesh, especially if the

wind blew from the east.

The selections negated their existence. In quiet lines they filed away to what they did not know--children, mothers, grandmothers, older men. It happened too fast to attribute meaning or locate discernible patterns. David remembered two of his five cousins standing behind him. One was a young mother.

> At the beginning, if a young woman, say twenty [years old], had a baby, they took the baby and gassed it because they knew the mother could work. See, remember the Germans were short of manpower by this time, so every able body was in the war effort. So they needed the women. [But if] they took the baby away, that caused a problem because most women would not give up their child and there was a tug of war. They [the inmates] were grabbing the children away, the mothers wouldn't let them. So, orders came in 1943 not to argue with the mothers. If they want to keep the babies, let them go to their deaths with the babies.

> I had a cousin... had five cousins at Auschwitz. We were standing behind the rest [getting off the cars]. Rose was the oldest. She was married with a child. She was about twenty-two. Raisa was sixteen or seventeen and she was single of course. Rose was holding the baby in her arms and the baby was crying. So Raisa says, "Rose, why don't you give me the baby?" She goes to her death and Rose survives!

David started out by saying that one thing survivors had in common was luck, but it was a mixed blessing-- beloved others perished while they had lived. He had chosen to sit in an ill-lit corner of the living room so that the chance breach of a tear would not betray his stoic composure. But the tears came anyway, softly in his voice and in unbidden pauses.

When his family got off the freight cars at Auschwitz his parents were gassed immediately while three brothers and a sister survived selections. Only he and his sister lived to return home. Survival hinged on so little. There were no distinctive behaviors which unequivocally held survival value. A chance act, seemingly insignificant, could mean the difference between life and death. David spoke of how such an anomaly separated his survival trajectory from his brothers.

> [We were standing in groups at the selection] one group here another group there, doctors and lawyers here... When they said "cabinetmakers" I volun... I was standing with my two brothers, you know when they said "cabinetmakers" [setting up a work detail]. I put my hand up. So I went with

the cabinetmakers. I left my two brothers there. That was the first act of self preservation that I... I... performed. If I had stayed with them, I could have perished the way they did, or I could have saved them. I have to live with that. But that was a selfish act.

His brothers and he were separated from that point on. David went to a work camp in the Auschwitz complex which used his skill in carpentry on various work details; his brothers were sent to a sub-camp of Mauthausen. In the slave labor system of the Nazi camps, not having a needed skill could mean your death. Being the oldest, David had acquired one, his younger brothers had not. In light of their eventual death, his being alive made him feel guilty of something; his choosing to live was reflected in simply showing he was a carpenter.

In the context of a death camp, the will to live which in ordinary times we take for granted, fell under scrutiny. It is difficult to imagine having no choice or a choiceless choice (Rittner and Roth 1993). It is natural for humans to assume the option of control even in situations where they really have none. David needed to believe he could have done more. Perhaps his unwillingness to accept being bested by circumstance was a character trait he gained in childhood. As a very young boy, and the first child of very young parents struggling to eke out a living, he had been sent to live with more established relatives, never staying long with any of them.

His mother and father had met and married in their late teens. His father had come from a rabbinical lineage but had left home at an early age to make his own way. David's mother, already a talented seamstress when she married, kept the family together with the little extra she earned. By the time he was five or six years old, his mother decided that it would be helpful for them if David were to stay with her relatives who were doing a little better than they were.

> The reason I was picked to go away, I am told by my older sister later on, was that I was appealing to strangers [knew how to get along]. I was quite cute. And my mother just thought that, with five children, I was the most likely to make it on my own. My mother gives me six pennies. A penny to buy a pencil, a penny to buy and eraser, and another penny to buy a postcard, and, "I want you to write once a month." They used to get these postcards already stamped, so. "And a Monday you go to uncle Simon's, a Tuesday you go to uncle Moishe's, and a Wednesday..." Every day I ate at a different place. I was there for one full year by myself. Six years old. I was so small, they put together two chairs with a pillow and a coat. That's what I slept in. And I went to Hebrew school there.

He had finished elementary school by the time laws prohibiting Jews from attending high schools and universities were enacted. His mother, not to be outdone by this turn of events, decided that David could still take cabinet-making and get ahead with his life.

> So I finished grade seven. That's as far as I went to school there. So my mother says, "You will learn a trade. It's something." So I went back to this little town [to train as a cabinetmaker].

By the time the knock came at the door in the early morning asking them to assemble in the street, David had completed his trade and was working at cabinet-making, earning a little money and, finally, at home with everyone together.

> Once I graduated from a trade in cabinetmaking, I went home. In 1943, I went home and I stayed home. Actually, those were my happiest days, because I was working as a cabinetmaker; I was making a little bit of money. It was nice to be in the family again. I missed out on a lot [as a child]. I was away from the ages of six to seven and a half, and I was away again from the age of thirteen to sixteen, you know. So I missed out on all this. I just took things as they were, you know. But in the Spring of '44 [I was at home again], that's how I happened to be sleeping in the kitchen... I happened to be there when they knocked on the door.

Because of being thrown on his own resources at a young age he had learned to remain open, flexible and even spirited while not controlling what was happening. More than any other feature of his biography this may have given him a sense of timing and savvy that helped him survive the concentration camps. He described a relationship he formed as part of this.

> A friend of mine and I teamed up so that we sort of hedged our bets. He would steal one day, and I would steal the other. He was standing behind me when I got tattooed, you know and I'm 12373 and he's 12374. So we kind of teamed up and we had a deal going whereby like at twelve o'clock sharp, the horn would sound. Dinner... lunch was served, if you like, which consisted... there was a... a SS officer downstairs with a barrel of soup, cabbage soup or whatever, and people ran upstairs and stood in line to get the soup to be the very first in line. Run upstairs, hide it under a bench and run down again and stand on line the second time. I did it once, he did it once. Now this was risky 'cause if they recognized me, you got a bullet...you-me. Or if somebody squealed, you got the bullet. We always changed. For instance, if you had

the jacket on the first time, you had the jacket off a second time around. I went one day, Marvin went the other day.

The metaphor of gamesmanship continued in the narrative downplays the risk involved. "Teamed up" is used rather than "organized," "had a deal going on," rather than "we were downtrodden and had to try something." David's choice of terms could be describing a game of poker. Such discursive stratagems masked survivors' vulnerability and limited agency in the trauma context. It also underscores the importance of self-pride to those utterly diminished. When asked about the importance of cooperation and helpfulness to survival, David dismissed the idea. Like many concentration camp survivors the overwhelming bitterness of camp existence made these virtues seem puny, valid only for other realities. Instead, he saw assertiveness or aggressiveness as having survival value there--the aggressive person found the means to survive using whatever means were at hand. But David was patient, wise, forbearing-- not aggressive. Fifty years after release from the camps, David was still not ready to give an unequivocal statement on what it took to survive a condition that went beyond known limits of terror. Nor would he acknowledge resistance or "organizing" as realistic options for captives. He was willing to accept the notions of risk and luck. "Winning" a limited goal, "not getting caught" were what the situation might bear. Moreover, the imagery propelled him.

> Never got caught! Never got caught!! It worked.

> You would see, we had so-called selections every month or so. We had to... we were examined by a doctor. We weren't examined [as in a physical]. We went through a corridor and [the "doctor"] kept a stick in his hand and anybody that showed ribs, they'd yank them out of the line up, not to be seen again. They were replaced with stronger ones, you know, and... that's... I used to be afraid of [this], you know.

Though he would not refer to it as "organizing," David would sneak into the kitchen and take potatoes or whatever could be found around the soldier's mess when it was relatively safe to do that. When asked if he considered that resistance, David replied,

> No. [Laughs] That was a form of self preservation. Resistance? I was so afraid of the Germans, you have no idea. I was beaten up once by an officer. Curfew was at seven o'clock sharp and I was maybe fifty seconds off. He caught me. I was running into the block, and he caught me and gave me such a

beating. I'm telling you... I lost three teeth and my nose was out of joint, and he only gave me one, with his fist into my face. I was terrorized when I saw SS. There was no way I wanted to tangle with this. Perhaps this is why I am here today.

He acknowledged that there was organized resistance but judged it a form of suicide. At the very least he considered it a rare event. Resistance was for those who had extraordinary strength and courage along with the vision of noble rebels. Resistance seemed to be for David something of a spiritual stance. At Auschwitz-Birkenau he had seen this kind of greatness in the distance as his fellow prisoners were punished for blowing up one of the crematoria.

> It was three in the afternoon. The sirens were blowing [pause] and we didn't hear any planes. So why the sirens? The sirens were blowing because they wanted us to go back to the camps where they had control over us, you see. Because we used to sleep and eat in the camps and work outside the camps. So by bringing us in there, they had control over us. They didn't need the manpower. The manpower were needed to go and fight sonderkommandos, and I understand that there is three or four SS that were shoved into the fire. And next day there was several hundred girls that were actually working in the munitions factory [whose participation was essential to the uprising], and they had them stand outside in the cold and snow for some twenty-four hours because the girls decided that they'll either kill us all or they'll let us live, but there is nobody who is going to admit to this thing. Finally seven girls stepped forth and they hung them-- in the men's camp.

The women working in the munitions factory had smuggled gunpowder to the men for the resistance operation. The explosion was successful, and the rebel sonderkommandos did accomplish a form of vindication against the SS. These men were killed but did not reveal the identities of the women accomplices. As David witnessed, these seven women were hanged where it might do the most emotional damage to other captives. He quietly reverenced them. Active resistance in the camps was rare because of the likelihood of outright failure. It seemed wisest, David thought, to have few ties and take no action whatsoever except what could be risked for physical survival.

> I had a lot of things going for me in addition to being [even] tempered; [one of these was] living on my own. A father who knew that his wife and children were gassed yesterday was totally destroyed psychologically. He gave up immediately. But not so the children who knew that their fathers and mothers were gassed. Therefore, there were more survivors among the young [as he was]

than were among the older, even though they [the elders] were smarter, physically probably more fit and all that, they had more experience, all that did not help. The will to live wasn't there after their family went.

Though there was little opportunity to expand social relations in the camp, even so there were shared understandings and sympathetic identification among the victims, which helped them. He felt marginal to a lot of it, but it was there.

> I used to look forward to our ration. That was my... You know, "What time is it? Another hour, two hours from now we get our ration." That was the main thing. There was absolutely nothing from the day we got up 'til we went to sleep at night that I could say [was social life]. We couldn't play cards. I wasn't a believer. Some guys would read the Bible, stuff like that. Pray? I couldn't do that. I didn't have the confidence to do that. There was no joking. There were discussions among adults which I did not partake in. Politics? I was afraid to open my mouth. There was a band that we all marched to on the way to work in the morning, and at night there was a band, a brass band. It was there for us to march in unison so they could count us. We were all counted when we left. We were all counted when we returned.

Though David did not participate, among those sharing the barracks there were discussions, some music, prayer, political debates and some observed religious holidays. Similarly, birthdays might sometimes be remarked. Stories would be told and retold to commemorate someone's bravery or wit, or highlight the best way to optimize one's chances in a crisis. What was lacking in this death camp context was an atmosphere in which these actions, which normally celebrated the self, could offer any real sense of pleasure; there was too much fear, grief, and repression.

He had been in the camps for a little over a year and remained "a virgin" throughout. But while there was little that could pass for sexual interaction amongst the inmates he knew, there was a lot of talk whenever some of the camp "elite" sought out new excitement. "When you are starving, sex is not on the list of priorities," he averred. But some in the camp were not starving; being "discovered" by them meant that David got, for one quick interlude, a very welcome hot water bath and a window on a world within a world.

> I was many times approached by gay people. Not forcibly. These were German intellectuals. Kind people. They happened to be gay, and they would wine you and dine you, and if you felt like it's worth it, you went for it, and if you didn't, you didn't. I had friends who befriended gays who were in high

positions, positions to help. And they went for it. And I would be the last person to condemn it. I myself was once approached and, to tell you the truth, I was so naive, I just didn't know what this man wanted from me. He invited me up to his office, and he gave me a tremendous meal and he said, "Would you like to have a bath?–We have one." "Oh my God. Would I ever!" you know, because it used to just be a wash in cold water in the morning. He said, "Okay I'll run it for you."

And he ran a bath for me. There was nice bubbles in there. It was nice and warm, and he says, "I'll wash your back." And then he washed my back. And he washed my front and he said, "I'll be back in a minute." While he was away, I got out of the bathtub, put on my clothes and, just as he was coming back he says, "Where are you going?" "Well, I got to get back to work." That was the end of that.

This kind of encounter could become a generator of gossip affirming what passed for a status system in the camps. Since Jews were a social category definitely slated for death, any among the dispossessed might surpass them. In this case, the reluctant target plumbed the moment with great caution. David continued with his work and kept in the background, simplifying his expectations to a minimum. At liberation, he weighed less than ninety pounds.

By winter 1945, a forced march was ordered from the Auschwitz-Birkenau complex to Melk, a sub-camp of Mauthausen. On the way, he and the other captives made overnight stops at several other camps.

We were hoping we would stay there and have the Russians liberate us. But no way. They took us... inhumane behavior... on this so-called march of death. At this time I didn't know it was an historic march. I thought it was just a march. It was Polish winter. Without food, without clothes, they walked us from Auschwitz to the Czechoslovakian border. Two days, two nights. It was sheer hell. People died on the way. People gave up. And, nobody was left alive if they couldn't march. Those were the orders. Keep up with the others and don't leave anybody behind. Keep up with the column.

So, there is people left and right. So it was just from one camp to another. They kept pushing us back and forth. Each camp was worse than the next. Finally, I ran into the camp where my two brothers were.

I was so happy when I got there. I ran into some people from my hometown. I says, "Hey! Where are my two brothers?" And they say, "Yes, they're here." And I couldn't go back to see them because they had locked us in after curfew. Next morning, I was told by those close to them that they ... they didn't make it. See, they didn't know they were dead. And, finally this place also got

> liquidated. I was by this time weighing forty kilograms [roughly eighty pounds]. I gave up really. I was just... My brothers died. I said, "What's the use? I'm not going to last anyhow."

He was in despair with the news. It completely drained him of his remaining energy. Loss of family was something he commented on directly throughout the interview. He knew engaging in strong feelings could deplete a person's existing reserves; he had seen physically strong men who lost their families give up and die, but he could not alter what he felt. Had liberation not come when it did, he believed he could not have endured much longer. But it did come.

> The Americans were moving fast towards our camp, and one day we just heard the tanks come up the hill. This gorgeous Austrian little city was on a plateau and you could see the highway and we all got up [to see] and this thing... tank... with the American [star] approached the gates, and instead of going through the gates, he [the driver] just backed up and went right through the fence, you know. Destroyed it! This was something like a message to us, a symbolic gesture to have us believe or convince us that we were free people, because there was a lot of people who had trouble accepting this. We just got there a couple of weeks ago, but there were some who had been there five, six, seven or eight years [in the KZ system] and it was hard for them to accept the fact that they were free.

> So we were told not to do anything that would jeopardize our health, our stomachs [had] shrunk, and to wait 'til tomorrow as a crew of dieticians [were on there way]. There was an outfit called UNRA, United Nations Rehabilitation,--something like that. It was some governmental agency that wouldn't... and they took tremendous care [of us]. God bless them, all these people.

He was liberated in June and by August was strong enough to travel back to Transylvania. His sister returned there shortly after. It was a difficult homecoming for them. They were the only survivors among his family of seven. Only memory would at this juncture bring all of them together again. What made it even worse was the fact that the family home was no longer "their's." When they were taken captive, in the spring of 1944, the houses and property of those "resettled" from his neighborhood had been confiscated by the Nazi state and allotted to others.

> When I went home, I entered the kitchen, the very same kitchen, and I entered the room, and I just stood there and I looked. And the furniture was all gone, and there was another room off from it. The door was still the same.

> And she [new owner] kept sending me looks I didn't understand, "Can I help you? What is it you want?"
>
> I stood there and... and for a minute I saw the room the way it was over three years ago with my mother by the stove and the bed and the credenza over there.
>
> And she [the present occupant]... "What is it you want? Can't you talk to me?"
>
> And I just broke down and cried and ran out of there and never returned. *I don't want any part of this.* There is nothing here that I want to see, that I want to do. Start from scratch.

Once more the family of his youth slipped away from him, this time in a shroud of tears--out of reach, gone forever. His longing to find home once again was symbolized in the image of his mother; his bitter loss was summoned in the specter of the stranger replacing what had been his.

> So those were the hard times when you were faced with the reality... you went back to the same kitchen and you... and all of a sudden reality sets in, and you see another woman, not your mother, and you're just a nobody. You're on the outside. *You don't belong here*, you know. You don't belong here.

He crossed from Hungary, then into Austria and eventually France. In Paris he found out that the XX- Jewish Congress were taking one thousand people under eighteen years of age into North America and placing them with local families. Officials were having a difficult time locating people to fit these specifications because so many had been gassed. So even though the age specification did not exactly fit him, David found room for himself and his sister with a group of young survivors heading westward to North America.

At the start of his new life he set up a business in a town where the landscape was filled with mile after mile of wheat and rich farmland. He married a woman who was born there, and they had three sons. Today, David is admittedly very happy and successful. He has flourished, transcending the past in many ways but not forgetting it, still dealing with the scars.

> I broke down three times in the last forty-four years. The first time was when I went home [after liberation]. That was the first time. The second time, I was in Israel. I was looking for the camps where my brothers were killed. Yad Vashem has a place with the "Eternal Light," and I think they

[have records on] about twenty-five camps there. And I was looking for Melk and I couldn't find it, and I ran out and I started to cry. *There isn't even a place for them on this earth.* No one will ever know that they ever existed. I went into the office. I started to yell. I says, "How dare you have a memorial here for the camps and yet have nothing for my brothers to tell us where they perished?" And the other time I told my wife, I said, "I don't understand why... but that's it, yesterday's news, new chapter."

Part of the pain such a survivor faces is the unassuaged sense that there will never be justice for what happened; what was done can neither be reversed nor vindicated. He shared very little of the past with his wife who had wanted so much to learn of his experiences. David believed in keeping the past and present as far apart as possible. He treasured the memories of his parents' world in which he grew to manhood. But the sights and sounds of the camps like a million shards of glass litter the path between these worlds.

I keep recalling events, sounds and sights, as vividly as if they happened yesterday. The sound of steel on steel as they opened up the door at Auschwitz, the sliding steel door. Bang! against the steel. The sound of the railroad wheels. You know how the rail is... is... bumps up against each other, and when the wheel hits that where its joined, it makes clickety-clack, clickety-clack noise. That noise bangs in my head.

To this day the sight of seven thousand people in this ghetto... And the sight of the last day in the camps when everybody was half dead and people would just fall out of their bed, you know. Or, if they didn't fall out, the others... there were three to one bed, so if one died, they would shove him out of bed. And I still see those skeletons at the end of the barracks piled up like sardines. They were still breathing when they put them there. I can still see people up against the wires, electrocuted.

It's amazing how I didn't really deal with this before. It never even... but recently it has been coming in. Perhaps it's why I'm talking about it. [Pause] The sights and sounds and smells, they keep coming back.

I've seen people [pause] being beaten. I've seen certain girls that were hung in our camp. I see them hanging. Beautiful girls, their heads shaven. [Pause] They hung them. There is a sign on them. "This will happen to anyone who defies the Third Reich." I remember the girls that were in our camp to entertain the German soldiers. There was one [pause] blonde. Whenever we came home from work or went to work they were always up on top. Pretty little girls. And they were there to keep the soldiers happy.

Adults--The Young Men

He stayed in touch with his best buddy in the camps over the years. They had both made it to North America, but were thousands of miles apart. They had each gone their separate ways. But in the camps they felt the bitterness of good faith betrayed in every sense by every part of the human community.

> We fantasized about being free, about having all the food in the world, doing what we wanted to do. And there's one thing we decided. If we ever survive, we would never be Jewish again! We would simply melt into the population and live like the rest of the world. "Why shouldn't we?" we said to each other. "What did Judaism do for us? It got us into this mess." "Why are we here? Sixteen, seventeen years old, what have we done to deserve this? Because we're Jews. And through the centuries Jews have suffered." We said, "Why?" We agreed, "Finished!"

These remonstrations born of anguish and pain have now faded. Today he and his friend are both active participants in the traditions of Judaism. They practice their faith in different ways, however. His friend got involved in Jewish orthodoxy, while David's gentle love of diversity and tolerance led him toward a more conventional expression of their faith.

> We call each other up at least once or twice a year. He's got four children. He's got a son a doctor-- brilliant young man. His daughter is a lawyer. Then they have one "black sheep" sort of hippie type--she wants to be an artist. She moved in with somebody.

> The Orthodox people live by a set of rules... they're very, very strict you know, and then they will not accept children who do not... and he hopes that some day she is going to turn... he just won't tolerate... which is sad.

Tolerance is a touchstone for David's life. He believed we have to care for each other as members of different ethnicities, religions, and lifestyles as well as within the family.

> We ought to care for our brothers because... for...for the human race. Speak up if there is... if there is any injustice done anywhere, because the world now is very small.

> Nobody spoke up for us during the Holocaust. Nobody did. Neighbors didn't; governments didn't.

His favorite space at home still seemed to be the kitchen, for both himself and his wife. They rounded out the interview there with cheering conversation, high spirits, strong coffee, and a wonderful homemade apple pie. Hanging on the wall of his spacious living room was the work of an Israeli artist. The subject was shtetl life. Its focus, a rabbi and his son. It was his silent tribute to his parents' world.

CHAIM

Chaim Feldman was born in Satoraljaujhely, on the Hungarian border with Czechoslovakia, to a very religious family. He was raised in the Hasidic tradition. His family ran a dairy farm which had four cows. Twelve people had shared his childhood home: two parents, one grandmother, three sisters and five brothers and himself. One sister and three brothers survived transport to Auschwitz. His sister survived Ravensbruck; Chaim and one of his brothers survived Mauthausen. The third brother was rescued by Raoul Wallenburg who was then with the Swedish embassy in Budapest.

Chaim was the youngest child in the family. He worked hard both on the farm and at school. He began learning the alphabet and aspects of religious life at an early age.

> So I was three. I remember my father took me on his arm, brought me down to the school and took me to the teacher, and the very same day, we started. Teacher took me aside, and the first three letters of the [Hebrew] alphabet-- they had put chocolate on it. He had already cut out [the letters] and we [ate] them.

> In one year we already read fluently in Hebrew. Oh, everything in Hebrew. By the age of six, I already studied the Talmud. It's just like a body of law. I may not have comprehended the deep meaning of every difficult passage to a point of law, but it started there. It's just like a chip, a microchip. Later on, I utilized it. It was all there when I started to understand more in life.

By age six he went to one of the two public schools run by the community. He studied in the Hasidic tradition, attending public school in the morning and Hebrew school in the afternoon. They worked hard and lived simply.

> My father brought up his family on four cows. Relatively speaking, we were rich compared to neighbors. The cows, the four cows, were not to give us milk every morning, but to sell, and from the little money... to live on it. I delivered every morning the milk and butter that my mother was making. I

never ate it. And I was jealous of the other kids. How come I deliver the milk to them? And I come home and I asked my mother, "I saw on their bread there was honey, jam and butter. How come I have not even bread?" So my mother said, "That's the way God wants it!" [laughing]

He felt proud of their self-reliance and strength. It toughened him to have to stand up against the odds like this. Religion had leant sanctity to their idealism and dignified their humble way of life on many levels. It had brought order and nuance to a spartan lifestyle.

> Our happiest day was the Sabbath because our whole week's effort was towards one goal. The whole week was very dreary. Even as a child, I spent [a lot of time] at school. But in addition to all this, I had from the age of eight... I was part of the economic unit, too. So, since early morning, I went out and cut hay. At noon, I had a half hour, I went out to the field... it wasn't too far... and turned the hay. I saw the sun go, in the evening collecting it. When the Sabbath came, [pause] no matter how, no matter what, the house was full of light.

> My sister always lit ten candles. I don't know how she could afford it, but there was never shortage of candles. Always there. We worked towards it all week, towards Friday, to be able to get a chicken. And my mother was such a master. For one chicken, she had to make five times a meal for ten people. So maybe a little wing here a little throat there. But it was happy and light... And, on the Sabbath we went to synagogue in the morning, the whole family. We came back singing and dancing. We went out to the fields looking after the sheep and the cows. And, my buddies, we went out to the field [practicing] the high jump. This kind of thing.

> It was like any other childhood. Money to buy a ball, we didn't have, but we had lots of socks that we tied together, made a football out of it. So this was the way we were.

Anti-Semitism clouded all inter-ethnic relations. Religion condoned it. The ordinary tiffs and misunderstandings of childhood peers were expressed in terms of religion's dynamics.

> They were [others boys] singing some funny songs that were about Jews-- "dirty stinking Jew." They made a song out of it.

Chaim was well conditioned physically by farm work and not slow to take the advantage when the cause was just and a fight was on. This put him at odds with his father, who believed in turning the other cheek, or at least taking a different way home. Chaim laughed at this now.

> Somehow, some reason, when they approached me, I didn't wait for them to make the first move [laughing]. I got the first punch. Because I am going my way. If you guys want to fight, you'll get it. So I used to go home with torn shirts, and then I got more from my father because he couldn't afford to buy me shirts, you see. He always told me, "When you see them, go to the other side of the street." So I told him, I says, "What?! Why should I go on the other side? He's no different from me. Just because I have two earlocks!"
>
> This was his [father's] lifestyle. He was the same person on the way to Auschwitz. Didn't realize. He was so imbued with religion, that God was good to him all the time. And my argument with him you see was, if somebody is... I believe in self-defense.

For the family, everyday problems loomed larger than the sociopolitical issues generated regionally and globally. Their religion forbade them to have radios and newspapers. They knew little of what was happening around them. So while Chaim was dealing in his own way with age peers, he was growing up almost completely within the dramas of his father's world. There was a healthy relationship between the two of them, each respecting the other's symbolic domain.

> I don't recall ever talking to him as an adult, one to one, because always he was very stern and strict. And he was very proud. I was a little son of a gun. So, obviously, I being mischievous and bad, a son of a gun. I was #8 and my father had problems how to feed us--he needed to be tough with me. I guess I got too much energy. But he was very proud of me. Each time he came to school, hearing all the praises I got and the prizes. My name was in the teacher's book always with block letters, you know. Those who got A's always, their name was on the class list in block letters. So he was very proud.

He was very proud of his religion and its tradition; conflicts with outsiders only served to enhance his solidarity with community. "My circle of friends were not Gentiles," he said. Yet despite this, he did help bring both communities together across their divisions when he organized a town athletics fair. He was this proud of who he was, knowing he would bring honor upon his father's house by acknowledging the other.

> We organized them [the games] ourselves in the summer, the Christian kids and myself. I proved to them that in high jumping and in broad jumping and in 100 meter dash, I'm better than they are. And we had this competition and [my father] didn't like this either. This was the only interaction that I had

with them. I did get some respect afterwards from my peers.

He was unabashed in his joy at setting ambitious goals and reaching them. He was also a budding financier at an early age. He would find ways to exchange something he had for an item worth more in trade and keep this up until he got a fair little sum. He would sell candies at school, and though such activity was frowned upon, it gave him an edge in the father-son bond.

> You know, my biggest kick was that I, a little smarkotch, as they say in Yiddish, a nobody... On Wednesday, since the age of eight and a half years, my father comes to me, "Can you give me a few pennies to buy flour for the Sabbath to make a white bread?" To me!! [With this acknowledgement] I was king, you see!

He was seventeen years of age when he and his parents were put on the first transport out of their city to an unknown destination, which turned out to be Auschwitz. The last words his father shared with him on the way had to do with comporting himself honorably as he had been taught to do.

> I remember my father asked me to remain Jewish. By that he meant living like one and a few other things. [Sighs]. Three things he told me: not to sign up for anybody, not to mix too much in politics, and to remain Jewish.

German tanks had entered his town out of Kosice in Czechoslovakia on March 19, 1944. At first they had taken forty hostages, representing a third of Jews in the town, demanding money. Two different collections were taken up in order to meet the extorters' demands, but the hostages were never released. Instead, the whole population of Jews were rounded up a few days later.

> They came in. They gave an order that everybody should be ready this morning to get... to go into the ghetto. They took four streets and established that this is going to be the ghetto. If a Christian happened to be living in that area, he had to move out. They forbade us to take anything other than what's on your back and one or more pairs of pants if you want. We were in a [modest] house, around ten families. Three days after, they allowed me to go back and bring at least two cows to the ghetto so that for the children there will be milk.

The ghetto had been created March 24, 1944. There was little they could do as civilians against a fully organized army. Even people with some weaponry found themselves outmaneuvered and terrorized. Brutal examples taught them obedience.

> In my hometown was a big jail. A lot of Partisans, Yugoslav Partisans ended up there. Somehow a breakout was organized. They had weapons. They were trained. I wasn't a soldier. I was a kid. I saw them in the afternoon being brought back on big wagons with shot heads, piled up in the wagons. Killed them. So. Where could you run? If they couldn't make it, where could I go? I remember the next day when the Germans came in, my next door neighbor's kid was pointing "Jude! Jude! Jude!" The general population was very anti-Semitic. You couldn't go anywhere anyways because you can't fight with your bare hands against machine guns.

All this had happened the day before the town's six thousand Jews were assigned to the ghetto. Nevertheless, small acts, symbolic of escape and resistance, could be risked, and Chaim got a chance to try.

> I worked with the cows for the ghetto, and I stole away my mother's jewelry because I had a feeling that something not good [was brewing], and I buried it in that barn where the cows were. I said, "Maybe if I come back, I'll find it."

There was very little to eat for the few weeks they shared the ghetto. They were not organized for a long sojourn. By early April, the Jewish ghetto was cleared. People were rounded up again and marched to the synagogue.

> Around four o'clock in the morning, they come to the [ghetto] gate. "All rise!" And, to the synagogue courtyard. As we arrived to the synagogue, again the same story. Everybody had to empty everything just to make sure that no valuables are going out of town. Marched down to the railway station. We went in a wagon with about ninety-five in a wagon.

They had no way of understanding the overall plan. People were in a state of shock. As they were being loaded onto the cattlecars, authorities attempted to keep the whole operation out of sight, carrying out the whole operation in a large roundhouse area for the trains. The heat from the engines eventually made the cars unbearable.

> In order to take away the semblance of human feelings, dignity, right away on the railway station they pulled into a big hanger, and they closed the

hanger after the train was in it, and they didn't put in gas, but heat was such, they must have put heat in there. It was intolerable, and many died right there, before even the train moved away from my hometown.

As captives, they could do little more than suffer the abuse. Three days later the transport arrived in Auschwitz. As the doors opened, Chaim jumped out. One of the inmates meeting the train spoke to him in Yiddish, telling him that he would be asked two questions: one was his age--answer eighteen; the other was his profession-- answer farmer. Chaim complied. After the selection on the railway platform, Chaim went in one direction, his parents the other. His group of young men were then taken and processed. Afterwards, they stood outside waiting for uniforms and shelter.

> That night we arrived, before getting our clothes, naked they kept us for thirty-six hours in the rain. And the way we kept warm, we huddled. I still have a spot on my lung from that night. Raining. You can imagine, the beginning of April in Poland, in the cold. And that night, we heard all the shouting from the next barricade. They were German Gypsies. They killed them all the same night.

> Next day we got our striped pants and a jacket and also striped shirt. They were lining us up all the way, asking this and that. They wanted volunteers. I said "I volunteer nowhere." I was just standing my ground because you don't know what volunteering means. Finally... I think I was altogether four days at Auschwitz... again, line us up... train... this time we were travelling towards Austria. Near Linz... twenty kilometers from Linz... there is a place called Mauthausen [this is where they stopped].

Chaim spent the rest of his internment at Gusen II. Gusen was a little town which had two different camps near it. The more primitive one, which had to be constructed when the prisoners arrived, was the one to which Chaim was sent. The inmates were given a number which was stamped at various parts of their body for individual identification in case only body parts were recoverable after a mishap. The work pace was vicious.

> At a town called St. George was a mountain. Our job was to dig into the mountain and build the airplane plant. I must tell you that in one year we built a whole city underground. Why underground? Because the American reconnaissance came everyday, and they bombed us. But they didn't harm us because the material in this mountain was like salt. The tunnels were reinforced with concrete. So they bombed us--never with any success. It was

called Herman Goerring Werk.

It was heavy, rough work. Sometimes it involved displacing large chunks of rock by hand. Chaim worked the jack hammer. There was very little food for the prisoners, and even this small amount varied with how well things were going on the war front. When things were going well for Germany, there was a third of a loaf of bread per person per day. When things went badly, there was one-eighth of a loaf per person, usually supplemented by half cooked beet leaf soup which Chaim suspected of contributing to the dysentery in the camp. Starvation itself has many complex symptoms (Helwig-Larsen, Hoffmeyer, Kielar et al., 1952); diarrhoea is among them. To control the diarrhoea Chaim ate charcoal which he could pick up as he jumped out of the wagon that brought them to the tunnel each day. He said it tasted like margarine and was brown like peat. More than starvation moved him to this strategy.

> It was such a horrible thing to see one or two of my teachers and they... they didn't make it. Because once you get it...that was the biggest killer... They [camp authorities] say anybody who feels he cannot work... is sick... should come and, "we will take him back to a good place," you know. They put them back [to the death camp]! I never saw them after. I remember a neighbor of mine, I begged him, "Don't go. Stay." He and his son both of them gone. They had no problem getting more people. They used to come... more, and more, and more.

Seemingly innocent choices and diseases of simple origin preyed upon the exhausted prisoners so that they ended up at the camp "hospital" to be picked up and disposed of at extermination station. He said he had watched others from his town, teachers, other professionals and religious leaders, die the slower kind of death, watching those they love perish. But he also witnessed other kinds of cruel deaths of neighbors.

> My... my family's dentist, they knocked him down there [in the camps]. It was in Gusen. And... they put a two-by-six [2 x 6 plank] on his neck. Somebody had to stand on it. Poor guy just choked. His stomach became like this [illustrates] bloated. That was his fun, the SS. Chaim tried not to let the anguish of watching this wear him down. He used lessons and practices treasured in the past to steady him in the camp.

> Survivors depended on will--strong will, and being young, and not to take it seriously in your head--that was very important. Not to think of this. I never... I was either singing or reciting [prayer] during work. I was always

praying. Either it was for amusement, making it not so monotonous [or for something deeper]. When you do this for nine hours with that hammer... And also I organized services. I knew it by heart.

Built like a tank, he had an indomitable physique. He was a natural leader, but he also knew when to become unobtrusive--"I made like a little snail, hiding." Strong when others were weak and focused when the context was chaotic, he led himself and others through the worst of times. On the one hand, he organized Jews to celebrate Yom Kippur and other special days of the Jewish calendar or to just pray together. On the other hand, if a crisis happened at work, he took over. There were costs and benefits attached to this. For organizing prayer, he was given twenty-five lashes on the buttocks; for heroics at work, he gained the respect of everyone, both guards and inmates.

One night as I was working the nightshift, I was up digging. On the bottom was a rubber band, a conveyor belt that all the material that was coming down went on out of the tunnel to the courtyard. And somehow... the people whose job was to shovel for the conveyor belt, they either were out, they had no strength or... The main thing is the conveyor belt choked. When one conveyor belt stops the whole plant stops. So the SS comes [sighs] vrmmm vrmmm. When the work stops, they don't like it. They want to see what the source is. So finally guy looks up to me, calls me down. He says to me in German, "Jew! I want to see this shit in one minute gone." So, I was accustomed to [using] the scythe. I took a shovel from a guy who was maybe fifty pounds. He was already on his last days, and shovelled. That material was like salt. I just shovelled it. I don't think I made it in a minute, but in five. He called me aside after, when the thing moved again, took my number. From that day on I got every week ten cigarettes. [Pause] Ten cigarettes meant life. The Jews [ordinarily] didn't get cigarettes.

Since he did not smoke, the cigarette was only useful in trade within informal camp circles. With it he could buy an apple, or thread to mend his pants. More significantly, it gave him a little bit more on which to survive.

There were many prisoners who did not get cigarettes. So I made the deal with them. They gave me a piece of meat, ham or something, and I bought it for five cigarettes. I smuggled it in my pants [laughs] to the camp and sold it for ten cigarettes from two other guys inside who were our blockaltestes. They were in charge those supervisors, those murderers. Now before I went out to work near the wash area, that was the market, every day, for a cigarette, I could buy an apple or a thread to mend my pants. Bread? Bread was not for sale. Nobody ever sold bread. I could get here a little soup or there something else. So that's the way the cigarettes helped me. That went on for a year.

No matter how bad conditions got, Chaim showed fewer signs of wear than many others. He was strong from years of working on his father's farm. Eventually, however, the lack of food and absence of vitamins took a toll. He developed two large abscesses, one under his right arm and the other on his ankle. He tried to fight the inevitable by small measures, but the swelling on his ankle eventually kept him from walking. It was late winter, 1945.

There was no washbasin [for inmates], so I improvised. I washed myself with snow. [But the abscesses] caused me a big fever. And it sent me to the infirmary. Now to the infirmary, I didn't go with great rejoicing because that infirmary had a reputation--you do not come out alive. But I had no choice [quiet]. They pushed me in.

I befriended a Spanish doctor and a Polish Jewish boy. This was two weeks before the end of the war. [The doctor] said to me, "They will ask you to go, to march. Don't stay here." That's all he told me. I couldn't walk, but that Polish Jewish boy says, "Don't worry. I'll carry you on my shoulder." So we lined up again. The purpose was to collect the Jews back up to Mauthausen and have the Final Solution there or twenty miles further on.

The Final Solution at Mauthausen did not take place; no one quite knows why. Chaim described a situation there at the end where people who held positions of authority, acting by omission, confusion or self interest, slowed down what was supposed to have been the implementation of a gotterdammerung. Inmates who could walk were moved toward a more central point further into Germany. At first, Chaim was among those forced to march, but he was weak by then.

As we... again, you have to march through the gate, and they [Nazis] did not want to have shame [prisoners had to appear healthy enough to walk on their own]. So I didn't piggy-back him [the Polish boy]. I was just hobbling. I don't think they noticed, otherwise they would not let me through the gate. Once through the gate marching, he took me piggy back. As we walk, halfway, SS comes around, and he sees how I am riding piggy back. Now they don't want this kind of sight on the main highway. So he ordered him to throw me on the side of the road. Being a little bit imbued with religion, I started to say the last rite. I know the prayer by heart. I still know it. Then the SS comes. I recognize the guy. "Do you remember me, that you gave me cigarettes because I was a good worker?" He looked at me a second and then put back the gun in its holster. A farmer came with his horse and buggy, stopped him, and he threw me on it. That took me into the camp.

The guards shot those who could not walk on their own. With those who could walk being weak from exhaustion and starvation, it was a march of invalids, and given that the Allies were almost upon them, more latitude may have fallen to the individual officer or soldier. Chaim had nothing to lose by addressing the guard he recognized. His message had to be short and incisive. He used work as a reference point. The gambit succeeded, and so Chaim went on living for another few hours.

Once in the camp again, Chaim was brought to a central area where there was a makeshift tent. Some who could walk were taken further up the mountain. Chaim was sent to another spot.

> Everybody moves away. Only the cripples stay. Some dead, some crippled. Then it comes a military truck again, and they say, "Anybody who can even crawl, come out." So I crawled. They threw me on the truck; and it was painful. I was the first one on. Everyone else was crowded on me. I saw stars, because even to touch [the abscesses] was painful. Those who could walk, they went into the camp; those who could not were put on this truck. Suddenly I see the truck stop by a ship on the Danube. [Pause] Now in that there was... it was a kind of a tanker from grain or oil. We were ordered to climb down into the tanker. Again, I don't know if the intention was to burn it or sink it. I don't know. They closed the top. It was just like a manhole to go down. Nothing else.

> As I go down, there are other people there dead. Oh God. So [many] bodies. Sick. I wasn't healthy either, but at least my mind was there. And they close it [the top]. Well, they created a hell. No air. No nothing.

> Don't ask what happen overnight. I don't know what happen. But I wake up... with the little bit I could see... with two dead guys on me... around me. And they opened... they [guards] lowered the rope. Now, "Anybody who can come up, come up." I can't; I stayed. Two or three times this was repeated. "Even if you can crawl, come up." I crawled up the ladder. There must have been something already in the air because they brought food there. Don't ask. I didn't eat the food because some animal--I don't blame him now, grabbed... I was incapacitated. I was immobile... so what is it to steal from me? Just grabbed it away from me and ate it. So I didn't get anything.

> Again, those who could walk went on foot and those who couldn't they took by truck. Those who walked didn't make it because they were already weak and sick. So they couldn't make it because they had to walk up. The Danube is

> down on sea level. We had to get up the mountain to Mauthausen. So they didn't make it. Shot that way. I was taken with a few more to the trucks and as we arrived... took us to the shower, [pause] and for the first time I was put in a bed with sheets.

Inmate medics lanced the huge abscesses but had nothing to put on the wounds. A male nurse carried him to a bed. He had survived the sepsis, attributing the healing to a most unlikely source.

> Talking about lice, to give the blessing to the lice, too, because the lice got into my [abscesses] and they were eating it. And I was told there was a big hole there, the way they were moving all the time and eating it. They were... they disinfect by their activities... kept it clean. A blessing to the lice. They kept it [the wound] until later the Americans gave better treatment! It healed up slowly. I have scars.

Having survived the tanker, he could afford to bless the lice that others cursed. Meanwhile, he noticed the infirmary was under new management. The SS, anticipating that the Allies were closing in on them, had bolted.

> It was May 6, 1945, because I recall that two days after, I heard rumbling again. Climbed up, I was on the third bed, and I looked out through a little window. I saw four American tanks coming. Only one stayed. Three more were rumbling for the town. The Americans came in and took pictures, and there were bodies like this [shows stacking] piled there. The SS ran away already two days before. We knew there was a change because the Wehrmacht had taken us over. There was no SS around when the Americans came.

Some prisoners broke into the storerooms and ate whatever they found. For many this proved fatal. So an order was given regarding food, that all prisoners should have the full variety of whatever was available for meals, but in small amounts.

> They gave everything, five peas, five something else... just a little bit. And I got from them immediately an I-V [intravenous feeding], some sugar I guess. In the last two weeks [before liberation] I really went down. My teeth, I just could take them out one by one. All loose. Scurvy.

Many SS had tried to steal away when the Allies approached. Many were recaptured and brought back to face the prisoners. There were different responses on the part of the inmates to this reversal of fate. Chaim had a great capacity for anger, but at the same time a deep store of his father's wisdom.

> I recall it was two or three days after liberation, and some of the Germans were captured and made to serve us. One came and asked me for water. Now if I would be a revengeful person, I would tell him to go to hell. I gave him from my water.
>
> [Wife: "I wouldn't have." Chaim: "Well that's cause you're a woman" (laughs). Wife: "Still it is said, he who comes to kill you, you rise up and kill him."]
>
> Well this time he didn't come to kill *me*. He *didn't* come to kill me. He was out of that league now, and for some reason, I could not... I just could not....

He had a complex system of distinctions in the situational ethics he constructed. These shored up the walls of his inner sanctuary. He saw that there were good and bad among the prisoners. There would also be variation among the guards.

> There was, for instance, a man in charge from the army, the Wehrmacht. Wasn't an SS. He was around forty-five-ish, and he was in charge of my barrack. What was his job? To make sure that the food is given out to the prisoners. The other bosses stole the bread. If somebody wanted a whole bread, all he had to do is kill three people, he had the bread.
>
> This Wehrmacht, whenever he could... First of all, he's always telling me, "Have faith. Slowly we are getting to the end of the war." Whenever he could, whenever there was left soup in the bottom of the kettle, he called me. Whatever you put in your stomach meant another day survival.

These unlikely signs of humanity among the guards meant life to him, but being able to show such flexibility meant having a strong sense of one's own identity. In the year Chaim spent at Mauthausen, the last of the war, there were more contradictions. One of these was with his barrack commander, who like the Wehrmacht officer was also older.

> He helped me survive, not because he loved me. I was mending his socks! My mother taught me. She said, "Some day it will help you." I mended his socks [laughing], and I sang for him. He liked Hebrew melodies. I sang for him. So, while I mended his sock and I was his singer, he threw me a morsel each time. He got parcels from home. So he gave me a little piece of cake or something. Every little thing helps.

Later, when he got into Vienna, it was under Russian control. He tried to get in touch with this former guard. Having located the house where the guard resided, Chaim talked to his wife. Though he never got to share a beer with the man who gave him comfort of a kind, he observed that the house was in a courtyard and right next door to a Jewish cantor who had lived there before the war. It helped Chaim understand. The man had lived most of his life with the sound of Jewish melodies all around; they symbolized home to him in the alienation of the camps.

Though it was not typical for Chaim to treat an enemy as a friend, he had the strength to be flexible. Following an old proverb, he had hoped to turn an enemy into a friend. In any case, he was exacting of himself, and as much as it might have given momentary release to seize a moral high ground and turn away when his enemy was vanquished, he chose not to rigidly categorize and hate. Survival had been an act of will and ingenuity each day at Mauthausen. He had learned to stand by his own principles with his own strength.

> I was squeezing my teeth every day to get out of there. Those people that gave in, they were after a week gone. They had to have this strong will, "I'll never give in, never give in." I never gave in!

He had begun to learn to appreciate surviving. As we spoke, more than forty years after liberation from Mauthausen, he had recently revisited Hungary. He and his wife had stayed in Budapest at a hotel called the Britannia, infamous for its association with Eichman and his torture rooms between 1943 and 1945. It now gave him a certain satisfaction to know that it was he rather than Eichman who comfortably slept in its elegant appointments.

Just after returning from the camps in July, 1945, there had been no sense of this transcendence when he returned home.

> There was no sense of purpose. I was dazed for a while. I didn't find my place for a year. After that I went up to Budapest. I had no purpose for a year. I had, for at least two months after getting back, nightmares. I was talking [in my sleep] about the things that happened.

Just after liberation, it was difficult for survivors like Chaim to know what was happening to them. Medical science had only begun to consider traumatic shock a response to prolonged extremity and offered little knowledge on the subject. Chaim fought the nightmares, hardly guessing their nature or purpose.

On their return home, survivors had very little infrastructure in place on which to secure new means to start over. Families had disappeared, property they once owned had been taken, and neighbors from the past were uncommunicative. In eastern Europe, the old religiously based way of life went without teachers, clergy or intact structures to house their functions. But Chaim nevertheless put great priority on resuming his religious studies. To support himself, Chaim banded together with a few buddies, generating cash by selling odd items. It was by his own initiative that he rebuilt his life.

> I made it alone. I shouldn't say alone because the Joint Distribution Committee--it's American--without them, getting free room and board and, not only that, they paid also my private tutor, I wouldn't have been able to do this.

> The JDC looked after us, and I was safe. First month, I was weak all the time... always sweating. Then slowly... I didn't do anything for a month. The JDC provided us with food twice a day. Then started... A few guys came back, and we formed a little organization, and eventually all of us decided to go up to Budapest to go to high school.

During the day he attended Rabbinical School; at night he did courses to obtain a high school diploma. He joined a twenty month program to help those displaced by war. The Joint Distribution Committee funded his progress. Now he is a judge.

He married an Israeli, having emigrated there from Hungary shortly after his return home. They settled in North America in the 1950s. His family now includes two sons and two daughters. One of the daughters practices law in her father's firm.

His family was anxious to learn about what he had been through. As part of this, one of their daughters had visited Germany and spent some time at Mauthausen in the 1980s. Her mother related the experience.

> It was in fall, 1983, she was in Europe, and she took the bus to Mauthausen to the concentration camp, just because her Dad [had been] there. She wanted to see it. While she was talking about it [on her return] she hysterically broke down and cried, which I've never seen her like this. How it happened, we were looking at an album at her aunt's place and we were looking at sisters and mothers. Somebody said,"You look like your father's sister, Leora, who died [at Riga]."

> [Chaim: She looks exactly like her. She was just a year older than me when she died.]
>
> She said that people were made to carry stones up twenty or one hundred steps and when they got there the SS would just shoot them.
>
> [Chaim: When you were assigned to the quarry, your life wasn't worth much.]

Most of the family had been taken to Riga and killed. Chaim had been taken by another route to Auschwitz and then Mauthausen. In his narrative, surprisingly little space is given to pathos. Chaim was above all a practical person committed to simple ways. After liberation it seemed too costly to gaze into that well of sorrow. Even today, he says very little about the sadism of the guards. However, near the end of what he had to say, he mentioned something that happened one day on the way to work in the tunnels of Mauthausen.

> He [the guard] hit me for no reason as we went in the morning just boarding the trains--the cattle train that took us to work every day--just to have fun, you see, and anybody who happened to be in the way of the rifle... The other train was coming. I obviously was stunned for a second, and I was down on my back. Instinctively I jumped when I saw it [butt of the rifle] coming. Just for fun, you know!
>
> The SS women were worse than the men, they were killing people then taking their heads and boiling them. Then they decorated their desks with somebody's shrunken skull. I saw the ugly side of human beings in this environment.

He did not make a quarrel with his Creator about the wisdom of evil. Nor did he rail against Heaven for his father's death which pained him greatly. Instead he said that he was thankful that he did not have to watch his father die a slow and painful death, thankful he did not have to endure that "test of faith and will." Clearly, it is a fortunate person, who having been abused, tortured and daily threatened with painful death, holds on to treasures of faith and self composure. Even today, he could only deal with most of the images of horror in silence.

On returning to his hometown in the late 1980s, he sensed the town was "dead." He went straight to the graveyard where there was a memorial to those who had perished in 1944-45. His feelings were mixed.

> I felt like rejoicing... but also sadness and revenge. I was... Because I

came to a city which used to be a bustling city [but they gave us] no room on the sidewalks [then]. We came in [now] and it's empty. Dead!

I was sorry to see the city be dead, but on the other hand, I said, "Good [enough] for you!" That's the way it should be, if you couldn't stand up and stop this thing then.

Chaim found it difficult to balance feelings of sadness and revenge against the love he was commanded by religious principle to observe. Contradictory emotions seem appropriate in this case, however, even though the inner turmoil they generate might cast a shadow that could turn the quickened heart to ice. It took strength to remember those brutally murdered and for more than fifty years bear witness to their misery. Chaim did at least that and somehow gained an equanimity.

I'm really very happy. Anybody asks me how are you, I say, 'Fine.' I don't do it just because that is the thing to say. Because since 19 March, 1944, every day to me is a gift. Why should I complain? It's always good. Failure?! --I say it's only money. I lost it, I'll make it again.

PARTISANS
LEON

Leon Arganic was a bright and ambitious son of a successful dairy farmer with large land holdings in the rural area surrounding Grodno. It was in a region on the 1939 border between Poland and Russia. The town nearest the farm was small, with about six thousand people of whom about sixty percent were Jewish. He was sixteen when the German front approached the town and stopped about one hundred and fifty miles away. That was June 22, 1941. From that time until liberation in June of 1944, as the Russian armies regained lost territory, he no longer had a home. He was the only survivor in his family of five.

When the Germans invaded Poland and they stopped at oh... I would say one hundred and fifty miles from us, the Russians came in and got us [pushed westward]. Then a tremendous influx of refugees running away from occupied Poland told us of all the atrocities and everything. We were petrified. Now when the Germans attacked Russia, it happened so fast that nobody could go any place. June 23, 1941, the Germans were already in our town. They dropped paratroopers and... and you know, how far does it take to travel one hundred and fifty miles?

So the Russians, just all of them, left. They escaped and just disappeared. As soon as the Germans came in, they handed over the civil administration to the Lithuanians, and the persecutions and the savagery that those people showed is impossible to describe.

Whatever calm they could lay claim to after this point was fleeting. They had at first imagined they would be able to hold against the predations of an invader passing through on the way to the Russian interior.

My father said, "As far as the Star of David is concerned, they can put twenty on me. I know who I am and some of the Polish farmers [nearest neighbors] know who I am. Taking away the belongings, they can take everything. As long as they don't take our lives, we will survive."

The family's idea of surviving was based on limited engagements of armies in the past, not one whose policy toward the people was strictly genocide. Three months after the invasion of the area, Nazi einsatzgruppen organized the *sonderbehandlung* of Jews. Having heard so many stories from passing refugees, locals were leery of complying with any order. When people were ordered to a round up of population in their small town, Leon's family thought of what they might do to avoid complying. His father sketched a limited risk operation that involved sending the women into town, with him and his sons going in separate directions and following separate strategies.

We had three synagogues in town, three big buildings. Everybody has to assemble there you know. Now my mother felt all the time, you know, that they're not going to hurt women and children. They are going to take the men maybe for work to Germany. So my mother, my sister, and my grandmother went to the synagogue. My father dressed up as a peasant with a rope in his hand. They surrounded the town with Lithuanian police. They could get in, nobody could get out.

He [father] spoke perfect Lithuanian. Because our part was in Poland, you know, there weren't many people who could speak Lithuanian--that was [always] a disputed area between Poland and Lithuania. The Lithuanians always wanted it, and the Poles would never give it to them. So the Germans were very "kind." They gave it to the Lithuanians. My father was very fluent in Lithuanian, so he came up [to the men carrying out the operation]. They didn't recognize him. He was dressed like a farmer and he had a rope in his hand. They said, "Where the hell are you going?" He said, "I'm going to get my cow. It's in the field." So they let him through.

Having fooled his captors once and gotten a sense of how the operation was organized, Leon's father later found a way to get the women of the family out of the synagogue area and back to relative safety. But Leon and his brother had not left the family farm. They chose the barn roof so as to have a vantage point overlooking the property. Here their journey into terror took shape.

> As children we used to play hide and seek. All of us do at one time. And we had a favorite hiding place... two buildings... the roofs, you know. Pick the roof, right in there... that's where we climbed up and that's where we hid. We hid there for two days, and without any food. We took two apples with us. We were so stupid. We thought it was just going to happen, it's just passing.
>
> So we were lying there. We could hear everything that was going on, the way our neighbors came into our house and... robbing the houses... boys that I went to school with... hollering... screaming, "Look what I got... look what I got." Then shooting, shooting, and shooting all the time. Screams and people hiding and being pulled out of the hiding places.
>
> We were there for two days and almost three nights, and the third night my brother and I said "We are going to starve to death, you know. So it's no use. Let's see if we can run away."

Just months before this, Leon's greatest worry was to stand up to the high school bullies as he got ready for graduation and university. He planned to enter a mechanical engineering program. The advancing Nazi front had changed all that. Now, as they set out under the cover of darkness, they had no particular place in mind to go except away from the houses. Their farm had enjoyed a wide popularity throughout the land, and the family had lived there for centuries. People would travel there in summer to holiday and enjoy the rich food. Right around them they had been less sure of neighbors' well wishes. On that particular night, with people frightened by the new occupiers, their thought was to avoid being murdered.

As they zig-zagged across the fields, they ate anything they could find, mostly a few vegetables, and they were hungry. It was getting on towards morning as they finally reached the edge of the town and crossed the little river which marked its boundary. At that point, the old Catholic cemetery with the quarry nearby seemed a fine place to hide through the day until they could ascertain where the others in the family were. They had no doubts about finally getting everyone together again at that time.

It wasn't used anymore... approximately a mile from our town. So both of us decided that would be a good place. I don't think anybody would look there... and it's abandoned, you know, and its overgrown. So that's where we headed, and that's where we made it to. Next to the cemetery was an old [pause] unused, gravel pit... that was... the gravel was already taken out, and it was unused also.

The next morning, I would say about 9-9:30 in the morning, we could hear a tremendous amount of noises coming from not far, you know. It was getting closer and closer and closer, and we stood up in amongst the bushes, you know, just looked out. There was a road leading towards the cemetery and towards the gravel pit, and again, this is one of the things that gets burned into your mind, that I'll never forget, I saw a cavalcade of wagons and... and... [swallows] and people walking. [Pace is slowing] All the women of our town were being herded in our direction, the women and the children.

Now, we didn't know what was going to happen, but we guessed, you know. Some of them were being on wagons, the older ones, you know. The children were on wagons. The women were being whipped and hit with rifles, you know, to move faster. And they brought them up to the little bushes, close to the gravel pit. Over there, they made the women undress. They made them walk up to the pit. And in groups of one hundred, they used to shoot them. And they were falling into the pits.

Now, before they shot them, the Lithuanians, because most of the killing was going on was being done by the Lithuanians, there were very few Germans amongst them, they were doing... the Lithuanians were doing all the killing... they raped the women repeatedly. I remember my cousin. She was the most beautiful girl. I just found a picture... a picture of her. [He shares the photo of her.] That was my mother's... my mother's sister's daughter, you know. She must have been at this time, what, eighteen or nineteen years old, you know. She was repeatedly raped. So was her mother. She was also a very beautiful woman.

What I cannot understand, if I am of the mind that I want to kill you, I want to execute you, and I put you against the wall and I shoot you, this is execution. Those savages, in addition to raping both the women, they cut their breasts off. They put rifles in the vaginas of women. They shot them. What I saw there, it's something that will burn into my mind forever.

Fifty years later Leon was still locked into the images he described. He was outwardly cheerful, though what he said was not.

When tears came, his face did not dissolve into anguish. He kept going quickly, hurling invective at the men who were committing the crimes, something he could not have done as freely that morning as he stood with his brother, staring at the carnage from the edge of the quarry.

> Now, thing is, I was standing there. Cemetery was a little raised up, it was higher ground and it was surrounded... big wall and completely overgrown. I was standing almost like in a balcony, you know, seeing what's happening there below. My brother was trying to pull me down. He almost sat on me. He said, "Don't look, don't look, don't look anymore." Because he already saw what was happening there.
>
> I couldn't stop looking. I wanted to scream. There's no... no... My mouth, you know, my throat was so dry that I couldn't scream. I wanted to shut my eyes. I couldn't keep my eyes shut, you know. Just to see what was happening over there. And that went on for, I don't know, six or eight hours, until they killed close to three thousand women. I'm guessing three thousand women because of the population. One thousand children were left. When I'm talking children, I'm talking children from the age of five until babies, because the other ones, they were already taken over. And, I'll tell you what happened there. [Deep breath] Now this was something to witness.
>
> The children were milling around and the Lithuanians were herding them together, just hitting... to [get them to] stay in one place, and then, all of the women were gone, and the turn of the children came. I saw the chief of police of our town that walked over to some of the Germans, and I could see they were shaking their heads. Then he spoke to some Lithuanians, and finally he donned a smock, a white smock, just like a doctor, and with another group of Lithuanians, a small group--it could be under ten, they proceeded of killing the children.
>
> Some of them they just threw in live, little ones... light... into... into the ditches. Some of them they grabbed them by the legs and smashed them against the wall of the Catholic cemetery... rocks there... smashing their brains out. And some of them, he just picked them up by a leg, shot them in the leg, in the head, and just threw them into the pit. That took three hours. And, I'm guessing, they killed close to one thousand kids. Farmers... Polish farmers were standing all around watching what was going on. Men and women. And then, finally, what they did is they shovelled dirt on top of it. Pardon me, before they did the dirt, they spilled, I would say, a truckload of lime on top of the bodies, and then shovelled dirt on top of it, and that was the end of it... that was the end of the women [and their children].

For Leon, time stood forever still at this moment. The lime is still falling on bodies not yet cold. He observes how "light" the children are, how much easier for the murderers to physically manipulate than their mothers. His pain was for the victims, but how could these men live on after committing such a heinous crime. What court would forgive them, what water wash away the blood of the innocents. He said, "The chief of police [among the perpetrators] had a family and children. He went home. Sunday he went to church, went to confession..." The stones themselves cried out the infamy.

He did not say what passed between his brother and himself the rest of that day. Their father was trying to get word into the marketplace, so as to alert the family that he was waiting. A solution came through a business contact of his father's.

> We had... my father had a very close friend, a Lithuanian that was in the police. He liked my father. So, he came into the main marketplace where all the people were there, looking for my Dad, and my father wasn't there because, as I said, my father got out first. So somebody brought him [the policeman] to my mother, my grandmother and my sister. And he said, "Where is your husband?" So. My mother was afraid to say he is already escaped. So, she said that they took him away and killed him. So, he says "Come, I will take you out from here."

Leon's mother tried to get some of her relatives to join her but they refused. Seeing that their husbands and brothers had been taken, they would not leave. She only managed to save Leon's grandmother and sister. They knew the most likely place to meet up with the others would be a certain Polish woman's farm. This woman and her family served as a place of refuge because the grandparental generation had been close. They proved invaluable allies for the short term.

> That Polish woman was almost like my grandmother. She was [still a] very kind old lady [then]. But anyway, at that time we all ran away to her... used to run to her. So the... all three of them [mother, grandmother and sister] went there. I'm jumping a little bit ahead because my brother and myself, after everybody was killed and we were at the cemetery, we also went to that Polish woman.

The time span for all of this action to occur involved several days. By this time, plans made earlier had been overtaken by tragedy. Rendezvous points were now compromised. They were scattered with no means of communication. Leon's father, fearing he had lost everything, had thought it best to seek out relatives in another village.

> So he [father] went to that little town called Radwig. My... my brother, myself, we both arrived [at the Polish lady's house]. We stayed there. The son of that lady took us to Radwig. We arrived, and my father was he... he my father aged fifty years in... in two days, you know. Anyway, we arrived there. My father was very glad to see us. We were crying and went into a house of some kind of relatives of ours, you know.
>
> The same day we arrived, that town got surrounded by Germans looking for escaped Jews from our town. Anyway, they rounded up some people, and while they were rounding everybody up, my brother and I-- my father wasn't there, he went to buy some cigarettes... tobacco, you know. My brother and I ran out in a garden. [Sighs] Never forget that one either [sighs tiredly]. We jumped into bushes of poison ivy!

They were now being hunted. Unaccustomed to this and how to manage their emotions wisely they found the comic and tragic working together. Even hunters go to lunch, and embattled patriots can stumble into a patch of poison ivy. They managed to evade their captors and heal their wounds that day, but the outlook for the future seemed bleak.

> Run! Where the hell do we run? So we run... try to run back to this Polish farmer... to this lady again. On the way now, the son of that Polish farmer who brought us to Radwig... and, you know, when somebody takes you, you don't pay attention. On the way back we couldn't find our way. So we were knocking on windows of Polish farmers asking for directions. Was suicide, because they would point us in the direction of the Nazis. Anyway, we had no choice. It was at night. So finally at daybreak we made it to that little village that we couldn't make it to [the day before]... the farmer's house... because people would see us... the farmers getting up so early. So we know that the lady's daughter is engaged to another man at another farm. So we went to his farm, and he put us up. So he said, "Stay here." [Through the efforts of neighbors, eventually the whole family gathered at this farmhouse].
>
> We weren't happy to see each other because, what's the purpose? They killed everybody there. They already *killed everybody there. Where are we to go?*

They were at a point emotionally where it took immense effort to rise up once again and find another shortlived hiding place. The destruction of community and the fragmentation of the basis for trust wore down what was left of their spirit. He echoed his bereftness with, "They killed everybody..." They felt driven and humiliated, endangering themselves and others in trying to hide. But the alternative was a vicious death.

> We lived in that town for nine months. [Pause] Same thing happened again. [Tears in his voice] "Everybody up!" And [sighs] this time they [authorities] didn't have any ditches dug. So they went from house to house and they took men to go dig ditches. My father was amongst them. They give them shovels. They give them pick-axes and so on and on. They led them to a cemetery again, a Jewish cemetery, about a mile out of town. My mother and some of the people that were in amongst the hundred people from our town, they already knew what was going to happen. So while they were walking, there was a man, a blacksmith, a very, very skookum guy. So he said, "Look. They're going to kill us anyway, you know." There was a rock pile, you know. He says, "When we get... get by the rock pile, we are going to smash them with the axes, with the shovels and run for life. If we get killed, we get killed." That's what they did. They killed all the policemen. Two Germans on horses escaped and the other seventy-four ran away into the forest. My father survived.

The routing was a short-lived success and the survivors knew it, but it bought them time. They were not prepared yet to live in the forest. So they found a building with an attic and hid in it with several others. The Nazis in the meantime were directing local administrators to see that all Jews were registered, so that they could more effectively round them up. Treachery and bitter compromise dogged them endlessly.

> Now my mother, my sister, my brother and my grandmother hid in a flat roofed building that had a very, very small attic. There were close to seventy Jews on that attic with us. We survived [pause].

> They came back and took another hundred people to go and dig ditches, and this time, they watched them, they didn't give them any shovels until they brought them to the ditches, and what they did is they said to them, "You dig the ditches, and we will let you and your families live." And that's what they did. They dug the ditches and then the whole town, all the Jewish people of the town, were brought out. So they told them, "You can only take your wife and your children. No mother, no father. Nothing." So out of the one hundred people digging ditches, approximately five hundred survived, and they brought them back into town. Now these people, the Jewish people, were running from house to house hollering, "If anybody is hiding, come on down and register" --they made them go to City Hall and register. This is how our family got down, and we registered and we stayed there, I don't know, for about three, four, weeks, and that's when the edict came out that we are going to be "resettled."

The Jews still alive were ghettoized. Known touchstones of cooperation hardly made sense anymore. Euphemisms that masked the raw

Adults--The Young Men

fact of genocide--"registration," "resettlement"--were, tragically, the only assurances of a way out of danger. With hiding being increasingly risky and tedious, the family decided that with winter coming on they would go into the ghetto with others from their area. Leon helped them do this but did not stay. By this time, he had made contact with the Partisans and arranged to go with them into the forests. He trained under Russian military insurgents and began to follow the guerilla lifestyle this demanded. Then word came that the Grodno ghetto where he had left his family was about to be liquidated.

> My father, my mother, my sister got into the Grodno ghetto a short time when the same thing [round-up] happened, only there they had seventy-five thousand Jews. Ghetto is completely surrounded. Sealed off completely by the Germans. [Pause] We were looking around, just walking around the perimeter, looking where is an opening to get out. We found a house that was completely bombed out during the war, you know, and over there just piles and piles of rock and... demolished house... windows and so on. And on the bottom, two guards were marching back and forth. That was Christmas of 1942.

> Cold... snow... just terrible... [breathes out heavily as though warding off the feeling]. And about every fifteen or twenty minutes one of them used to come up to have a smoke and used to come up in front of the bombed out [pause] house and standing with his back against... a window, you know... like a bombed out window.

> My father was in his forties, my brother was older than me, and there was another couple that was running away with us, a young man... must have been in his twenties... and his sister. And we decided that the only way we can run away is by killing the two guards. [Pause] And the finger was pointed at me. I'm seventeen years old at that time.

Leon observed that the guards were not following strict military guidelines in guarding the perimeter, leaving a short period of time in which each was out of eyeshot of the other. This would be the weak point that Leon would try to turn to advantage for those relying upon him. Their escape from the ghetto would not be easy.

> Now, I never killed anybody in my life yet. And not only that, we didn't have a gun or anything at all. We had those big butcher knives that you could find in the ghetto. [Pause] I didn't know how to do it, you know. All I can... I used to visualize it.

> I crawled into the house, in the snow and I [hid] behind the parapet of that

window. When he came up—he was dressed... quite heavy, he was walking with a rifle. He took out a cigarette, lit a cigarette, and he was standing like that against the wall. I grabbed him. I cut and dropped him. He fell right in the snow, forward, you know [his anxiety and discomfort have increased].

Now I was standing there retching my guts out because to me it was such a terrible thing what I have done. I don't know the man. I don't know if he was a good man. I don't know if he's a bad man. Has he got children? Has he got a wife? Has he got parents. Who is he, you know. I didn't even see his face! I don't know what he looked like. [Distressed]

The other German... the fifteen minutes passed by and the guy didn't come down... started calling, "Hans. Zie vu ist tu? zie vu ist tu?" He was calling him, and finally he came up and he noticed that he was lying flat in the snow. There was no blood, you know, that you could see because everything fell over to the front, you know. So he bent over for him... over him. I jumped on his back, knifed him in the back, and I killed the second one. [He is no longer cheery but tense]

My father and the others came up already. They could see it. They were watching what was happening. And, in pairs we walked out. My sister and the other lady, my brother and the other boy, and my father and I were walking out.

Leon had been trained to set explosive devices to blow up rail track or wreak some general havoc on the German troops. Hand-to-hand combat was a grotesquerie he never managed to accept. His limited training had been sufficient to get him through the demands of that night, however, and he took the seven people he was trying to protect into the town of Grodno then decorated for seasonal festivities.

Life in Grodno was normal. It was Christmastime. People were going and people were laughing and bells were ringing. And here we were walking right through the center of the city. We walked out.

That night, we walked close to forty kilometers to hide. The people that... the boy and the girl, they were from that vicinity, you know. So they took us to a lady that lived in a one-room house dirt floor. That place looked like a palace to me in those days. She gave us hot milk. There was honey and things like that, that we didn't see for years.

It was a study in contrasts: the gaiety of the holiday with the terror of killing, the rigidity of need to escape with the suppleness of the victim, victims having to victimize in order to walk away. Throughout the rest of his life, Leon mourned the men he killed that evening. He did not try to diminish the pain with denial or numbing of emotions. He had come a great inner distance from the terrified figure at the edge of the gravel pit. Now he had learned to accept that the situation would not change without active involvement, and this would mean bearing fear, guilt, grief and revulsion.

Leon's stories of life with the Partisans strikes a completely different picture than the tragedy and pain of being with family, fruitlessly trying to protect them against an overwhelming force. With the Partisans he shared the risks of war; with his family he watched the horror of being a people targeted for eradication in genocide.

Living with the Partisans, he worked in a group of six men whose mission was to blow up the trains carrying German supplies to the Russian front. They covered an area approximately one hundred miles from their camp. The mines had to be set by hand and the pin pulled just as the train approached. Timing was extremely important. But as the movement at the front changed, so did the known schedule for the running of the trains. One day they ran into trouble.

> My partner and I, we used to place the mine and wait for the train to approach. We didn't place the mine when the train was approaching because we needed some time to place the mine. Here we were, lying in the bush close to the railway. All of a sudden, we heard a train coming. So we run to that railway, without digging out, without taking up the rocks [that hid the device]. We just stuck the mine on the railway, on the ties, and we run back. Turned out the train was going the other way, wasn't [laughs] coming our way. Now what I mentioned to you, the pin, the safety pin was taken up and the commanding officer said, "Who is going to volunteer to go and take out the mine?" That was suicide. To put that pin... it was as thin as a needle... the slightest little move... you get blown up. Anyway, my partner and I went back--the guy was just fearless, nerves of steel. He put the needle back in!

> So we grabbed the mine, and we started going back to the forest, you know. Now, it is in the middle of summer, the forest is very dry. So every time you step, you crack [make a noise] you know. So when we were cracking at night it carries. All of a sudden, a fusillade opens up on us because the guards on the trains [hear], and they shot up flares. But it's a forest. We were running like crazy.

His unit scattered, each moving by a different way toward another rendezvous point. This was all very typical. As a unit of irregulars they had none of the information normally available to the conventional military. At any time they might happen upon an unanticipated regrouping of the enemy. Flexibility and the capacity to retreat successfully was as favored a strategy as any by them--that and a good sense of humor to see them through the hazards and limitations.

> We were travelling always at night, never during the day. One time we had to travel during the day, but we didn't want to go six [the size of their work team] because it's a group [and might look suspicious]. So we broke up, three and three. So Mishka, [close friend], myself and a Ukrainian by the name of Symba, three of us, and the other three went [by another way], and we made up to meet at a little bridge on the river there, you know, in the woods. And during the day when we were travelling, Mishka and I had an argument as far as the direction we had to go. He said we had to go to the right. I said we have to go to the left because I am from that area... born in that area. And the Ukrainian, Symba, agreed with me. So we... he said, "Okay, if you want to go that way, you go your way, I'll go mine."
>
> I carried a heavy machine gun... Russian machine gun, and the Ukrainian carried the discs for the machine gun. Anyway, after about an hour's walk, we are walking separately. [Illustrates] We are walking in along the forest right here. It's all the way around. This is an open field. So we are walking this way in here. All of a sudden we look to the side. We see Mishka! coming across the way here. And we decided that we will intercept him somewhere here. Keep in mind that I am eighteen... nineteen years old you know. -- Everything we lost, but we didn't lose our sense of humor. So we... I decided to pull a fast one on Mishka. So I said to the Ukrainian "Let's hide in the bush here. When he comes up close by, I will holler in German, "Halt you cursed Jew." [Laughing] Stupidity! Because he could have turned around with a gun and fired right into me, you know.
>
> So we were standing right there... and another thing too, you see when you are walking by yourself, your nerves are as tight as ropes, you know, because he was carrying the rifle... he was carrying the mine on his back and he was dragging the rifle in the grass. People from far away couldn't see that he was carrying a rifle. The mine on his back it's like a rucksack, you know. Anyway his nerves all up. He was walking. All of a sudden I hollered in German, "Halte verfluchte Jude!" And the same moment that I hollered, I hollered "Mishka! Mishka!" Forget it! I chased him for a mile! [Laughing] First of all, he just took up the mine and he flung it right away so he can run, and he just took off like a shot. So I came back. Symba and myself are killing ourselves [laughing], [but] we were sorry that we scared him like that.

Adults--The Young Men 267

> Anyway all day long we walked. We came to that little river, and we were sitting... dark at night already, we were sitting and having something to eat and drink, some nice stream water. In comes Mishka, just like you see a deer that charges [when it is] shot at. Muddy from top to bottom you know. His hair a mess. Everything, you know. And both of us broke out laughing, the Ukrainian and I. So he looked at us, "What the hell are you laughing about?" So I said, "Halte verfluchte Jude!" you know, the way I said it before. Well, he grabbed the rifle, the bullet in the chamber [gales of laughter]. He was going to shoot me! The Ukrainian wrestled him [Mishka] down.

In the joke they relived their most feared dangers: discovery by the Nazis, and, killing one another in error. It played upon the trust bond on which so much depended. The strong relationship he had with his buddies in the forest was fortunate since, during the course of the three years, from the time the Nazis entered his town until the Russians retook that territory in June, 1944, he lost all of his family. Without prefacing what was to follow with a warning statement, he described the episode in which he saw his father and sister killed.

> My father, when I went into the fighting, my father and my sister remained with the family group and the family group was living from day to day under the kind of sponsorship of the fighting men. But the Lithuanians and some of the German groups used to come into the forest. We used to run away, as I told you. Some of the family groups never got the messages or sometimes didn't get the messages, and they were the ones that were taking the brunt of the losses. But the Lithuanians especially [were] coming into the forest, hunting for Jews.

> Now my father and a small group of men used to move out of the big forest, go into the smaller forest, another forest. But I was coming from my camp, from my central camp when I was in laying the mines. I always was in the area where my father was hiding and I used to be in touch with them through my contact man.

> So, one day I came with our group there, and, at night, we came in and found my father with a group of people who were sitting there in a small forest, and we stayed with them overnight. In the morning--we put up sentries, you know, [sighs] never slept without sentries standing up. And there were... there were... we teamed up with another small group, also six people... So, there were twelve of us and there must have been about eight or nine [civilians], my father, my sister, and other people. Again, women and men, [sniffs] and the sentries were standing... it was a forest about this size here [illustrates]... and the sentries were standing there. We were sleeping and here again was an open field. All of a sudden the sentries came running to

tell us that we are being attacked.

So far in the story the scene is typical of the kind of lives they lived with danger always at hand and calm of any kind purchased by high preparedness. They were discovered by their local enemies, because one of Leon's group foolishly told a farmer who seemed onsides where they were putting up for the night. When it was not clear just why someone victimized by the Nazis could possibly be enemies of the Partisans, such misjudgments were all too likely to happen.

> Anyway, those two guards come running, telling us that we were being attacked. We didn't know who it was, but we moved up closer to the edge to see who it was. There were 150 Poles attacking us [deep breath]. Now we had machine guns and so on. So we fought them for a while. We ran out of bullets, so we started running. My... I was already trained a little bit in the tactics of war, you know. So I wasn't running. I went out into the open, and I dropped on my belly and turning around shooting and just moving... shooting and moving. [By contrast] My father was just like a deer, you know. He was running right straight out, and they hit him with a dumdum bullet. A dumdum bullet is a bullet that explodes. And when he was running beside me he said, "Take a look." He was pouring blood from his [mid torso]. Must have been as big as a grapefruit. He came out, he pulled down his shirt. He was pouring blood.

> He was a very powerful man. He was only in his forties, you know. So he was running with me through this opening. And I run into another little forest, and he says, "Where's Frieda?" So I turned around and I could see two Poles chasing her with the bayonets right behind, chasing my sister. I shot and I killed both of them. A third one started chasing her again, you know... fourteen, fifteen year old girl. What in the hell could she do to anybody, you know? I started shooting again. My Russian gun jammed! He run after her with the bayonet. He run the bayonet right through my sister. And she fell to the ground right like a wounded little bird, you know. I was standing there saying, "God in heaven why? why? why?" [Crying].

> That was the end of my father. My father was wounded and lived with me for six days. He died [in my arms]. My sister I never found. The farmers dug a ditch and threw her in, plowed it over. I never found [her body].

After the war he went back to the area where they were killed and reburied his father and brother in a Jewish cemetery; he could never find his sister's remains. It was an emotional scene which put him once again at the edge of the quarry, unable to close his eyes, unable to scream, unable to undo the injustice.

As the war intensified, life became more complicated. The Jewish Partisans Leon had worked with had allied with and been trained by the Russians. There were also Lithuanians and Poles in the forests, fighting, who had chosen to go with the Nazis. Still others among the Partisan units were purely nationalist and organized only to fight in a given region. With the Nazis losing the war, it seemed in their own best interests for some of these other units to seek the protection of the Russian Partisans. One night some of them sent an emissary to Leon and his buddies.

> That night, a farmer came to see the miller and said to him. "Listen. I know that you're connected with the Partisans. I know that you know where to find [them]." He didn't know that we were there, because we were hiding. "I have a group of seventy-two Ukrainians, [pause] German collaborators... German uniforms... that are willing to cross over to the Partisans."
>
> So the miller was very afraid, because nobody was supposed to know that he was a contact man, you know, because they would denounce him to the Nazis. So he told the guy, "I don't know nothing about Partisans." He denied everything, and the guy laughed.
>
> The miller came down to us and said, "What should I do?" So. We advised him that the time is getting [near] the end. We told him what happened on the roadway and that maybe what you can do is go back and tell them that you have contacted some Partisans and they would be willing to meet with the Ukrainians.

It was a dangerous gambit. Leon's unit was small and away from homebase. Seeking to gain the status of prisoner-of-war might be a ruse. No kind of armistice had been declared, and few were really sure that the Nazis were retreating from Russia. If this group was disbanded and on the run, they might pose another kind of threat, this time preying on the local population. Nothing was clear.

> Now we are six, they are seven. How do you handle things like... you know. Now they were already on the run. We didn't know exactly what was happening, and we were petrified to approach them. So we told the miller to go back to the farmer and tell them that we would like to meet with the leaders of the seventy-two, and they should come without any weapons, you know. And in the middle of a field...
>
> Anyway, they came, and we could see that they were sincere. Young people,

> very young people that they were sincere. Now, we knew one thing. The Nazis didn't force anybody... the Ukrainians to come into the army. The Poles volunteered to come out there, you know, to fight against the Russians and to kill Jews, wherever they could find them. Now, the deal that we made with them was like that. They have to come out in the field, right in the open, and shed everything they have, grenades and bullets and guns and take off the jacket so we could see they're not hiding anything, and then walk over to the place designated. And they did that, you know. We searched every one of them... body searched, to see that they're not carrying any pistols. That was unnecessary, because they meant it. And we dug a big ditch and buried all their ammunition, rifles... because you couldn't carry it anyway. And we took the seventy-two, and we started going in the direction of our camp which is a two- or three-day walk, you know. While we were walking on the road, during the day bombing was going on--strafing. Just fantastic!

Some time before that, he and his men had, unbidden, almost run into a column of Nazi soldiers in retreat. It confirmed that the war was swinging in a new direction. With the young prisoners, they had done the humane thing. These were people roughly their own ages who with them were eagerly anticipating the war's end. Nor was it lost on Leon's unit that mere days before, these same people would likely have betrayed them to the Nazis. But reason did prevail as long as no one else but themselves were involved.

> Young people are young people. Three days, we became almost friendly with each other. Finally, on the second day, we came... we came to the... to a village. We were in the forest, you know. It was just amazing you know. We came in the forest, and we run up on a shepherd with his cows. So we said to [him], "What's happening there," you know? And he says he doesn't know where they [Nazis] are now. Anyway, he said, "There are soldiers there in his village right now that are wearing epaulets... they are wearing stars and they got a star on their hat [Russian soldiers]"

> Anyway, we said to this shepherd, "Leave the cows, we will look after your cows." We were afraid to go, because we didn't know who was in the village, and we were walking with seventy-two people wearing German uniforms!

> Well, an hour later, two guys, two Russian officers with the farmer are walking towards us. I'll never forget. I'm seeing the end of the war for us. [Pause] They come into the forest... Russian army. The hugging and the kissing like you see it sometimes, that's what went on there. I get emotional when I think of it. The way they were calling us heroes--"You helped us win the war." And they were looking at the Ukrainians and calling them the worst names in the world, you know.

Anyway, they took us into a village... the village where they were stationed. They locked up the seventy-two... seventy-four Ukrainians in a barn. [Pause] What happened to them is tragic, you know. Because you become friendly, you know, to an extent, young people with young people. The next morning, they took them all out and shot them. [Pause.] Executed all them. [Very quiet]

Inadvertently, roles had gotten reversed, and Leon was now thrown in with those who shot unarmed people who had given him and his men their trust. This terrible incident had not left him comforted. There was for him no acceptable justification for what had been done; the experience left him torn. However, it was different in dealing with the farmer who had betrayed him the morning of the attack in which his father and sister were killed.

That farmer, the Polish farmer, that N--sczi, that came out to the forest that brought those [sighs] killers upon us when I lost my father and my sister. I... a group of us... twenty of us Partisans went to his home about two weeks or three weeks later, and... hate to talk about it, [whispered] but I paid him back.

[Q: Did you speak to him?]

I spoke to him, but he denied everything. He said, "I didn't do it." [Sniffs] The funny part is that I thought I killed him, you know, because I didn't shoot him. I took the bayonet.

Killing had never been easy for Leon; he could not dehumanize others, even the enemy. But he had seen his sister being bayonetted as she ran, and sat with his dying father through six days of agony, and this would not leave him. He sought out the man who had betrayed his position on the fateful day when they had been attacked at daybreak.

I just hit him as many times as I could with a bayonet. And I abhor knives. I never... hand to hand fighting, I abhor it. [But too] impersonal when you shoot somebody, you know [even if] you feel the bullets hitting him. It was too easy for him to die [that way] for what he did to me... [quiet] to my family, you know. So I stabbed him so many times that I thought I killed him. It turned out that I didn't kill him. He lived. He lived a worse... worse life than being dead. He would have been better off to be dead.

Vengeance was a mean feast, and Leon sought to leave it behind him when he came to North America. In the value system of his parents, killing another human being was an ultimate crime that marked whoever committed it. Even killing that was part of the logic of war would not be fully absolved. On the other hand, to not carry out justice would be equally reprehensible.

In order to be able to carry on a new life and attempt to feel normal, he cast a boundary between the worlds of then and now. Then he had to kill to live; now he just had to learn to live well. Despite his resolve, the gap between the two worlds which he tenaciously kept separate floods with memories that roar into his present, full of pain and horror.

> I don't carry hate in my heart because hate is... destroys you, you know. If you hate people... I mean, if I hate you, you know that I hate you, and I cannot transform my hate to you. I cannot say to you that I hate you. But in the meantime, my guts, my heart, you know, everything destroys me from the inside. So you cannot go on hating, because it will destroy you.

> I don't believe in collective guilt. I don't believe all Germans or all Lithuanians or all Ukrainians... I can say that you are a bad person, but I wouldn't say that all Ukrainians are bad people. So I don't hate the Germans.

He makes certain compromises in order to be at peace in his Jewish faith and heritage, but he is attacked by memories, by the words of his father as they were stormed by the Poles, "Hold them back! Hold them back!" when his gun jammed. Through no fault of his own he is part of what happened and cannot escape agony in his loss. When a crowd at a football game roars encouragement, tumultuous emotions of another time reverberate in his mind.

> The whole scene comes back of my father hollering "Hold them back!" [as the crowd roars for the team on the one yard-line]. I... I travelled, and I go across railway tracks, carloads and carloads of cattle on the way to the slaughter houses. I don't see cattle, I see people. [Pause] This thing like... I am... mostly... the most like [voice is clutched] the worst thing that happens to me.

> I'm a symphony goer. I have symphony... I see and listen to the music, and it just kills me. It comes all back... all the scenes... all the tapes that you got in your head... come all back when I... Completely, completely relaxed, and I am enjoying what I'm listening to...[then the memory]. I avoid going to symphonies.

He fights now for his happiness. He is still gregarious, still believes in being a strong and contributing part of his community. He did become a mechanical engineer and developed a successful business firm. He married a woman who as a child had visited his father's dairy farm in her father's arms. Leon met her by chance in New York after the war at an event honoring Partisans and survivors in the Manhattan Ballroom. A year later they married. He is now a proud grandfather.

> I don't live with it [the hurt] every day, you know. I'm a very happy man. I've got three children. Those are my three [shows photos]--my two sons, and I got one little grandchildren. Financially very successful, you know. I been in this business... thirty years. I started out with B-- [business company] as a salesman. I wound up as being the president of their construction company, and I was very successful financially. From that point of view, God has been very good to me. Wonderful wife, wonderful children. I don't know what made me... what chased me... why did I survive? Because, when you think of it, see, in my town there were six thousand Jews. Out of the six thousand, 150 survived.
>
> So, I consider myself very lucky. I consider myself that I'm not afraid of death because, from the point of view, as far as dying, well all of us have to die someday, but I feel that if death would strike me tomorrow, I've had forty-five years more... gifted years... than my brother or my sister, or my father, because, basically, I should have been dead with all the rest of them. But I'm not. I've been given extra years.

DISCUSSION

These young men--David, Chaim and Leon, whose narratives were examined in this chapter were members of a community targeted for extermination. The dreams and wishes of their adolescence went unfulfilled as they faced the realities of a genocide aimed against them. Between 1939 and 1945, they had been caught up in a cruel maelstrom of a severity they could not have imagined. Unable to alter the course of history as those they loved were killed and all they cherished was taken from them, they cast about to first find a means to survive, then to seek some kind of justice, and finally to build a new life. These narratives represent survival accomplished by men who, so far from being passively driven to do so by various forces beyond their control, instead were actively thinking and strategizing how to help themselves and others achieve it. They told of physical stamina and endurance, all of which has its own place in the lore of manhood. In the survival process they described, they took action while being persecuted, they spoke of hurt while managing emotions and took courage when all that passed invited little more than terror.

CHAPTER 7

REFLECTIONS; THE CHALLENGED IDENTITY MODEL

> Berek Obuchowski was... among those deported from the Lodz ghetto to Birkenau in September 1944... 'I was taken with some men and boys,' he recalled. ...into a field where we were told to sit down by the Germans. After a few hours they picked out twenty-five young boys like myself. We were taken to a hut and made to undress completely for inspection to see if we were fit enough for work. I was in a fearful state of terror as the defect I had was in my right buttock, a part of which had decomposed while I was in a coma for six days in the Lodz ghetto... The flesh had deteriorated and fallen out, leaving a large gap to the bone... The other boys immediately and automatically came to my aid by standing behind, in front and at the side of me.'
> **Martin Gilbert**, *The Boys; The Untold Story of 732 Young Concentration Camp Survivors*, 1997:181.

SURVIVORS AND THE NARRATIVES

The survivor of a "successful" genocide is by definition something of an anomaly. There were few European Jews who survived the 1933-1945 period. In the Nazi KZ system (Chalk and Jonassohn 1990), eye-witness accounts tell us that it was mainly the youngest able-bodied workers who were retained; the rest were killed. Ninety percent of Jews who entered the death camps died there (Rubenstein and Roth 1989). Many of those who survived, in hiding, in exile, with the Resistance, or in the camps, had been under eighteen years of age at the time of their initial exposure to persecution related trauma. All had their socialization interrupted. They faced fragmentation and dissolution of their social worlds, watched loved ones be murdered and experienced physical demands that pushed the limits of their endurance.

Quite often the older the age of a young person, the more developed her/his socialization. When that expectation holds the older the age of the individual confronted by trauma, the more likely the narrative to reflect an interpretive richness and to reveal a gift for nuance, flexibility and emotional sophistication. But it is also true that children may develop faster than their years, given certain circumstances. In the present work, the survivor's age when first immersed in persecution affected what they remembered and the degree of specificity and nuance in their description. The younger the child, the greater the likelihood that unresolved traumatic memory would be shoved into silence for want of the discursive means at the time of the violence to understand themselves, what was happening, or their own responses to it. Degree and kind of isolation from family influenced the terms in which the pain was conceptualized and situationally managed. For all of them, exclusion and stigmatization in public life had the potential to sponsor retreat from trust. In addition, increased vulnerability due to community meaning frameworks being eroded by terror meant that there was no automatic safe haven possible with others or within the self. At such an extreme, the will to personify the other, or to translate feeling and emotion into understanding, might very well have been eclipsed by shock, denial and anger, especially in the very young and the very isolated. However, survivor narratives in this work showed the importance of transcendence processes focused on family, religious heritage and being with others sharing their fate.

Child survivors in various other documents often mentioned that what they went through was largely left unarticulated or expressed in the imagic, poorly differentiated wholes of primary memory. Child survivor narratives in this work showed some evidence of this kind of effect. They tended to be focused narrowly on the concerns of childhood and to describe factual scenes without detailed elaboration of their possible meanings. By contrast, young adult and adolescent narratives were more detailed and historically resonant--they had a deeper sense of what was happening to them and painted a larger more complex picture of the event frame.

Overall, each narrative presented in this work contributed something to a socially dimensioned model of surviving prolonged threat and extreme privation. They each referenced the eclipse of reason, told of society run amok and described a nightmarish reality that repelled the definitions learned in their earlier lives. They spoke of a world in which a thousand people could "disappear" in the smaller part of an hour, where children could be thrown live into burning pits, and pregnant women could be savaged by dogs while "authority figures" looked on. In that kind of ghoulish space, the thinking, feeling self retreats at least temporarily. Rene dreamt of escaping to his father more than he worried about some monster finding him and taking him where they took his mother. Chaim prayed as he operated a jackhammer for his enemy. Polla struggled to keep her baby alive. Each story showed the inner landscape which responded to the encompassing horror. In their words we can see how discursive processes are part of interactive strategies that help maintain the integrity of the self during crisis. Each illustrates how strategic identity during persecution and abuse works toward meeting specific instrumental goals or may just add something to emergent solidarity with others. Within the social worlds of misery and pain that configure each of the contexts of persecution these survivors described, the struggle to remain whole was a compelling quest for each individual until sheer physical exhaustion absorbed consciousness.

How may we put these concepts of self, identity and meaning together in the light of what the survivors said? The Challenged Identity Model attempts to formally sketch an answer. First the model is briefly stated and then it is discussed in terms of the narratives.

THE CHALLENGED IDENTITY MODEL

At the start of this work we said that the *challenged identity model* involved three major problematics: 1) developing a *challenged identity*; 2) mobilizing *interactional emergents*; and 3) generating a *survival communality*. Challenged identity itself is a concept which points to how we might understand surviving extremity, with the self mobilizing meaning so as to act constructively during terror, persecution, and the destruction of social worlds. Survivors spoke of setting limited goals and meeting them, managing fear and other emotions. Interactional emergents are ideas suggested by interactional episodes that serendipitously allow for the creation of survival strategies. They are innovative bits of the discursive stream between self and other that help challenged identity form. Generated out of the flow of interaction rather than individual intentionality, they have a logic and content that reflect collective level dynamics. Survival communality is a field of meaning that fosters social solidarity and fellow feeling among the oppressed so that they may bring off a countercultural effect that supports rather than undermines their survival in a setting inimical to it. In the survival process, challenged identity, interactional emergents, and survival communality are tied together.

Challenged Identity

Identity as a general category locates people in interpersonal terms (Lindesmith, Strauss and Denzin 1991:234; Stone 1981:188; Strauss 1969) so that they may handle the normal flow of interaction with efficacy and dispatch. By contrast, *challenged identity* pushes the self to confront rather than capitulate to duress and diminishment. Whereas in everyday life, names, titles, roles, or characteristic ways of doing things act as tags which identify us to others and are part of who we are to them, during times of ordeal the survivor must actively construct a new set of definitions to form a support for the self in the face of contention and threat. Challenged identity forms gradually, one situation at a time, building into a configuration of the self as agent, meeting self-affirming goals. It springs from definitional or reflective processes within a conflict situation where shock, alarm and severe danger are prevalent features of the social landscape and must be handled as responsibly as possible to protect life.[1] At the level of awareness, the motives associated with it are addressed in terms of "pulling the self together," "doing something" or "being helpful". Whatever the strategies are which articulate the challenged identity, they will consist of actions that can be risked.[2]

Challenged identity gradually mobilizes the self to replace the lost scaffolding of routine social life that once supported it with new frameworks for establishing meaning in the coercion context. With it, individuals are guided to look for resources to help them act credibly and with growing effectiveness as they formulate tractable routines and manageable expectations. Challenged identity lends to a self stance that mitigates against simple victimage to form limited strategies like "organizing" a bit of extra food, supporting someone in distress, and forming relationships of various kinds.

This kind of identity fosters survival from one ordeal to another and constitutes a unique patterning of self resources. Its elements grow out of a wider community of reference in which social identity (Goffman 1963) is defined. For Jews in the Holocaust, for instance, it would have been generated out of the symbols of Judaism and the historical expressions of Jewish identity as well as from socialization to gender worlds and general cultural references. Challenged identity emerges out of a) a set of conditions related to a shared humiliating fate,[3] b) a readiness to symbolically confront structures or practices that bring diminishment, and c) a willingness to embrace transcendence that turns physiological displacement toward a disciplined inward control which anticipates a readiness to resist.

Interactional Emergents

Interactional emergents are limited, spontaneous, dialogic episodes or gestural sequences, bits of social life out of which the survivor, at a self depleting extremity, finds meaningful orientations to maximize survivability. The process is already familiar to individuals as language users inasmuch as from our earliest socialization language is part of how we selectively define and respond to the world around us. We use the symbols of language to define and negotiate encompassing situations of various kinds. The concept of interactional emergents is anticipated by Goffman's work on the interaction order (1983; see also 1955) which references limited stabilities in interpersonal interaction loosely responsive to the larger cultural context. In the limited "stabilities" of a hiding place or concentration camp barracks, for instance, given human resilience and creativity, we might expect more than simple compliance to coercion at the level of interpersonal interaction. Using their own points of reference, survivors might discursively identify one another in terms of images of justice, rehash events that just happened, or rehearse strategies for the future or engage in survival humor (see also Weisman 1980) among other things, and so demonstrate what is referred to here as interactional emergents.

Interactional emergents represent the negotiated or fluid nature of social order rather than its capacity for becoming formally structured. They are spontaneous and random rather than organized or planned, fed by successful improvisation between at least two people. Though they are elemental and accrue in unintended ways, interactional emergents are not irrelevant or trivial but are *growing points for adaptive modes of thinking and relating*. Effective use of interactional emergents has both immediate and long-range effects as they lend to the partial resolution of some imminent problem, point to limited practical solutions, and tacitly affirm the importance of survival as a goal.

Survival Communality

Survival communality is generated in much the same way as any naturally occurring consensus. Erikson (1976:186-245), in his study of natural disaster in the Buffalo Creek flood, described "communality" as a sociocultural synthesis in which many individuals had before the disaster held similar meanings together as a social whole. Using shared meanings they acted with a special degree of resonance, much like having a "sixth sense"; they could anticipate how events might more than likely transpire and know what someone was most likely to do before they did it and align their own actions accordingly. *Survival communality* is similar in effect to what Erikson describes, but it grows out of a chaotic social space. Within it those who are oppressed come to share a more confirming ground in each other than a destructive context would otherwise afford. Such a framework of meanings guides single individuals in a risky and threatening environment to act as with the force of many.

The concept of survival communality is not fully anticipated by what traditional sociology calls social structure but represents a kind of focused sociality revolving around staying alive during prolonged extremity. Since it is responsive to a shared threatening circumstance, values critical to it highlight endurance and remaining whole. The feelings and emotions that feed it are stirred by surrounding events as survivors recognize something of their own plight in each other's suffering. Eventually typical sequences of action take on a meaning and purpose responsive to helping self and others survive.

Summary: Taken together, these concepts--challenged identity, interactional emergents, and survival communality, are part of the process of survival from a relational, socially dimensioned standpoint. We find them present in the narratives examined in this work, where individuals were moved from being merely victims to becoming agents for their own and others' good, capable of turning aspects of their limited spheres of action to some more affirming posture during threat and persecution. From this point of view, surviving engaged a dialectic between beliefs, norms and values from the past and their complete obfuscation in the coercion context. Within the self as well as in the flow of interaction with others similarly situated, a new picture of the coercion setting was formed in which the self was recast to turn all other goals toward a central one of their own making. The profoundly threatened survivor acquired the means to rename the coordinates of existence and identify others within them. This conceptualization of survival allows us to anticipate that, even in a power vacuum, discursive social processes in some minimal ways would 1) direct self resources toward a more resilient integrity; 2) suggest ideas for surviving; and 3) generate a shared perspective fostering a commonweal of the dispossessed.

Taking this model and examining each of its main concepts in terms of age categories--children, adolescents, young women and young men, within various conditions of survival--the camps, hiding, exile, with the Resistance or the Partisans, we will attempt to clarify the social dimensions of surviving during the Holocaust.

CHALLENGED IDENTITY

Children

Tracing the development of challenged identity in each of the narratives, Robbie started out with the identity of "the baby" in his family. This identity shackled him as the Holocaust fully set in and the family could no longer control its own fate. In the work camps, partly in response to his father's urgings, he developed the new identity, "wunderkind." Robbie eventually went beyond wunderkind. In the bread and marmalade episode a deeper part of himself began to develop. He defined the unexpected gift of a stranger as a "great blessing," satisfying more than his physical hunger. Symbolically it joined him to a wider community of justice and hope. When he took pains to share the extra food with his sister he amplified its worth even more. Each week when he did this, he risked his life, but, as he did, new identities of protector and provider emerged.

On his own, after the death of most of his family, when he was digging antitank ditches, he added once again to the dimensionality of his challenged identity. In the episode of the murderer's apple, he showed himself to be a moral arbiter, wise judge, and witness to truth. Standing within inches of a fellow prisoner who had just been shot, and fighting a paralyzing sense of anxiety, he saw the guard move toward him. Instead of a bullet, the guard gave him an apple. He was relieved beyond the power of words to express, but instead of a vacuous show of thankful self abasement, like a miniature rebbe, he interpreted the episode as a midrash on the text of living in a time of death. The miraculous contradiction took him beyond himself toward what he little understood, but with dignity. In these incremental ways, his survival came to be connected with the growth of inner strength.

With regard to attachment to family during ordeal, Rene, like Robbie, was eventually left with strangers, the difference between the two being that Rene believes his father is alive; Robbie has seen his vanish. Rene's father was with the Resistance and had successfully kept him hidden. The development of challenged identity for Rene included three elements: 1) identity fostered onto him by others, 2) the identity he longed for, and, 3) the identity that emerged in ongoing interaction. In the struggle between the given and what might have been, reality was indeed bleak for him but nevertheless open to interpretation. The part of identity which his parents fostered onto him was one he refused; he could not bear the thought of parting from them, regardless of the harsh times. His intransigence on this point proved a great threat to himself and others as he revealed in the episode of the railroad station, when he was rescued but his mother was captured and led away. The second is expressed in the longing he would never relinquish, that is, of being happy once again with his parents. He never gave up identity longed for, to the point that at times it became his reality, eclipsing events he could not bear to consider. His crippling emotional loss at the capture of his mother was signalled in his almost fatal illness that followed. The third became his challenged identity, that is the child planning escapes from safe havens and all the horror they were keeping at bay. There was an essential, uplifting romance in this identity which brought him out of his doldrums and showed him to be, not a victim displaced by persecution, but a survivor capable of daring escapes, with a fantastic father to visit--a father full of mystery but also very loving, who could, even years later, still shape his dreams.

Louise was more passive than Rene in her roles within the trauma context. She survived by faithful obedience to her family's wishes. Like Robbie and Rene she had to displace her resentment of being treated like a child, a *quantite negligeable*, when it came to decision-making. She did this by holding a clear sense in her own mind that her compliance was for the good of the family. Her challenged identity involved seeing herself as protector of her family and wise sage. Like other survivors of extremity she saw herself as both inside and outside the situations she encountered, but not contained by them; she could be the obedient child but felt resilient and independent. She had a rich inner life to balance out the starched emptiness of her endless days in hiding without books or friends or freedom of movement.

Challenged identity for Harry involved holding to his ideal of the strong silent man, one who did not complain, who kept on going against whatever came, whose endurance of threat and abuse was ensured by courage coupled with good luck. He represents an heroic construal of survivor identity which highlights a self that remains intact despite the mirk in which it is cast, one which can be found celebrated universally in transcendence myths. What he chose to say of the past revealed no sense of the rhetoric of accusation that helped order chaotic and violent times in memory. There is something noble about his style, but also something hidden, associated with unhealed wounds.

Mariette, though aware of a tenuous connection to family through their shared participation in the Resistance, is essentially isolated. In fact she is the archetype of the traumatized child. She decided to keep the past and present closed to each other, identifying one with the identity of Mariette and the other with Marie. Perhaps this device oversimplifies an abyss of traumatic memory which she leaves unexplored, but she can relate to others in terms of latitudes this artifice allows, helping her to have the worlds of both the past and the present without compromising either. Trying to describe the past involved her in a confusion of unworded bits of experience which her truncated socialization and her sparse ties to family during her ordeal helped keep attenuated. She did manage a challenged identity as Mariette the courier, the precocious child, the escape artist, the mime, the lucky survivor.

Adolescents

Little about existence under coercion can be changed by the victim, but the impact of events can be altered by the interpretive process in which they are grasped. The adolescents have a clearly well- developed discursiveness that explores both fateful and negotiable aspects of surviving. In Leo's case, the fateful part of survival trauma is indexed with the remark, "I talked to a young man who... who was castrated." Medical experiments were conducted at many camps in the KZ system, with Auschwitz mainly specializing in what passed for racial testing. Twin experiments were a sadistic exploitation of human subjects for trifling kinds of questions. Subjects were sacrificed, some dying in excruciating agony. The negotiated aspect of existence in such a frightful space might involve trying to get a little more food, or feeling lucky for having no particular test being done that day. In such a place, being "lucky" meant feeling a little better off than others maimed or dying. Leo had no identity that sat well with him other than cheating the torturer just a little. It surprised Leo when the identity "twin" helped him escape a beating. The protected status terrified him as well as made him feel a little bit lucky. As he amplified what might be risked, he gathered strength, visiting others through the barbed wire separating the blocks of inmates in the camps. Gradually his challenged identity grew until, with a buddy, he had the self command to hide rather than go on the last forced march out of Auschwitz. He is certain now that this decision saved his life.

Serge, though two years younger than Leo and in hiding, like Leo valued self-reliance and luck, configuring it into protector-keeper roles within the group sharing the cellar shelter. Michel's challenged identity formed in the company of captives he came to so highly esteem. Though not with his family as Serge was, his challenged identity had a similar dimensionality, highlighting themes of protector, provider, fighter, brother, man of faith and honor. In part, this grouping of elements is congruent with Michel's age, in part with the young soldiers he fell in with at Birkenau. Out of his resolve to gather to himself the things of a man, he attracted to himself companions with similar longings and sympathies and for whom he could make brave choices.

Peter and Klara, though different in gender and personality, both for different reasons stumbled upon a similar pattern in their challenged identity. It involved self mastery, controlling the ability to give all that the situation might call out from them. Though Peter was aggressive and Klara muted in style, they both managed emotions carefully. Peter planned and strategized while Klara quietly and efficiently mobilized her inner resources. To their great amazement, despite whatever happened around them, whatever exigency came upon them, they were still alive when the morning dawned each day. They stoically bore whatever misery that put upon them.

Young Women
Like challenged identity in the other age groups, each of the women contribute something in their narratives to the idea of reconstructing the self during ordeal. Bertha learned immense compassion that had the power during ordeal to help her reflectively analyze the block leaders and women commandants as well as her fellow survivors. Her challenged identity focused on nurturing and being nurtured. Using inner discursive strategies, she would not grow cynical nor would she allow herself the hate she saw in others, not even for the guards. This commitment carried through after liberation when, despite the aching pain that went with loneliness and grieving for her murdered family, she carried on, got a job, formed a Zionist association and made her beliefs constructively reshape a bleak external reality for herself and others. The child weeping for her mother on the way to Birkenau was transformed into a woman mourning for her people.

Vera had seen her family suddenly dispossessed, their citizenship taken away, landholdings confiscated. Her family were sent packing "with their bare minimums" while neighbors stared at them through curtained windows. No one helped. This had left her in an altered state which she could not shake off. Yet from this time of inner frailty to the emergence of the heroic self we find depicted at Plaszow, her challenged identity had formed. Within the limits of roles she could legitimate, she fostered in herself the challenged identity of rescuer to her mother and those others she meant to sustain and protect. At Plaszow, she became known for her brave deeds--stealing a pair of shoes for someone with none, getting extra food from local townspeople to share with members of her work detail. She earned the respect of the other women for her courage and daring, despite the depredations of a sadistic female lieutenant. Her buoyancy and confidence reemerged under persecution, along with a strong sense of humor.

Elsie's survival strategy centered on remaining as invisible as she could. Despite this, she did develop a fighting stance as weaver of hopes and dreams in the stories she constructed or the wisdom she shared. In this role she assumed a challenged identity that touched other lives even as the horrors of the Krakow ghetto unfolded.

Ruth formed a challenged identity as she tried to deal with the upheaval in her personal life brought on by the Nazi rise to power in the 1920s and 30s. She used reason and critical insight to take the stance of "rebel" against a sociopolitical reality primed for genocide. She worked with a natural tendency to confront problems. Full of fiery spirit uncontaminated by illusion, she managed to save her nephew and herself despite what it cost in emotional terms to stand up against her whole family as they struggled to remain loyal to a Germany that had disappeared.

Polla was a natural for the formation of challenged identity. She had always resisted whatever seemed unjust. The first year of her imprisonment in the Russian gulag was a turning point for her. She found a way to rebound from the shock of capture, trial, and imprisonment. She accepted the mentorship of a nurse in the camp hospital, and with this base of encouragement remained functional in that world of cold and bitter suffering until, in 1944, after her transfer to the Black Sea area, she escaped with her child. Her resilience throughout this part of her ordeal is at least remarkable. She kept her wits about her and with each new obstacle mustered a clearer, stronger commitment to her original goals. Resurgence seemed to be Polla's way of responding to eradication of hopes and dreams. For one set of dreams lost, she found another and wove survival out of the bits of life that were still intact. This is the essence of a challenged identity. It fosters the individual capacity to be autonomous, to be able to make independent judgements in the face of pernicious normative trends or coercive dictates.

With challenged identity, all of these women survivors became transformers of reality, growing beyond their limitations to new depths of strength and courage.

Young Men

For the young men in these narratives, more than other survivors, there is a full blown emphasis placed on luck, good gamesmanship, coordination and deftness. Their interpersonal interaction in the situations of their ordeal was influenced by a framework of values from the past as well as the logic of hardship. They favor rhetorics of individuality, power, and strength to account for how they handled situations described in their narratives. In terms of the self process associated with survival, each young man found a unique way of mobilizing pluck and character in confronting the ineffable. After 1945 their narratives indicate they each could weave together a worldview that recognized values learned in childhood, and rescue their future from the ravages of persecution.

In the first three days of hiding during the Nazi invasion of his area, Leon's survival or challenged identity as a Partisan began to unfold. His experience of the slaughter of the women and children moved him out of passivity to find a way to fight back. He trained with the Russian military, and within a few months those who knew him saw his potential as a brave and wily fighter emerge. It was this image that he wove into the many contexts he mentioned, rescuing, protecting, or attacking as the situation warranted.

David was normally of a quiet and determined character--witty and humorous, but insightful. As he developed a challenged identity he learned flexibility and bearable compromise. From a very young age he was able to buoy against difficulty and in small ways turn events in his favor. He drew on this store of insight during ordeal, conducting himself as a practical sage, vigilant in all situations. This was his challenged identity. He would see the optimal effort required to put a corrective to a problem, always informed by measured decency. Through each moment of inner crisis, he summoned strength for the next. Somewhere in the course of confronting his pain and loss he had decided that ultimate victory over the dehumanizing conditions of genocide would only come by forming loving, caring knots of people dedicated to each other's well being across social categories. Out of his sorrow came his keen awareness of the need for a radical philosophy of humanism.

Chaim saw himself as a strong man and a capable worker. At Mauthausen this identity had survival value. He engaged in passive resistance as he confronted the rejection of his religious faith and ethnic roots by the oppressor. Praying alone as he worked a jack-hammer or over others as they lay sick or dying, he kept his faith and his tradition alive in his heart. This, as much as his natural strength and resilience, formed a sustaining base for his survival. It meant that he never became the beaten kind of person the captors expected to create in the survivor, nor was he defiant. In his challenged identity, he was a man who could lead others from all walks of life, and, in the face of stigma and oppression, be at peace with himself. His identity frame became his springboard for surviving atrocity and constructing a vital moral career that spanned divergent realities and bridged his way back into conventional life.

INTERACTIONAL EMERGENTS
Children

Robbie's survival from the start was responsive to interactional emergents. His family searched for ways to protect him, for being the youngest of the family there were fewer means available to protect him. They tried out many shaky strategies, from having him hide on someone's farm to letting him serve as courier for the Polish resistance around Skarczysko. In the course of events Robbie became expert at sensing weak spots in strategies and appearances. Above all, he learned to work faster and more efficiently than the others. In the early days of the forced labor system this protected him from random scrutiny and his father protected him during official selections.

In terms of interactional emergents, Harry, surviving in the relative shelter of Theresienstadt, had much less than Robbie to negotiate. Though Theresienstadt was a showpiece camp where the wealthiest families were sent, it was also Auschwitz's waiting room. Most who entered Theresienstadt eventually did go further east to their deaths. Of the 140,000 people sent there, 33,000 died there; 88,000 were sent to their deaths at Auschwitz. They were permitted to set up a school for the children, emphasizing art, poetry and music. They set vegetable gardens from which only camp administrators were allowed to eat. The half-starved men and frozen bodies Harry saw returning westward in open boxcars left him with few doubts about the overall scheme of things. A silent terror and frozen calm characterized his survival stance. What he did to stand up to this nightmare he kept to himself, making veiled reference to a special block in the camp that he and his pal had come to know. Through their information network they heard of the resistance in the woods surrounding the camp and kept a balanced perspective. He still, however, remains a man of few words.

Mariette became an independent, inventive child under the pressures of her ordeal in hiding and with the resistance. She still carefully guards the access roads to her inner self at all times. After liberation, she did not suffer the reordering of her world by anyone. During the 1939-45 period she survived by using different languages to carry messages for the Resistance. When caught, she showed daring and imagination as she slipped through the hands of the Gestapo to safety. She withstood betrayal, murder of her friend and endless, anxiety-laden uncertainty as she passed from one hiding place to another.

It was relatively late in the war in Holland when, in 1943, Louise's family decided to go into hiding. Interactional emergents that sustained her survival sprang from everyday life with others sharing close quarters. They had used a series of contacts known to her mother's family to successfully leave Amsterdam and find someone connected with the Dutch Underground to hide them. Fortuitous coalitions between the Dutch Underground and Christian fundamentalists made their initiative work. Nevertheless, the link between the host and the hidden was fragile; there were no protocols by which to place guarantees on desirable outcomes. There were no standards for action, and Louise found it hard to settle in, to eat only at night, to keep no reading materials around, to rarely wash clothes and move about only when others were sleeping. She had to learn how to balance long periods of boredom with a readiness to flex with sudden situation shifts. Family solidarity emerged out of their strategizing.

Mariette, Rene and Louise spent a great deal of their experience under persecution in hiding. Hiding imposes peculiar limitations on those who are forced into it. Sometimes, as with Louise and her family, it demanded the management of appearance and identity as well as the specific cultivation of invisibility. With only an intuitive logic and quick wittedness to guide them, they adjusted to the pressures and surprises of becoming and remaining "invisible." Survivors who went into hiding, in many cases, had to appear to be part of a way of life which formerly was completely foreign to them, convincingly representing new customs, manners and rituals as though these were their own. Looking and acting like those native to the situation also meant speaking correctly the language and the dialect of the region where they were hiding. If the hiding involved total seclusion, they had to, in a sense, "die" to relatives and former friends (see also Frank 1995). Hiding meant learning to be skillful at negotiating impromptu situations. It meant having the discipline and the courage to take a risk when no one was sure how far the others involved could be trusted.

The Adolescents

Interactional emergents are not so much what any one person does but unexpected combinations of symbols that suggest new ideas and solutions in an unclear, risky kind of context. Klara's stories tell of the women collectively organizing to help the youngest among them be vigilant, to remember that they could be horribly damaged as culture bearers before being killed as physical bodies. Without such caring insight, these teenagers might not have as readily attuned themselves to the incredible shifts in identity the progression of a genocide had placed upon them. Though Klara was shocked and disoriented, she eventually came to accept this caring even when directed toward her by others her own age. Klara's narrative also reveals that there was a processual, interactive unfolding of nurturant orientations, sympathy and protectiveness as the women grew more aware of their shared plight until gradually it almost became routine. Referring to lines formed at early morning appel as well as at various points throughout the day, she said, "Each morning we took turns, always another person was standing in the middle. You see, the one in the middle, at least she was a bit warmed by the two bodies next to her." They actively tried to bolster optimism by, in the barracks, telling stories of being saved by noble strangers, finally being avenged by an outraged world at last made aware of what was happening to them. Such little acts of respect and love were the acts of resistance, courage and ingenuity they gradually learned to prize as important.

Peter, who so prized his self-reliance, mentioned interaction sequences that got him into work details he could bear. Knowing what to fear as part of the flow of interaction in the camps led him to keep on working when he had a seeping head wound. Staying connected to a "prominenz" in the camp ranking system got him in the line leading the forced march out of Auschwitz. He stayed very aware in order to not miss the slightest chance to use whatever opportunity presented itself to stave off fatal effects of hunger and thirst or to be selected. When he had used up all the physical strength he had in fighting off typhus he developed tuberculosis. Similarly Michel in his anecdotes spoke of a terror that was unrelenting, a world of pain and degradation eased only by a mesh of small acts of support from barracks mates.

Leo had to fight against the caged bird effect of being kept as an experimental subject. It kept him isolated from the larger community of captives. But, gradually, he began speaking to others through the wire fences, talking anxiously to other human subjects and learning to look for lucky solutions to immediate problems until finally he was strong enough to make the decision to hide from the last forced march out of Auschwitz, a choice that likely saved his life.

Young Women

Like the other survivors, Bertha, Elsie, Vera, Polla and Ruth mentioned luck, an unheralded emergent from ongoing streams in the flow of activity. They also pointed to the importance of self reliance and a certain healthy selfishness in uncertain times. These are assessments derived from interaction that proved successful in some way. In Polla's case, other women of various rank in the gulag system showed her signs of caring--bringing a carrot or giving a kind word, or allowing her privacy to perform her toilet. Similarly, Bertha was particularly painstaking in showing how her thinking changed in response to the flow of interaction, moving her first into shock and isolation and then back once again to a balance from which she could take perspective and reach out to others.

Vera, by the time she reached Plaszow, was ready to find whatever ways she could to keep her mother alive and protected. Elsie had started out that way, trying to find strategies to protect her mother and mother-in-law using the work permit system. Until the multi-step liquidation of the Krakow ghetto occurred, this worked. She protected children trusted to her care until they were taken to Auschwitz. She admitted to always trying to find a small bit of wriggle room, a hole in the oppression structure that afforded escape from its full force. Finally, in Auschwitz, her humor and sense of what the others needed for hope allowed her to build salient imagery into the stories she would tell in the barracks.

In exile, it might at first seem that Ruth would not represent interactional emergents related to a survival communality. But in the 1930s, through a gradual sifting process, those who held the view that Germany under the Nazis was a threat to life as they treasured it became part of a growing public that either sought means to escape Germany and help others do the same. Ruth's experience fit this pattern. During the 1930s, while still in Germany, she strove to warn her family of the danger she saw looming and the likelihood that at the very least they should make a special effort to protect her nephew, their child and grandchild. Having arranged her own plan of escape, she only sought to use it when she had exhausted all means of convincing those she loved to come with her. Urged by her ailing father to follow through on her plans herself, she got on the last steamship to sail from Europe as the war closed in upon them.

Young Men

Leon experienced interactional emergents from the point of view of a guerrilla unit. Sometimes help emerged out of nowhere, or in the heat of a crisis amazing talents possessed by a comrade might come to light and save the day. Mostly such emergents had to do with building team solidarity, or unearthing information about hidden enemies that might keep the unit from harm.

David spoke of Auschwitz as a suffocatingly pernicious environment that turned living human beings into nonpersons to be violated at will. Captives he felt were kept from freely communicating with and helping each other across most situations. Despite being determined to give no compromise to the enemy, he found himself saying he was a carpenter when asked. He was chosen to work in the Buna section of Auschwitz. His brothers, equally determined not to give an inch, were younger than David and received none of training he had. They did not make any admission of talent and were taken into hard labor at camps farther west. Had they been given the smallest opportunity to confer, he might have been able to change matters. As it was, the trifling difference in choices taken in the twinkling of an eye separated David's fate from that of his brothers. Oppressive structures at Auschwitz precluded any real possibility of expressing human emotions or relationships that could be counted on through thick or thin. Nevertheless, in the trammel of endless misfortune and hunger he developed and sustained a relational tie to at least one other person. Disappointing as it was to realize how much more might have been done had only interaction between captive been unfettered, even David admitted "organizing" extra food rations with a buddy. He said that he had been attuned to flexibility by having to adapt to changing conditions as a child.

Chaim, by contrast, represents the prototype of interactional emergents in the camps. He was strong and quietly gregarious. Like david, he had learned early in life to be adaptive, to on his own swiftly change from one set of situational handicap to another without second thought. But he was also able to turn to others, to open to whatever small sign of humanity there might be in anyone around him in any part of the camp structure. He was willing to chance risky leads and primitive intuitions that only made sense in the shifting currents in the flow of violence, to save his life. From mending socks to helping those on their last to die as he prayed with them, he showed the value of interaction even at such an extreme. And somehow this orientation helped him even to the point of escaping certain death as he crippled along on a forced march out of Mauthausen. Chaim clearly exemplifies what he and other survivors called good luck. He made the most of moments marginal to the camp's instituted order to find some reprieve. Chaim's story of the older guard who gave him not just a bowl of soup but certain encouragement is an example of this kind of "luck" amidst fluctuating anomalies.

An infallible logic is not the trademark of the emergent interactional order, but practical efficacy in conduct may be. Interactional emergents in the anecdotes Chaim shared include a) fortuitous grafting of individual initiative on forced relationships, b) momentary bursts of caring within and between layers of the camp's status system especially as the fortunes of war changed, and, c) simple codes such as "be alert," and "look for ways to help yourself," all were reflections of individuals casting about for alternatives to a situation which was becoming increasingly difficult.

SURVIVAL COMMUNALITY
The Children

The development of shared orientations in response to extreme conditions and the growth of interactional novelties that spurred the emergence of a communality of survival were clearest under conditions of captivity in the camps. But, nonetheless, they prevailed as well in each of the other survival contexts. Survival communality was expressed by Mariette in her ties to the Resistance, several of whom were members of her family, and she made reference to them as one who was never alone and always alone--in the midst of 'friends' but always guarded. During the train scene when she was deftly rescued by her brother, or suddenly, when out of nowhere, she received word to leave a compromised hiding spot, for instance--these were signs that someone within the Resistance was protecting her.

Though connected to the Resistance, Rene seldom thought of himself in such terms. Rather he saw himself clearly as a Jewish boy amid his heart-of-France Catholic rescuers. He was a bright child, and his teachers doted on him. They were his survival communality--not like him but for him. His father's contacts formed yet another layer in this whole which was always present yet always hidden within the flow of life and summed up in the sentinel image of the woman who always came to get him eventually, no matter where he was hidden. Though he did nothing in particular, he was supported by those who saw him through that terrible time of fear, horror, and loneliness.

For Louise and her family, the resistance workers and their hosts formed a small core of a larger survival communality held together by the Resistance and Dutch Underground. Within this, the family stayed afloat in a sea of shifting risks and demands in hiding. The family gingerly felt their way through this kind of ambivalence and anxious misgivings when a second family joined them in their hiding space. They got through Louise's dental emergency. Similarly, they worried their way past her sister's hiding place being compromised. Each of these events had the potential to sunder their plans and required different kinds of adjustments. They met all of these crises with discipline and a certain poise. Her father's awareness of how to get through the worst of times bolstered their confidence. He was at the center of their survival communality and his reference point as an ideal community based on justice, ethics, law, and beyond the grip of Nazism.

Robbie's references to a survival communality at first were deflected through family, but this gradually opened up to include other people from various parts of the camp system. By contrast, Harry's survival communality came from beyond the camps where the Partisans and local resistance functioned. They appeared in his remarks as he spoke about the end of the Theresienstadt camp. Across the cases, though a ready opportunism was easily associated with survival communality, unspoken codes of conduct were legitimized in terms of a "goodness principle" that tied back to what they had valued in their former lives. Strategic closeness in pseudo-family units put strangers together as friends. Sometimes this helped heal emotional and physical wounds generated by the trauma; at other times it at least gave a diffuse back region in which to generate affirming relationships.

The Adolescents

For those in hiding, survival remained focused on a small array of persons, but in the concentration camps and with the resistance or the Partisans this broadened to include many who never met each other in any face-to-face way. Lacking support generated within the instituted order, survival communality grew out of survivors helping, caring and protecting one another as relative strangers. There were within this knots of friends who also articulated the rhetoric of survival communality but within a closed circle, moreso. To the extent that they represented networks of "surrogate families," they, in the sense intended here, supplied limited sources of tenderness, affection, and practical generally to whoever they could, given the limits of their resources. Schmolling (1984:114; see also Klein 1983:122) also noted that within the context of the group, a prisoner became whole again, and self was redefined against the unity of a larger community framework. Through involvement in group life, the individual was lifted out of the despair bred by powerlessness. This brought them reflectively beyond a sole reliance on fantasy (Abram, 1970:53) to a point where the individual could consistently make a distinction between what Goffman (1963) referred to as "felt" and "social" identity, between what they knew themselves to be authentically and their situated self expressions in interaction. The survival communality guided the identification process and facilitated within its survival rhetoric a heightened sense of worth for each captive (see also Frankl 1965:91-108; Kanter 1972:282).

During the early part of her internment, Klara could not bring herself to eat or drink. She was sickened by the loss of her family. She kept to herself, letting interpersonal distance give her the appearance of strength. But the other women intervened, helping her to balance this austerity. Gradually the discursive sense of a survival communality took hold, each person recognizing the others' situated needs in terms of their own. Klara's survival was premised on this slim collective of caring for which she had initially felt nothing but distance. It eventually became clear to her that placing a sense of trust in these strangers was necessary for survival. The relatively older women assumed a nurturant role toward the younger ones who were still girls like Klara. She illustrated survival communality when she mentioned the importance of belief. She referred to a sense of there being "a little family" among the women to help each person get through whatever arose. She survived because of the unity she shared with five other women. Survival communality is exemplified in many ways in Klara's narrative which at the same time also highlights how interactional emergents sustain it. In the cloth of caring episode where, having been left without a smock or shoes until the next bath four weeks later, Klara was given pieces of her friends' dresses with which to warm her heart if not her body. She did survive this impossible situation because of a blanket and the symbolism shared. Survival of the body in Klara's narrative was preceded by the collective strengthening of the spirit.

The "solution" to any given problem did not come from any one person but rather from the general state of understanding which grew out of interaction in their group. Interactional emergents flow into survival communality and back. Michel acknowledged this, as with each new obstacle he developed strategies to aid survival. Peter described a scene in which these interactional emergents, made meaningful within the logic of a survival communality, turned his likely death by typhus into a rescue. "I was helped," he said. Peter had fallen unconscious with typhus and could not defend himself; he had been selected for extermination when the young Slovakian who was in charge of the block asked an older man who had been overlooked in the last selection but who was at death's door if he would go to the gas in Peter's stead. He agreed. Similarly, in Michel's narrative there is also a sense that helping one another was valued among the prisoners. Though Russian soldiers under the Commissar Order of 1941 (Levin 1990:47-48), were themselves scheduled for specific abuse and death once captured, they had reason to fear that Michel, of slight build and gentle ways, Jewish from birth, would be treated far worse on his own than with them. Soon they were on their way to Nordhausen together. This camp was a terrifying, frozen spot where workers were hanged for the slightest trifle, their bodies left in plain view for the next shift of workers to see. Michel's conception of himself involved building solidarity, feeling grateful that he got a whipping rather than a hanging. His camarades protected each other from descent into complete barbarity, and this was part of what made him think of them as a company of heroes. By ingenious means and, at times, profound sacrifice, survival communality worked.

Young Women
Being brave and reaching out to others were characteristics of self comportment that Bertha, Vera, Elsie, Polla and Ruth valued. Each of the women in turn tacitly acknowledged survival communality, some referring to it directly. Vera spoke of the evening lecture series the women prepared for one another on various topics, the "feast" the women in her barracks prepared for her birthday, her own dedication to keeping her mother alive. The communality of caring that these acts bespeak is also referenced in Bertha's comments about women in her barracks when they "adopted" her, seeing that her shock was so great she could hardly speak anymore. Bertha reached back to life because of this, letting her own capacity for understanding and insight inform a variety of people and activities. Elsie was the optimist and humorist who found stories to bolster others and inspire a limited solidarity. Modestly, but with grace and sophistication, she analyzed a situation bereft of all but tragedy and turned it into manna for the wounded soul. And Polla, too, working within this kind of social process, working with the other prisoners in the Russian camps, underwent a personal transformation, becoming a careful mother, nurse and friend, one who could listen to others. Pawelczynska (1979) refers to ties between prisoners in her concentration camp experience being guided by a wider frame of reference than was structurally anticipated, allowing for the growth of a diffuse esprit de corps. "Regardless of how isolated a prisoner felt or how aware he was of the support of his fellow-prisoners, that support existed. In the beginning the chance to give material help was almost nonexistent, but there was at least sympathy" (1979:101).

Young Men
Survival communality was recognized to some extent in all the narratives, but men were much less willing than women to credit interpersonal ties with helping them stay alive during terror and abuse. In

their analytical remarks they tended to take for granted the will to survive, or any but themselves being involved in their own survival. That being noted, their anecdotes were heavily peopled. There was always a "we," either directly referenced or implicit, especially where survival seemed most problematic. In their narratives they could isolate the key experiences which were turning points in their knowledge of life, self and others during their ordeal, suggesting that what we are calling survival communality was present and vital. They referred to feelings and emotions, taking seriously the way they managed them. In their depiction of themselves during ordeal they were the bearers of community the representatives of humanity, standing, as it were, at the gates of hell yet witnessing, judging, reflecting, beating back their terror, and within the floating stream of suffering around them, finding the means to endure. Their stories were of family, simple courage, caring and fierce inner commitment.

Remarks that centered on survival communality for Leon at first referenced a network of relatives, friends, neighbors and members of the Jewish community providing a flow of information that kept them from being captured. Later he spoke of life as a guerrilla fighter, setting mines, fighting skirmishes, protecting who they felt they could. Beyond a certain point in the chaos--just after the Nazis occupied the Grodno area on their way eastward--he had joined the Partisans. Thereafter, the lifestyle that choice demanded structured his survival. His story of the joke they played on Mishka showed the flexibility of the buddy relationship and the great reliance of the Partisans on one another. Outside of the solidarity of his comrades and fellow soldiers, death was almost a certainty, as he observed through what happened to his family and kindred.

Chaim had a much richer acknowledgement of a field of others and framework of symbols that highlighted community values from the past, even if just a little. Chaim in so many of his anecdotes showed his own and others' caring, emphasizing faith and spirit to hold against the force of the crime being committed against them. David was different. He had been taken to Auschwitz very shortly after the occupation of their region by Nazi forces. His boyhood had taught him buoyancy and creativity where there were few strong social supports. He quite naturally chose in the camps to keep his own counsel, to depend almost completely on his own experience, powers of observation and ability to remain invisible by blending into the mass of life around him. With a buddy he shared anger, grief, resentment, and extra rations. There were chance references to diffuse acts of helpfulness among the oppressed in his description, but generally, survival communality was a much foreshortened reference in his account. Like Chaim, he depended on community of the past to supply him with a store of symbolic meanings to support him until the last vestiges of physical stamina would have to carry him.

Summary: Though there are differences in style across the individual narratives as well as variation in terms of conditions of persecution, yet we have been able to flesh out the conceptual elements of the challenged identity model using all of the cases. What we know of survival through these narratives is a tribute to the dignity of those who endured unimaginable, unwanted fates. They assure us that by their own efforts, ordinary social actors may keep their humanity whole and intact under threat, humiliation, and terror.

CONCLUSION

The material in this work provides a socially dimensioned conception of surviving extremity. It suggests that personal characteristics and moral states of the individual should be considered as we attempt to understand the survival of trauma associated with persecution, captivity and abuse. In the narratives, the interactional "order" (see also Goffman 1981) of survivors in various coercion contexts provided a stream of face-to-face actions which sustained its own framework of meanings and contributed to the emergence of a counter-order--that of the victims. Interactional emergents helped bridge the gaps between the survivors' past and their longed-for futures. The present and the future were part of a selective reconstruction of life, emphasizing transcendence through a variety of activities including those of care-giving and support for one another. As a result, assault on the internalized order of the selves of survivors referred to by other researchers, e.g., Eitinger (1974), Niederland (1968; 1964) and Krystal (1968), did not completely determine the fate of these survivors. Survival was, in fact, a far more complex process than we have heretofore allowed ourselves to see, with survivors pitching their battle against obliteration on many planes, one day, one situation at a time.

While, therefore, this is an exploratory approach to the study of the social dimensionality of survival, it suggests that survivors used beliefs, practices and values from the past to allow social definitions part of community life to inform constructive sociality within the trauma context. This suggests that recovery after exposure to trauma may be examined in terms of symbolic frameworks and social structures facilitating some level of agency within the simple flow of interaction.

Healing, like physical survival, may be influenced by strategies individuals have taken during exposure to extremity. Survivors variously rework their connections back to life and wholeness by acting in ways that opened them to interpersonal dynamics and community values that could be in some way continued during their ordeal.

ENDNOTES

CHAPTER SEVEN

1. In this work we are discussing the role of transcendence for people who were captives and marked for death. Passive or spiritual resistance may have been the most they could have hoped to achieve with responsible conduct. As readings like Borowski's tell us, it is difficult to look or act heroic while being eyed by a sadist with a whip. And yet, even in Borowski's anecdotes there are those who put their lives on the line to help others. For instance, there is Ivan who saves the Greek (1955:79) in "A Day at Hermenz." It is problematic that those trying to survive would develop a challenged identity, and even when they do, it may not look like anything too spectacular. But with it people are saved, the goal of survival for both self and others is emphasized, and individuals become more than mere victims-- they fight back, and this is in no grander form than passive resistance. To develop a challenged identity brings dignity in the face of diminishment.

2. Chances at developing an agentic orientation toward an oppressor occur serendipitously, and the sense of what might be risked becomes fuller and more trustworthy with practice. *Rescuers* in Tec's work (1986:150-193), for instance, may be seen as having assumed a challenged identity in order to be capable of performing any of their life-saving activities. Most of these had set out modestly, even timidly, upon a journey that started first with a prevailing sense of limited agency. From this, as chances to participate in the resistance efforts or their own individual initiative continued, experience may have gradually expanded their domain of effective agency.

3. As noted by Rittner and Roth (1993:69-119), Olga Lengyel (1947) in her firsthand account of Auschwitz, and Terrence Des Pres are among the many who depict the humiliation victims and survivors suffered. As for confronting what was happening to them, it was difficult for the powerless even to define correctly what the parameters of their subjugation were. Shackled by lack

of information, it was difficult to effectively analyze even seemingly trivial situations. They could, however, form a compassionate solidarity with others who were similarly burdened. They could together use shared beliefs and values from the past to comfort one another.

Otherwise, Lawrence Langer's reference to "choiceless choices" sums up the terrible situation left to the persecuted. Survivors made choices during selections or torture, or in merely preparing to get loved ones through their ordeal, which turned out to be fatefully flawed. They were powerless, yet had been given the illusion of choice by their captors. The illusion more than reality stayed with them in the form of survivor "guilt," a component of their bond to those now lost to them which needlessly freighted the selves they constructed after liberation with doubt and grief.

APPENDICES

METHODOLOGICAL APPENDIX I

Survivors Background Characteristics
　　The goal of this narrative analysis of surviving the Holocaust is to provide insight into the social dimensions of surviving extremity. The survivors mentioned in this paper were Jewish children or young adults who adapted to threat and persecution during the 1933-45 period by a) hiding, b) joining the Partisans or Resistance, c) getting transported to the concentration camps, d) going into exile, or some combination of these. Most of the countries of Europe then under Nazi occupation--including Lithuania, Bessarabia, Russia and Poland, Holland, Belgium, Germany and France--are represented by these people. In terms of raw numbers, according to Martin Gilbert (1986), by 1983 there were just over fourteen million Jews worldwide, three and a half million in Israel, six million in North America. Just under six million were estimated by this same source to have perished between 1939-1945 in Nazi dominated Europe (see also Gutman 1990 and Dawidowicz 1984 [1975]). In terms of its design, which combines ethnography with in-depth interviews, this work is intended to be exploratory, to generate new insight as well as amplify already existing understanding about the social aspects of surviving the persecution and abuse associated with genocide.
　　In the first table (see Table 1), survivors are compared in terms of age category, country of origin and condition of persecution. Following a tradition long honored by ethnographers, the anonymity of participants is guaranteed; only the survivors' first names are authentic; the surnames have been altered to preserve their privacy. The survivors, on the other hand, had taken upon themselves the task of being interviewed as an act of witness (see also Des Pres 1976; Ozick 1988) and were quite willing to sacrifice their anonymity for the purpose of remembering those who had died and the bitter events which had passed. It was, however, their narratives rather than their personal identities which I felt would most surely accomplish this goal.
　　Looking at each of the categories used in Table 1, "Age" refers to how old the respondent was on first encountering the Nazi system. I listed the person who was between twelve and eighteen years of age when Nazis entered their area as "adolescent," if twelve or younger, "child," if seventeen or older, "adult." "Country" refers to their country of origin. Because of flight or emigration, this at times differed from where they lived or were taken captive. "Condition" refers to where the survivor spent

the main part of his or her time under persecution. Since survivors quite often had complex survival patterns, many started out in hiding or in ghettoes or with the Resistance or Partisans but ended up in the death camps. Condition of persecution refers only to *what they viewed as their chief situation of persecution*. The place name where they hid, served with the Partisans or Resistance, or were imprisoned or exiled, is given next to their country of origin.

Table 2 compares respondents by age and length of time spent in what they identified as the context in which they chiefly experienced the Holocaust. Because of this emphasis, the table tends to inadequately reflect the full length of persecution endured. For example, in Mariette's case, she was born into a family fleeing Poland. Her father was killed trying to help others flee and find safe haven after they arrived in the west. She fell clearly under the category of those in hiding yet at the same time she was running messages for the Resistance. Technically speaking, she had experienced persecution from birth, but because her most intense isolation and deprivation occurred after her seventh birthday when her mother and many of her brothers had been taken to Auschwitz, four years and not eleven were given as the duration of her privation--a conservative estimate by any count.

Table 3 completes the background information with a stratificational profile in terms of social class (e.g., NORC's General Social Surveys, 1972-1991; Cumulative Codebook, 1991; Macionis 1993:239-289) indicating lifestyle variation for respondents. "Respondent's Class" refers to indicators of social position obvious at the time of the interview. "Father's Class" relates to the lifestyle the family shared before persecution. As many of the respondents varied in terms of rural-urban and traditional-modern factors influencing community of origin, this treatment of class represents an attempt to enhance clarity overall. Helmreich (1992:86-119) provides a more detailed approach to work and occupation patterns of Holocaust survivors who came to the United States. While survivors in my study seem to have held their own or gone beyond the level of their fathers, with around ten percent (10%) of these now being professionals of some kind, Helmreich showed a greater proportion of artisans and blue collar workers in his sample.

Table 1. The Respondents: Age Category, Name, Country, Condition of Persecution

Respondents	Country	Condition
Children		**Hiding**
Rene	Luxembourg	France
Mariette	France	Paris-Brussels
Louise	Holland	Holland
		Camps
Harry	Czechoslovakia	Theresienstadt
Robbie	Poland	Buchenwald
Adolescents		**Hiding**
Serge	Romania	Romania
		Camps
Peter	Vienna	Auschwitz
Michel	Russia	Auschwitz
Klara	Hungary	Birkenau
Leo	Hungary	Birkenau
Adults--Women		**Exile**
Ruth	Germany	America
Polla	Poland	Russia
		Camps
Bertha	Czechoslovakia	Birkenau
Elsie	Poland	Auschwitz
Vera	Hungary	Auschwitz
Adults--Men		**Partisans**
Leon	Lithuania Russia	
		Camps
Chaim	Poland	Mauthausen
David	Transylvania	Auschwitz

Table 2. Respondents by Age and Duration of Condition

Name	Age	Condition	Years
Children			
Harry	11	Camps	1
Robbie	8	Camps	4
Rene	6	Hiding	5
Louise	10	Hiding	3
Mariette	7	Hiding	4
Adolescents			
Leo	15	Camps	1
Peter	14	Camps	3
Michel	14	Camps	4
Klara	15	Camps	1
Serge	13	Hiding	3
Adults-Women			
Bertha	18	Camps	1
Polla	20	Exile	4
Elsie	21	Camps	4
Vera	19	Camps	4
Ruth	18	Exile	6
Adults-Men			
David	17	Camps	1
Chaim	18	Camps	1
Leon	16	Partisans	3

Table 3. Respondents by Class and Father's Occupation

Age Group	Respondent's Class	Father's Class
Children		
Harry	Upper middle	Lower upper
Robbie	Upper middle	Upper middle
Rene	Upper middle	Lower middle
Louise	Upper middle	Lower upper
Mariette	Upper middle	Lower middle
Adolescents		
Peter	Upper middle	Upper middle
Michel	Upper middle	Middle
Leo	Middle	Lower middle
Klara	Upper middle	Lower upper
Serge	Middle	Middle
Adults-women		
Bertha	Middle	Lower middle
Polla	Middle	Working
Elsie	Middle	Upper middle
Vera	Upper middle	Lower upper
Ruth	Upper middle	Upper middle
Adults-men		
David	Upper middle	Working
Chaim	Upper middle	Farm
Leon	Upper middle	Farm

METHODOLOGICAL APPENDIX II
RESEARCH DESIGN AND METHOD

Design and Techniques

The research that generated the survivor narratives in the present work had an ethnographic base. For a year and a half before the interviews were conducted I visited the research site attempting to learn as much as possible about a Jewish way of life both today and in the past. In addition, I began to develop a wide familiarity with the Holocaust literature, emphasizing firsthand accounts at first and then going on from there. The second part of the research contains the actual interviews.

All of my survivors are North American, citizens now of either Canada or the United States. Having started the research design with an ethnographic "frame," I went each mid-week and Sabbath to join the local Jewish community at a small and very old structure that served as both synagogue and community center near where I worked and close to the larger area where many of the survivors in the study presently live. Through them I was put in touch with the regional Jewish Congress and the regional Holocaust Memorial Society, and, in this way, using legitimate community ties I gained access to those who provided the in-depth interviews on which the narrative analysis in this work is based.

The in-depth interviews were taped, with a great effort made to keep formality and discomfort to a minimum. The survivors chose the place where the interview was conducted, and most of the interviews took place in their homes, anywhere from late morning to early evening between Monday and Thursday. I began each interview by asking the survivor to describe her or his life from earliest childhood through the Nazi period and up to the present time. In keeping with Cicourel's (1974) approach to the sensitive interview, survivors were allowed to proceed with their accounts unfettered by any prescribed set of questions (see also Bar-On and Gilad 1994; Reinharz 1992). The "conversation" with each survivor lasted anywhere from ninety minutes to three hours, with taping starting when I entered the house. I kept notes of any details that occurred but were not taped. Once the interviews were concluded I transcribed the tapes.

The process of translating and making sense of very intensely emotional material should not be taken for granted. For a qualitative sociologist, part of the verstehen method involves awareness of ones own feelings and actions (see also Kleinman and Copp 1993; Kleinman 1991). As I listened to the harrowing experiences of these otherwise ordinary seeming people, I realized the courage it had taken for them to return to their past and attempt to share it with others. For one reason or another, most of the survivors I met had remained "silent" most of their lives, sharing only small bits of factual information about their experience when others asked. Doctors and therapists were now able to assure them that such an effort to externalize the trauma would help them heal any lingering wounds they might still have. Many also wanted to respond to the increasing Holocaust revisionism around them. All of them wanted testify to the reality of the Holocaust as they had each experienced it. Going in a somewhat different direction, my overarching goal was multifaceted, informed by my discipline as well as by our shared moment in history. I wanted this work to be in part an analysis of self structure while under extreme condition, an examination of traumatic memory, and, above all, a chance to model a socially dimensioned conception of survival. As complex as surviving might be, and as unworthy as my efforts to grasp its fullness might prove, this work would be my quest for the next several years. I wanted to learn new ways to richly and precisely represent the human document associated with individuals confronting the ineffable.

Verstehen Sociology and the Lifestories

The practice of *verstehen* method in sociology is part of the interpretive tradition associated with Max Weber's sociology of culture. The methodology stemming from the verstehen approach is found in many fields, and in sociology involves research practices ranging from participant observation to the in-depth interview (see also van Maanen 1988). Qualitative inquiry (Bruyn 1970:306; Schwartz and Schwartz 1955:350) is guided not only by a closeness to the empirical world but by a sympathetic alignment with those who are being studied. Using empathetic communication and imaginative participation in the life of the observed, the researcher tries to gain as full an understanding as possible of the subject under study. Many such qualitative approaches to the study of social life have been pursued by those attached to the Chicago School tradition in American sociology (see also Blumer 1970; Becker 1970; Denzin 1970:415-418; Denzin and Lincoln 1994; Fine 1995). Survivor narratives as I have constructed them in the present work follow this orientation in research and theory, locating wider epic social processes as they impinge on a particular person in fateful times. As such they are part of a collective level action constituting culture while at the same time representing individual life in a specific historical moment (see also Denzin 1991; Gergen and Gergen 1988; Maines 1993:17-22; Maines and Ullmer 1993). They are tied to extreme experience, to turning points in life which crystalize sentiment and insight and yet are assembled with the belief that, as unique as the story is, it can be revealed whole and tractable from one person to another.

Narratives in the present work reflect the experience of those excluded from the social worlds of which they had once been part and brought to an unimaginable point where all that represented life to them was either destroyed or jeopardized. In the particular case of these Holocaust survivors, while survival was an issue suddenly forced upon them, each reflected a preoccupation with regaining the symbolic coordinates to maintain self in the coercion setting; the body was simply a part of this rather than being the survivors' sole consuming focus (see also Fisher 1991; Goldenberg 1995). The commitments the victims assumed as they engaged life in fateful times significantly influenced them and left an indelible mark upon their lives.

BIBLIOGRAPHY

Abram, Harry S. 1970. *Psychological Aspects of Stress*. Springfield Illinois: Charles W. Thomas Publisher.

Allen, William Sheridan. 1984 [1975].*The Nazi Seizure of Power; the Experience of a Single German Town 1922-1945*. New York: Franklyn Watts.

Abzug, Robert H. 1985. *Inside the Vicious Heart: Americans and the Liberation of Nazi Concentration Camps*. New York: Oxford University Press.

Amery, Jean. 1980. *At the Mind's Limits: Contemplations by a Survivor of Auschwitz and Its Realities*. Translated and edited by Sidney and Stella Rosenfeld. Bloomington Indiana: University of Indiana Press.

Arendt, Hannah. 1958. *The Human Condition*. Chicago: University of Chicago Press.

Arendt, Hannah. 1963. *Eichmann in Jerusalem; A Report on the Banality of Evil*. New York: Viking.

Auerbahn, Nanette C. and Dori Laub. 1987. "Play and Playfulness in Holocaust Survivors." *Psychoanalytic Study of the Child*. 42:45-58.

Bar-On, Dan and Noga Gilad. 1994. "To Rebuild Life: A Narrative Analysis of Three Generations of an Israeli Holocaust Survivor's Family." Pp.83-112 in *Exploring identity and Gender; The Narrative Study of Lives* edited by Amia Lieblich and Ruthellen Josselson. Thousand Oaks, CA: Sage.

Bauman, Zygmunt. 1991. *Modernity and Ambivalence*. Ithaca, NY: Cornell University Press.

Bauman, Zygmunt. 1989. *Modernity and the Holocaust*. Cambridge: Polity Press.

Bauman, Zygmunt. 1988. "Sociology after the Holocaust." *The British Journal of Sociology* 36 :472-497.

Bauer, Yehuda.1982. *A History of the Holocaust*. New York: Franklyn Watts.

Becker, Howard S. 1970. "The Relevance of Life Histories". Pp. 419-428 in *Sociological Methods: A Sourcebook* edited by Norman K. Denzin. Chicago:Aldine.

Becker, Howard S.1967. "Who's Side Are We On." *Social Problems* 14:239-47.

Bernstein, Basil.1964. "Aspects of language and Learning in the Genesis of the Social process." Pp.251-263 in *Language in Culture and Society* edited by Dell Hymes. New York: Harper and Row.

Bettelheim, Bruno. 1980. *Surviving and Other Essays*. New York: Knopf.

Bettelheim, Bruno. 1960. *The Informed Heart*. Glencoe, Illinois: Free Press.

Bluhm, Hilde O. 1948. "How did they Survive? Mechanisms of Defense in Nazi Concentration Camps." *American Journal of Psychotherapy* 2: 3-32.

Blumer, Herbert.1979. *Critiques of Research in the Social Sciences: An Appraisal of Thomas and Znaniecki's The Polish Peasant in Europe and America*. New Jersey: Transaction.

Blumer, Herbert G. 1970. "Methodological Principles of Empirical Science". Pp. 20-39 in *Sociological Methods: A Sourcebook* edited by Norman K. Denzin. Chicago: Aldine.

Blumer, Herbert. 1969. *Symbolic Interactionism: Perspective and Method*. Berkeley: University of California Press.

Bonhoeffer, Dietrich. 1971 [1953]. *Letters and Papers from Prison*. Edited by Eberhard Bethge. New York:MacMillan.

Borowski, Tadeusz. 1976 [1959]. *This Way for the Gas, Ladies and Gentlemen*. London, England: Penguin Books.

Brittan, Arthur. 1973. *Meanings and Situations*. London: Routledge and Kegan Paul.

Bruyn, Sevryn T. 1970. "The Methodology of Participant Observation." Pp.305-327 in *Qualitative Methodology: Firsthand Involvement with the Social World* edited by William J. Filstead. Chicago: Markham.

Buber, Martin. 1988 [1965]. *The Knowledge of Man; Selected Essays*. Atlantic Highlands, NJ:Humanities Press International, Inc.

Caplan, Sophie. 1985. "Psychological and Spiritual Resistance in Nazi Concentration Camps: The Example of Rabbi Benjamin Gottschal." *Australian Journal of Politics and History* 31(1):109-127.

Camus, Albert. 1956. *The Rebel*. New York:Random House.

Chalk, Frnk and Kurt Jonassohn. 1990. *The History and Sociology of Genocide; Analyses and Case Studies*. New Haven: Yale University Press.

Charmaz, Kathy. 1994. "Identity Dilemmas of Chronically Ill Men." *The Sociological Quarterly* 35:269-288.

Cicourel, Aaron. 1974. *Cognitive Sociology*. New York: Free Press.

Cicourel, Aaron V. 1974. *Theory and Method in a Study of Argentine Fertility*. New York: John Wiley and Sons.

Cicourel, Aaron. 1964. *Method and Measurement in Sociology*. New York: Free Press.

Davidson, Shamai. 1979. "Massive Psychic Traumatization and social Support." In *Psychological Aspects of Stress* edited by Harry S. Abram. New York: Charles Thomas Publisher.

Dawidowicz, Lucy S. 1975. *The War Against the Jews 1933-1945*. New York: Holt Rinehart.

Deak, Istvan. 1992a. "Witnesses to Evil." *New York Review* 22 October.

Deak, Istvan. 1992b. "Strategies of Hell." *New York Review* 8 October.

Denzin, Norman K. 1992. *On Understanding Emotion*. San Francisco:Jossey-Bass.

Denzin, Norman K. 1991. "Representing Lived Experience in Ethnographic Texts." *Studies in Symbolic Interaction* 12:59-70.

Denzin, Norman K. 1989. *Interpretive Interactionism*. Sage: Newbury Park.

Denzin, Norman K. 1985. "Emotion as Lived Experience." *Symbolic Interaction* 8(2):223-240.

Denzin, Norman K. 1977. *Childhood Socialization*. San Francisco: Jossey-Bass.

Denzin, Norman K. 1972. "The Genesis of the Self in Early Childhood." *Sociological*

Quarterly. 13:291-314.
Denzin, Norman K. 1970. *Sociological Methods: A Sourcebook*. Chicago: Aldine.
Denzin, Norman K. and Yvonna S. Lincoln. 1994. *Handbook of Qualitative Research*. Thousand Oaks CA: Sage.
Des Pres, Terrence. 1976. *The Survivor; An Anatomy of Life in the Death Camps*. New York: Oxford University Press.
Dimsdale, Joel E. 1974. "The Coping Behavior of Nazi Concentration Camp Survivors." *American Journal of Psychiatry* 131(7):792-797.
Donat, Alexander. 1967. *The Holocaust Kingdom*. New York: Holt, Rinehart and Winston.
Dreifuss, Gustav. 1980. "The Psychotherapy of Nazi Victims." *Psychotherapy and Psychosoma* 34:40-44.
Eckhardt, A. Roy with Alice L. Eckhardt. 1982. *Long Night's Journey into Day*. Detroit: Wayne State University Press.
Eitinger, Leon. 1974. "Coping with Aggression." *Mental Health Sociology* 1: 297-301.
Ehrenhaus, Peter. 1993. "Cultural Narratives and the Therapeutic Motif: the Political Containment of Vietnam Veterans." Pp.77-96 in *Narrative and Social Control: Critical Perspectives* edited by Dennis Mumby. Newbury Park CA: Sage.
Eliach, Yaffa. 1982. *Hasidic Tales of the Holocaust*. New York: Oxford University Press.
Ellis, Carolyn. 1990. "Sociological Introspection and Emotional Experience." *Symbolic interaction* 14(1):23-50.
Erikson, Kai T. 1976. *Everything in its Path; Destruction of Community in the Buffalo Creek Flood*. New York: Simon and Schuster.
Ezrahi, Sidra DeKoven. 1980. *By Words Alone; The Holocaust in Literature*. Chicago: University of Chicago Press.
Ezrahi, Sidra DeKoven. 1978. "The Holocaust Writer and the Lamentation Tradition: Responses to Catastrophe in Jewish Literature." Pp.133-149 in *Confronting the Holocaust; The Impact of Elie Wiesel* edited by Alvin H. Rosenfeld and Irving Greenberg. Bloomington, IN:Indiana University Press.
Fackenheim, Emil L. 1982. *To Mend the World: Foundations of Future Jewish Thought*. New York: Schocken.
Fackenheim, Emil L. 1978. *The Jewish Return into History; Reflections in the Age of Auschwitz and a New Jerusalem*. New York: Schocken Books.
Fackenheim, Emil L. 1970. *God's Presence in History: Jewish Affirmations and Philosophical Reflections*. New York: New York University Press.
Fein, Helen. 1976. *Accounting for Genocide; Victims and Survivors of the Holocaust*. New York: The Free Press.
Filstead, William J. 1970. *Qualitative Methodology: Firsthand Involvement with the Social World*. Chicago: Markham.
Fine, Ellen S. 1990. "Women Writers and the Holocaust: Strategies for Survival." In

Bibliography

Reflections of the Holocaust in Art and Literature edited by Randolph L. Braham. Boulder Colorado: Social Science Monographs.
Fine, Gary Alan. 1993. "The Sad Demise, Mysterious Disappearance, and Glorious Triumph of Symbolic Interaction." *Annual Review of Sociology* 19:61-87.
Fisher, Josey G. 1991. *The Persistence of Youth; Oral Testimonies of the Holocaust.* New York: Greenwood Press.
Freidman, Paul. 1949. "Some Aspects of Concentration Camp Pathology." *American Journal of Psychiatry* 105:601-605.
Frankl, Viktor E. 1965. *The Doctor and the Soul.* Translated by Richard and Clara Winston. New York: Alfred A. Knopf.
Funkenstein, Amos. 1993. "The Incomprehensible Catastrophe: Memory and Narrative." Pp. 21-29 in *The Narrative Study of Lives* edited by Ruthellen Josselson and Amia Lieblich. Newbury Park, CA: Sage.
Gallant, Mary J. 1997. "Prolonged Trauma in Children: Effects Fifty Years Afterwards; Adult Narratives from the Holocaust." Tampa, FL: *27th Annual Scholar's Conference on the Holocaust.* March.
Gallant, Mary J. 1994. "Children and Adolescents Experience the Holocaust: Effects of Trauma." Presented at *Erinnerung an die Zukunft II,* Berlin, FDR: University of Berlin.
Gallant, Mary J. 1987. "Challenged Identity and Community Bonds." Presented at *American Sociological Association Roundtables.* Chicago.
Gallant, Mary J. and Jay E. Cross. 1992. "Surviving Destruction of the Self: Challenged Identity in the Holocaust." *Studies in Symbolic Interaction* 13:221-246.
Gallant, Mary J. and Sherryl Kleinman. 1983. "Symbolic Interactionism vs. Ethnomethodology." *Symbolic Interaction* 6:1-18.
Gergen, Kenneth and M. Gergen. 1988. "Narrative and the Self as Relationship." *Advances in Experimental Social Psychology* 21:17-55.
Gill, Anton. 1988. *The Journey Back from Hell; an Oral History.* New York: William Morrow and Company, Inc.
Gilbert, Martin. 1987. *The Holocaust; the Jewish Tragedy.* London:Fontana/ Collins.
Goffman, Erving. 1983. "The Interaction Order." *American Sociological Review* 48:1-17.
Goffman, Erving. 1967. *Interaction Ritual.* Chicago:Aldine.
Goffman, Erving. 1963. *Stigma; Notes on the Management of Spoiled Identity.* Englewood Cliffs, N.J.: Prentice-Hall, Inc.
Goffman, Erving. 1961. "The Moral Career of the Mental Patient." Pp. 128-169 in *Asylums: Essays on the Social Interaction of Mental Patients and Other Inmates.* Garden City NY: Doubleday.
Goffman, Erving. 1955. "On Face-work: An Analysis of Ritual Elements in Social Interaction." *Psychiatry* 18:213-231.
Goldenberg, Myrna. 1994. "Lessons learned from Gentle Heroism; Women's Holocaust Narratives." Presented at *Erinnerung an die Zukunft II,* Internationale Konferenz: University of Berlin. Berlin, FDR.

Bibliography

Goldenberg, Myrna. 1991."Different Horrors, Same Hell: Women Remembering the Holocaust." Pp. 150-166 in *Thinking the Unthinkable: Meanings of the Holocaust*, edited by Roger S. Gottlieb. New York: Paulist Press.

Goldhagen, Daniel J. 1996. *Hitler's Willing Executioners; Ordinary Germans and the Holocaust.* New York:Alfred Knopf.

Greenspan, Henry. 1998. *On Listening to Survivors; Recounting and Life History.* Westport CT: Praeger.

Gutman, Israel. 1990. *Encyclopedia of the Holocaust.* New York:Macmillan.

Hass, Aaron. 1995. *The Aftermath; Living with the Holocaust.* New York:Cambridge University Press.

Heinemann, Marlene. 1986. *Gender and Destiny: Women Writers and the Holocaust.* Westport, Connecticut: Greenwood Press.

Helmreich, William B. 1992. *Against All Odds; Holocaust Survivors and the Successful Lives they Made in America.* New York: Simon and Schuster.

Helweg-Larsen, Per, Hendryk Hoffmeyer, Jorgan Kielar, Eigil Hess Thaysen, Paul Thygesen, and Munke Hertel Wulff. 1952. "Famine Disease in German Concentration Camps: Complications and Sequelae." Acta Psychiatrica et Neurologica Scandinavica. Supplementum 83. Ejnar Munksgaard: Copenhagen.

Herman, Judith Lewis. 1992. *Trauma and Recovery.* New York:Basic Books.

Hertz, J.H. 1987. *Pentateuch and Haftorahs.* New York: The Soncino Press.

Hilberg, Raul. 1991. "The Discovery of the Holocaust." Pp. 11-19 in *Lessons and Legacies* edited by P. Hayes. Evanston IL: Northwestern University Press.

Hilberg, Raul. 1985. *The Destruction of the European Jews.* New York: Holmes and Meier.

Hochschild, Arlie Russell. 1983. *The Managed Heart; Commercialization of Human Feeling.* Berkeley: University of California Press.

Hocking, F. 1970. "Extreme Environmental Stress and its Significance for Psychotherapy." *American Journal of Psychotherapy* 24: 4-26.

Holliday, Laurel. 1995. *Children in the Holocaust and World War II. Their Secret Diaries.* New York:Simon and Schuster.

Hutter, Mark. 1966. "A Symbolic Interaction Perspective on the Chinese Thought Reform Experience." Unpublished Paper.

Jaffe, Ruth. 1963. "Group Activity as a Defense Method in Concentration Camps." Israel *Annals of Psychiatry and Related Disciplines* 1(2) October.

Joas, Hans. 1990. Mead's Position in Intellectual History and His Early Philosophical Writings. In *Philosophy, Social Theory, and the Thought of George Herbert Mead* edited by Mitchell Aboulafia. Albany: State University of New York.

Josselson, Ruthellen and Amia Lieblich (eds.) 1993. *The Narrative Study of Lives.* Newbury Park CA: Sage.

Katovich, Michael A. and William A. Reese. 1993. "Postmodern Thought in Symbolic Interaction: Reconstructing Social Inquiry in Light of Late-Modern

Bibliography

Concerns." *The Sociological Quarterly* 34:391-411.
Kanter, Rosabeth Moss. 1972. *Communities and Commitment.* Cambridge MA: Harvard University Press.
Kielar, Wieslaw. 1971. *Anus Mundi; 1,500 Days in Auschwitz/Birkenau.* New York:Times Books.
Krystal, Henry. 1968. *Massive Psychic Trauma.* New York: International Universities Press.
Klein, Hillel and Ilany Kogon. 1986. "Identification Processes and Denial in the Shadow of Nazism." *American Journal of Psychoanalysis* 67:45-52.
Lang, Berel. 1988. "Writing the Holocaust: Jabes and the Measure of History." Pp.245-260 in *Writing and Holocaust* edited by Berel Lang. New York: Holmes and Meier.
Langer, Lawrence. 1991. *Holocaust Testimonies: The Ruins of Memory.* New Haven: Yale University Press.
Langer, Lawerence. 1978. "The Divided Voice: Eli Wiesel and the Challenge of the Holocaust." Pp. 31-48 in *Confronting the Holocaust; The Impact of Elie Wiesel* edited by Alvin H. Rosenfeld and Irving Green. Bloomington, IN: Indiana University Press.
Latour, Anny. 1981. *The Jewish Resistance in France.* New York NY: Walden Press Inc.
Leitner, Isabella. 1978. *Fragments of Isabella.* New York: Schocken.
Levi, Primo. 1965. *The Reawakening.* Translated by Stuart Woolf. New York: Collier Books.
Levin, Nora. 1990. *The Holocaust Years: The Nazi Destruction of European Jewry 1933-1945.* Malabar, FL: Krieger.
Levinas, Emmanuel. 1979. *Totality and Infinity.* Boston: Matinus Nijhoff.
Lifton, Robert Jay. 1986. *The Nazi Doctors; Medical Killing and the Psychology of Genocide.* New York:Basic Books, Inc.
Lindesmith, Alfred R., Anselm L. Strauss and Norman K. Denzin. 1991. *Social Psychology.* Englewood Cliffs NJ: Prentice-Hall.
Littel, Franklin H. 1986 [1975]. *The Crucifixion of the Jews; The Failure of Christians to Understand the Jewish Experience.* Macon GA: Mercer University Press.
Littel, Franklin H. and Hubert Locke (eds.) 1974. *German Church Struggle.* Detroit, Michigan: Wayne State University Press.
Lofland, Lyn. 1973. *A World of Strangers.* New York: Basic Books.
Macionis, John J. 1993. *Sociology.* Englewood Cliffs, NJ:Prentice Hall.
Maines, David R. 1993. "Narrative's Moment and Sociology's Phenomena: Toward a Narrative Sociology." *The Sociological Quarterly* 34:17-38.
Maines, David R. and Jeffrey T. Ullmer. 1993. "The Relevance of Narrative For Interactionist Thought." *Studies in Symbolic Interaction* 14: 109-124.
Mead, George Herbert. 1934. *Mind, Self and Society.* Chicago: University of Chicago.

Michener, James A. 1965. *The Source.* New York: Fawcett Press.
Muller, Filip. 1979. *Auschwitz Inferno; The Testimony of a Sonderkommando.* London: Routledge and Kegan Paul.
Neher, Andre. 1978. "Shaddai: The God of the Broken Arch". Pp.150-158 in *Confronting the Holocaust; The Impact of Elie Wiesel* edited by Alvin H. Rosenfeld and Irving Greenberg. Bloomington, IN:Indiana University Press.
Niederland, William G. 1968. "Clinical Observations on the 'Survivor Syndrome'." *International Journal of Psycho-Analysis* 49:313-315.
Niederland, William G. 1964. "Psychiatric Disorders among Persecution Victims; A Contribution to the Understanding of Concentration Camp Pathology and Its After-Effects." *Journal of Nervous and Mental Disease* 139:458-474.
Nomberg-Pryztyk, Sara. 1985. *Auschwitz: True tales from a Grotesque Land.* Chapel Hill, NC: University of North Carolina Press.
NORC. 1993. *General Social Surveys, 1972-1993: Cumulative Codebook.* Chicago: National Opinion Research Center.
Orenstein, Anna. 1985. "Survival and Recovery." *Psychoanalytic Inquiry* 5(1):99-130.
Pawelczynska, Anna. 1979. *Values and Violence in Auschwitz; A Sociological Analysis.* Berkeley: University of California Press.
Perl, Gisella. 1948. *I was a Doctor in Auschwitz.* New York: International University Press.
Plummer, Ken. 1990. Herbert Blumer and the Life History Tradition. *Symbolic Interaction* 13:125-144.
Perinbanayagam, Robert S. 1991. *Discursive Acts.* New York:Aldine.
Porter, Jack Nussan. 1982. *Genocide and Human Rights; A Global Anthology.* Lanham NY: University Press of America.
Raicin-Klebanow, Galina. 1991. "Report of a Slaughter of Jews in latvia given by a Child in Camp Kaiserwald: Memoirs." Pp.139-149 in *The Unfinished Road: Jewish Survivors of Latvia Look Back* by edited by Gertrude Schneider.
Roth, John K. and Michael Berenbaum (eds.) 1989. *Holocaust; Religious and Philosophical Implications.* New York: Paragon House.
Reynolds, Larry T. 1987. *Interactionism: Exposition and Critique* Dix Hills, New York: General Hall Inc.
Riessman, Catherine Kohler. 1993. *Narrative Analysis.* Newbury Park CA: Sage.
Ringelblum, Joan. 1990. "Thoughts about Women." In *Thinking the Unthinkable: Meanings of the Holocaust* edited by Roger S. Gottlieb. New York: Paulist Press.
Rittner, Carol and John K. Roth (eds.) 1993. *Different Voices; Women and the Holocaust.* New York: Paragon House.
Rochberg-Halton, Eugene. 1986. *Meaning and Modernity; Social Theory and the Pragmatic Attitude.* Chicago: The University of Chicago Press.
Rosenblatt, Roger. 1983. *Children of War.* Garden City NY: Doubleday/Anchor.
Rosenfeld, Alvin H. and Irving Greenberg. 1978. *Confronting the Holocaust; The Impact of Elie Wiesel.* Bloomington, IN: Indiana University Press.
Rosenfeld, David. 1986. "Identification and its Vicissitudes in Relation to the Nazi

Bibliography

Phenomenon." *International Journal of Psycho-Analysis* 67:53-64.
Rosenthal, Gabriele. 1993. "Reconstruction of Life Stories: Principles of Selection in Generating Stories for Narrative Biographical Interviews." Pp.59-91 in *The Narrative Study of Lives* edited by Ruthellen Josselson and Amia Lieblich. Newbury Park CA:Sage.
Roth, John K. 1999. *Ethics after the Holocaust: Persepctives, Critiques, and Responses*. St. Paul MN: Paragon House.
Rubenstein, Richard L. 1978. *The Cunning of History; the Holocaust and the American Future*. New York: Harper Colophon Books.
Rubenstein, Richard L. and John K. Roth. 1987. *Approaches to Auschwitz: The Holocaust and its Legacy*. Atlanta: John Knox Press.
Schmolling, Paul. 1984. "Human Reactions to the Nazi Concentration Camps: A Summing Up." *Journal of Human Stress* Fall:108-120.
Schwartz, Morris S. and Charlotte G. Schwartz. 1955. "Problems in Participant Observation." *American Journal of Sociology* 60 (January).
Segev, Tom. 1993. *The Seventh Million; The Israelis and the Holocaust*. Translated by Haim Watzman. New York: Farrar, Strauss and Giroux.
Shotter, John. 1993. *Conversational Realities; Constructing Life through Language*. London:Sage.
Singer, Isaac Bashevis. 1982. *The Collected Stories*. New York:Farrar Strauss Giroux.
Stone, Gregory P. 1981. "The Play of Little Children." Pp.249-256 in *Social Psychology through Symbolic Interaction* edited by Gregory P. Stone and Harvey A. Farberman. New York:John Wiley and Sons.
Stone, Gregory P. 1977. "Personal Acts." *Symbolic Interaction* 1: 2-19.
Strauss, Anselm, 1969. *Mirrors and Masks*. San Francisco: Jossey-Bass.
Sullivan, Harry Stack. 1953. *The Interpersonal Theory of Psychiatry*. New York: W.W. Norton.
Szalet, Leon. 1945. *Experiment "E"* translated by Catherine Bland Williams. New York:Didier.
Tec, Nechama. 1992. *In the Lion's Den; the Life of Ostwald Rufelsen*. New York: Oxford University Press.
Tec, Nechama. 1986. *When Light Pierced the Darkness: Christian Rescue of Jews in Nazi-Occupied Poland*. New York: Oxford University Press.
Tec, Nechama. 1984 [1982]. *Dry Tears; The Story of a Lost Childhood*. New York: Oxford University Press.
Terr, Lenore. 1990. *Too Scared to Cry; Psychic Trauma in Childhood*. New York: Harper and Row.
Van Maanen, John. 1988. *Tales of the Field; On Writing Ethnography*. Chicago:University of Chicago Press.
Weinberg, Werner. *Self-Portrait of a Holocaust Survivor*. Jefferson, NC:McFarland and Company Inc., Publishers.
Wiesel, Elie. 1972. *Souls on Fire; Portraits and Legends of Hasidic Masters*. New York:Random House.

Wiesel, Elie. 1970. "Snapshots". Pp. 46-47 in *One Generation After*. New York: Random House.
Wiesel, Elie. 1969. *Night*. New York: Avon.
Wiesel, Elie. 1968. "The Death of My Father". In *Legends of Our Time*. New York: Holt, Rinehart, and Winston.
Weisman, Eric. 1980. *The Rhetoric of Holocaust Survivors: A Dramatistic Perspective*. PhD. Dissertation: Temple University.
Williamson, Clark M. 1993. *A Guest in the House of Israel; Post-Holocaust Church Theology*. Louisville, Kentucky: John Knox Press.
Weber, Louis. 2000. *Holocaust Chronicle; a History in Words and Pictures*. Lincolnwood IL: Publications International.
Wyman, David S. 1985. *The Abandonment of the Jews; America and the Holocaust 1941-1945*. New York: Random House.
Young, James E. 1988. "Holocaust Documentary Fiction: The Novelist as Eyewitness." Pp.200-215 in *Writing and the Holocaust* edited by Berel Lang. New York NY: Holmes and Meier.

INDEX

Age
    of survivors in this work tables 1-3, Appendix 1
Antiman
    survivor as 6
Anti-Semitism
    Bertha 165
    Elsie 188-192
    Mariette 93-94
    Michel 123, 124
    Polla 211
    Rene 53
    Serge 153
Anti-Judaism
    Chaim 241-242
    Polla 199
    Robbie 36-37
Auschwitz (see also Birkenau) 99-103, 110-114, 168, 179, 181, 188-192, 226, 228, 245, 254
Belgium 52, 83
Bertha 164-178
    anti-Semitism 165
    Auschwitz-Birkenau 168
    deportation 167-168
    ghettoized 167
    loss 168
    liberation 174-176
    lingering effects 175-176
    new world 176-178
    religious conviction 171-173
    relationships 165-167, 168-174
    song of generations 177
Bialystock 122-124
Birkenau (see also Auschwitz) 125-130, 138-146

Chaim 240-255
    anti-Judaism 241-242
    Auschwitz 245, 254
    Danube 249
    death march 248-249
    deportation 244
    early years 240-241
    Eichman 252
    ghetto 243
    Gusen II 245
    hostages 243
    hunger 244-245
    Joint Distribution Committee 253
    last days of Mauthausen 248-252
    liberation 250, 252
    lice, a blessing upon the 250
    lingering effects 250
    marriage 253
    Mauthausen 245-251
    Partisans 244
    religious conviction 241-243, 247, 251-252, 255
    relationships 251-252
    return home 252
    Riga 254
    Satoraljaujhely 270
    shock 244
    terror 243-244
    Vienna 252-253
Challenged identity 14, 275-297
Czechoslovakia 29
David 226-240
    Auschwitz 226, 228
    deportation 226

early years 230-231
forced march 235
ghettoization 227-228
liberation 231
lingering effects 238
loss 229, 237-238
marriage 240
Melk 235
new world 237-240
relationships 230-232, 234, 239
resistance in the camps 233
survivor guilt 230, 236
selections 229
Transylvania 226
Elsie 186-198
   Auschwitz 188-192
   ghetto 180-188
   Goeth, Amon 193
   Krakow 186
   loss 188-189, 197
   liberation 195
   marriage and children 197-198
   postwar Krakow 196-197
   relationships 157, 187-190
   religious conviction 193-195
   Schindler's ghetto industries 187-192
Endlosung 5 n2
Harry 29-35
   Czechoslovakia 29
   individualism 31
   Israel 33
   liberation 32, 33
   luck 31
   Theresienstadt 29-30
   transports 30-31
Klara 137-151
   anti-Semitism 137
   Birkenau 138-146
   cloth of caring 146
   deportation from Hungary 138-139, 142
   generational loss 151
   house arrest 137
   liberation 147-148
   lingering effects 148-149, 150-151
   loss 139-140
   marriage 149
   mountain of corpses 147
   new family 149-151
   relationships 144, 146
   selections 141-142
   slave labor 146-147
   return home 148-149
KZ system 5 n1, 6 n7
Leo 98-106
   Auschwitz 99-103
   diminishment 101
   liberation 101, 103
   lingering effects 99, 106
   loss 99
   medical experiments 100
   new world 104-105
   twin sister 104
Leon 255-273
   collaborators 269-271
   early years 255-256
   einsatzgruppen 256
   Grodno ghetto 263-265
   hidden by neighbors 260-262
   lingering effects 272-273
   loss 258, 265, 268
   new life 268, 272
   Partisans 263-270
   racial cleansing 256-262
   sonderbehandlung 256
   shock 258, 264, 268
   slaughter of the women and children 258-260
Louise 67-83
   Amsterdam 67
   anti-Semitism 71, 81
   Dutch underground 75-76
   confiscation of property

Index

71-72
  decision to hide 75
  ghetto 72-74
  hiding 76-78
  liberation 79
  lucky 80
  marriage 82
  resettled 72
  return to normalcy 80-82
  Rotterdam 67-89
  sealing the ports – no escape 68-70
  survivor guilt 82
Luxembourg 52-53
Lyons 64
Mariette 83-94
  anti-Semitism 93-94
  Auschwitz 83
  Brussels 83
  capture 85
  escape 85
  foster parents 62-63
  hiding 84, 86-87
  illness 86-87
  lingering effects 93
  marriage 91-93
  Marie 88, 91, 92
  new life 88
  relationships 85, 87, 88-89, 90-94
  resistance 83, 84, 85-86
  shock 87
Michel 122-137
  anti-Semitism 123, 124
  Bialystock ghetto 122-124
  Birkenau 125-130
  Birkenau transport 124
  Kanada kommando 129
  company of heroes 130
  ethical conviction 130-134
  liberation 134
  lingering effects 135-137
  loss 125
  luck 128, 129, 131
  marriage 136
  Nordhausen 130
  parents 122-123, 125
Peter 106-122
  Anschluss 106
  Auschwitz 110-114
  Brussels 106
  capture by Gestapo 108-109
  Dachau 116-117
  death march 115-116
  deportation 109
  hiding 106-107
  liberation 118
  lingering effects 119
  luck 108, 119-120
  marriage 121
  relationships 116, 120-121
  starvation and thirst 115-116
  work camps 114-118
Polla 198-212
  anti-Judaism 199
  anti-Semitism 211
  baby Laura 207
  capture 204
  early years 198-200
  escaping Warsaw 203-204
  1938-39 201-203
  flight 168-171
  grandchildren 211-212
  gulag 205-209
  husband 199, 209
  invasion of Poland 201-202
  letters home 206-207
  loss 207, 209
  lucky 211
  new world 211
  pregnancy 205, 207
  prison 205-206, 207
  relationships 206-209
  religious conviction 199-200

Index

return to Brest 210
round-ups 198, 202
Rene 52-67
  anti-Semitism 53
  Barbie, Klaus 61, 63, 65
  capture 56-57
  childhood joy 52-53, 60
  community of children 58
  Chateauroux 59-60
  escape 54, 56, 58
  flight 54-56
  Free Zone 56
  invasion of France 58
  hiding 58
  last train to Auschwitz 63, 65
  liberation 61-62
  Limoges 57-58
  loss 57, 63, 64
  Luxembourg 52-53
  Lyons 64
  the Milice 62
  nobody came 63, 65
  new life 66
  Occupied Zone 55
  refugees 54-56
  round-up 56
  Resistance 60-62, 63
  Vichy France 58
Robbie 35-52
  anti-Judaism 36-37
  Buchenwald 49
  captive (or slave) labor 38-50
  captive labor 43-49
  civil liberties lost 39
  early life 35-38
  forced march 49
  ghetto 39-41
  liquidation of 42
  gift 45-46
  hiding 40-41
  invasion of Poland 37
  liberation 49-50
  lingering effects 48-49
  loss 42, 48
  marriage 50
  new life 50
  Polish Partisans 44-45
  religion 51-52
  selections 43-44
  shock 39, 47
  Skarszysko 35
  Treblinka 40, 42
  work permits 38
  work camps 43, 45, 46
Romania 151-155
Rotterdam 67
Ruth 212-221
  anti- Semitism 213
  Bad Freienwald 212
  Berlin 212-215
  early years 212-214
  exile 216-217
  last ship out 216-217
  lingering effects 217, 219-221
  loss 216-221
  luck 216
  nephew in hiding 215, 217
  new world 217
  rescue 215
Serge 151-161
  anti-Semitism 153
  Antonescu 153
  Bar Mitzvah 151
  hiding 155-156
  Iasi 152, 155
  lingering effects 156, 160
  Nazi invasion 151-155
  new world 160
  Ploesti oil fields 156
  Polonoj 152
  relationships 157-159
  religious conviction 159-160
  Romania 151-155
  self-reliance 157-158, 160
  torture of Jews 151-155

Index

Theresienstadt 29-30
Transylvania 226
Treblinka 40, 42
Vera 178-186
    Auschwitz 179, 181
    Budapest 178
    deportation 179
    father 179
    ghetto 179
    Leipzig 183-180
    liberation 184-185
    mother 178-179, 180, 184
    Munich Pact countries 178
    Plaszow 180
    relationships 180-182, 185
    starvation and thirst 179, 181
Vichy France 58
Work camps (captive labor)
    Bertha 168-174
    Chaim 245-251
    David 29-234, 235
    Elsie 187-192
    Klara 140-148
    Michel 129-134
    Peter 114-118
    Robbie 43-49